The Real MCTS SQL Server 2008 Exam 70-433 Prep Kit

Database Design

Mark Horninger Technical Editor
**Valentine Boairkine and
Herleson Pontes** Lead Authors

Dinesh Asanka
Denny Cherry
Justin Langford
Steve Long
Bret Stateham
Sylvia Vargas

PUBLISHED BY
Syngress Publishing, Inc.
Elsevier, Inc.
30 Corporate Drive
Burlington, MA 01803

The Real MCTS SQL Server 2008 Exam 70-433 Prep Kit

Transferred to Digital Printing, 2010

ISBN 13: 978-1-59749-421-2

Publisher: Laura Colantoni
Acquisitions Editor: Rachel Roumeliotis
Technical Editor: Mark Horninger
Developmental Editor: Gary Byrne
Indexer: SPi

Project Manager: Heather Tighe
Page Layout and Art: SPi
Copy Editors: Adrienne Rebello,
Leslie Crenna, Betty Pessagno
Cover Designer: Michael Kavish

For information on rights, translations, and bulk sales, contact Matt Pedersen, Director of Corporate Sales, Elsevier; email m.pedersen@elsevier.com.

Library of Congress Cataloging-in-Publication Data
Application submitted

Technical Editor

Mark Horninger (A+, Net+, Security+, MCSE+I, MCSD, MCAD, MCDBA, MCTS, MCITP, MCPD) is manager of database operations at Internet Pipeline, Inc. He is also the founder of Haverford Consultants, Inc. (www.haverford-consultants.com/), located in the suburbs of Philadelphia, PA. He develops custom applications and system engineering solutions, specializing primarily in Microsoft .NET technology and Microsoft SQL Server. He is a contributing author to *Securing SQL 2005, Configuring and Troubleshooting Windows XP Professional MCSE Windows 2000 Professional Study Guide* and *Designing SQL Server 2000 Databases for .NET Enterprise Servers* published by Syngress, an imprint of Elsevier Inc. Mark has also served as an adjunct professor at Kaplan University teaching Web design.

Mark has over 20 years of computer consulting experience and has passed 50+ Microsoft Certification Exams.

He lives with his wife, Debbie, and son, Robby, in the Philadelphia area.

Mark would like to thank his wife, Debbie, for her infinite patience, love, and support during this project.

Lead Authors

Valentine Boiarkine (MCSE, MCDBA, MCSD, MCT) is a founding partner at Blade Ltd., a software consulting firm based in Wellington, New Zealand. She is the lead architect of the revolutionary Blade File Transfer System file transfer technology. Valentine has over 10 years' consulting and software development experience, and she specializes in enterprise software integration, security, IT alignment, and unified communications. She has designed distributed software solutions for financial, legal, and government organizations.

Valentine is the author of numerous technical training courses, guides, and white papers for Microsoft Corp. and Quest Software, including SQL Server Microsoft Official Curriculum titles. She is also an accomplished trainer and presenter. She frequently trains support engineers at Microsoft and Microsoft partners worldwide. Her technology expertise lies in SQL Server, .NET development, Exchange Server, and Office Communications Server. Valentine resides in Auckland, New Zealand, with her husband, Keith, and children Spencer and Alexander.

Herleson Pontes (MVP, MCT, MCITP, MCTS, MCP, MOS) is an IT consultant, writer and trainer of desktop, Web, and mobile environments, with more than eight years of expertise. He currently provides technical consulting and IT training to companies and Microsoft CPLS all over Brazil. His specialties include Microsoft SQL Server, Microsoft Windows Server System, Windows Desktop Client, Microsoft Desktop Optimization Pack, database design and implementation, strategic BI planning, system architecture and design, and IT environment troubleshooting and optimization. Herleson is a key speaker, writer, and contributor to many publications and Microsoft communities of Brazil.

Herleson holds a bachelor's degree in information systems and is a student working toward his master's degree in applied informatics from the University of Fortaleza. Herleson currently resides in Fortaleza, Ceará, with his wife, Priscila, and family.

Contributing Authors

Dinesh Asanka (MVP SQL Server, B.S. [Eng], MBA [IT]) is a database architect at Exilesoft (Pvt) Ltd. He is primarily involved in designing databases in SQL Server. Dinesh has been working with SQL Server since 2000 starting from version 7.

Dinesh is a regular columnist for popular Web sites, including sql-server-performance.com, sqlservercentral.com, and sqlserveruniverse.com. Besides writing, Dinesh is actively involved in presentations for the SQL Server Sri Lankan User Group (SS SLUG).

Dinesh holds a bachelor's degree in engineering and an MBA from the University of Moratuwa, Sri Lanka.

Denny Cherry (MCSA, MCDBA, MCTS, MCITP) is a senior database administrator and architect for Awareness Technologies. He currently handles all database change design and implements changes to both the companies' ASP solution as well as the consumer hosted versions of the product. In addition Denny manages the Infrastructure Team, which maintains the 100-plus server environment. Denny's background includes database administration and database engineering positions at MySpace.com, IGN.com, GameSpy.com, and EarthLink Networks.

In 2008 Denny was named to the Quest Software Customer Advisory Board, and in 2009, Denny was named as a Microsoft MVP. Denny has written dozens of articles related to SQL Server, both for print magazines and various Web sites.

Justin Langford (MCSE, MCITP, MCDBA, SNIA, CCNA, ITIL) is a principal consultant for Coeo Ltd, a Microsoft Gold Partner in London. Coeo provides SQL Server consulting services for upgrade, performance tuning, scalability, and availability solutions for all versions of SQL Server. Coeo offers remote DBA services to customers who outsource management and 24×7 operations of their SQL Server platforms. Justin delivers and maintains SQL Server solutions for customers in many different industry sectors throughout Europe.

Prior to joining Coeo, Justin spent three years working at Microsoft UK as a premier field engineer. In this role, Justin delivered SQL Server support consulting to some of Microsoft's largest finance and government customers in Europe. Justin has also coauthored *Wrox IT Pro: SQL Server Performance Tuning*.

Steve Long is a senior software engineer/systems analyst at Wilmington Trust. Steve has over 14 years of database and application design and development experience. He currently provides database and application support to trading applications and processes using Microsoft technologies. He also serves as technical lead on significant projects in addition to lending his infrastructure, project management, and business process expertise to all initiatives. Before making a full-time switch to the information technology field, Steve spent a number of years working in the accounting field.

Steve holds a bachelor's degree from Goldey-Beacom College in Wilmington, Delaware, and a Client/Server Technology certification from Pennsylvania State University. He is currently working toward his graduate degree at Goldey-Beacom.

Steve wishes to thank his coworkers for putting up with him every day and his family for their understanding and support during his writing.

Bret Stateham (MCT, MCSE, MCTS, MCITP) is the owner of Net Connex Technology Training and Consulting, LLC, located just outside San Diego, CA. Net Connex provides consulting and training services that are focused primarily on Microsoft server platforms. Bret has over 20 years of experience in the industry and over 10 years as a trainer. He has been working with SQL Server since version 6.5 and has been teaching SQL Server since version 7.0. Bret has contributed to multiple Syngress SQL Server publications starting with *Designing SQL Server 2000 Databases for .Net Enterprise Server*. He stays involved with the community by helping to organize the Socal Code Camp and he is a frequent speaker at Code Camps and User Groups. Bret lives in Ramona, CA, with his wife, Lori; son, Chase; and daughter, Katie.

Sylvia Vargas has been working with information technology since 1981. Sylvia's experience in SQL Server started in 1997, although she has over 20 years' experience in other relational database technologies, including IBM SQL/DS, Digital Equipment Corp.'s RDB, and Oracle.

She has worked for state and local governments; Fortune 500 companies, such as Boeing, Disney, and Texaco; and a broad number of industries, including finance, manufacturing, Internet, and utilities.

She has been a developer, DBA, and manager on everything from a SQL/DS running on an IBM/Oracle system running UNIX to SQL Server and DB2 installations.

Sylvia has an undergraduate degree from Fordham University and an MBA from Pace University in New York. She has worked at Microsoft since 2006.

Sylvia lives in Seattle, WA, and enjoys bicycling, genealogy, and the great theatre in the Seattle area. Sylvia also teaches part-time at the University of Washington's Extension Certificate Program teaching SQL Server Development.

Contents

Companion Web Site: An appendix with coverage of other components in SQL and a more detailed answer key for the Self Test questions in this book are available on the Web. Go to www.elsevierdirect.com/companions/9781597494212.

Chapter 1

MCTS SQL Server 2008 Exam 433

New Features in SQL Server 2008

Exam objectives in this chapter:

- New Feature Overview
- Reporting Services

Exam objectives review:

- ☑ Summary of Exam Objectives
- ☑ Exam Objectives Fast Track
- ☑ Exam Objectives Frequently Asked Questions
- ☑ Self Test
- ☑ Self Test Quick Answer Key

Introduction

Congratulations on your journey to become certified in SQL Server 2008. This book will help prepare you for your exam and give you a practical view of working with SQL Server 2008.

SQL Server 2008 is a fantastic product when you think about all it does. I've worked with SQL Server since the days of 6.5, and it's come a long way since then.

In this chapter, we will briefly review the new features in SQL Server 2008. There are quite a few enhancements to SQL Server, many of which will make the job of the DBA much easier. One of these, the new performance data management system, allows for database statistics and performance information to be automatically captured across an enterprise.

While this chapter covers the new features in SQL Server 2008, bear in mind many of the "basic" features of SQL will also be covered on the test. This book will not only cover the new features but also the topics from earlier versions of SQL Server that have not changed, as you will also need to know these items.

Head of the Class...

Know and Understand All SQL Server 2008 Features

Be sure you understand all of the topics in this book before attempting the test. It will cover old and new features, so don't limit your studying to just the new features. This will help you not only when it comes to the test, but also in using SQL Server 2008 in general.

A Word About the Test

On your testing day, make sure you arrive rested and ready to sit for the exam. Be calm and read each question carefully. Microsoft doesn't try to trick you; however, the questions and answers are presented in such a way that you should think about each question before answering it.

When you take your exam, be sure to leave no question unanswered. Most questions are multiple choice, so if you can narrow it down to two possible answers, you have a 50–50 chance at getting the question right—although this book will do an excellent job of preparing you for the exam.

If you are not sure of the answer to a question, sometimes it's good to skip that question and move on and come back to it. Another question may jog your memory, and when you come back to the first question the answer is much clearer.

When you go in for your test, don't bring pagers, laptops, cell phones, and so on. They will not allow you to bring them in. Also be sure to bring two forms of ID. Most testing centers have video cameras, and you are taped during the exam to deter cheating.

Test Day Tip

Be sure to read each question completely before answering! Sometimes there is a more "correct" answer than the first answer in the list. While there may be more than one correct answer, one solution may be better than another.

New Feature Overview

SQL Server 2008 has many new features for the DBA and database developer. With these features, Microsoft was able to achieve its vision of managing data more efficiently.

The following section is meant to provide a high-level overview of many of the new features found in SQL Server 2008.

Test Day Tip

Make certain you know which features go with which edition. You can be sure that some answers will be presented in such a manner as to test your knowledge of editions.

Installation

The new SQL Server Installation Center offers many more options. Figure 1.1 will familiarize you with the new tool.

Configuring & Implementing...

The New SQL Server 2008 Installation Center

The new SQL Server 2008 Installation Center has a different look and feel as compared to previous versions. The overall look and feel is much more user friendly than the old installation methods, and it's also more centralized.

Figure 1.1 The SQL Server Installation Center

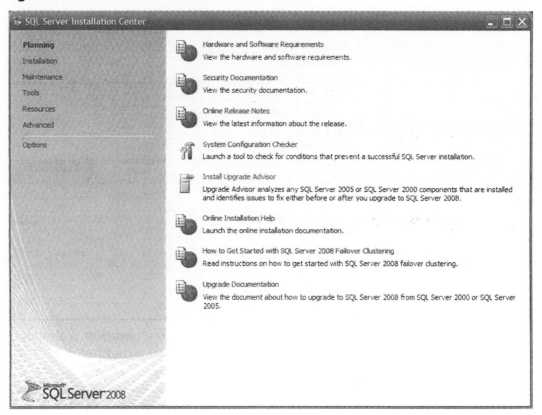

The SQL Server installation tool is used to create a new installation, or to make changes to the existing installation. Keep in mind many of the changes require you to have the installation media to complete the change.

EXAM WARNING

Be sure you have walked through installing SQL Server 2008 before attempting to complete the exam! The terms and questions asked will be much more familiar to you if you have.

Compressed Backups

Compressed backup is a great new feature in SQL Server 2008. By compressing backups, you can save time and disk space. Initial thoughts may lead you to believe that compressed backups would take longer, as during the backup process the disk is usually the bottleneck; however, since less data is being written to the disk, backup time is usually reduced.

New & Noteworthy...

Compressed Backups

Compressed backups are an exciting new feature in SQL Server 2008. While these have been available for a long time from third-party vendors such as Red Gate, Quest, and many others, they are now built into SQL Server. With compressed backups built in, we expect they will become the standard for most companies.

It's a relatively simple process to use compressed backups. During the backup you would select **Compress backup** (see Figure 1.2). Bear in mind that if you are working with a SQL 2005 database this feature will not be available.

Figure 1.2 The Compress Backup Option

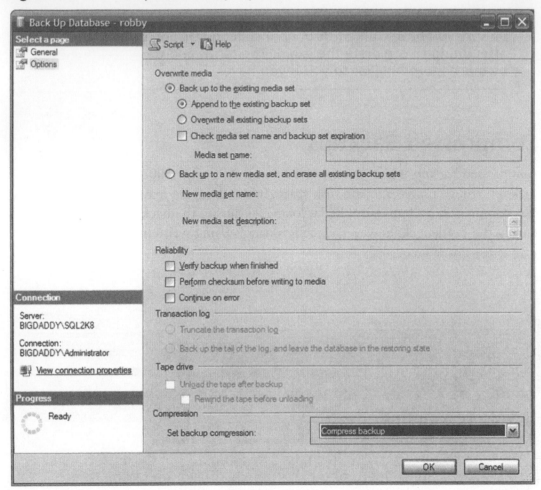

When using T-SQL to create the backup, you'd use:

```
BACKUP DATABASE [robby] TO DISK = N'C:\Backup\robby.bak' WITH
NOFORMAT, NOINIT, NAME = N'robby-Full Database Backup', SKIP,
NOREWIND, NOUNLOAD, COMPRESSION, STATS = 10
```

Either approach will produce the same result. It's a good idea to understand how to work both in the GUI and using T-SQL.

While we are on the subject of backups, it's also important to understand how Copy Only Backup works, and why and when you'd want to use it. Copy Only Backup is especially useful for taking "one-off" backups for development or testing—the advantage is it doesn't affect transaction log backups or differential backups.

Keep in mind it also cannot serve as a base for differential or transaction log backups when restoring either.

To select Copy Only Backup, simply check the **Copy Only Backup** option in the GUI (see Figure 1.3).

Figure 1.3 The Copy Only Backup Option

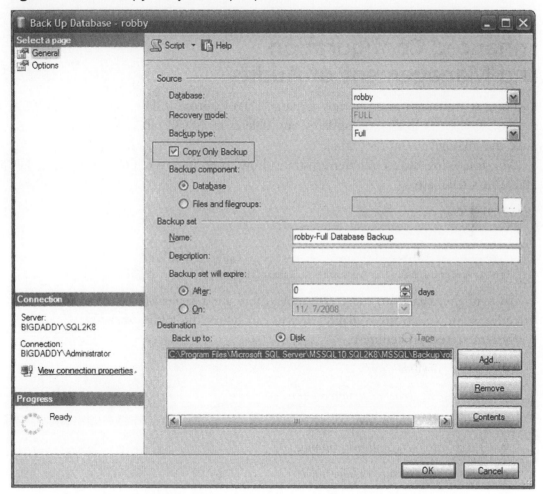

The T-SQL procedure to do a Copy Only Backup would look like this:

```
BACKUP DATABASE [robby] TO DISK = N'C:\Backup\robby.bak' WITH
COPY_ONLY, NOFORMAT, NOINIT, NAME = N'robby-Full Database Backup',
SKIP, NOREWIND, NOUNLOAD, STATS = 10
GO
```

Enhanced Configuration and Management of Audits

Auditing is available using the new Change Data Capture (CDC) feature. CDC can be used to capture insertions, updates, and deletes in a SQL table in a database and place the changes in another table.

The following SQL code demonstrates how to configure CDC for auditing of a table in a database:

```
--Activate CDC
   EXEC sys.sp_cdc_enable_db_change_data_capture
   --Enable CDC on table
   EXEC sys.sp_cdc_enable_table_change_data_capture @source_schema =
   'dbo', @source_name = 'myTable', @role_name = 'cdc'
```

To read the data from the CDC table, there are a series of system stored procedures and functions available, or you can query the tables directly.

System stored procedures:

- *sys.sp_cdc_add_ job*
- *sys.sp_cdc_ generate_wrapper_ function*
- *sys.sp_cdc_change_ job*
- *sys.sp_cdc_ get_captured_columns*
- *sys.sp_cdc_cleanup_change_table*
- *sys.sp_cdc_ get_ddl_history*
- *sys.sp_cdc_disable_db*
- *sys.sp_cdc_help_change_data_capture*
- *sys.sp_cdc_disable_table*
- *sys.sp_cdc_help_ jobs*

- *sys.sp_cdc_drop_ job*
- *sys.sp_cdc_scan*
- *sys.sp_cdc_enable_db*
- *sys.sp_cdc_start_ job*
- *sys.sp_cdc_enable_table*
- *sys.sp_cdc_stop_ job*

System functions:

- *cdc.fn_cdc_ get_all_changes_<capture_instance>*
- *sys.fn_cdc_has_column_changed*
- *cdc.fn_cdc_ get_net_changes_<capture_instance>*
- *sys.fn_cdc_increment_lsn*
- *sys.fn_cdc_decrement_lsn*
- *sys.fn_cdc_is_bit_set*
- *sys.fn_cdc_ get_column_ordinal*
- *sys.fn_cdc_map_lsn_to_time*
- *sys.fn_cdc_ get_max_lsn*
- *sys.fn_cdc_map_time_to_lsn*
- *sys.fn_cdc_ get_min_lsn*

TEST DAY TIP

You can count on questions about Change Data Capture on your exam. This new feature makes tracking down changes and auditing much easier than it has been in the past.

New Table Value Parameter

The ability to pass tables as parameters has been a long time coming. The new table type can be passed to a stored procedure. This will solve quite a few problems!

Here's an example.

To declare a Table User Defined Type in the database:

```
create type MyTableType as table
(
    Name          varchar(150),
    City          varchar(20),
    AddressID     int
)
```

And here's the stored procedure that consumes it:

```
create procedure InsertFriends
(
    @MyTable MyTableType readonly
)
as
    insert
    into Friends (Name, city, AddressID)
    select Name, city, AddressID
    from @MyTable;

--To fill create and fill the temp table:
declare @MyBestFriends_temp MyTableType
insert into @MyBestFriends_temp values ('Debbie', 'Havertown', 2)
insert into @MyBestFriends_temp values ('Chris', 'Philadelphia', 1)
insert into @MyBestFriends_temp values ('Tom', 'Garden City', 11)
insert into @MyBestFriends_temp values ('Greg', 'Lansdowne', 6)
insert into @MyBestFriends_temp values ('Steve', 'Wilmington', 6)

--And finally, to execute:
execute InsertFriends @MyBestFriends_temp
```

FileStream Data Types

FileStream data types are a new, interesting feature in SQL Server 2008. Basically, the database engine will store all of the data associated with the column in a disk file as opposed to the actual database. You might have used a similar home-grown scheme in earlier versions of SQL, but this integrates everything nicely into SQL Server.

In order to use FileStream, you must first enable it. This is accomplished via the *sp_FILESTREAM_configure* system stored procedure, or via the GUI in Management Studio under **Advanced settings**.

Once FileStream is enabled, a file group must be added to the database in order for it to be able to use FileStream data types.

FileStream has the following limitations:

■ Database mirroring cannot be configured in databases with FileStream data.

■ Database snapshots are not supported for FileStream data.

■ Native encryption is not possible by SQL Server for FileStream data.

EXAM WARNING

Be sure you remember the limitations of FileStream data types!

Sparse Column Support

Sparse columns are a new addition to SQL Server. Sparse columns allow for the optimized storage of null columns. Sparse columns can be a good thing, but be sure to enable them only on columns that contain sparse data, or your storage requirements may go up instead of down.

To enable a column as a sparse column, use the create statement in SQL or change the properties in the column to *Sparse* (see Figure 1.4).

Figure 1.4 Enabling a Column as a Sparse Column

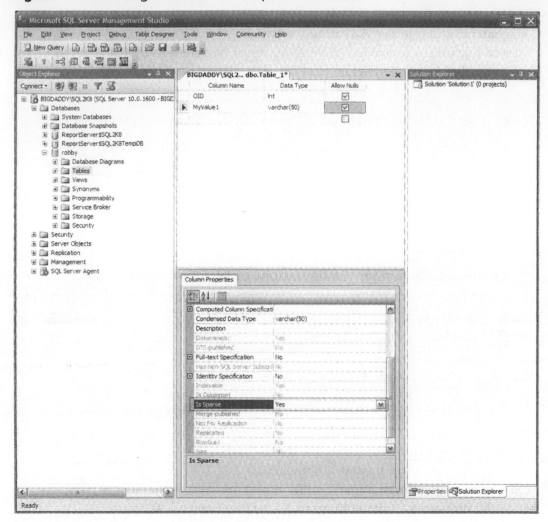

The SQL to accomplish this is as follows:

```
CREATE TABLE dbo.Table_1
    (
    OID int NULL,
    MyValue1 varchar(50) SPARSE NULL
    ) ON [PRIMARY]
GO
```

Encryption Enhancements

In the past, to use whole database encryption efficiently, it was necessary to purchase a third-party product such as NetLib. There are many other products out there that can be used for this as well.

Transparent data encryption (TDE) is available in SQL Server 2008. TDE allows you to easily encrypt the contents of your database and is designed to provide protection to the entire database. With TDE, you can encrypt the contents of your database with no changes to your application.

To enable TDE, you need to first create a master key and a certificate. Once the master key and certificate are set up, use the following to enable TDE:

```
ALTER DATABASE myDatabase SET ENCRYPTION ON
```

Once TDE is enabled, it's designed to be transparent to the application.

Key Management and Encryption

Encryption requires keys to secure the database. These keys must be protected and backed up so that in the event the system needs to be re-create, the data will still be accessible. An enterprise key management system can be incorporated where you use a hardware security module to store the keys in separate hardware.

Encryption is covered in greater detail in Chapter 5.

High Availability

There are quite a few new features when it comes to higher availability in SQL Server 2008. *Mirroring* has been improved, *Hot Add CPU* has been added, and *Hot Add Memory* is available. This means you can add a CPU or memory without switching the server off. Special hardware is required to take advantage of Hot Add CPU and Hot Add Memory, and these are supported only in the Enterprise Edition of SQL Server 2008.

SQL Server 2008 can also take advantage of the new failover clustering enhancements available in Windows 2008.

It's important to note that not all features are available in all of the SQL Server editions. For example, failover clustering is not available in the Web Edition or Workgroup Edition.

Performance

There are a number of performance enhancements in SQL Server 2008. Many of these upgrades are internal to SQL Server 2008, but there are a few worth mentioning.

Performance Data Management

Performance data management is a new tool available in SQL Server 2008. Performance data management allows you to collect performance-related data from your SQL Server servers over time. Performance data management consists of a warehouse database (for storing the results) and the data collector, and collection is usually scheduled to run at specific times.

Resource Governor
(Similar to Query Governor)

Resource Governor is a nice new feature to help manage workload by limiting the resources available to a process. To use the Resource Governor, the DBA creates a workload group and a resource pool. Workload groups are containers to hold user sessions. Workload groups are mapped to resource pools.

User sessions are mapped to workload groups based on classifier functions. The classifier functions can be by IP address, username, application name, and so on.

Figure 1.5 shows at a high level how it all fits together.

Figure 1.5 Managing a Workload with Resource Governor

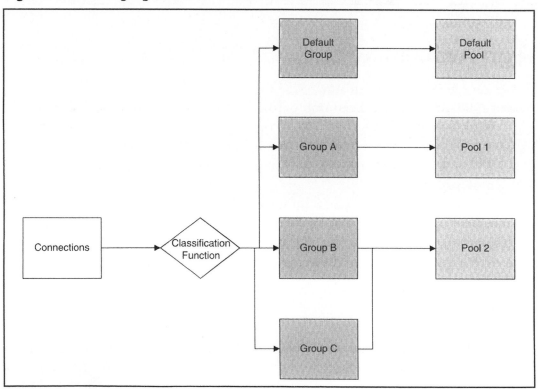

Freeze Plan

Freeze plan is a cool (pardon the pun) new feature in SQL 2008. Plan freezing is meant to offer greater predictability when it comes to executing a particular query in SQL Server 2008.

By executing a few lines of code, you can create a plan guide, which is basically a cached plan that is kept around and used for a particular query.

First, you need to create the data warehouse, which is fairly easy. There's a wizard that will guide you through the steps in the management console. The wizard's main dialog is shown in Figure 1.6.

Figure 1.6 Creating a Data Warehouse

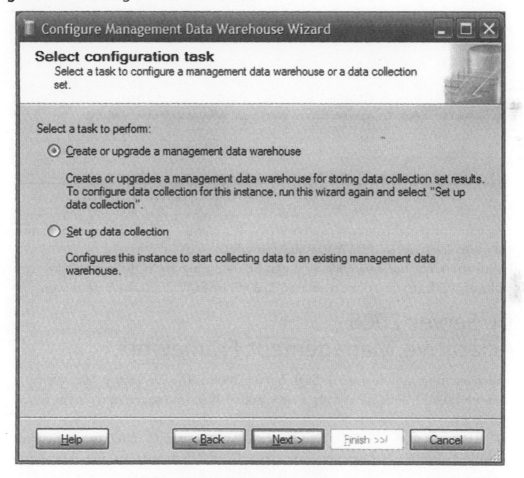

The actual *how to* is found later in this book; it's worthwhile knowing how to use this new feature.

Figure 1.7 is a sample of one of the reports available in the data collection set.

Figure 1.7 A Data Collection Report

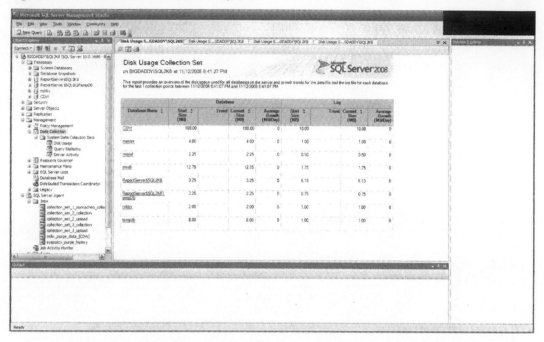

As you can see, this report can be useful. It provides quite a bit of information about your databases and their size and growth.

Unfortunately, the data collection can be used only on SQL Server 2008 servers. It will not work if you connect to a SQL 2005 or SQL 2000 database server.

SQL Server 2008 Declarative Management Framework

Another exciting new feature in SQL Server 2008 is the *Declarative Management Framework* (DMF). This is basically a new policy-based management system for SQL Server 2008.

The DMF is very similar to Windows policy; however, it's much more focused on SQL Server specifics. For example, you can enforce a particular naming convention for stored procedures and a different naming convention for tables.

There are three main components to the DMF: policies, conditions, and facets. See Figure 1.8.

Figure 1.8 DMF Components

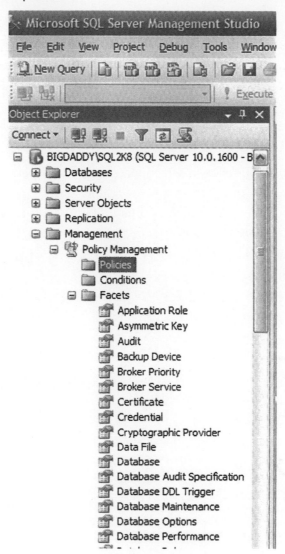

To create or apply a policy, you would right-click on the **policy node** and proceed from there. In the following screens, you'll be prompted to use facets and conditions to create a policy.

Development Improvements

Now we'll discuss a few development improvements that were made to SQL Server 2008.

LINQ Support

LINQ is a new technology. It's more of a programming language than T-SQL. It's basically a mapping of the database object to programming objects. This allows for a more object-oriented approach to dealing with database objects than in the past. This is a cool new feature and is covered in greater detail later on in this book.

MERGE Statement

The *MERGE statement* performs insert, update, or delete operations on a target table based on the results of a join to a source table.

For example, you can synchronize two tables by inserting, updating, or deleting all of the rows in one table based on differences in the other table.

Here is an example of *MERGE* code:

```
MERGE MyDatabase.Inventory AS target
USING (SELECT ProductID, SUM(OrderQty) FROM mySales.Orders AS o
    JOIN mySales.mySalesOrderHeader AS soh
    ON o.mySalesOrderID = soh.mySalesOrderID
    AND soh.OrderDate = @OrderDate
    GROUP BY ProductID) AS source (ProductID, OrderQty)
ON (target.ProductID = source.ProductID)
WHEN MATCHED AND target.Quantity - source.OrderQty <= 0
    THEN DELETE
WHEN MATCHED
    THEN UPDATE SET target.Quantity = target.Quantity - source.OrderQty,
        target.ModifiedDate = GETDATE()
OUTPUT $action, Inserted.ProductID, Inserted.Quantity,
Inserted.ModifiedDate, Deleted.ProductID,
    Deleted.Quantity, Deleted.ModifiedDate;
```

More on *MERGE* can be found in Chapters 6 and 9.

Spatial Data Type

The *spatial data type* is a new data type available in SQL Server 2008. The spatial data type is used to store location-based data. This could be a boon to applications that do geocoding.

Analysis Services Improvements

In *Analysis Services,* some of the new improvements are a better cube designer, an improved dimension and attribute designer, and enhanced data mining structures.

ETL/SSIS Enhancements

Many of the new features carry over to SSIS, like Change Data Capture and the *MERGE* statement. Another good new feature is being able to script in C# instead of only VB.NET. This will make things a bit easier for those of us who really like C#.

Reporting Services

There have been a few improvements to *SQL Server Reporting Services.* The configuration has changed; for example, it now supports rich text format.

In addition, SharePoint integration Reporting Services now will integrate closely with Microsoft SharePoint.

No Longer Requires IIS

This is a key new breakthrough. In the past, IIS needed to be installed to host Reporting Services. Most of the time, this involved running IIS on the database server that had the reporting databases on it.

Better Graphing

Reporting Services supports graphing, which is great when creating dashboard style reports, charting sales, tracking growth, or doing anything better suited to a graph. This will make the Reporting Services reports an enterprise-class solution.

Export to Word Support

Reporting Services now has the ability to export to Word. This is a cool new feature, because in the past, you needed to purchase a third-party product such as OfficeWriter in order to export to Word.

Deprecated Features

The following is a list of deprecated features that are still available in SQL Server 2008, but will not be in future versions. Remember that while these will still work in SQL Server 2008, they are not a recommended best practice.

- BACKUP {DATABASE | LOG} WITH PASSWORD
- BACKUP {DATABASE | LOG} WITH MEDIAPASSWORD
- RESTORE {DATABASE | LOG} … WITH DBO_ONLY
- RESTORE {DATABASE | LOG} WITH PASSWORD
- RESTORE {DATABASE | LOG} WITH MEDIAPASSWORD
- 80 compatibility level and upgrade from Version 80
- DATABASEPROPERTY
- WITH APPEND clause on triggers
- Default setting of disallow results from triggers option = 0
- *sp_dboption*
- FASTFIRSTROW hint
- *sp_addremotelogin*
- *sp_addserver*
- *sp_dropremotelogin*
- *sp_helpremotelogin*
- *sp_remoteoption*
- *@@remserver*
- SET REMOTE_PROC_TRANSACTIONS
- *sp_dropalias*
- SET DISABLE_DEF_CNST_CHK
- SET ROWCOUNT for INSERT, UPDATE, and DELETE statements
- Use of *= and =*
- COMPUTE / COMPUTE BY
- *sys.database_principal_aliases*
- sqlmaint Utility
- The RAISERROR (Format: RAISERROR integer string) syntax is deprecated.

EXAM WARNING

Be sure you are aware of deprecated and removed features, as these may be the "correct" way to answer some of the questions that relate to earlier versions of SQL Server. They would not be the "correct" answer when working with SQL Server 2008.

Discontinued Features

The following is a list of features that are no longer available in SQL Server 2008:

- *sp_addalias*
- Registered Servers API
- DUMP statement
- LOAD statement
- BACKUP LOG WITH NO_LOG
- BACKUP LOG WITH TRUNCATE_ONLY
- BACKUP TRANSACTION
- 60, 65, and 70 compatibility levels
- DBCC CONCURRENCYVIOLATION
- *sp_addgroup*
- *sp_changegroup*
- *sp_dropgroup*
- *sp_helpgroup*
- Northwind and pubs
- Surface Area Configuration Tool
- *sp_makewebtask*
- *sp_dropwebtask*
- *sp_runwebtask*
- *sp_enumcodepages*

Summary of Exam Objectives

In this chapter, we reviewed the new features in SQL Server 2008. While most of these features will be found on your test, it's important to understand all of the content in this book. You can expect that the test will cover both the new features and some of the older features in earlier versions of SQL Server.

There are a number of deprecated features in SQL Server 2008. Know what they are and expect them to be "wrong" answers on your test, even though they still work in SQL Server 2008.

Be sure you know what features are no longer available in SQL Server 2008. Know what they are and expect them to be "wrong" answers on your test.

Exam Objectives Fast Track

New Feature Overview

- ☑ There are quite a few new features in SQL Server 2008, such as Change Data Capture and Declarative Management Framework.

- ☑ Reporting Services no longer requires IIS.

Reporting Services

- ☑ Deprecated features are features that will soon be removed. To that end, you should not use any of the deprecated features, for while they will work in SQL Server 2008, they will most likely be removed from the next version.

- ☑ Deleted features are no longer available. They may have worked with the last version of SQL Server, but they are no longer available and cannot be used.

Exam Objectives
Frequently Asked Questions

Q: Can I use the new Declarative Management Framework to enforce a naming convention across my mix of SQL 2005 and SQL 2008 servers?

A: No, the DMF can only be used on SQL 2008 servers.

Q: Can I use the new Change Data Capture feature across my mix of SQL 2005 and SQL 2008 servers?

A: No, the Change Data Capture feature can only be used on SQL 2008 servers.

Q: Can you use compression when backing up a SQL Server 2005 database?

A: No, compression is a new feature available in SQL Server 2008.

Q: Will backup compression take longer to complete?

A: The answer to this is complicated. In general, the disk is the bottleneck, so in most cases, backup compression will actually speed up your backups.

Q: We use an application that uses SQL 2005 DMVs. Will it work with SQL 2008?

A: For the most part the DMVs remain intact. However, you should test your application to be certain.

Self Test

A Quick Answer Key follows the Self Test questions. For complete questions, answers, and explanations to the Self Test questions in this chapter, as well as the other chapters in this book, see the **Self Test Appendix**.

1. You are setting up security for your new SQL Server 2008 installation. Management is concerned about security. What approach should you take to ensure security settings are optimal?

   A. Use the Surface Area Configuration Tool to secure the installation.

   B. Use the new Security Analysis tool to secure the installation.

   C. Use SQL Server Configuration Manager to secure the installation.

   D. Use Windows Service Manager to enable and disable the appropriate services.

2. You have been tasked with setting up standards for your SQL Server 2008 installation. You need to enforce a table naming convention. What is the best way to accomplish this in your SQL Server 2008 environment?

   A. Use Windows Group Policy.

   B. Create DDL Triggers.

   C. Create DML Triggers.

   D. Create a Declarative Management Framework policy.

3. You have been asked to create a backup of your production database and restore it on a development server. Your production server is using the full recovery model. Full backups are taken Monday and Wednesday. Transaction log backups are taken every hour. Today is Friday. The backup needs to be created as quickly as possible. What's the fastest way to get the latest database copy while minimizing impact to production?

   A. Create a normal backup. Use that to restore to development.

   B. Create a Copy Only Backup. Use that to restore to development.

   C. Use the Wednesday backup. Restore the transaction log backups since Wednesday.

   D. Copy the .mdf and log files and use *SP_attach*.

4. You have a SQL Server 7.0 database and would like to move it to a new SQL Server 2008 instance. The database is part of an FDA-validated system and cannot be changed at all. How can this be accomplished?

    A. Restore the 7.0 database on your new server and set the compatibility mode to 7.

    B. You must upgrade the database to SQL 2005 or greater.

    C. Restore the 7.0 database on your new server and set the compatibility mode to 6.5.

    D. Copy the .mdf and log files and use *SP_attach*.

5. You have an application that is being upgraded from SQL Server 2005 to SQL Server 2008. You notice that some stored procedures are not working correctly. An excerpt is as follows:

```
SELECT *
FROM Territories, Region
WHERE territories.regionid *= region.regionid
```

    What should you do to resolve the issue?

    A. There is no issue. The problem lies elsewhere.

    B. The join syntax is incorrect. Replace with left join.

    C. The select is incorrect. You need to enumerate the fields.

    D. The where clause should be = not *=.

6. Your disk is almost full on the transaction log drive for a database server. How can you resolve this issue?

    A. Use BACKUP LOG WITH TRUNCATE_ONLY.

    B. Change the mode to simple and shrink the log.

    C. Reinstall SQL.

    D. Drop the database and restore from the last backup.

7. You want to enforce a standard naming convention for stored procedures. What's the best way to do this in SQL Server 2008?

    A. Create a DDL trigger.

    B. Use the performance data warehouse.

    C. Create DML triggers.

    D. Use the SQL Server 2008 Declarative Management Framework.

8. You want to enforce a standard naming convention for tables and stored procedures. Your company has two SQL 2008 servers and 60 SQL 2005 servers. You need to use the same solution on all servers. What's the best way to do this in SQL Server 2005 and SQL Server 2008?

    A. Create a DDL trigger for all servers.

    B. Use the performance data warehouse.

    C. Create DML triggers.

    D. Use the SQL Server 2008 Declarative Management Framework.

9. You have a database table with a varchar(600) field in it. Most of the records in the table have a null value for this field. How can you save space?

    A. Move the data into a second table.

    B. Use sparse columns.

    C. Install a third-party tool on the machine to compress the data.

    D. Use the SQL Server 2008 Declarative Management Framework.

10. You have a database table with a FileStream field in it. Most of the records in the table have a null value for this field. What's the best way to save space?

    A. Move the data into a second table.

    B. Use sparse columns.

    C. Use the SQL Server 2008 Declarative Management Framework.

    D. None of the above

11. You need to store images for a Web site using SQL Server 2008. How can you accomplish this?

    A. Use a FileStream data type, and the images will be stored on disk.

    B. Use a varchar data type and store the images in that field.

    C. Use an int data type and store the images in that field.

    D. Use an nchar data type and store the images in that field.

12. You are responsible for a system that is used for both online transaction processing (OLTP) and reporting. When reports run on the server, the OLTP process slows way down. How can you allow reports to be run on the server and minimize impact to the OLTP processes?

    A. Use the Resource Governor.

    B. Use a DDL trigger.

    C. Use a DML trigger.

    D. Use processor affinity masks.

13. You are creating an application to track crime in different locations throughout a large city. What data type could prove useful for storing location data (longitude and latitude)?

    A. Varchar

    B. int

    C. Char

    D. Spatial

14. You are running out of space on the drive used to store backups. All of the servers use the same network location. What can you do to save space with your backups while maintaining the same number of backups?

    A. Use data compression.

    B. Use compressed backups.

    C. Use full backups.

    D. Use a third-party tool.

15. You need to store sensitive data in your SQL Server database. The application has already been written and works fine. What's the easiest way to do this without having to change your application?

    A. Modify the stored procedures to use *xp_encryptstring*.

    B. Use transparent data encryption.

    C. Use a third-party tool.

    D. Use a trigger.

16. Within your application, you need to log all changes to one table. DDL and DML changes must be logged. What's the best approach to solve this problem?

    A. Use the built-in auditing capability.

    B. Create a DDL trigger.

    C. Create a DML trigger.

    D. This cannot be accomplished.

17. You have a server that supports Hot Add CPU. The current CPU utilization is 95 to 100 percent most of the time. The server is mission-critical and cannot be shut down. SQL Server 2008 Standard Edition is installed. What should you do?

    A. Use the Hot Add CPU feature to add another CPU.

    B. Use the Hot Add CPU feature to add two CPUs.

    C. Add more memory to the server.

    D. Schedule an outage and add another CPU to the server.

18. You are contemplating using data compression on a table. You would like to know how much space this will save. How can you determine the savings?

    A. View the table properties.

    B. Enable compression, then check the table size.

    C. Use *sp_estimate_data_compression_savings*.

    D. Use *sp_check_compression*.

19. You have a server that supports Hot Add Memory. Performance is sluggish, and you believe adding more memory will help. The server is mission-critical and cannot be shut down. SQL Server 2008 Standard Edition is installed. What should you do?

    A. Use the Hot Add CPU feature to add another CPU.

    B. Use the Hot Add CPU feature to add two CPUs.

    C. Add more memory to the server.

    D. Schedule an outage and add memory to the server.

20. You have a SQL Server 2008 installation, and you want to create a high-availability solution. What are the ideal approach(es) to solve this problem?

A. Backup and restore

B. Replication

C. Mirroring

D. Clustering

Self Test Quick Answer Key

1.	**C**	11.	**A**
2.	**D**	12.	**A**
3.	**B**	13.	**D**
4.	**B**	14.	**B**
5.	**B**	15.	**B**
6.	**B**	16.	**A**
7.	**D**	17.	**D**
8.	**A**	18.	**C**
9.	**A**	19.	**D**
10.	**D**	20.	**C** and **D**

Chapter 2

MCTS SQL Server 2008 Exam 433

Implementing Objects

Exam objectives in this chapter:

- Understanding DDL and DML Language Elements
- Working with Tables, Constraints, and Indexes
- Creating and Managing Views, Stored Procedures, Functions, and Triggers

Exam objectives review:

- ☑ Summary of Exam Objectives
- ☑ Exam Objectives Fast Track
- ☑ Exam Objectives Frequently Asked Questions
- ☑ Self Test
- ☑ Self Test Quick Answer Key

Introduction

SQL Server 2008 is a mature enterprise data platform, providing objects for storing, accessing, and modifying data. In this chapter you will discover how to create tables, indexes, views, stored procedures, functions, and triggers. Designing database objects and writing scripts for their creation is a key task of database developers. As a database developer, you must understand the concepts behind database objects and have the skills necessary to create and modify them. This chapter will provide you with these key skills.

Database objects are divided into two broad categories: storage and programmability. *Tables* are units of data storage, structured by *columns* and *rows*. Each column in a table stores data of a specific *data type*. You can choose from many built-in data types, or you can create custom *user-defined data types* if necessary. Tables can store large amounts of data, which can take a long time to query. To maximize query performance, you can create fast lookup structures known as *indexes*. Indexes are created on columns that are frequently searched on and enable quick traversal when looking for particular values within a table, similar to the index you will find at the end of a printed book.

You can associate *constraints* with table columns. Constraints define the rules to which data in a particular column or columns must adhere. For example, you can use a constraint to specify that values stored in the **EMailAddress** field are of a particular format. Unique constraints ensure that data for a particular column is unique across the table. For example, you may ensure that product names are always unique in the Products table. Constraints can also define relationships between tables, such as the necessity to have a Customer entity associated with every Order entity. These are known as *FOREIGN KEY constraints*.

Some database objects allow you to define Transact-SQL statements that can be reused again and again. *Views* are based on Transact-SQL *SELECT* statements. They represent a way of viewing a data set and show data from one or more underlying tables. Views can be updated, allowing you to write data to the view and to update underlying tables.

Understanding DDL and DML Language Elements

Transact-SQL is the language used to create objects and access data in SQL Server. Data Manipulation Language (DML) is part of the Transact-SQL language that allows you to insert, modify, and delete data in SQL Server tables. The core statements that comprise DML are *INSERT, UPDATE, DELETE*, and *MERGE*. These statements are covered in Chapters 7 and 8 of this book.

Data Definition Language (DDL), a subset of Transact-SQL, deals with creating database objects such as tables, constraints, and stored procedures. You will examine these statements in depth as they are mapped directly to the exam objectives. SQL Server 2008 Management Studio provides a rich user interface for creating these database objects. However, not all functionality is available within the user interface, and often you will use DDL scripts to create your database objects. The SQL Server 2008 Management Studio user interface simply allows you to create an underlying DDL statement using the appropriate GUI component. Figure 2.1 shows the user interface for creating a table. The DDL statement for creating the same table is shown in Example 2.1.

Figure 2.1 SQL Server Management Studio User Interface

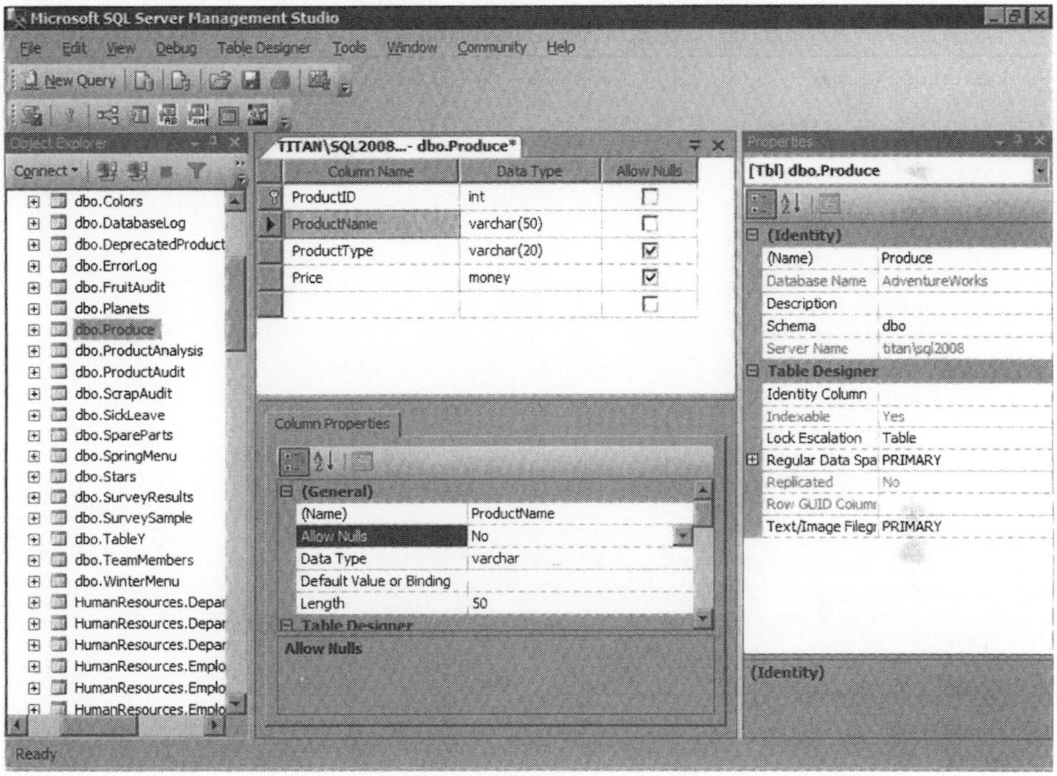

TEST DAY TIP

Remember that the user interface provided by SQL Server 2008 Management Studio allows you to visually design DDL statements. Any task available in SQL Server 2008 Management Studio can be completed using a DDL script, but not all options available within a DDL script are available within the user interface. You must be familiar with the DDL statements of *CREATE, ALTER,* and *DROP* for objects including tables, user-defined data types, views, triggers, functions, and stored procedures.

The key *DDL* statements are *CREATE, ALTER*, and *DROP.* The *CREATE* statement creates a SQL Server database object, such as a table, view, or stored procedure. Example 2.1 creates a new table named Produce and a new view named Fruits. In this example, we also use the *INSERT* DML statement to add three rows into our new table.

Example 2.1 Using the *Create DDL*
Statement to Create a New Table and View

```
USE AdventureWorks;
GO

-- Use the CREATE DDL statement to create a new table named Produce
CREATE TABLE Produce
(ProductID int PRIMARY KEY,
ProductName varchar(50),
ProductType varchar(20))

-- Use the INSERT DML statement to add rows to the Produce table
INSERT Produce VALUES
(1, 'Tomato', 'Vegetable'),
(2, 'Pear', 'Fruit'),
(3, 'Kiwifruit', 'Fruit');
GO

-- Use the CREATE DDL statement to create a new view named Fruit that shows
us only produce of type 'Fruit'
CREATE VIEW Fruit AS
SELECT * FROM Produce WHERE ProductType = 'Fruit';
GO

-- Use the SELECT statement to view the data in the Fruit View
SELECT * FROM Fruit
```

```
-- Results:
-- ProductID         ProductName        ProductType
-- -----------       ------------       -----------
-- 2                 Pear               Fruit
-- 3    Kiwifruit        Fruit
```

The *ALTER DDL* statement changes an existing object, and it can be used to add or remove columns from a table. You can also use this statement to change the definition of a view, stored procedure, trigger, or function. Example 2.2 adds a Price column to the Produce table we have created in Example 2.1. In this example we also redefine the view to include the new Price column. Do not confuse the *ALTER* statement, which changes an object definition, with the *UPDATE* statement, which changes data in a table.

Example 2.2 Using the *Alter DDL* Statement to Add a New Column to a Table and Redefine a View

```
-- Add a new column
ALTER TABLE Produce
ADD Price Money;
GO

-- Use the UPDATE statement to set prices
UPDATE Produce SET Price = 2.50 WHERE ProductID = 1;
UPDATE Produce SET Price = 3.95 WHERE ProductID = 2;
UPDATE Produce SET Price = 4.25 WHERE ProductID = 3;
GO

-- Redefine the view
ALTER VIEW Fruit AS
SELECT ProductID, ProductName, Price FROM Produce WHERE ProductType = 'Fruit';
GO

SELECT * FROM Fruit
-- Results:
-- ProductID         ProductName        Price
-- -----------       ------------       ----------------------
-- 2                 Pear               3.95
-- 3    Kiwifruit        4.25
```

The *DROP DDL* statement removes an object from the database. If other objects depend on the object you are attempting to drop, this statement will not succeed and an error will be raised. Example 2.3 deletes data from the Produce table and then removes both the Fruit view and the Produce table from the database. In this example, we also attempt to drop the Person.Contact table. This operation will fail, as other objects depend on Person.Contact. Do not confuse the *DROP* statement, which removes an object from the database, with the *DELETE* statement, which deletes data from a table.

Example 2.3 Using the *Drop DDL* Statement
to Remove Tables and Views from a Database

```
DELETE FROM Produce;
SELECT * FROM Fruit;
-- Results:
-- ProductID       ProductName          Price
-- -----------     -----------          ------
-- (0 row(s) affected)
DROP VIEW Fruit;
GO

DROP TABLE Produce;
GO

DROP TABLE Person.Contact;
-- Results:
-- Msg 3726, Level 16, State 1, Line 1
-- Could not drop object 'Person.Contact' because it is referenced by a
FOREIGN KEY constraint.
```

Performing a Conditional Drop

In real-life situations, you frequently need to drop the object from the database but only if it already exists. If not, you don't want to receive an error stating that the object does not exist. How should you test for the existence of your object, before attempting to drop it? Query the system views for the existence of your objects. System views belong to the *sys* schema. Useful system tables include:

- sys.Tables
- sys.Columns

- sys.Databases
- sys.Constraints
- sys.Views
- sys.Procedures
- sys.Indexes
- sys.Triggers
- sys.Objects

These object names are self-explanatory. The sys.Objects view contains a row for every object in the database. The key columns are *name*, *object_id*, *type_desc*, *type*, *create_date*, and *modify_date*. Table 2.1 lists the values of the type column, along with the explanation of each type.

Table 2.1 sys.Objects Object Types

Type	Description
C	CHECK constraint
D	Default constraint
F	Foreign Key constraint
FN	Transact-SQL scalar function
FS	Clr scalar function
IT	Internal table
P	SQL stored procedure
PK	PRIMARY KEY constraint
S	System table
SQ	Service queue
TF	SQL table valued function
TR	SQL trigger
U	User table
UQ	Unique constraint
V	View

Example 2.4 uses the EXISTS function to check whether a table named Produce exists. It also uses the OBJECT_ID function to obtain the ID of the Produce table. If the table is found in sys.objects, the next statement will drop the table. Later, the example also creates the table, but only if it does not exist.

Example 2.4 Performing a
Conditional DROP Operation Using sys.objects

```
IF EXISTS (SELECT * FROM sys.objects WHERE object_id = OBJECT_ID(N'[dbo].
[Produce]') AND type = N'U')
DROP TABLE [dbo].[Produce];
GO

IF NOT EXISTS (SELECT * FROM sys.objects WHERE object_id = OBJECT_ID(N'[dbo].
[Produce]') AND type = N'U')
CREATE TABLE Produce
(ProductID int PRIMARY KEY,
ProductName varchar(50),
ProductType varchar(20));
GO
```

When you are preparing for the exam, ensure you have practiced using the *CREATE, ALTER*, and *DROP DDL* statements and have achieved a good understanding of the DDL syntax. The AdventureWorks sample database is a great tool for learning Transact-SQL without the risk of damaging your live databases. Exercises in this chapter are based on the AdventureWorks database. Perform all exercises to get hands-on experience in writing and executing DDL queries.

Working with Tables, Constraints, and Indexes

Tables store data. For each column in the table, you must select a built-in or a user-defined data type. Indexes are created on tables to maximize query performance. Constraints are associated with table columns and define the rules to which data in a particular column or columns must adhere. Constraints can also define relationships between tables, like the necessity to have a Customer entity associated with every Order entity. These are known as *FOREIGN KEY constraints*. In this section we'll provide you with details about tables, constraints, and indexes.

Working with Tables and Views

Tables are the database objects that store data in a SQL Server database. Tables are structured as columns and rows, like a spreadsheet. The columns define the type and length of data they can store. Every table must have at least one column. Column names must be unique within a table; that is, you cannot specify ProductName column to appear twice in the Product table. Tables store the underlying data within the .mdf and .ndf data files as pages and extents. (These are discussed in more detail in Chapter 7.) Columns are sometimes associated with constraints; for example, *PRIMARY KEY, UNIQUE,* or *DEFAULT.* Types of constraints will be explained later in this chapter. You can also mark columns with the following special attributes:

- **Identity columns** Values for these columns are generated automatically in sequence by incrementing every time a row is added. Usually, values 1, 2, 3, *n* are used, but you can define your own seed (starting value) and increment value for the IDENTITY column.

- **Computed columns** These columns do not store any data; instead, they define a formula that calculates the column value at query time.

- **Timestamp columns** These columns are used as a mechanism for version-stamping table rows and tracking changes.

- **UniqueIdentifier columns** These columns store globally unique identifiers (GUIDs). GUIDs values are used for replication and are guaranteed to be unique. GUIDs values can be generated using the *NEWID()* built-in function. This function is covered in depth in Chapter 8 of this book.

When defining columns for a new or existing table, you can specify column *nullibility*. A column is said to be nullible if it allows storing null (empty) values. You can choose to mark a column as not nullible. If anyone attempts to insert a *NULL* value into this column, an error will be raised, and the *INSERT* operation will fail. To mark a column as nullible, use the *NULL* keyword when defining the column in the *CREATE TABLE* or *ALTER TABLE* statements. To mark a column as not nullible, use the *NOT NULL* keyword. By default, columns are nullible. Columns designated as primary keys cannot be nullible.

Creating Tables

Tables can be created and modified using the SQL Server Management Studio table designer or the *CREATE TABLE* or *ALTER TABLE* statements. To access the SQL

Server Management Studio graphical table designer, in Object Explorer expand the database if you wish to create the table. Then, right-click **Tables** and click **New Table**. To modify an existing table, right-click it and then click **Design**. The table designer shows the columns that will be created for your table at the top and the properties of the selected column in the **Column Properties** pane, usually located at the bottom of the screen. Figure 2.2 shows the use of SQL Server Management Studio to create a new table.

Figure 2.2 Using the SQL Server Management Studio Table Designer

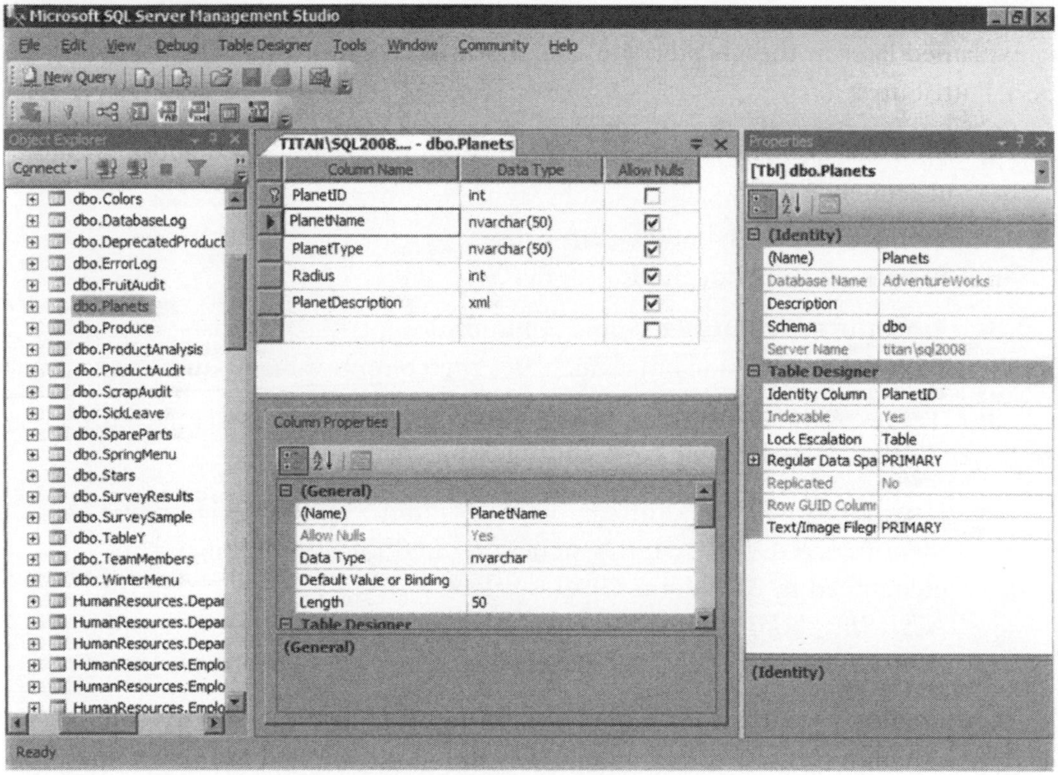

To create a table using DDL, use the *CREATE TABLE* statement along with the syntax shown in Example 2.5.

Example 2.5 *Create TABLE* Statement—Syntax

```
CREATE TABLE [database_name].[schema_name].table_name
(column1_name data_type [NULL | NOT NULL] | [PRIMARY KEY] | [IDENTITY],
Column2_name data_type [NULL | NOT NULL],
[<computed_column_definition>]
```

In this statement, the *table_name* is the name of the table you wish to create. When defining columns, you can specify whether or not they will allow *NULL* values. You can also state that a column will be designated as the *PRIMARY KEY* for the table and whether it will contain automatically incrementing values, known as *IDENTITY* columns. The *computed_column_definition* is the formula for a calculated column. When defining columns, you must designate a data type, like varchar or int, and in some cases a length.

Table 2.2 summarizes built-in data types that are available to you when you are defining columns.

Table 2.2 Built-In Data Types

Numeric	Character	Dates and Times	Other
Tinyint	Char	Datetime	Binary
Smallint	Nchar	Smalldatetime	Bit
Int	Varchar	Date	Cursor
Bigint	Nvarchar	Datetime2	Xml
Smallmoney	Text	Datetimeoffet	Smalldatetime
Money	Ntext	Time	Varbinary
Decimal		Timestamp	Uniqueidentifier
Double			Hierarchyid
Float			Rowversion
Real			Sql_variant
			Image

Some of the data types shown in the table also allow you to specify the length or precision for the data stored in the column you are creating. For example, a column of type *char(1000)* allows you to store up to 1,000 characters per row. A column of type *decimal(10)* allows you to store up to 10 digits on either side of the decimal point, while *decimal(10,5)* allows you to store numbers of up to 10 digits with up to 5 digits to the right of the decimal point. Variable-length data types, like *varchar*, *nvarchar*, and *varbinary*, consume only the space that the characters stored in the column take up. Fixed-length equivalents of *char*, *nchar*, and *binary* consume a fixed amount of space regardless of the amount of actual data contained in the column. Data types prefixed with "n"—*nvarchar* and *nchar*—store Unicode text and can be used to store characters from multiple languages in one column.

Computed Columns

Computed columns are used when you need to store a calculated value in a table. As a best practice, you should never physically store a value in a table that can be derived from other data within the table. If you do so, you will be consuming disk space unnecessarily. You will also open yourself up to logic errors, when the base columns have been updated, but the column storing the derived value is not, and vice versa. SQL Server offers the computed column feature to overcome these challenges. Use computed columns when you don't want to manually calculate a column's value in every query and when you wish to simplify your query syntax.

A computed column is based on a formula that can reference the values of noncomputed columns in the same row of the same table. Scalar functions can also be used in the definition of a computed column. A computed column cannot reference data in other tables or contain a subquery.

By default, computed columns are virtual, and the values in them are not stored on disk. The values are calculated every time the computed column is queried. When it is more efficient to store the values of computed columns on disk, you can use the PERSISTED keyword to instruct SQL Server to physically store the column values. PERSISTED columns are updated when other columns they are based on are updated, or when new rows are inserted into the table. Only computed columns using deterministic functions can be marked as PERSISTED. A function is deterministic when it is guaranteed to return the same value, if you pass it the same parameters. For example, the AVG function is deterministic, while the GETDATE function is not. Whether or not the computed column is persisted, you can never write directly to it. Persisted computed columns can be indexed. This is useful if you need to search and sort by the values of this column.

Creating User-Defined Data Types

Sometimes you need to create your own data types that are based on the built-in data types introduced earlier. Custom data types are also known as user-defined data types. User-defined data types are especially useful when you must store the data with the same length or precision over and over again. For example, you can create a new user-defined data type to represent people's names. This user-defined data type can be based on *nvarchar(50)* and cannot contain nulls. This user-defined data type can now be bound to any column that is to contain people's names and will be consistent throughout. Create your user-defined data types in the Model system database, so that it is automatically inherited by all new databases you create. User-defined data types are created using the *CREATE TYPE* statement. The syntax is shown in Example 2.6.

Example 2.6 *Create TYPE* Statement—Syntax

```
CREATE TYPE [schema_name. ]type_name
{FROM base_type([precision],[scale])
  [NULL | NOT NULL]
}
```

Example 2.7 shows the syntax used to create a user-defined data type named PersonName and to create a table that contains two columns of type PersonName.

Example 2.7 Using the *Create TYPE* Statement

```
CREATE TYPE PersonName
{FROM varchar(50)
  NOT NULL
};
GO

CREATE TABLE TeamMembers
(MemberId int PRIMARY KEY,
MemberName PersonName,
ManagerName PersonName);
GO
```

Use the *ALTER TYPE* statement to change the definition of your user-defined types. The *DROP TYPE* statement should be used to remove the user-defined data types you no longer need in the database. You cannot remove user-defined types from the database while there are tables with columns based on these types. If you attempt to use the *DROP TYPE* statement to remove a data type that is in use, you will get an error message similar to: "Msg 3732, Level 16, State 1, Line 1. Cannot drop type 'PersonName' because it is being referenced by object 'TeamMembers'. There may be other objects that reference this type."

Working with Constraints

Constraints are data validation rules that are bound to a column or a set of columns in a table. Constraints can also be used to enforce a relationship between two entities represented as two tables. The available types of constraints are as follows:

- **CHECK constraints** These constraints validate the integrity of data in a column by checking it against a valid comparison. For example, you can use a *CHECK* constraint to ensure that no one in your Employees table has a

Birth Date earlier than 01/01/1880. You can also use a *CHECK* constraint to validate that an e-mail address is always at least seven characters long.

- **Primary Key constraints** *PRIMARY KEY* constraints represent the unique identifier column that will enforce the uniqueness of each row. For example, you can designate the CustomerID column as the *PRIMARY KEY* for the Customers table. If you get two customers that have the same values in the Name column and other columns, but represent different people, you will use the PRIMARY KEY to distinguish between them. It is a best practice to always have a PRIMARY KEY in each table and to use surrogate PRIMARY KEYs that have no meaning to the application.

- **Unique constraints** These constraints are similar to *PRIMARY KEY* constraints, except that you can have more than one unique constraint per table. For example, you can designate that the combination of FirstName, LastName, and TelephoneNumber is unique in the Customers table and that the EMailAddress column can only contain unique values.

- **FOREIGN KEY constraints** These constraints enforce a relationship between two tables. For example, you can use a *FOREIGN KEY* constraint to specify that any row in the Orders table must have a corresponding row in the Customers table and that the tables are linked through the CustomerID column, which is included in both tables. Once this *FOREIGN KEY* constraint is enforced, you cannot delete a row from the Customers table that has related rows in the Orders table.

- **Default constraints** Also known as "defaults," the *DEFAULT* constraints specify a default value to be inserted into a column if no value is inserted. Defaults can be bound to a column that is defined as *NULL* or *NOT NULL*. An example of a default is to use the value "Not Applicable" for the ProductColor every time someone adds a product to the Products table without specifying a color.

When you attempt to insert, delete, or modify data in a table that will result in a constraint violation, the statement will roll back. *DML* statements, like *INSERT*, *UPDATE*, *DELETE*, or *MERGE*, always succeed or fail as a whole. For example, if you were inserting 1,000 records into a table, but one violated a *PRIMARY KEY* or *UNIQUE* constraint, all 1,000 rows would roll back and nothing would be inserted. If a *DELETE* statement violated a *FOREIGN KEY* constraint, even on one row, the entire *DELETE* statement would fail and nothing would be deleted. You will never receive a partial result set from a *DML* statement. Example 2.8 shows the syntax used for working with constraints.

TEST DAY TIP

Remember that *DML* statements commit as a whole or not at all.
A constraint violation will cause the entire statement to fail and roll back.

Example 2.8 Working with Constraints

```
CREATE TABLE Stars
(StarID int PRIMARY KEY,
StarName varchar(50) Unique,
SolarMass decimal(10,2) CHECK(SolarMass > 0),
StarType varchar(50) DEFAULT 'Orange Giant');
GO
INSERT Stars(StarID, StarName, SolarMass)
VALUES (1, 'Pollux', 1.86);
INSERT Stars(StarID, StarName, SolarMass, StarType)
VALUES (2, 'Sun', 1, 'Yellow dwarf');
SELECT * FROM Stars
-- Results:
-- StarID       StarName    SolarMass     StarType
-- -----------  ----------  ----------    ----------
-- 1            Pollux      1.86          Orange Giant
-- 2            Sun         1.00          Yellow dwarf
INSERT Stars(StarID, StarName, SolarMass, StarType)
VALUES (2, 'Deneb', 6, 'White supergiant');
-- Results:
-- Msg 2627, Level 14, State 1, Line 1
-- Violation of PRIMARY KEY constraint 'PK__Stars__06ABC647542C7691'.
Cannot insert duplicate key in object 'dbo.Stars'.
-- The statement has been terminated.
INSERT Stars(StarID, StarName, SolarMass, StarType)
VALUES (3, 'Deneb', -6, 'White supergiant');
-- Results:
-- Msg 547, Level 16, State 0, Line 1
-- The INSERT statement conflicted with the CHECK constraint "CK__Stars__
SolarMass__58F12BAE". The conflict occurred in database "AdventureWorks",
table "dbo.Stars", column 'SolarMass'.
-- The statement has been terminated.
```

```
INSERT Stars(StarID, StarName, SolarMass, StarType)
VALUES (3, 'Deneb', 6, 'White supergiant');

SELECT * FROM Stars
-- Results:

--DROP TABLE Stars
-- StarID        StarName      SolarMass     StarType
-- ----------    ----------    ----------    ----------
-- 1             Pollux        1.86          Orange Giant
-- 2             Sun           1.00          Yellow dwarf
-- 3     Deneb   6.00    White supergiant
```

Enforcing Referential Integrity through FOREIGN KEY Constraints

A *FOREIGN KEY* constraint creates a relationship between two tables, based on a value held in a column or multiple columns. One of the tables participating in the relationship contains a PRIMARY KEY used in the relationship. The value of the primary key column can only appear once in this table. You can also use a *UNIQUE* constraint instead of a *PRIMARY KEY* constraint to define a relationship. Sometimes the table holding the PRIMARY KEY is referred to as the parent table or the "one" in a one-to-many relationship. The second table also has a column that contains the same values as the PRIMARY KEY column in the parent table. In the second table these values can repeat many times. This table is referred to as the child table, or the "many" table in a one-to-many relationship.

Consider this simple example. The Customers table may contain columns CustomerID, CompanyName, and StreetAddress. The CustomerID column is the PRIMARY KEY column and contains unique values. The Orders table contains an OrderID column, a CustomerID column, and an OrderAmount column. The CustomerID column in the Orders table contains the unique identity of the customer who has placed the order. To look up which customer an order belongs to, look them up by their CustomerID. To find all orders for a particular customer, look them up by their CustomerID. The CustomerID column in the Orders table is known as a *FOREIGN KEY* because it is a key of a foreign entity, an entity that does not belong in the table.

By creating a *FOREIGN KEY* constraint between two tables, their relationship is formalized. The rules of the constraint are applied to the relationship. By default, you cannot delete a parent record, if there are related child records in the child table referenced by a *FOREIGN KEY* constraint. You can also explicitly specify an action to take when the parent record is deleted or the key value of the parent record is updated. To do this, use the *ON UPDATE* and *ON DELETE* optional clauses when creating a *FOREIGN KEY* constraint. The following actions are available:

- **NO ACTION** This is the default action. No special action is taken, and if the FOREIGN KEY is violated, the statement rolls back.

- **CASCADE** Propagate the update or delete action to child rows. If you delete a parent row that participates in a cascading relationship, all child rows will be deleted. If you change a key value of a parent row, the corresponding child rows will also change.

- **SET NULL** Set the values of the FOREIGN KEY column to null for all related records.

- **SET DEFAULT** Set the values of the FOREIGN KEY column to its default values for all related records.

Configuring & Implementing...

Null FOREIGN KEYs and Self-Referencing FOREIGN KEYs

Columns marked as FOREIGN KEYs can contain null values. However, this practice is not recommended because when a FOREIGN KEY consists of two or more columns and contains null values, the constraint cannot be verified, and the integrity of your data cannot be guaranteed.

It is also possible for a *FOREIGN KEY* constraint to reference columns in the same table. This is known as a *self-reference*, and when querying a table in this arrangement it is referred to as a *self-join*. An example of a self-reference is a Generations table containing names of people with the columns PersonID, PersonName, and MotherID. The mother is also a person stored in the Generations table, and therefore, you can create a FOREIGN KEY relationship from the MotherID (FOREIGN KEY column) referencing PersonID (PRIMARY KEY column).

FOREIGN KEY constraints are frequently used by queries to join the parent and child tables. For this reason, it is recommended that you create a nonclustered index on every FOREIGN KEY contained in a table.

Example 2.9 creates two tables and links them by a *FOREIGN KEY* constraint.

Example 2.9 Working with *FOREIGN KEY* Constraints

```
CREATE TABLE Team(
TeamID int PRIMARY KEY,
TeamName varchar(50));
GO

CREATE TABLE TeamMember(
TeamMemberID int PRIMARY KEY,
FullName varchar(100),
TeamID int CONSTRAINT FK_Team_TeamMember
FOREIGN KEY REFERENCES dbo.Team(TeamID));
GO

INSERT Team VALUES (1, 'Development'), (2, 'Testing'), (3, 'Management');

INSERT TeamMember VALUES (1, 'Valentine', 1), (2, 'Bryant', 1), (3, 'Shane', 1),
(4, 'Keith', 3)
SELECT Team.TeamID, TeamName, FullName FROM
Team LEFT JOIN TeamMember ON
Team.TeamID = TeamMember.TeamID ;
GO
-- Results:
-- TeamID          TeamName          FullName
-- -----------     -----------       -----------
-- 1               Development       Valentine
-- 1               Development       Bryant
-- 1               Development       Shane
-- 2               Testing           NULL
-- 3               Management        Keith

DELETE FROM Team WHERE TeamID = 2;
GO
-- Results:
-- (1 row(s) affected)

DELETE FROM Team WHERE TeamID = 3;
GO
-- Results:
-- Msg 547, Level 16, State 0, Line 1
```

```
-- The DELETE statement conflicted with the REFERENCE constraint "FK_Team_
TeamMember". The conflict occurred in database "AdventureWorks", table "dbo.
TeamMember", column 'TeamID'.
-- The statement has been terminated.
ALTER TABLE TeamMember
DROP CONSTRAINT FK_Team_TeamMember;
GO

ALTER TABLE TeamMember
ADD CONSTRAINT FK_Team_TeamMember
FOREIGN KEY(TeamID) REFERENCES dbo.Team(TeamID)
ON DELETE CASCADE;
GO

DELETE FROM Team WHERE TeamID = 3;
GO
-- Results:
-- (1 row(s) affected)
DROP TABLE TeamMember;
GO
DROP TABLE Team;
GO
```

Head of the Class...

Using CHECK and NOCHECK options

When you add *FOREIGN KEY* or *CHECK* constraints to an existing table that already contains data, by default all data in the table is validated against the constraint. Depending on the amount of data in your table, this may take a long time. If you wish to instruct SQL Server not to validate data integrity, and just create the constraint, you can specify *WITH NOCHECK*. The constraint will apply to new and modified rows, but the existing rows will not be examined. Data integrity is not checked when reenabling a previously disabled constraint.

Continued

It is not recommended that you specify *WITH NOCHECK* as this may result in erratic behavior when updating existing data. For example, you may be updating a column that has nothing to do with the constraint, and you may receive constraint violation errors. Only use *WITH NOCHECK* in situations that explicitly require it.

You must understand that constraints that were defined *WITH NOCHECK* are not used by the query optimizer to create efficient queries. To allow the query optimizer to use these constraints, you must reenable them using the *ALTER TABLE* statement with the *CHECK CONSTRAINT ALL* clause.

Creating Indexes

An index is a lookup structure created on a table to optimize, sort, and query performance. Indexes are created on a particular column or columns and store the data values for this column or columns in order. When raw underlying table data is stored in no particular order, this situation is referred to as a *heap*. The heap is composed of multiple pages, with each page containing multiple table rows. When raw underlying data is stored in order, sorted by a column or columns, this situation is referred to as a *clustered index*. For example, if you have a table named Customer, with a clustered index on the FullName column, the rows in this table will be stored in order, sorted by the full name. This means that when you are searching for a particular full name, the query optimizer component can execute the query more efficiently by performing an *index lookup* rather than a *table scan*. Only one clustered index is allowed per table; usually this is created on the column designated as the PRIMARY KEY.

You can also create additional *nonclustered indexes* on a table that is stored either as a heap or as a clustered index. A nonclustered index is a separate lookup structure that stores index values in order, and with each index value, it stores a pointer to the data page containing the row with this index value. Nonclustered indexes speed up data retrieval. It makes sense to create nonclustered indexes on all frequently searched fields in a table. The trade-off with indexes is write performance. Every time a new row is inserted, the index must also be updated. When writing data to a table with nonclustered indexes, sometimes the pages within the table have to be rearranged to make room for the new values. In addition, indexes are storage structures that take up disk space. Indexes are created using the *CREATE INDEX* statement. Example 2.10 shows the syntax for creating an index.

Example 2.10 *CREATE INDEX* Statement—Syntax

```
CREATE [ UNIQUE ] [ CLUSTERED | NONCLUSTERED ] INDEX index_name
ON table_or_view ( column1 [ ASC | DESC ], column2, ...n)
[ INCLUDE (additional_column_name, ...n) ]
[ WHERE filter_clause]
[ WITH OPTIONS]
```

The *CREATE INDEX* statement creates a clustered or nonclustered index on a specified column or columns. You can choose to create the index as *UNIQUE*, which will enforce a *UNIQUE* constraint on the index columns. A *filter_clause* can be specified to create indexes only on a subset of data that meets specific criteria. This is useful for a very large table, where creating an index on all values of a particular column will be impractical. Table 2.3 summarizes index options that can be used with the *CREATE INDEX* statement.

Table 2.3 Index Options

Option	Explanation
PAD_INDEX = ON | OFF	When this option is *ON*, free space is allocated in each page of the index. Allows for new values to be inserted without rearranging a large amount of data. The amount of free space allocated is specified by the *FILLFACTOR* parameter. When this option is *OFF*, enough free space for one row is reserved in every page during index creation.
FILLFACTOR = fill factor percentage	Specifies the percentage of each page that should be filled up with data. For example, a fill factor of 80 means 20% of each page will be empty and available for new data. The fill factor is used only when you create or rebuild an index. Fill factor and index padding are discussed in detail in Chapter 7.

Continued

Table 2.3 Continued. Index Options

Option	Explanation
SORT_IN_TEMPDB = ON	OFF	Specifies whether the data should be sorted in the tempdb database instead of the current database. This may give performance advantages if the tempdb database is stored on a different disk to the current database.
IGNORE_DUP_KEY = ON	OFF	Specifies that duplication errors should be ignored when creating unique indexes.
STATISTICS_NORECOMPUTE = ON	OFF	Specifies that optimization statistics should not be updated at this time.
DROP_EXISTING = ON	OFF	Specifies that the existing index with the same name should be dropped and then be re-created. This equates to an index rebuild.
ONLINE = ON	OFF	Specifies that the underlying table should remain online and accessible by users while the index is being built. This option is only available in SQL Server 2008 Enterprise or Developer edition.
ALLOW_ROW_LOCKS = ON	OFF	Specifies whether locks should be held on each row, as necessary.
ALLOW_PAGE_LOCKS = ON	OFF	Specifies whether locks should be held on each page, as necessary.
MAXDOP = max_degree_of_parallelism	Specifies the maximum number of processors that are to be used during the rebuild operation.
DATA_COMPRESSION = NONE	ROW	PAGE	Use data compression at row or page level of the index. Data compression is discussed in detail in Chapter 7.

Example 2.11 creates a clustered index (by star name) and a nonclustered index (by star type) on the Stars table we created in the previous example. Figure 2.3 shows how the *IX_Star_Name* can be created using the interface of SQL Server Management Studio.

Example 2.11 Working with Indexes

```
--Create the table specifying that the PRIMARY KEY index is to be created
as nonclustered
CREATE TABLE Stars
(StarID int PRIMARY KEY NONCLUSTERED,
StarName varchar(50) Unique,
SolarMass decimal(10,2) CHECK(SolarMass > 0),
StarType varchar(50) DEFAULT 'Orange Giant');
GO

CREATE CLUSTERED INDEX Ix_Star_Name
ON Stars(StarName)
WITH (PAD_INDEX = ON,
FILLFACTOR = 70,
ONLINE = ON);
GO

CREATE NONCLUSTERED INDEX Ix_Star_Type
ON Stars(StarType)
WITH (PAD_INDEX = ON,
FILLFACTOR = 90);
GO
```

Figure 2.3 Creating an Index Using SQL Server Management Studio

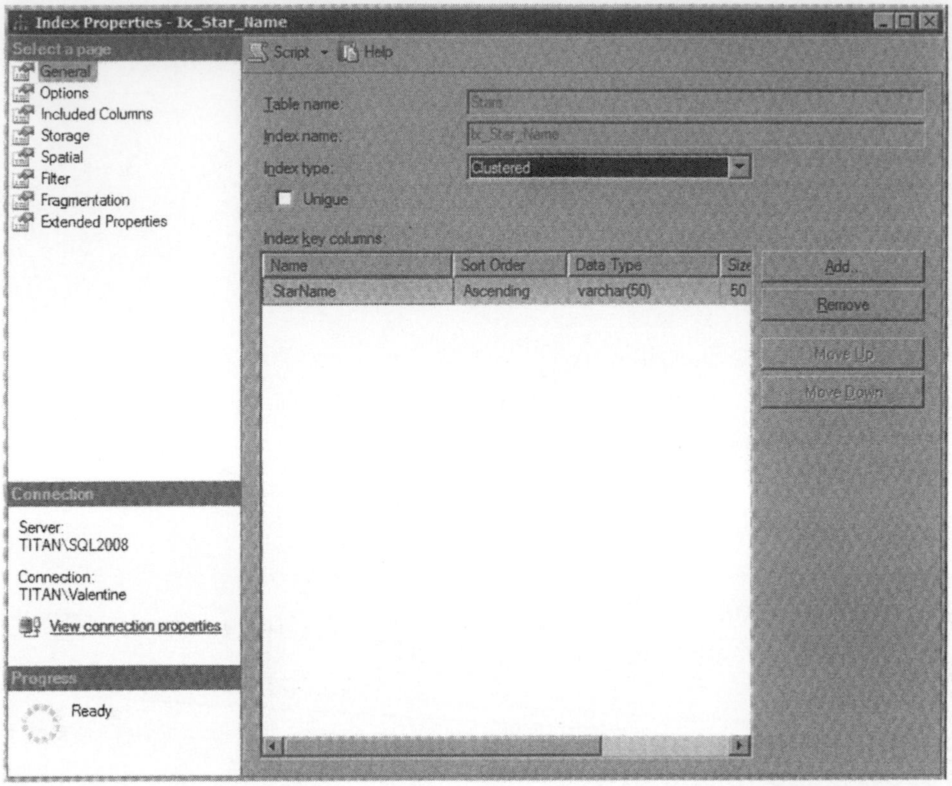

When you are creating a *PRIMARY KEY* constraint, an index on the column(s) designated as *PRIMARY KEY* will be created automatically. This index will be clustered by default, but this can be overridden when creating the index by specifying the **PRIMARY KEY NONCLUSTERED** option. As a best practice, it is recommended that you accept the default of the clustered PRIMARY KEY column, unless you have a specific reason to designate another column as the clustered index key. Usually, the automatically created index is named *PK_TableName_<Unique Number>*, but this can be changed at any time by renaming the index. For example, a newly created Stars table with a *PRIMARY KEY* of StarID automatically has an index named *UQ__Stars__A4B8A52A5CC1BC92*.

Remember that when creating a table, a unique index will be automatically created on the columns designated as the *PRIMARY KEY*. If you wish to avoid the long rebuild time associated with building a clustered index, or if you wish to create the clustered index on a column different from the *PRIMARY KEY,* you must explicitly specify the **PRIMARY KEY NONCLUSTERED** option. The *PRIMARY KEY* will always be unique.

Working with Full-Text Indexes

Standard indexes are great when used with the simple *WHERE* clause of the *SELECT* statement. An index will greatly reduce the time it will take you to locate rows where the indexed column is equal to a certain value, or when this column starts with a certain value. However, standard indexes are inadequate for fulfilling more complex text-based queries. For example, creating an index on StarType will not help you find all rows where the StarType column contains the word "giant," but not the word "supermassive".

To fulfill these types of queries, you must use full-text indexes. Full-text indexes are complex structures that consolidate the words used in a column and their relative weight and position, and link these words with the database page containing the actual data. Full-text indexes are built using a dedicated component of SQL Server 2008—the *Full-Text Engine*. In SQL Server 2005 and earlier, the Full-Text Engine was its own service, known as full-text search. In SQL Server 2008, the Full-Text Engine is part of the database engine (running as the SQL Server Service).

Full-text indexes can be stored on a separate filegroup. This can deliver performance improvements, if this filegroup is hosted on a separate disk from the rest of the database. Only one full-text index can be created on a table, and it can only be created on a single, unique column that does not allow null values. Full-text indexes must be based on columns of type *char, varchar, nchar, nvarchar, text, ntext, image, xml, varbinary*, and *varbinary(max)*. You must specify a type column, when creating a full-text index on a image, varbinary, or varbinary(max) columns. The type column stores the file extension (.docx, .pdf, .xlsx) of the document stored in the indexed column.

Example 2.12 amends the Stars table to include a Description column and creates a full-text index on this column. The *FREETEXT* function allows us to search on any of the words specified using the full-text index. This yields a similar user experience as using an Internet search engine.

Example 2.12 Creating and Using a Full-Text Index

```
ALTER TABLE Stars
ADD Description ntext DEFAULT 'No description specified' NOT NULL ;
GO

CREATE FULLTEXT CATALOG FullTextCatalog AS DEFAULT;
CREATE FULLTEXT INDEX ON Stars(Description)
KEY INDEX PK__Stars__06ABC6465F9E293D;
GO

UPDATE Stars SET Description = 'Deneb is the brightest star in the
constellation Cygnus and one of the vertices of the Summer Triangle. It is
the 19th brightest star in the night sky, with an apparent magnitude of 1.25.
A white supergiant, Deneb is also one of the most luminous stars known. It
is, or has been, known by a number of other traditional names, including
Arided and Aridif, but today these are almost entirely forgotten. Courtesy
Wikipedia.'
WHERE StarName = 'Deneb';

UPDATE Stars SET Description = 'Pollux, also cataloged as Beta Geminorum,
is an orange giant star approximately 34 light-years away in the constellation
of Gemini (the Twins). Pollux is the brightest star in the constellation
(brighter than Castor (Alpha Geminorum). As of 2006, Pollux was confirmed to
have an extrasolar planet orbiting it. Courtesy Wikipedia.'
WHERE StarName = 'Pollux';
GO

SELECT StarName
FROM Stars
WHERE FREETEXT (Description, 'planet orbit, giant' );
GO
-- Results:
-- StarName
-- -------------------------------------------------
-- Pollux
```

Partitioning Data

When working with large databases, query performance often becomes an issue, even if your indexing strategy is spot-on. If you have decided that indexing is not enough to produce your desired result, your next step can be data partitioning. Data partitioning separates a database into multiple filegroups containing one or more files. These filegroups are placed on different disks, enabling parallel read and write operations, thus significantly improving performance. Approach a partitioning strategy by separating different tables and indexes into different filegroups and placing them on separate disks. As a guide, always separate large, frequently accessed tables that are in a FOREIGN KEY relationship, so that they can be scanned in parallel when performing a join.

If the desired performance is not achieved by simple partitioning, this is usually due to very large single tables. You can employ a *horizontal* or *vertical partitioning* technique to split a single large table into multiple smaller tables. Queries that access this table will run quicker, and performance of maintenance tasks, such as backup and index rebuild, will also be improved.

Horizontal Partitioning

Horizontal partitioning splits a table into several smaller tables by separating out clusters of rows, based on a partitioning function. The structure of the smaller tables will remain the same as the structure of the initial table, but the smaller tables will contain fewer rows. For example, if you have a very large table that has 100 million rows, you can partition it into 10 tables containing 10 million rows each. Date columns are often a good choice for horizontal partitioning. For example, a table could be partitioned historically by year—each year stored in a smaller table. Thus, if a query requires data for specific dates, only one smaller table needs to be scanned.

Analyze the data and how your users are accessing this data in order to derive the best horizontal partitioning strategy. Aim to partition the tables so that the majority of the queries can be satisfied from as few smaller tables as possible. To join smaller tables together, *UNION* queries are required, and these can degrade performance.

Vertical Partitioning

Unlike horizontal partitioning, vertical partitioning separates different columns of a single table into multiple tables. The resultant smaller tables have the same number of rows as the initial table, but the structure is different. Two types of vertical partitioning are available:

- **Normalization** Normalization is the process of applying logical database design techniques to reduce data duplication. This is achieved mainly by identifying logical relationships within your data and implementing multiple tables related by *FOREIGN KEY* constraints.

- **Row splitting** This technique separates some columns from a larger table into another table or tables. Essentially, each logical row in a table partitioned using row splitting is stored across two tables. To maintain integrity between the tables, use a *FOREIGN KEY* constraint when both the primary and FOR-EIGN KEY participants are unique. This is known as a one-to-one relationship.

If implemented correctly, vertical partitioning reduces the time it takes to scan data. Use row splitting to separate frequently used and rarely accessed columns into separate tables, and eliminate overhead. The drawback of vertical partitioning is the processing time and resources it takes to perform the joins, when needed.

EXERCISE 2.1

CREATING TABLES, CONSTRAINTS, AND INDEXES

In this exercise, you will use Transact-SQL statements to create a table named Planets. You will create constraints and indexes on the table to enable fast search and data validation. You will also create a full-text catalog on the TeamMembers table.

Before you begin, you must have the following software installed on your computer:

- SQL Server 2008—a free trial is available for download
- AdventureWorks sample database

1. Open SQL Server Management Studio. To do this, click **Start | All Programs | Microsoft SQL Server 2008 | SQL Server Management Studio.**
2. Create a new query against the AdventureWorks database,
3. Create the Planets table and insert three rows of data into it using the following statement.

```
IF Exists(SELECT * FROM sys.tables WHERE name = 'Planets')
DROP TABLE Planets;
GO

CREATE TABLE Planets
(PlanetID int IDENTITY PRIMARY KEY NONCLUSTERED,
PlanetName varchar(50) NOT NULL,
PlanetType varchar(50) NULL,
Radius int CHECK (Radius > 1000),
PlanetDescription varchar(max));
GO

INSERT Planets (PlanetName, PlanetType, Radius) VALUES
('Earth', 'Terrestrial Planet', 6371),
```

```
('Jupiter', 'Gas Giant', 71492),

('Venus', 'Terrestrial Planet', 6051);

GO
```

4. View the data in the Planets table using the following statement.

```
SeLECT * FROM Planets
```

5. Create a unique clustered index on the PlanetName column with 80% fill factor using the following statement.

```
CREATE UNIQUE CLUSTERED INDEX Ix_Planet_Name

ON Planets(PlanetName)

WITH (PAD_INDEX = ON,

FILLFACTOR = 80);

GO
```

6. Update the table to include planet descriptions. Create a full-text index on the PlanetDescription column.

```
UPDATE Planets SET PlanetDescription = 'Earth is the third planet
from the Sun. Earth is the largest of the terrestrial planets in
the Solar System in diameter, mass and density.' WHERE PlanetName
= 'Earth';

UPDATE Planets SET PlanetDescription = 'Jupiter is the fifth planet
from the Sun and the largest planet within the Solar System.' WHERE
PlanetName = 'Jupiter';

UPDATE Planets SET PlanetDescription = 'Venus is the second-
closest planet to the Sun, orbiting it every 224.7 Earth days.
It is the brightest natural object in the night sky.' WHERE
PlanetName = 'Venus';

GO

CREATE FULLTEXT CATALOG PlanetsFullTextCatalog AS DEFAULT;

CREATE FULLTEXT INDEX ON Planets(PlanetDescription)

KEY INDEX IX_Planet_Name;

GO
```

7. Use the *FREETEXT* function to locate the planet that contains the words "sky bright in the night."

```
SELECT PlanetName

FROM Planets

WHERE FREETEXT (PlanetDescription, 'sky bright in the night' );

GO
```

8. Do not delete the table, for you will use it in the next exercise.

Viewing and Modifying Data

A view is a database object that represents a saved *SELECT* statement and is also referred to as a virtual or logical table. Views can be queried in the same way as tables, and some types of views can be updated, too. Using views instead of tables can greatly simplify data access and decouple client applications from the underlying tables containing actual data. With the appropriate use of views, it is possible to completely change the schema of the database and redesign the tables without breaking any client applications. Think of views as an abstract interface between your physical database tables and the people or applications querying them.

Creating Views

SQL Server 2008 allows you to create views of the following types:

- **Standard view** This view is based on one or more base tables. The view may include joins, filter restrictions (using the *WHERE* clause), and row count restrictions (using the *TOP* and *ORDER BY* clauses). You cannot use the *ORDER BY* clause in a view without specifying the *TOP* clause as well.

- **Updateable view** A view that is based on a single underlying table can be updated directly. Executing *INSERT, UPDATE, DELETE,* and *MERGE* statements on this type of view will affect the data in the underlying table. You can also define an *INSTEAD OF INSERT, INSTEAD OF UPDATE,* and *INSTEAD OF DELETE* trigger on any view, which will perform a particular action when you attempt to insert, update, or delete data in the view.

- **Indexed view** Sometimes it is valuable to create one or more indexes on a view in order to optimize the time it takes to query the view. Indexes can be created on views using standard *CREATE INDEX* syntax. Indexed views must be created with the *SCHEMABINDING* option (see the "Using the SCHEMABINDING Option to Lock in a View's Underlying Schema" sidebar).

- **Partitioned view** A partitioned view joins data that is spread across a table partitioned horizontally—for example, if you have partitioned a table by OrderDate to store orders from five years ago and earlier in one partition, orders created within the last five years in another partition, and orders created this year in yet another partition. A partitioned view will join all the partitions together into one Orders virtual table containing data from all three partitions.

To create a view, use the *CREATE VIEW* statement syntax shown in Example 2.13.

Example 2.13 *CREATE VIEW* Statement—Syntax

```
CREATE VIEW [schema_name].view_name[(column_names)]
[ WITH ENCRYPTION | SCHEMABINDING ]
AS select_statement
[ WITH CHECK OPTION ]
```

Specifying the *column_names* in a view definition allows you to assign names to computed columns or to rename columns produced by the *SELECT* statement. This is useful for calculated columns and columns that may have ambiguous names. If you don't specify explicit column names, the view columns will inherit the same names as the columns in the *SELECT* statement.

Specifying the *WITH ENCRYPTION* option encrypts the view definition. This also prevents the view from being used in replication.

Configuring & Implementing...

Using the SCHEMABINDING Option to Lock in a View's Underlying Schema

Views are named *SELECT* statements and include one or more columns from one or more tables. What will happen if a column or table referenced by a view is dropped from the database? The view will become invalid and will return an error the next time it is queried. To lock the view into the schema objects on which it relies, add the *WITH SCHEMABINDING* option to your *CREATE VIEW* statement.

This option ensures that any table or column referenced by this view cannot be dropped or altered, until the view itself is dropped. This applies only to columns referenced by the view. You can freely add and remove columns from underlying tables, as long as they are not used in the view.

Only specify the *SCHEMABINDING* option when the view references tables from a single database. You must specify the *SCHEMABINDING* option if you wish to build indexes on the view you are creating.

Example 2.14 creates a view based on the Stars table using the *SCHEMABINDING* option. We then attempt to alter the underlying structure of the base table but receive an error. Figure 2.4 demonstrates how the same view can be created using the graphical view designer in SQL Server Management Studio.

Example 2.14 Working with Views

```
CREATE VIEW MyStarsView WITH SCHEMABINDING
AS SELECT StarName, StarType FROM dbo.Stars
WHERE SolarMass >=1;
GO

SELECT * FROM MyStarsView;
-- Results:
-- StarName        StarType
-- ----------      --------------------------------------------------
-- Deneb           White supergiant
-- Pollux          Orange Giant
-- Sun             Yellow dwarf
ALTER TABLE Stars
DROP COLUMN StarType;
GO

-- Results:
--Msg 5074, Level 16, State 1, Line 1
-- The object 'MyStarsView' is dependent on column 'StarType'.
-- Msg 5074, Level 16, State 1, Line 1
-- ALTER TABLE DROP COLUMN StarType failed because one or more objects
access this column.

-- This view is updateable, as it is based upon only one base table
UPDATE MyStarsView
SET StarType = 'White Supermassive Giant'
WHERE StarType = 'White supergiant'
GO

SELECT * FROM MyStarsView;
-- Results:
-- StarName        StarType
-- ----------      --------------------------------------------------
-- Deneb           White Supermassive Giant
-- Pollux          Orange Giant
-- Sun Yellow dwarf
```

Figure 2.4 Creating a View Using SQL Server Management Studio

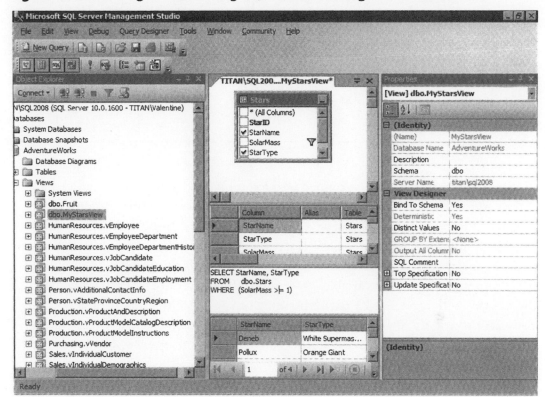

Creating Stored Procedures

Stored procedures are Transact-SQL statements that perform one or more actions and are saved in the database with a name. Stored procedures, used widely to encapsulate the logic of your database system, can accept parameters and return values. Stored procedures are the only database object that can update data by executing *DML* statements. For example, you may write a stored procedure named *AddCustomer* that accepts a *CustomerName*, *EMailAddress*, and *PhoneNumber* parameter. The logic within this stored procedure can check that the potential customer's details are valid, insert a new row into the Customers table using parameter values supplied, and then return the CustomerID of the newly created customer.

To create a stored procedure, use the *CREATE PROCEDURE* statement syntax shown in Example 2.15. The *CREATE PROCEDURE* keywords can be shortened to *CREATE PROC*. To change the definition or options of a stored procedure, use the *ALTER PROCEDURE* or *ALTER PROC* statement.

Example 2.15 *CREATE PROCEDURE* Statement—Syntax

```
CREATE PROCEDURE [schema_name].stored_procedure_name[ ; procedure_number]
[@parameter1_name parameter1_data_type [=default_parameter_value]
[ OUT | OUTPUT] [READONLY]
[@parameter2_name parameter2_data_type…]
[ WITH ENCRYPTION | RECOMPILE | EXECUTE AS]
AS [BEGIN] transact_sql_statements [END]
```

Stored procedures can be grouped into logical named groups. Each procedure within a group will have a unique *procedure_number*, while the entire group can be referred to using the *procedure_name*. The entire procedure group can be dropped at once using the *DROP PROCEDURE* statement. To use a single procedure, you can omit the *procedure_number*. In this case *procedure_name* will always be used to refer to it.

Parameters are named variables passed into the procedure. Parameter names always start with an @, and a data type must be specified for each parameter. You can also use the *default_parameter_value* to assign a default value to a parameter if the procedure was called without this parameter being supplied. The most common use of procedure parameters is to pass values to the stored procedure, so that it can use these values within the Transact-SQL statements that comprise it. Sometimes you must return values to the caller of your stored procedure. To do so, mark each parameter you wish to return to the caller as *OUTPUT* or *OUT* (the two are equivalent). If the parameter is not to be updated within the stored procedure, you can specify it as *READONLY*.

Similar to defining views, specifying the *WITH ENCRYPTION* option encrypts the stored procedure definition. Specify the *WITH RECOMPILE* option to instruct the database engine never to cache the execution plan for this stored procedure. Instead, the optimal execution plan will be calculated every time the procedure is called. The *EXECUTE AS* option allows you to run the procedure as an alternative set of user credentials, different from those of the caller.

Example 2.16 creates and executes a stored procedure to add a new row into the Stars table. The procedure accepts parameters for the star name, star type, solar mass, and description; and returns the ID of the newly created star.

Example 2.16 Creating and Executing a Stored Procedure

```
CREATE PROC AddNewStar
@ID int OUT,
@StarName varchar(50),
@SolarMass decimal(10,2),
@StarType varchar(50),
@Description ntext = 'No description provided.'
AS
BEGIN
  DECLARE @NextStarID int
  SET @NextStarID = (SELECT MAX(StarID) FROM Stars)
  SET @NextStarID = @NextStarID + 1
  INSERT dbo.Stars(StarID, StarName, SolarMass, StarType, Description)
  VALUES(@NextStarID, @StarName, @SolarMass, @StarType, @Description)
  SET @ID = @NextStarID
END;
DECLARE @NewStarID int
EXECUTE AddNewStar @NewStarID OUT, 'Sigma Octantis', 5.6, 'Giant'
SELECT @NewStarID as NewStarID
SELECT * FROM Stars
-- Results:
-- (1 row(s) affected)
-- NewStarID
-- -----------
-- 4
-- (1 row(s) affected)
-- StarID      StarName         SolarMass    StarType         Description
-- -------     --------------   -----------  --------------   -----------
-- 3           Deneb            6.00         White Supermassive  Deneb is the…
                                             Giant
-- 1           Pollux           1.86         Orange Giant     Pollux,also…
-- 4           Sigma Octantis   5.60         Giant            No description…
-- 2           Sun              1.00         Yellow dwarf     No description…
--(4 row(s) affected)
```

Creating Functions

Functions, like stored procedures, are saved Transact-SQL statements. Unlike stored procedures, functions cannot perform actions by executing *DML* statements. Functions always return a single value or a single table-valued expression. They are used by database developers to encapsulate and reuse calculations. For example, you may create a function to calculate the tax amount given a particular salary or to determine whether an e-mail address that has been provided is valid.

It is possible for a function to take no parameters, but often functions accept multiple input parameters and use the parameter values in the calculations which the particular function represents. Unlike stored procedures, functions do not support output parameters. The following types of functions are available within SQL Server 2008:

- **Scalar functions** These functions return a single value of any data type.

- **Single statement table-valued functions** These functions execute a single *SELECT* statement and return the result of this statement as a table-valued expression.

- **Multiple statement table-valued functions** These functions return several table-valued expressions created by one or more *SELECT* statements.

- **Built-in functions** SQL Server provides many built-in functions to perform common tasks. For example, the *GETDATE()* built-in function returns today's date and time. The *AVG()* function returns the average value of the column.

You can use the *CREATE FUNCTION* statement to create new functions using the syntax shown in Example 2.17. You can use the *ALTER FUNCTION* statement to change the function's definition.

Example 2.17 *CREATE FUNCTION* Statement—Syntax

```
CREATE FUNCTION [schema_name].function_name (
[@parameter1_name parameter1_data_type [=default_parameter_value],
[@parameter2_name parameter2_data_type…] )
RETURNS data_type
AS
transact_sql_statements
```

Example 2.18 demonstrates how to create and use scalar and table-valued functions.

Example 2.18 Working with Functions

```
CREATE FUNCTION ConvertKilogramsToPounds
(@Kilograms decimal(18,2))
RETURNS decimal(18,2)
AS
BEGIN
DECLARE @Pounds decimal(18,2)
SET @Pounds = @Kilograms * 2.21
RETURN (@Pounds)
END

PRINT dbo.ConvertKilogramsToPounds(5)
-- Results:
-- 11.05
```

Creating Triggers

Triggers are stored procedures that are bound to a table or view. They run when a *DML* statement is executed on the table or view. You can specify triggers as *FOR UPDATE, FOR INSERT*, and *FOR DELETE*. These triggers will execute immediately after *INSERT, UPDATE,* or *DELETE* operations. You can also create *INSTEAD OF UPDATE, INSTEAD OF INSERT*, and *INSTEAD OF DELETE* triggers. These triggers will execute without the data being actually inserted, updated, or deleted.

A trigger can query tables and views, execute *DML* statements, and include complex Transact-SQL logic. The trigger and *DML* statement that caused the trigger to fire occur within the context of a single transaction. It is possible to roll back *INSERT, UPDATE*, and *DELETE* statements from within a trigger. This is useful for complex data validation purposes. You can use triggers to manually cascade changes through related tables; to guard against malicious or incorrect *INSERT, UPDATE*, and *DELETE* operations; and to enforce other restrictions that are more complex than those defined by using *CHECK* constraints.

EXAM WARNING

Triggers should be used sparingly because they have severe performance implications. In addition, triggers can be difficult to maintain.

Unlike *CHECK* constraints, triggers can reference columns in other tables. For example, a trigger can use a *SELECT* statement from another table to compare to the inserted or updated data and to perform additional actions, such as modifying the data or displaying a user-defined error message. Triggers can evaluate the state of a table before and after a data modification and take actions based on that difference. Multiple triggers of the same type (*INSERT*, *UPDATE*, or *DELETE*) on a table allow multiple different actions to take place in response to the same modification statement. Triggers also allow the use of custom error messages.

Triggers can be specified as *FOR*, *AFTER*, or *INSTEAD OF*. The trigger action will fire during the *DML* statement, after the *DML* statement, or in place of the *DML* statement, respectively. Triggers can be specified for *UPDATE*, *INSERT*, *DELETE*, or any combination of these.

How do you know what data the user is attempting to insert, update, or delete within a trigger? The trigger can access special tables called INSERTED and DELETED. These virtual tables exist only while the trigger is executing. The INSERTED table contains the new values you are attempting to insert into the table, or new values of the row when you are attempting to update data. The DELETED table contains the row you are attempting to delete or old values of the row when you are attempting to update data. Make use of these tables by querying them to determine old and new values of the data being affected. To cancel the *DML* statement from within a trigger and roll it back, use the *ROLLBACK TRANSACTION* statement.

Example 2.19 demonstrates how to create triggers, and the effect they take after a *DML* statement is executed on the table to which the trigger is bound.

Example 2.19 Creating a Trigger on the Stars Table

```
CREATE TABLE StarHistory
(StarHistoryId int IDENTITY PRIMARY KEY, StarName varchar(50), OldType ntext,
NewType ntext, DateChanged DateTime);
GO
CREATE TRIGGER UpdateStarHistory
on dbo.Stars
AFTER INSERT, UPDATE
AS
BEGIN
   INSERT StarHistory (StarName, OldType, NewType, DateChanged)
   SELECT INSERTED.StarName, DELETED.StarType, INSERTED.StarType, GETDATE()
   FROM INSERTED LEFT JOIN DELETED on INSERTED.StarID = DELETED.StarID
END
GO
```

```
UPDATE Stars SET StarType = 'Burnt out' WHERE StarName = 'Sun';
GO

SELECT * FROM StarHistory
-- Results:
-- StarHistoryId    StarName    OldType        NewType       DateChanged
-- -------------    --------    ----------     -----------   ---------------
-- 1                Sun         Yellow dwarf   Burnt out     2009-01-21
                                                             11:56:29.530
```

Test Day Tip

You don't need to be able to write a trigger for the exam. Make sure that you understand the concepts behind triggers and why you may wish to use them. Remember that triggers can be defined on views as well. Creating *INSTEAD OF* triggers on a view that cannot be updated will allow you to perform actions when a user attempts to insert, update, or delete data in the view.

EXERCISE 2.2

WORKING WITH VIEWS AND STORED PROCEDURES

In this exercise, you will use Transact-SQL statements to create views and stored procedures that show and modify data in the Planets table that you have created in Exercise 2.1. Make sure that you have completed Exercise 2.1 before proceeding with this exercise.

1. Switch to **SQL Server Management Studio**.

2. Create a new query against the AdventureWorks database.

3. Create a view named **TerrestrialPlanets** that shows a planet name and planet description for only those planets where the type is "Terrestrial Planet" and insert a new row into the view. View the data in the underlying table to ensure the new row has been inserted. Use the following statement:

   ```
   CREATE VIEW TerrestrialPlanets AS
   SELECT PlanetName, PlanetDescription
   FROM Planets
   WHERE PlanetType = 'Terrestrial Planet'
   GO
   ```

```
SELECT * FROM TerrestrialPlanets;

INSERT TerrestrialPlanets

VALUES ('Mars', 'Mars is the fourth planet from the Sun in the
Solar System.')

SELECT * FROM Planets
```

4. Create a trigger that will update the PlanetType to "Terrestrial Planet" when a new row is inserted into the **TerrestrialPlanets** view. Use the following statement:

```
DELETE FROM Planets WHERE PlanetName = 'Mars';

GO

CREATE TRIGGER UpdatePlanetType

on dbo.Planets

AFTER INSERT

AS

BEGIN

  UPDATE Planets SET PlanetType = 'Terrestrial Planet'

  FROM Planets join INSERTED ON INSERTED.PlanetName = Planets.
PlanetName

END

GO

INSERT TerrestrialPlanets

VALUES ('Mars', 'Mars is the fourth planet from the Sun in the
Solar System.')

SELECT * FROM Planets
```

5. Create and test a stored procedure that will update the radius for a given planet. Use the following statement:

```
CREATE PROCEDURE UpdateRadius

@Radius int,

@PlanetName varchar(50) AS

BEGIN

UPDATE Planets SET Radius = @Radius WHERE PlanetName = @PlanetName

END;

GO

EXECUTE UpdateRadius 3376, 'Mars';

GO

SELECT PlanetName, Radius FROM Planets
```

Summary of Exam Objectives

In this chapter you have learned about creating database objects. As a database administrator, you must understand the types of objects that comprise a database system. Database objects are divided into two broad categories: storage and programmability. Tables store data and are created using the *CREATE TABLE* statement. For each column in the table, you must select a built-in or a user-defined data type. Indexes are created on tables to maximize query performance. Constraints are associated with table columns and define the rules to which data in a particular column or columns must adhere. Constraints can also define relationships between tables, like the necessity to have a Customer entity associated with every Order entity. These are known as *FOREIGN KEY constraints*.

Programmability objects allow you to define Transact-SQL statements that will be reused over and over again. *Views* are based on Transact-SQL *SELECT* statements. They represent a way of viewing a data set, and they show data from one or more underlying tables. Views based on a single underlying table can be updated. Specifying the *WITH SCHEMABINDING* option when creating a view prevents the underlying table from being modified, if the modification will affect the view. *Stored procedures* are compiled Transact-SQL statements that perform particular actions. Stored procedures can accept parameters and return values. *Functions* are similar to stored procedures, except that they always return a value, and they never update data. *Triggers* are actions defined on tables that will execute every time data in a table changes. Triggers can be created *FOR UPDATE, FOR DELETE,* and *FOR INSERT* opeations. You can also create triggers for *AFTER* and *INSTEAD OF DML* operations.

Exam Objectives Fast Track

Understanding DDL and DML Language Elements

- ☑ Data Definition Language (DDL) contains statements used to add, modify, and remove objects from the database. The *DDL* statements are *CREATE, ALTER,* and *DROP.* These statements can be used to create and manipulate tables, data types, indexes, views, stored procedures, functions, and triggers.

- ☑ Data Manipulation Language (DML) is a part of the Transact-SQL language that allows you to insert, modify, and delete data in SQL Server tables. The core statements that comprise DML are *INSERT, UPDATE, DELETE*, and *MERGE.*

- ☑ DDL manipulates database structure, whereas DML manipulates actual data stored in tables.

Working with Tables, Constraints, and Indexes

☑ Use the *CREATE TABLE* statement to define a table by listing columns in the table along with corresponding data types.

☑ Indexes are useful for quickly searching and sorting data. One clustered index is allowed per table, and the underlying table data is stored in the order of the clustered index. Nonclustered indexes are separate lookup structures that point to the table heap or the clustered index.

☑ Full-text indexes are used for specialized querying using functions like *FREETEXT*. Only one full-text index is allowed per table.

☑ Indexes and constraints can be defined separately and are bound to an existing table.

Viewing and Modifying Data

☑ A view is a *SELECT* statement saved with a name. A view can be updated if it is based on a single table, or if it has *INSTEAD OF* triggers defined on it. Indexes can be created on a view as well as on a table.

☑ A stored procedure is any Transact-SQL statement saved with a name. Stored procedures can update data by using *DML* statements.

☑ A function is a Transact-SQL statement that usually performs a calculation. Functions must return a value. Functions that return a single value are known as scalar functions, whereas functions that return a table-valued expression are known as table-valued functions.

☑ A trigger is a statement that runs automatically, when data in a particular table or view is modified. Triggers can cancel transactions by using the *ROLLBACK TRANSACTION* statement. Triggers can be specified as *FOR*, *AFTER*, or *INSTEAD OF*. You can access special *INSERTED* and *DELETED* tables within the trigger to find out the old and new values of rows that are being updated.

Exam Objectives
Frequently Asked Questions

Q: What is the best indexing strategy?

A: Indexing strategies vary depending on your data access pattern and parameters such as the size of your table. As a rule of thumb, it is recommended that you create a clustered index on the PRIMARY KEY column and multiple nonclustered indexes for other frequently searched-on columns.

Q: When should I use **FILLFACTOR** and **PAD-INDEX** options?

A: Use these options when creating or rebuilding an index. Bear in mind that *FILLFACTOR* and *PAD-INDEX* optimize write performance but slightly decrease read performance because more data pages have to be accessed. Do not bother padding indexes based on identity columns. In these cases, new values will never go in the middle of a page; they should always go at the end.

Q: Why would I use *FREETEXT* search function instead of multiple *LIKE* '*%value%*' comparisons?

A: Using *LIKE* comparisons is a highly time- and resource-intensive operation that always requires a table scan. The *FREETEXT* utilizes the full-text index structure and delivers much better performance than the *LIKE* comparison.

Q: What is the advantage of using an updateable view over updating the table directly, given that the updateable view will by definition always be based on a single table?

A: A view is more flexible. For example, you may wish to restructure the underlying tables without the need to change your client applications. You will only need to update the view in this case, not everything that referenced the tables being restructured.

Q: Why should I use stored procedures in preference to functions?

A: Stored procedures are usually used to perform an action, like update, insert, or delete, whereas functions are usually used to perform calculations. Functions cannot be used to execute *DML* statements.

Q: If I define multiple triggers on a single table, what is the order of the triggers firing?

A: The triggers will execute in random order; you cannot rely on the order of triggers firing.

Self Test

1. You are creating a view named WeeklySales. This view is used to create a sales report that is presented to management at the beginning of each week. You want to ensure that the underlying tables on which this view is based are not accidentally modified, causing the report to break. What is the easiest way to implement this view?

   A. Use a *CREATE VIEW WITH CHECK* constraint to create a view.

   B. Use a *CREATE VIEW WITH SCHEMABINDING* statement to create the view.

   C. Do nothing. When a view is based on a table, the underlying table cannot be modified until the view is dropped.

   D. Use a DDL trigger to roll back any statement that attempts to modify the table on which the view depends.

2. You have a view named YearlySales that lists all sales for the year. The reporting application your organization uses allows you to query the YearlySales view by CustomerName or by OrderDate. You receive unfavorable feedback from users that report generation is painfully slow. What is the best way to optimize report performance?

   A. Create indexes on CustomerName and OrderDate columns.

   B. Create a *UNIQUE* constraint on CustomerName and OrderDate columns.

   C. Create a *DEFAULT* constraint on CustomerName and OrderDate columns.

   D. Create a full-text index on CustomerName and OrderDate columns.

3. You have a table named Production that records every unit produced in a factory. Over time, the performance of the queries referencing the Production table has become unacceptably slow, despite your excellent indexing strategy. The row count in the table is approaching 1 billion rows. What should you do to maximize performance without impacting the existing application code?

   A. Design and implement a partitioning strategy for the table.

   B. Delete all indexes on the Production table and re-create them.

   C. Delete all *CHECK* constraints in the Production table.

   D. Delete all *FOREIGN KEY* constraints in the Production table.

4. You have a table named Products, which contains the ProductID, ProductName, Model, and Color columns. The ProductID is marked as IDENTITY. You wish to ensure that there are never two products with the same combination of name, model, and color. What is the easiest way to achieve this?

   A. Create a *PRIMARY KEY* constraint on the ProductName, Model, and Color columns.

   B. Create a *DEFAULT* constraint on the ProductName, Model, and Color columns.

   C. Create a *UNIQUE* constraint on the ProductName, Model, and Color columns.

   D. Create a trigger *FOR INSERT* that checks that the table does not already show a combination of name, model, and color.

5. You have two tables: PrizeDraw and Employees. Both tables have a PersonName column. You must ensure that employees cannot enter the prize draw. A record with the name that already exists in the Employees table cannot be inserted into the PrizeDraw table. What is the best way to achieve this?

   A. Create a *CHECK* constraint on the PrizeDraw table.

   B. Create a *CHECK* constraint on the Employees table.

   C. Create a trigger on the Employees table.

   D. Create a trigger on the PrizeDraw table.

6. You are tasked with creating a Reseller table, with the Commission column containing the commission percent. When a new reseller is added, the default commission level is 30%. What is the easiest way to implement this rule?

   A. Create a *FOR INSERT* trigger on the Reseller table.

   B. Create an *INSTEAD OF INSERT* trigger on the Reseller table.

   C. Create a *DEFAULT* constraint on the Commission column.

   D. Create a *CHECK* constraint on the Commission column.

7. You work for a geological exploration firm, managing databases that are populated by data collected using scientific instruments. The EarthSamples table contains over 1 billion rows of data collected over the last 10 years. The EarthElements database contains around 100 rows and is related to EarthSamples via a one-to-many relationship. The database is becoming

unmanageable and impossible to query. What is the best way to resolve this performance issue without impacting the existing application code?

A. Implement vertical partitioning. Partition the EarthSamples table so that the FOREIGN KEY column that relates to the EarthElements table is separated onto another filegroup.

B. Implement horizontal partitioning. Partition the table by date, separating it into 10 smaller tables—one for each year.

C. Separate EarthSamples and EarthElements tables into different filegroups for parallel scanning.

D. Join EarthSamples and EarthElements tables into the same filegroup for sequential scanning.

8. The HR manager has asked you to create a table that will store candidate resumes. These files are created using Microsoft Word 2003 or Microsoft Word 2007, and the HR manager wants them to be stored in this format. It is a requirement that the HR representatives are able to query the table using search engine-style syntax. How should you create the table?

A.

```
CREATE TABLE Resumes
(ResumeID int PRIMARY KEY NULL,
ResumeFile varbinary(max),
FileType varchar(10))
```

B.

```
CREATE TABLE Resumes
(ResumeID int PRIMARY KEY,
ResumeFile varbinary(max))
```

C.

```
CREATE TABLE Resumes
(ResumeID int PRIMARY KEY,
ResumeFile varbinary(max),
FileType varchar(10))
```

D.

```
CREATE TABLE Resumes
(ResumeID int UNIQUE NULL,
ResumeFile varbinary(max),
FileType varchar(10))
```

9. You have a table named TeamMembers containing the data shown in Table 2.4.

Table 2.4 TeamMembers Table

MemberName varchar(50) PRIMARY KEY
Valentine
Hayden
Matthew

MemberName is the *PRIMARY KEY* for the table. You execute the following statement:

```
INSERT TeamMembers Values ('Phil'), ('Valentine'), ('Peter')
```

Which team members will be present in the TeamMembers table after the statement executes?

    A. Valentine, Hayden, Matthew, Phil

    B. Valentine, Hayden, Matthew, Phil, Peter

    C. Valentine, Hayden, Matthew, Phil, Valentine, Peter

    D. Valentine, Hayden, Matthew

10. You have created a Customers table and an NZCustomers view using the following definitions:

```
CREATE TABLE Customers
(CustomerID int IDENTITY PRIMARY KEY,
CompanyName varchar(50),
Country varchar(50),
Notes varchar(max));
GO

CREATE VIEW NZCustomers AS
SELECT * FROM Customers WHERE Country = 'New Zealand';
GO
CREATE TRIGGER Trig_NZCustomers
ON dbo.NZCustomers INSTEAD OF INSERT
AS
```

```
BEGIN

   SELECT CustomerID FROM INSERTED

END

GO
```

You notice that when you insert data into the NZCustomers view, no error occurs, but the data does not appear in the table. What is the cause of the problem?

A. The *Trig_NZCustomers* must be dropped because it is preventing the insert operation.

B. The view cannot be updated because of the *WHERE* clause. Remove the *WHERE* clause from the view.

C. The *IDENTITY* column is preventing new CustomerIDs from being generated. Redefine the column not to use the *IDENTITY* attribute.

D. You must explicitly call *COMMIT TRANSACTION* within *Trig_NZCustomers*.

Correct Answer & Explanation: *A*. Answer *A* is correct because the *Trig_NZCustomers* is defined as *INSTEAD OF* and therefore is preventing the insert operation.

Incorrect Answers & Explanations: *B*, *C*, and *D*. Answer *B* is incorrect because as long as the view is based on a single table, it is updateable, regardless of the *WHERE* clause. Answer *C* is incorrect because the *IDENTITY* column does not stop update operations in any way. Answer *D* is incorrect because the transaction within the trigger commits automatically.

11. You are adding a Notes column to a table named Customers. You are instructed that the Notes column must always contain a value, even if the value is "No notes available." Unfortunately, many stored procedures you use to add data to the Customers table omit the Notes column, and it is impractical to redesign the stored procedures. What is the easiest way to ensure that the *Notes* column in the Customers table always has a value assigned?

A. Define the Notes column as *NULL*. Create a default constraint on the Notes column with the default value of "No notes available."

B. Define the Notes column as *NOT NULL*. Create a default constraint on the Notes column with the default value of "No notes available."

C. Define the Notes column as *NOT NULL*. Create a *CHECK* constraint on the Notes column.

D. Define the Notes column as *NULL*. Create a *CHECK* constraint on the Notes column.

12. You have a view that displays records from multiple tables within the same database. These tables are managed by different team members. Frequently, your view is inaccessible, when someone modifies the underlying tables. You are instructed by management that the view must work and be accessible at all times. You wish to prevent people from deleting or modifying the tables your view relies on. What is the best way to achieve this?

    A. Use an *ALTER TABLE WITH SCHEMABINDING* statement to update each of the source tables.

    B. Use an *ALTER TABLE WITH CHECK* statement to update each of the source tables.

    C. Use an *ALTER VIEW WITH SCHEMABINDING* statement to create the view.

    D. Use an *ALTER VIEW WITH CHECK* statement to create the view.

13. You have a large table named CustomerEnquiries. There is a clustered index on the CustomerName column. Unfortunately, your users inform you that it takes an excessively long time to add a new customer to the table. How should you resolve this issue?

    A. Use the *ALTER INDEX* statement with the *FILLFACTOR* and *PAD INDEX* options.

    B. Use the *DROP INDEX* statement to drop the index.

    C. Use the *ALTER INDEX* statement with the *NONCLUSTERED* option.

    D. Use the *ALTER INDEX* statement with the *REBUILD* option.

14. You have a table named Customers. When a new customer is added, you must check the CreditRating table for the proposed customer's credit rating. If the credit rating is below a certain value, you must not allow the customer to be added to the Customers table. What is the best way to achieve this?

    A. Create a *FOR INSERT* trigger.

    B. Create an *AFTER INSERT* trigger.

    C. Create an *INSTEAD OF INSERT* trigger.

    D. Create a *CHECK* constraint.

15. You must create a stored procedure that adds a row to the Customers table and returns the ID of the newly inserted customer. Select the statement that will declare the procedure parameters correctly.

    A.
    ```
    CREATE PROC AddNewCustomer
    @ID OUT,
    @CustomerName varchar(50),
    @Notes varchar(max)
    AS…
    ```

    B.
    ```
    CREATE PROC AddNewCustomer
    @ID int OUT,
    @CustomerName varchar(50),
    @Notes varchar(max)
    AS…
    ```

    C.
    ```
    CREATE PROC AddNewCustomer
    @ID int,
    @CustomerName varchar(50) OUT,
    @Notes varchar(max) OUT
    AS…
    ```

    D.
    ```
    CREATE PROC AddNewCustomer
    ID int OUT,
    CustomerName varchar(50),
    Notes varchar(max)
    AS…
    ```

16. You have a table named Orders that contains the OrderID, CustomerID, Amount, and OrderDate columns. You must retrieve all orders placed in the last seven days. What criteria should you use with the *WHERE* clause (select all that apply)?

    A. *WHERE DateDiff*("week", OrderDate, *GETDATE*()) <= 1

    B. *WHERE DateDiff*("day", OrderDate, *GETDATE*()) <= 7

    C. *WHERE GetDate*("day", OrderDate, *DATEDIFF*()) <= 7

    D. *WHERE GetDate*("day", OrderDate, *DATEDIFF*()) >= 7

17. You have a table named Orders. You must make sure that the order date for each order occurs before the ship date. What is the best way to achieve this?

    A. Create a *CHECK* constraint using a *CHECK (OrderDate > ShipDate)* statement.

    B. Create a *CHECK* constraint using a *CHECK (OrderDate < ShipDate)* statement.

    C. Create an *INSTEAD OF INSERT, UPDATE* trigger.

    D. Create a *FOR INSERT, UPDATE* trigger.

18. You always allow 50 Unicode characters for names of people, and you never allow names to be null. You wish to create a user-defined data type that will be used whenever a person's name must be stored. How should you create the data type?

    A. `CREATE TYPE PersonName { FROM varchar(50) NOT NULL }`

    B. `CREATE TYPE PersonName { FROM nvarchar(50) NOT NULL }`

    C. `CREATE TYPE PersonName { FOR varchar(50) NOT NULL }`

    D. `CREATE TYPE PersonName { FROM nvarchar(50)}`

19. In your database system, you must frequently convert from EURO currency to USD currency, using the exchange rate stored in the ExchangeRates table. What is the best way to achieve this?

    A. Create a function that accepts an *@EURAmount* parameter and returns the USD value.

    B. Create a stored procedure that accepts an *@EURAmount* parameter and selects the USD value using the *SELECT* statement.

    C. Create a view that accepts an *@EURAmount* parameter and selects the USD value.

    D. Create a stored procedure that accepts an *@EURAmount* parameter and returns the USD value using the *SELECT* statement.

20. You have two tables—Product and Category. The tables are related by CategoryID column, and many products can be assigned to a single category. You have created a *FOREIGN KEY* constraint named FK_Product_Category using the following code:

```
CREATE TABLE Product(
ProductID int PRIMARY KEY,
ProductName varchar(50),
```

```
CategoryID int CONSTRAINT FK_Product_Category FOREIGN KEY
REFERENCES Category(CategoryID));
GO
```

The category "Floppy Disks" contains over 100 products, but the entire category has been decommissioned. You are asked that the "Floppy Disks" category be removed from the database so that it does not appear in any reports. What code should you use to remove it (select all that apply)?

A.

```
ALTER TABLE Product DROP CONSTRAINT FK_Product_Category;
GO
ALTER TABLE Product ADD CONSTRAINT FK_Product_Category
FOREIGN KEY(CategoryID) REFERENCES Category(CategoryID)
WITH NOCHECK;
GO
DELETE Category WHERE CategoryName = 'Floppy Disks';
```

B.

```
ALTER TABLE Product DROP CONSTRAINT FK_Product_Category;
GO
ALTER TABLE Product ADD CONSTRAINT FK_Product_Category
FOREIGN KEY(CategoryID) REFERENCES Category(CategoryID)
ON DELETE CASCADE;
GO
DELETE Category WHERE CategoryName = 'Floppy Disks';
```

C.

```
DELETE Product
FROM Product
JOIN Category ON Product.CategoryID = Category.CategoryID
WHERE CategoryName = 'Floppy Disks';
GO
DELETE FROM Category WHERE CategoryName = 'Floppy Disks';
GO
```

D.

```
DELETE Category
FROM Product
JOIN Category ON Product.CategoryID = Category.CategoryID
WHERE CategoryName = 'Floppy Disks';
GO
```

Self Test Quick Answer Key

1. **B**

2. **A**

3. **A**

4. **C**

5. **D**

6. **C**

7. **B**

8. **C**

9. **D**

10. **A**

11. **B**

12. **C**

13. **A**

14. **A**

15. **B**

16. **A** and **B**

17. **B**

18. **B**

19. **A**

20. **B** and **C**

Chapter 3

MCTS SQL Server 2008 Exam 433

Programming Objects

Exam objectives in this chapter:

- Implementing Functions
- Implementing Stored Procedures
- Implementing Triggers

Exam objectives review:

- ☑ Summary of Exam Objectives
- ☑ Exam Objectives Fast Track
- ☑ Exam Objectives Frequently Asked Questions
- ☑ Self Test
- ☑ Self Test Quick Answer Key

Introduction

Microsoft SQL Server allows database developers to interact with databases using Transact-SQL (T-SQL) queries. With a single statement, you can easily manage objects (Data Definition Language [DDL]) and manipulate the data (Data Manipulation Language [DML]) of your databases. In addition, you can create scripts with many T-SQL queries and store them in files, which can be used for automation or documentation purposes.

Because SQL Server is easy to use, many applications work with SQL Server databases, calling T-SQL queries from within to process user requests. For example, you can create a report of the clients registered in your application. In this situation, you will use a simple *SELECT* and it is done.

For small requests, such as the one described in the preceding example, the use of simple queries fits the application needs perfectly, and the management of their code is easy. However, as time passes and your databases grow larger and more complex, simple queries will not satisfy the needs of your application. In addition, maintaining the code for T-SQL queries in this complex environment becomes a difficult and stressful job. As a database developer, you should be aware that a rich programming logic will be necessary to accomplish this task and to maintain the code in an efficient way.

To help us achieve these goals, Microsoft SQL Server provides three programmable objects focused on giving us ways to develop and maintain a rich programming logic in our T-SQL queries: functions, stored procedures, and triggers. Besides the built-in set of functions that we saw in Chapter 2, you can create *user-defined functions (UDFs)* to group pieces of code that perform some processing and results in a scalar value or a set of rows; this code will be reused across the application. *Stored procedures* also allow you to group pieces of code, but the return is not mandatory, and it allows us the creation of a secure interface between database and application. *Triggers* are event-responsive codes, which are executed according to database events.

In this chapter, we will present more information on these objects, including their features and uses. We will focus on the creation and management of these objects, and some best practices in preparation for creating them in the real world.

Implementing Functions

Chapter 2 showed you some of the most common built-in functions that can be used in your application, providing great functionality and minimizing the coding task. For example, you can use the *GETDATE()* function to return the current system date and time for use in your *INSERT* statements, or the *AVG()* function to return the average value of a column in your *SELECT*.

Although Microsoft SQL Server provides a great set of built-in functions, you can also create your own function to encapsulate a routine that performs an important action in your application, such as a complex calculation. For example, you can create a function that calculates the number of hours an employee worked in a month, based on his or her work schedule.

When you create a user-defined function, Microsoft SQL Server stores its definition (the code) inside the database. Every time you need to execute that piece of code, you j ust need to call the desired UDF: the routine inside this function is automatically executed, and the result is returned to you. Like the built-in functions, UDFs also can accept parameters. You define them at the creation of the UDF, and the user inputs them upon execution.

According to the return type, UDFs are classified in two groups: scalar functions or table-valued functions. *Scalar functions* return a single scalar value, such as a number or a date. *Table-valued functions* return a set of rows, like a table. A function always returns a result in one of these types.

Advantages and Limitations of UDFs

User-defined functions have many advantages for database developers like you and me. First of all, they allow you to create a function and to call it as many times as you want from your application. As a module of your application, UDFs can be modified independently of the application source code, and their changes will be propagated for all scripts that call these functions. They also reduce the compilation cost of the T-SQL code and accelerate the execution time by caching the execution plan and reusing them for repeated executions. As a result, UDFs don't need to be reparsed and reoptimized for every use. Also, when a function is invoked in the *WHERE* clause of a *SELECT* statement, it reduces the number of rows sent to the application, thereby cutting down on the network traffic.

Although user-defined functions have great advantages, they can only read data. Thus, the UDF cannot be used to insert, update, or delete data; nor can it be used to create, alter, or drop objects. Another limitation is the UDF's availability for only the database where it is stored. If you need to use an existing function for another database, you must re-create it in the desired database.

Scalar Functions

As you learned earlier, scalar functions are routines that return a single scalar value. This return can be any data type except text, ntext, image, cursor, and timestamp. To create a scalar function, you use *the CREATE FUNCTION* T-SQL statement. The syntax of the statement is as follows:

```
CREATE FUNCTION [ schema_name. ] function_name
( [ [ { @parameter_name [ AS ][ type_schema_name. ] parameter_data_type
    [ = default ] [ READONLY ] }
    [,...n ]
  ]
)
RETURNS return_data_type
    [ WITH <function_option> [,...n ] ]
    [ AS ]
    BEGIN
                function_body
        RETURN scalar_expression
    END
[ ; ]
<function_option>::=
{
    [ ENCRYPTION ]
  | [ SCHEMABINDING ]
  | [ RETURNS NULL ON NULL INPUT | CALLED ON NULL INPUT ]
  | [ EXECUTE_AS_Clause ]
}
```

Basically, the *CREATE FUNCTION* statement has a two-part structure: *header* and *body*. The header defines the function name, which must have a unique name that conforms to the rules for objects in SQL Server. The header also defines the input parameter names and data types, and the return parameter data type and optional name, although you don't have to define them to have your function. For each input parameter, you can define a default value and the *READONLY* option. When you define a default value, the function will be executed without specifying a value for that parameter. The *READONLY* option indicates that a parameter cannot be updated or modified within the definition of your function.

Configuring & Implementing...

Input Parameters

In the real world, it's rare to encounter a function without input parameters in your database. Parameters extend the functionality of functions, allowing you to create complex calculations and to customize the return, according to the input of user.

Usually, you will define one or more input parameters in your functions along with their respective data types.

Still talking about the header part, we have the *RETURNS* clause, for which you specify the data type of the scalar value that the function will return, and the optional clause *WITH*, for which you define some function options.

In the *WITH* clause, four options are available to you: *ENCRYPTION, SCHEMABINDING, RETURNS NULL ON NULL INPUT (CALLED ON NULL INPUT)* and *EXECUTE AS*. You specify the *ENCRYPTION* option when you want to encrypt the function definition. The *SCHEMABINDING* option prevents any object that your function depends on from being dropped. The behavior of your function when it receives a null input is defined by the *RETURNS NULL ON NULL INPUT* and *CALLED ON NULL INPUT* options. If you specify the first option, it indicates that SQL Server will return *NULL* when any of the input values received is null, without executing the body of the function. However, if you specify the second option, SQL Server will execute the body of the function, regardless of the null input. By default, when you don't specify anything, SQL Server will set the *CALLED ON NULL INPUT* option. The *EXECUTE AS* option specifies the security context under which the function is executed. Therefore, you can control which user account SQL Server will use to validate permissions on objects referenced in your function.

The body of the *CREATE FUNCTION* statement is the main part of it. It is here where you define the routine of actions that the function will perform. It contains one or more *T-SQL* statements that perform the function logic. This part is delimited by a *BEGIN...END* statement, where you place all the code, and the *RETURN* clause, which is responsible for outputting the value that the function returns as a result of it. Be aware about the read-only restrict that we discussed before. Although you can't use functions to change data and objects, you can use a function as part of a *SET* clause in an *UPDATE* statement, or a *WHERE* clause in a *DELETE* statement. Also, you can change objects local to the function, such as variables.

EXAM WARNING

Be careful about the *RETURNS* and the *RETURN* clauses. Although *RETURNS* specifies the data type of the output and belongs to the header of the function, *RETURN* is the output itself, and it is inserted in the body of the function.

Example: Creating and Consuming a Scalar Function

In the *AdventureWorks2008* database, you have the table *Product*, which is responsible for product data, such as name, color, and size. This table includes a column called *SafetyStockLevel*, which stores the minimal stock of a product (see Figure 3.1).

Figure 3.1 Structure of the Product Table

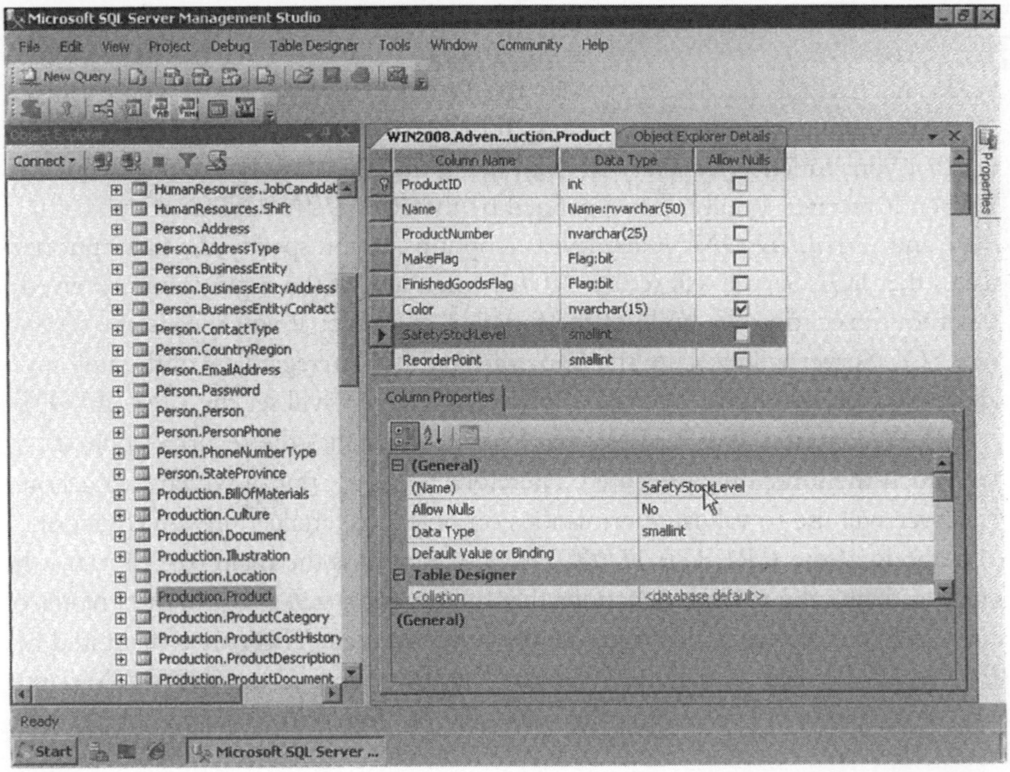

Imagine that you need to retrieve this stock level in many parts of your application. A single *SELECT* could solve the problem, as shown in the following:

```
SELECT SafetyStockLevel
FROM [Production].[Product]
WHERE ProductID = @ProductID
```

But what if you need to use this query ten times? Will you copy and paste it ten times? And if you need to change a name of the column *SafetyStockLevel* to *StockLevel*, will you alter your code ten times? And what if you need to use the return of this query as an argument of another?

As a database developer, you will use your knowledge and create a function that executes this *SELECT* and returns the desired value. Figure 3.2 shows how you can define a scalar-valued function that returns the safety stock level of a given product.

Figure 3.2 Creating a Scalar Function
That Returns the Safety Stock Level of a Product

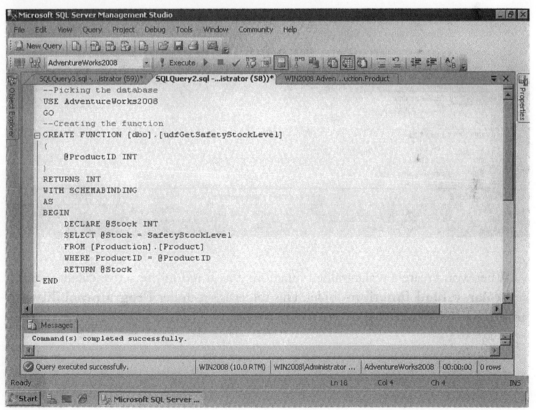

As you can see, the new function has the name *udfGetSafetyStockLevel* and the variable *@ProductID* as an input parameter and returns a value with the *INT* data type. It has the *SCHEMABIDING* option, and the routine is a *SELECT* statement.

Once created, you can use this function in many ways. You can call it using a *SELECT* statement, a *PRINT* command, or inside a *WHERE* clause of a *SELECT* statement, for example (see Figure 3.3).

Figure 3.3 Some Ways to Call the New Function

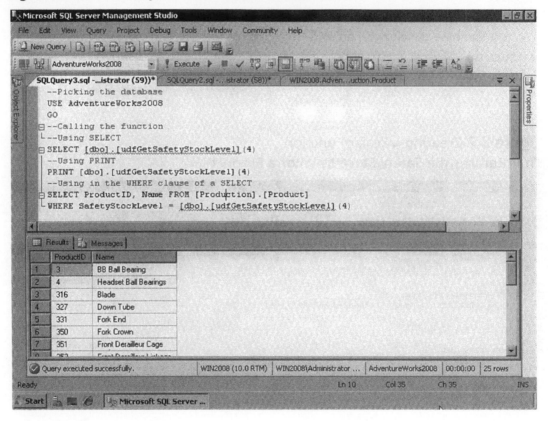

When you create a scalar-valued function, it is stored in the active database, inside the **Scalar-valued functions** folder. This folder is set under **Programmability | Functions** (see Figure 3.4).

Figure 3.4 The Folder Scalar-Valued Functions

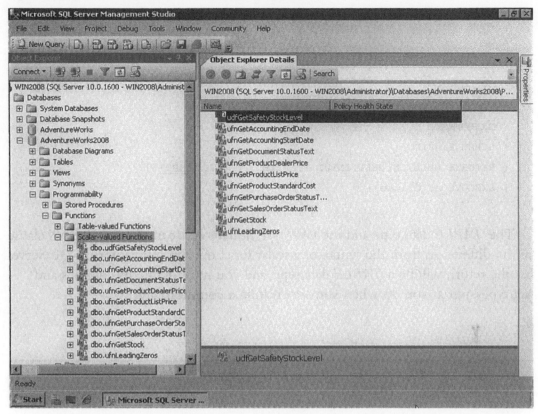

Table-Valued Functions

Table-valued functions have the same rules and options as the scalar function. The difference is that the table-valued functions return a table as output, allowing you to create complex calculations and return a set of rows. The general syntax of a table-valued function is as follows:

```
CREATE FUNCTION [ schema_name. ] function_name
( [ { @parameter_name [ AS ][ type_schema_name. ] parameter_data_type
    [ = default ] [ READONLY ] }
    [ ,...n ]
  ]
)
RETURNS @return_variable TABLE < table_type_definition >
    [ WITH <function_option> [ ,...n ] ]
    [ AS ]
```

```
    BEGIN
            function_body

        RETURN scalar_expression

    END
[ ; ]
<function_option>::=
{
    [ ENCRYPTION ]
    | [ SCHEMABINDING ]
    | [ RETURNS NULL ON NULL INPUT | CALLED ON NULL INPUT ]
    | [ EXECUTE_AS_Clause ]
}
```

The *TABLE* data type and the *table_type_definition* part in the *RETURNS* clause are the differences from the syntax of a scalar function. You must inform SQL Server that the return will be a *TABLE* data type, and you must define its columns and data types, just as you do when you are creating a common table.

Head of the Class...

Temporary Table vs. Table Variable

One of the most common areas of confusion that database developers create involves the definition and use of temporary tables and table variables.

Temporary tables are temporary table structures with data that are stored in the *tempdb* system database. These tables are removed from SQL Server only when a connection that was used to create the table is closed or when a user employs the *DROP TABLE* statement. You use temporary tables to store rows that must be available after its creation. For example, you can create a temporary table to store data of a report. This table can be created inside a function or a procedure, but this table will be available after the execution of the object.

On the other hand, *table variables* are table structures with data that are stored in memory. Unlike temporary tables, table variables only exist

Continued

in the local context of a function, stored procedure, or trigger, and they are removed from memory when the object that created it has exited. You use table variables to temporarily store rows inside a function or a procedure until its execution is complete. For example, you can create a table variable to store data of a *SELECT* statement that will be used inside the object later.

The return of a table-valued function is a table variable, although you can use temporary tables inside the routine for better data manipulation and memory optimization.

A special type of table-valued function, one that returns a table data type, can be used to achieve the functionality of parameterized views. This type is called the *Inline user-defined function*. You can use Inline UDF to support parameters in the search conditions specified in the *WHERE* clause, reducing the number of rows that SQL Server manipulates. The difference between Inline UDFs and views is that a view doesn't support parameters in the *WHERE* clause.

For example, imagine that you need to create a report that lists the clients of a given city. If you have seven cities in all, you will create seven views, one for each city; or you will create a single view with all clients, and filter them using the *WHERE* clause of a *SELECT* statement. The problem of the first way is that you will maintain seven objects. The second one will first select all the clients, and only after that, will it filter data, consuming resources. Using an Inline UDF allows you to have a single object to maintain, and it will only retrieve the data according to the city input by users.

Example: Creating and Consuming a Table-Valued Function and an Inline UDF

Returning to the *AdventureWorks2008* database, let's now collect the product name and number from the table *Products*. The table structure and its columns are the same as those shown in Figure 3.1. Your goal is to retrieve, given a product ID, its name and product number. In this case, you need to return an array of two values. Scalar functions can be used here, since they return a single scalar value. So, you conclude that the solution will be using a table-valued function. Figure 3.5 shows how you can define a table-valued function that returns the name and number of a given product.

Figure 3.5 Creating a Table-Valued Function
That Returns the Name and Number of a Product

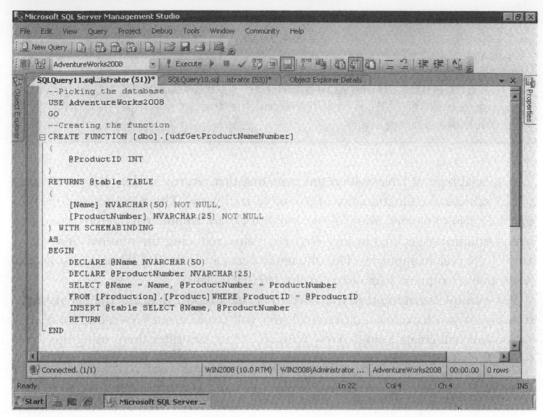

Let's take a better look at the code in Figure 3.5. After the definition of the name and the parameter, you see that the *RETURNS* clause has improved from the last example. Now it shows the definition of a return variable, called *@table*, whose data type is *TABLE* and the specifications of the table variable that the function will return to you. Be careful about the data type of columns: they must match the data they will receive.

In the body part of the function, there is nothing special until an *INSERT* statement appears. This query retrieves the value of the two variables selected before and stores them inside table variable *@table*. Then, the *RETURN* clause returns this variable and ends the function. You don't need to specify the variable that will be returned in the *RETURN* clause: it is already defined in the *RETURNS* clause in the header of the function.

Once created, you can call the function using a *SELECT* statement, specifying the function as the object of the *FROM* clause. When you create a table-valued function, it is stored in the active database, inside the **Table-valued functions** folder. Like the scalar-valued functions folder, the **Table-valued functions** folder is set under **Programmability | Functions**, as shown in Figure 3.6.

Figure 3.6 The Folder Table-Valued
Functions and the Execution of the New Function

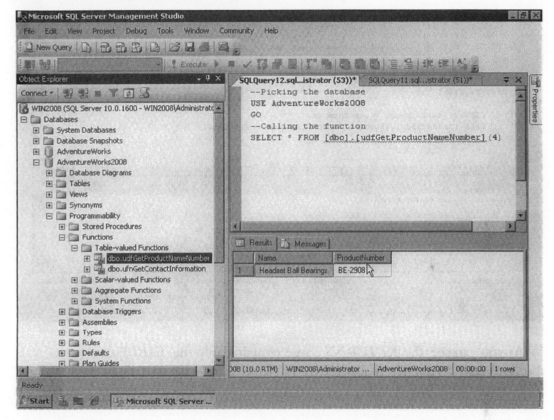

You can solve this problem using the Inline user-defined function too. Figure 3.7 shows how you can define an Inline UDF that returns the name and number of a given product, exactly the same return of the table-valued function.

Figure 3.7 Creating an Inline UDF
That Returns the Name and Number of a Product

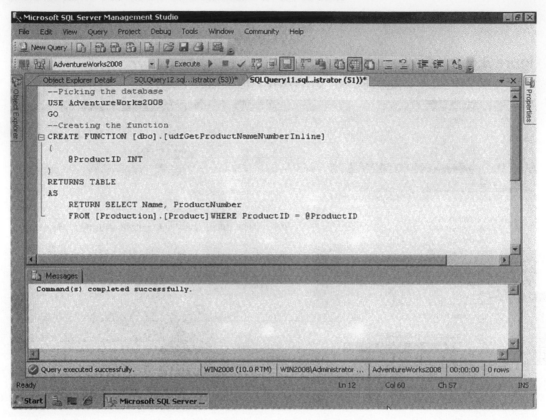

As you can see, the *RETURNS* clause contains only the *TABLE* data type.
You don't have to define the structure of the table variable because it's set by the format
of the result set of the *SELECT* statement in the *RETURN* clause. Also, observe that
there is no *BEGIN…END* statement delimiting the function. The whole function
consists of a single *SELECT* statement, and the result set of this query forms the
table returned by the function.

Managing User-Defined Functions

Managing the existing UDFs is a task as important as creating them. As a database
developer, you need to learn some basic important operations, such as altering a
function and viewing its definition. Basically, there are two ways to manage
functions: using the *SQL Server Management Studio (SSMS)* or using *Transact-SQL*
statements.

In *SQL Server Management Studio*, the functions are stored under
Programmability | Functions of the selected database. You can see the proper-
ties of a function right-clicking it and choosing **Properties** to open a new window.
In the **Function Properties** window, you can see some information about the
selected function, such as if its definition were encrypted (see Figure 3.8).

Figure 3.8 The Function Properties Window

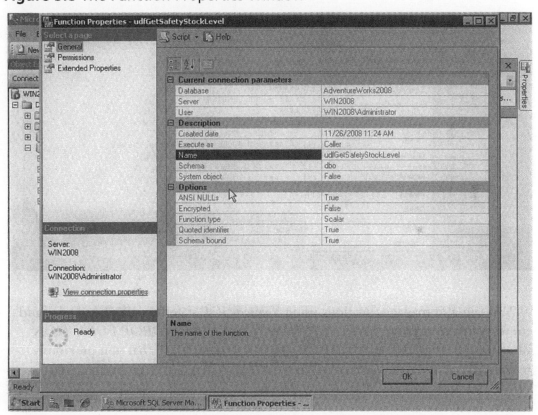

You can also alter the code of the function by right-clicking it and choosing
Modify to open a new query tab (see Figure 3.9). This tab shows the actual definition
of the UDF and allows you to make changes at this function as you wish. After the
changes are made, you can commit them by clicking on the **Execute** button. Also, to
drop a function, right-click the desired function and choose the **Delete** option. You
can see which objects depend on a function and which objects a function depends on
by right-clicking it and choosing use the **View Dependencies** option.

Figure 3.9 Modifying a Function Definition

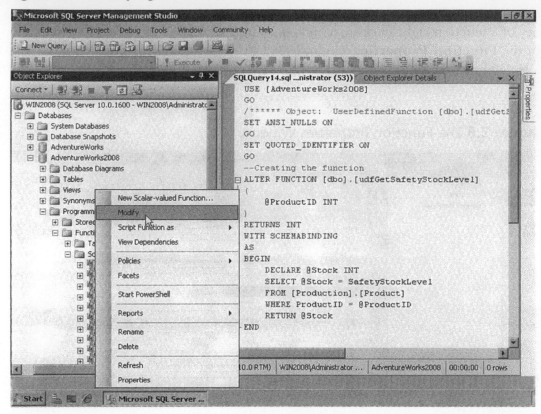

You can also manage functions using *Transact-SQL* statements. You can alter and remove a function using the *ALTER FUNCTION* and the *DROP FUNCTION* statements. The *ALTER FUNCTION* alters an existing UDF that you previously created by executing the *CREATE FUNCTION* statement, without changing permissions and without affecting any dependent functions, stored procedures, or triggers. Its syntax and options are the same as the *CREATE* statement. The *DROP FUNCTION* removes one or more user-defined functions from the current database. The syntax is as follows:

```
DROP FUNCTION { [ schema_name. ] function_name } [,…n ]
```

You can also use *system stored procedures* and *catalog views* to provide information about functions and their definitions. Some of the most common system procedures that you can use to retrieve the function definition and properties are the *sp_help* and *sp_helptext*. The first procedure lets you view information about a user-defined function. The second allows you to view the definition of a user-defined function.

The following example shows you how to retrieve the definition of and information on the scalar-valued function *udfGetSafetyStockLevel*, created in the first example:

```
--View the definition
sp_helptext udfGetSafetyStockLevel

--View the information
sp_help udfGetSafetyStockLevel
```

Managing User-Defined Function Security

As with all objects in SQL Server, you must specify the security context of functions. Every time you call a UDF, SQL Server first verifies if you have the permission to execute it. Once verified and approved, SQL Server then checks whether you have permission to access the objects involved in the routine of the function. Therefore, you should establish the security context of a function and set up the permission for users; these are two essential tasks that you, as a database developer, should execute to protect your functions and the objects involved. Table 3.1 shows the permissions available for a user-defined function.

Table 3.1 User-Defined Functions Permissions

Permission	Description
EXECUTE	Execute a scalar-valued function.
SELECT	Select the data returned by a table-valued function.
VIEW DEFINITION	View the information and definition of a function.
ALTER	Alter the properties of a function.
CONTROL	Assign the permission of a function to other users.
TAKE OWNERSHIP	Take ownership of a function.

You can set the user's permission using the *GRANT, REVOKE,* or *DENY* T-SQL statements. These three statements are components of the *Data Control Language (DCL)* and are responsible for setting the permission of users in objects. The first statement grants permissions on a securable to a principal; the second statement removes granted permissions; and the last statement prevents a user from gaining a specific permission through a *GRANT.* The following two examples show how to grant a user permission on a function:

```
--Grant EXECUTE to a user (Scalar-valued Function)
GRANT EXECUTE ON [dbo].[udfGetSafetyStockLevel] TO Priscila

--Grant SELECT to a user (Table-valued Function)
GRANT SELECT ON [dbo].[udfGetProductNameNumber] TO Herleson
```

Working with Deterministic and Nondeterministic Functions

As a database developer, it's important for you to know whether a function you are using is deterministic or nondeterministic. A function is *deterministic* when it always returns the same value any time for a specific set of input values. On the other side, a function is *nondeterministic* when it returns different values for the same set of input values every time you call.

For example, the built-in function *DAY*, which returns an integer that represents the day of a date, is a deterministic function: it will always return the same value if you input the same date. However, the built-in function *GETDATE*, which returns the current database system timestamp as a *datetime* value, is a nondeterministic function: it will generate a different value every time you call it.

Several properties of the UDF determine SQL Server's ability to index the results of your function, and the determinism of a function is one of these properties. For example, you can't create a clustered index on a view if this view calls a nondeterministic function. Therefore, to maintain and optimize database transactions, it's important that you keep these two concepts in mind.

Test Day Tip

The functions *CAST, COVERT, CHECKSUM, ISDATE,* and *RAND* can sometimes behave as a deterministic function and at other times as a nondeterministic function. Although it's important for you to know when these functions are deterministic, the exam 70–433 doesn't cover this behavior. You only need to know when a function is deterministic or nondeterministic, and functions will be a piece of cake to you.

EXERCISE 3.1

CREATING FUNCTIONS

In this exercise, you will create a scalar function to return the average due value of a given customer. You will then create an Inline UDF that selects the sales according to their values. At the end, you will review these functions' information and definitions.

1. Launch SQL Server Management Studio (SSMS), connect to the instance, open a new query window, and change the context to the *AdventureWorks2008* database.

2. Create the scalar function *udfGetAvgCustomer* by executing the following code:

```
CREATE FUNCTION [dbo].[udfGetAvgCustomer]
(
    @CustomerID INT
)
RETURNS MONEY
AS
BEGIN
    DECLARE @Amount MONEY
    SELECT @Amount = AVG(TotalDue)
    FROM [Sales].[SalesOrderHeader]
    WHERE CustomerID = @CustomerID
    RETURN @Amount
END
```

3. Test the created function calling it using the *SELECT* statement, as follows:

```
SELECT [dbo].[udfGetAvgCustomer](29825)
```

4. Now, let's create an Inline UDF to see the information about the highest sales. Execute the following code to create the *udfGetSales* function:

```
CREATE FUNCTION [dbo].[udfGetSales]
(
    @Amount MONEY
)
```

```
        RETURNS TABLE
AS
        RETURN
        SELECT SalesOrderID, CustomerID, TotalDue
        FROM [Sales].[SalesOrderHeader]
        WHERE TotalDue > @Amount
```

5. **Test the created function calling it, using the *SELECT* statement, as follows:**

```
SELECT * FROM dbo.udfGetSales(170000)
```

6. **To finish, view the information and definition of *udfGetSales* function using the following code:**

```
sp_help udfGetSales
sp_helptext udfGetSales
```

Implementing Stored Procedures

The favorite programming objects used by the database developers so far, *stored procedures,* are compiled SQL routines that are stored in a database and act like an independent program within SQL Server when called. Stored procedures are essential for the security and accessibility of data for applications because they allow you to use them as an interface from your database to your application.

An interface between a database and an application enables you to control the user's access to your database and objects, as well as to protect and isolate your code, resulting in high security and easy maintenance. For example, you can create a stored procedure that inserts the client's data into the table clients. The application will only call the stored procedure responsible for the insert: developers don't need to know the T-SQL code behind this operation, protecting your database and code. Another advantage of this interface is that you will maintain only the code of the stored procedure, regardless of how many times an application refers to your stored procedure: no changes will be necessary in the application if you edit the procedure's code.
In addition, you can grant a user permission to execute a procedure, without having to give permission to realize the actions within the procedure, thereby increasing the security of your database. In other words, you can grant a user permission to execute a procedure that selects data from a table, without granting him the *SELECT* permission on that table: users can execute the procedure but cannot execute a *SELECT* statement in this table.

Creating Stored Procedures

You can use stored procedures to modify data, return a scalar value, or return a result set. Unlike functions, however, the return in stored procedures is not mandatory. Also, stored procedures support almost all commands of SQL Server inside their routines. To create a procedure, you will use the *CREATE PROCEDURE* statement. The general syntax for creating a stored procedure is the following:

```
CREATE { PROC | PROCEDURE } [schema_name.] procedure_name [ ; number ]
    [ { @parameter [ type_schema_name. ] data_type }
        [ VARYING ] [ = default ] [ OUT | OUTPUT ] [READONLY]
    ] [,…n ]
[ WITH <procedure_option> [,…n ] ]
[ FOR REPLICATION ]
AS { <sql_statement> [;][ …n ] }
[;]
<procedure_option> ::=
    [ ENCRYPTION ]
    [ RECOMPILE ]
    [ EXECUTE AS Clause ]
<sql_statement> ::=
{ [ BEGIN ] statements [ END ] }
```

When executing procedure statements, you can use only the word *PROC* as an alias of *PROCEDURE*. Like functions, the structure of the *CREATE PROCEDURE* statement has two parts: *header* and *body*. The header starts with the procedure name, which must have a unique name that conforms to the rules for object in SQL Server. In the header you can define the input parameter names and data types, which are used within the procedure as local variables. The user must supply the value of each declared parameter when the procedure is called, unless a default value is defined or the value is set to equal another parameter. You can also indicate that a parameter cannot be updated or modified within the definition of your procedure, using the *READONLY* option.

You can also define parameters as the output of a procedure, although you don't have to define them. The *OUTPUT* option indicates that the parameter is an output parameter. You can create as many output parameters as your application needs. *OUTPUT* parameters can be any data type, except text, ntext, and image data types.

EXAM WARNING

Although functions can also return scalar value or tables, remember that only procedures can modify data and objects in a server.

The *WITH* clause offers three options for your procedures: *ENCRYPTION*, *RECOMPILE*, and *EXECUTE AS*. You specify the *ENCRYPTION* option when you want to encrypt the procedure definition. The *RECOMPILE* option indicates that SQL Server does not cache a plan for this procedure, and it will be compiled each time the procedure is executed. The *EXECUTE AS* option specifies the security context under which the procedure is executed.

Configuring & Implementing...

When Do You Use the *RECOMPILE* Statement?

When a stored procedure is executed, SQL Server compiles the procedure and stores it in the query cache. The compilation process creates a query plan and an execution plan, allowing SQL Server to reuse them in the subsequent executions, decreasing the answer time of a procedure.

When you use the *RECOMPILE* option, SQL Server will discard the stored query plan and create a new one in each procedure execution. This option is useful when you make changes that bring benefits to the procedure performance, such as the addition of a new index in a table that the routine within the procedure will use. You should use the *RECOMPILE* option in the *ALTER PROCEDURE* statement; you should avoid using it at the creation process.

The body of the *CREATE PROCEDURE* statement is the main part of this statement. This is where you define the routine of actions that the procedure will execute when called. This part is delimited by a *BEGIN...END* statement, where you place all the code. You can execute any T-SQL command, except *SET SHOWPLAN_ TEXT*, *SET SHOWPLAN_ALL* and *USE* statements.

Example: Creating and Consuming a Stored Procedure

The *AdventureWorks2008* database has a table called *ProductCategory*, which shows the categories available for products. Figure 3.10 shows the table structure and its columns. All the columns, except the *Name*, are filled in automatically.

Figure 3.10 The ProductCategory Table Structure

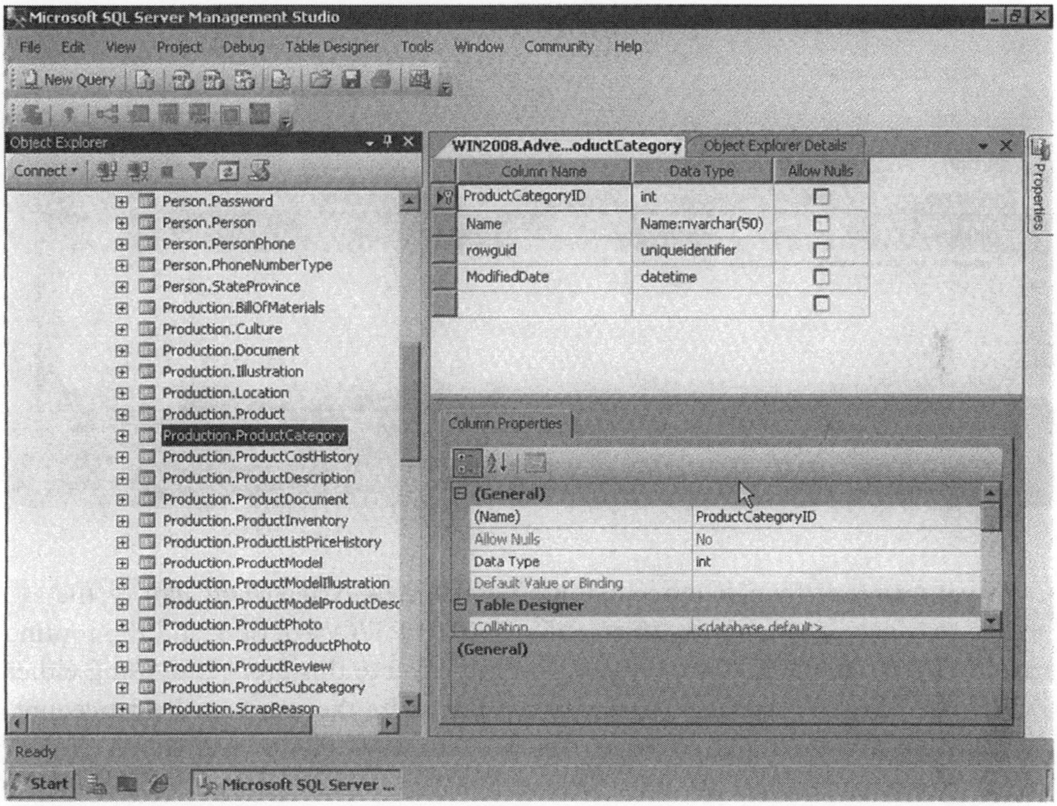

As a database developer, you decide to create a stored procedure to insert new categories into the table *ProductCategory* for your application. With this object, you intend to ease the maintenance of your code and secure your code and data from developers and users. Figure 3.11 shows how you can create a stored procedure that executes an *INSERT* statement in the desired table. When you create a procedure, it is stored in the active database, inside the folder **Stored Procedures**, set under the **Programmability** folder.

Figure 3.11 The Creation Syntax of the Stored Procedure

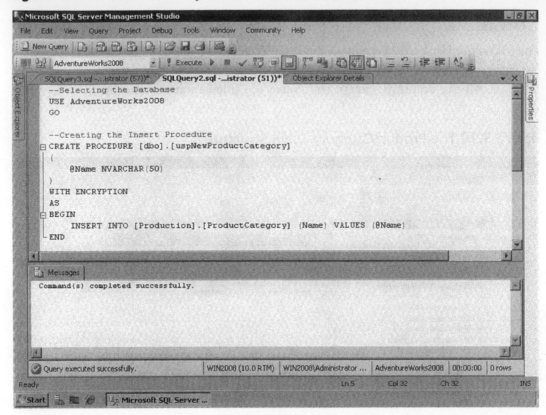

As you can see, the new procedure has the name *uspNewProductCategory*, the variable *@Name* as an input parameter, the *ENCRYPTION* option, and the routine is an *INSERT* statement. Once created, you can execute this procedure using either *EXEC* or *EXECUTE* statements, or you can just write the name of the procedure. Also, you can pass the input parameters in different ways. Figure 3.12 shows the ways to pass parameter values and a *SELECT* that returns the inserted category.

Figure 3.12 Executing the Procedure and Viewing the Inserted Value

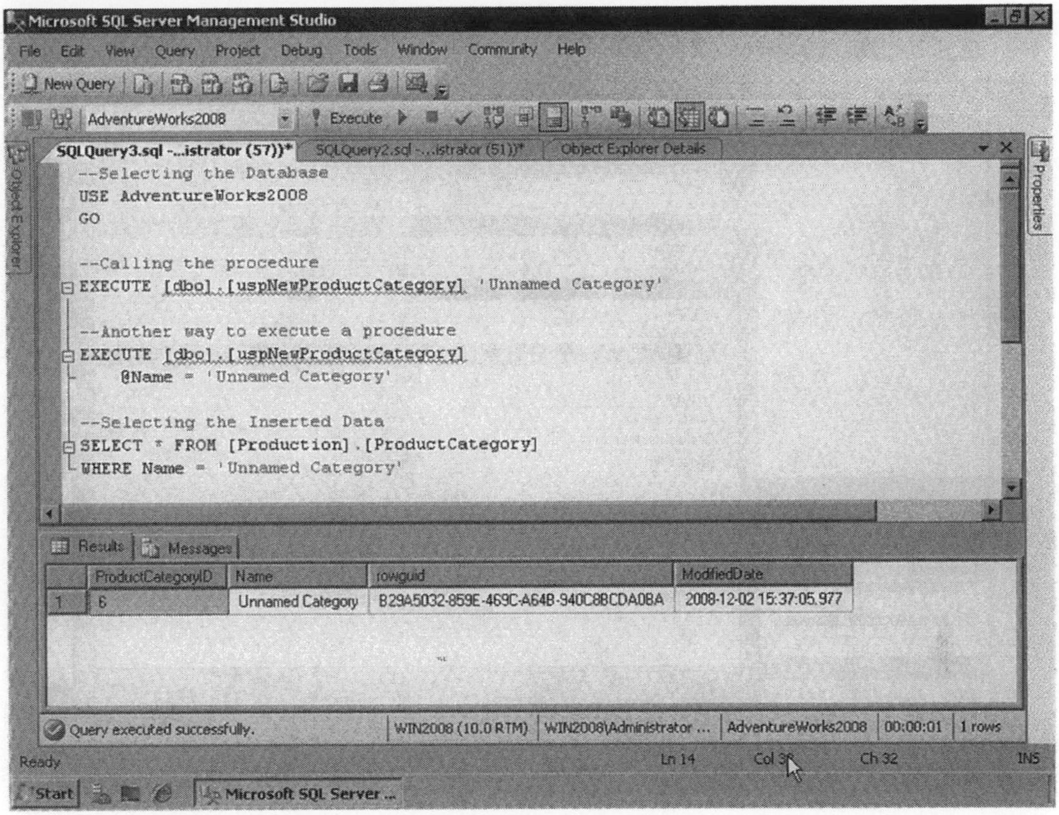

Managing Stored Procedures

As a database developer, you need to learn some basics about managing stored procedure objects, such as altering a procedure and viewing its definition. Basically, there are two ways to manage these procedures: using the *SQL Server Management Studio (SSMS)* or using *Transact-SQL* statements.

In *SQL Server Management Studio*, the procedures are stored under **Programmability | Stored Procedures** of the selected database. You can see the properties of a procedure by right-clicking it and choosing **Properties** to open a new window. In the **Stored Procedure Properties** window, you can see some information about the selected procedure, such as if its definition is encrypted (see Figure 3.13).

Figure 3.13 The Stored Procedure Properties Window

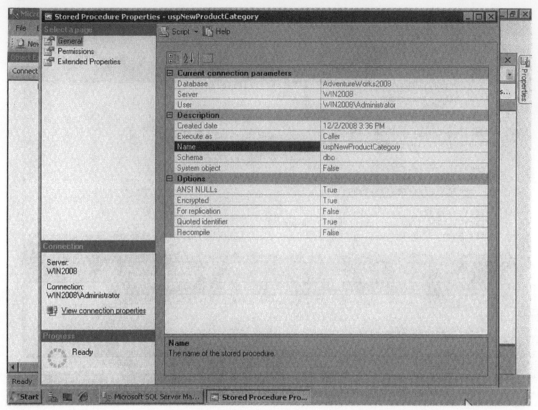

You can alter the code of the procedure by right-clicking it and choosing
Modify to open a new query tab. This tab shows the actual definition of the stored
procedure and allows you to make changes at its code. After you complete the changes,
commit them by clicking on the **Execute** button. Also, to drop a procedure, right-click
the desired object and choose **Delete**. You can see the objects that depend on a
procedure and the objects that a procedure depends on by right-clicking it and
choosing the **View Dependencies** option.

You can also manage procedures using *Transact-SQL* statements. You can alter
and remove a procedure using the *ALTER PROCEDURE* and the *DROP
PROCEDURE* statements. The *ALTER PROCEDURE* alters an existing stored
procedure that you previously created. Its syntax and options are the same as the
CREATE PROCEDURE statement. The *DROP PROCEDURE* removes one or
more procedures from the current database. The syntax is as follow:

```
DROP { PROC | PROCEDURE } { [ schema_name. ] procedure } [ ,...n ]
```

You can also use *system stored procedures* and *catalog views* to provide information about stored procedures and their definitions. Some of the most common system procedures that you can use to retrieve procedure definition and properties are the *sp_help* and *sp_helptext*. The following example shows you how to retrieve the definition of and information on the stored procedure *uspNewProductCategory*, created in the example:

```
--View the definition
sp_helptext uspNewProductCategory

--View the information
sp_help uspNewProductCategory
```

Managing Stored Procedure Security

The stored procedure, as an object, allows you to grant users permission to use it. However, procedures have a security mechanism called delegation, which acts in a special way about the permissions of objects within the procedure and the stored procedure itself. When you grant a user the *EXECUTE* permission, SQL Server automatically delegates your permissions to the objects and statements referenced inside the routine, making the execution of the procedure possible to this user. The user receives these permissions only when executing the procedure, and these permissions don't affect the permissions that you set directly in these objects.

Let's take, for instance, the *uspNewProductCategory* that you created in the example. This procedure inserts rows into the *ProductCategory* table. You have the *INSERT* permission on the table and have also created the procedure. Let's say that users of your application have no permission on the *ProductCategory* table but need to insert new categories inside the table. So, when you grant the *EXECUTE* permission to such users, they can execute this procedure normally because the insert permissions necessary to execute the routine are delegated to them. However, they cannot execute an *INSERT* statement directly, once they have no permission on *ProductCategory*.

The security delegation provided by stored procedures gives you a powerful and secure mechanism, enabling you to create an interface of stored procedures that applications will use. With this interface, users will not access data and tables directly, unless they use the stored procedures you have created and provided. Also, these delegated permissions are still dependent on the code within the procedure, allowing you to validate the input parameters, avoid attacks such as SQL Injection, and execute specific tasks according to the user who is calling the procedure.

Besides *EXECUTE*, stored procedures have other permissions, focused on their administration (see Table 3.2).

Table 3.2 Stored Procedure Permissions

Permission	Description
EXECUTE	Execute a stored procedure
VIEW DEFINITION	View the information and definition of a procedure
ALTER	Alter the properties of a procedure
CONTROL	Assign the permission of a procedure to other users
TAKE OWNERSHIP	Take ownership of a procedure

Like functions, you can set the user's permission using the *GRANT, REVOKE* or *DENY* T-SQL statements. The following two examples show how to grant a user permission on a stored procedure.

```
--Grant EXECUTE to a user
GRANT EXECUTE ON [dbo].[uspNewProductCategory] TO Priscila
```

Adjusting Transaction Isolation Levels

As you have seen, stored procedures have an essential role in the development of databases, creating a secure interface between your database and your application. Most of the procedures that compose this interface execute data manipulation commands: *SELECT, INSERT, UPDATE, DELETE,* and *MERGE* statements.

When you are manipulating data, SQL Server provides isolation levels for the transactions that are being executed. This isolation defines how these transactions will access the resources and how SQL Server will solve concurrency between transactions. The transaction isolation levels control how locks will be taken when data is read, how long the read locks will be held, and how a read operation will reference rows modified by another transaction.

The isolation property is one of the four properties—atomicity, consistency, isolation, and durability (ACID)—that a logical unit of work must display to qualify as a transaction. It is the ability to shield transactions from the effects of updates performed by other concurrent transactions. The level of isolation can actually be customized for each transaction.

Every transaction that you execute always gets an exclusive lock on any data it modifies, and it holds that lock until the transaction is completed. For read operations, transaction isolation levels primarily define the level of protection from the effects of modifications made by other transactions.

If you define a lower isolation level for a transaction, it will increase the ability of many users to access your data at the same time, but it will increase the number of concurrency effects users might encounter, such as dirty reads or lost updates. At the same time, a higher isolation level reduces the types of concurrency effects your users may encounter, but requires more system resources and increases the chances that one transaction will block another.

Concurrency causes three basic side effects: *dirty read*, *nonrepeatable read,* and *phantom read*. A *dirty read* occurs when a second transaction selects a row that is being updated by another transaction. The second transaction is reading data that has not been committed yet and may be changed by the transaction updating the row. A *non repeatable read* occurs when a second transaction accesses the same row several times and reads different data each time. A *phantom read* occurs when an insert or a delete action is performed against a row that belongs to a range of rows being read by a transaction. The transaction's first read of the range of rows shows a row that no longer exists in the second or succeeding read as a result of a deletion by a different transaction.

An example of a *dirty read* is when you are making changes to a table. During the changes, a user creates a new table that is a copy of the table that includes all the changes made to that point. You then decide that the changes that have been made so far are wrong and you remove the changes. The table created by the user contains changes that no longer exist and should be treated as if they never existed. An example of a *nonrepeatable read* is when you read the same table twice, but between each reading a user changes the data. When you read the table for the second time, it has changed. The original read was not repeatable. An example of a *phantom read* is when you propose changes to a table, but when the changes are incorporated into the table, you discover that a user has made other changes to the table without your consent.

As a database developer, you must choose the appropriate isolation level of your transactions and routines within your stored procedures, considering the data integrity requirements of your application and the overhead of each isolation level. The highest isolation level, *SERIALIZABLE*, guarantees that your transaction will retrieve exactly the same data every time it repeats a read operation, but it does this by performing a level of locking that is likely to impact other users in multiuser systems. The lowest isolation level, *READ UNCOMMITTED*, may retrieve data that has been modified but has not been committed by other transactions. All of the concurrency side effects can occur in read uncommitted, but because there is no read locking or versioning, overhead is minimized in your environment.

SQL Server supports the transaction isolation levels defined in SQL-92. The transaction isolation levels are as follows:

- **READ UNCOMMITTED** Specifies that statements can read rows that have been modified by other transactions but not yet committed.

- **READ COMMITTED** Specifies that statements cannot read data that has been modified but not committed by other transactions. This prevents dirty reads. Data can be changed by other transactions between individual statements within the current transaction, resulting in nonrepeatable reads or phantom data. This option is the SQL Server default.

- **REPEATABLE READ** Specifies that statements cannot read data that has been modified but not yet committed by other transactions and that no other transactions can modify data that has been read by the current transaction until the current transaction completes.

- **SNAPSHOT** Specifies that data read by any statement in a transaction will be the transactionally consistent version of the data that existed at the start of the transaction. The transaction can only recognize data modifications that were committed before the start of the transaction. Data modifications made by other transactions after the start of the current transaction are not visible to statements executing in the current transaction. The effect is as if the statements in a transaction got a snapshot of the committed data as it existed at the start of the transaction.

- **SERIALIZABLE** Specifies that the statements cannot read data that has been modified but not yet committed by other transactions; no other transactions can modify data that has been read by the current transaction until the current transaction completes; and other transactions cannot insert new rows with key values that would fall in the range of keys read by any statements in the current transaction until the current transaction completes.

Table 3.3 shows the concurrency side effects enabled by the different isolation levels of a transaction:

Table 3.3 Isolation Levels and Their Side Effects

Isolation Level	Dirty Read	Nonrepeatable Read	Phantom
READ UNCOMMITTED	Yes	Yes	Yes
READ COMMITTED	No	Yes	Yes
REPEATABLE READ	No	No	Yes
SNAPSHOT	No	No	No
SERIALIZABLE	No	No	No

TEST DAY TIP

On the day of your exam, review the isolation levels and their side effects table so that you will know the relationship between levels and effects. You will see that the questions about isolation will be very easy.

You can define the isolation level of a transaction using the *SET TRANSACTION ISOLATION LEVEL* statement. You use this command before the transactions that you will execute. The syntax is as follows:

```
SET TRANSACTION ISOLATION LEVEL
    { READ UNCOMMITTED
    | READ COMMITTED
    | REPEATABLE READ
    | SNAPSHOT
    | SERIALIZABLE
    }
[ ; ]
```

EXAM WARNING

The 70–433 exam will include at least three questions about transaction isolation levels, given the importance of this topic. So be careful about the use of each isolation level and the concurrency side effects each causes.

EXERCISE 3.2

CREATING STORED PROCEDURES

In this exercise, you will create a stored procedure that will update a product category, according to a given ID. You then will alter this procedure, creating an output for it. At the end, you will review the procedure definition.

1. Launch *SQL Server Management Studio (SSMS)*, connect to the instance, open a new query window, and change the context to the *AdventureWorks2008* database.

2. Execute the following statement to view the rows of the *ProductCategory* table.

```
SELECT * FROM [Production].[ProductCategory]
```

3. Create the stored procedure *uspUpdateProductCategory* by executing the following code:

```
CREATE PROCEDURE [dbo].[uspUpdateProductCategory]

(
    @ProductCategoryID INT,

    @Name NVARCHAR(50)
)

AS

BEGIN

    UPDATE [Production].[ProductCategory] SET Name = @Name

    WHERE ProductCategoryID = @ProductCategoryID

END
```

4. Update the product category using the *EXECUTE* statement, as follows:

```
EXECUTE uspUpdateProductCategory 4, 'Others'
```

5. Now, let's alter the created procedure, adding a new parameter as an output. This output will be a message to the user about the success or failure of the procedure. Execute the following code:

```
ALTER PROCEDURE [dbo].[uspUpdateProductCategory]

(
    @ProductCategoryID INT,

    @Name NVARCHAR(50),

    @Message NVARCHAR(20) = 'None' OUTPUT
)

AS

BEGIN

    BEGIN TRANSACTION

    UPDATE [Production].[ProductCategory] SET Name = @Name

    WHERE ProductCategoryID = @ProductCategoryID

    IF (@@ERROR = 1)

    BEGIN

        SET @Message = 'An error occurred!'

        ROLLBACK TRANSACTION

    END
```

```
        ELSE

        BEGIN

              SET @Message = 'Category updated'

              COMMIT TRANSACTION

        END

    END
```

6. Update the product category using the *EXECUTE* statement, as follows:

```
DECLARE @Var NVARCHAR(20)

EXECUTE uspUpdateProductCategory 4, 'Acessories', @Var OUT

PRINT @Var
```

7. Now create a new user and grant him or her the *EXECUTE* permission, as in the following code:

```
CREATE USER Herleson WITHOUT LOGIN

GRANT EXECUTE ON [dbo].[uspUpdateProductCategory] TO Herleson
```

8. To finish, view the definition of the *uspUpdateProductCategory* function using the following code:

```
sp_helptext uspUpdateProductCategory
```

Implementing Triggers

A *trigger* is a T-SQL routine stored on the server that is executed automatically in response to an event within SQL Server. You can use triggers to evaluate data before or after a manipulation, to maintain data integrity, to control server operations and access, to audit a server, and to implement business logic. Unlike procedures and functions, you cannot execute triggers directly: they are attached to an object.

You can create three types of triggers: *Data Manipulation Language (DML)*, *Data Definition Language (DDL),* and *Logon triggers.* DML triggers run in response to data manipulation events, such as inserting, updating, and deleting data. DDL triggers fire in response to server events, such as creating, altering, and dropping an object. Logon triggers fire in response to the *LOGON* event that is raised when a user session is being established. Whereas DDL and Logon trigger a response to events in a server, DML triggers only exist inside a table or a view. Triggers support recursive and nesting. Recursive occurs when a trigger calls itself inside its routine, and nesting takes place when a trigger executes a statement that fires another trigger.

Creating DML Triggers

A DML trigger fires as a response to the execution of *INSERT, UPDATE*, and *DELETE* statements. When you create a DML trigger, you attach it to a table or a view, and you define which event will elicit a response. Triggers can fire in two different ways: *AFTER* and *INSTEAD OF*.

You use an *AFTER* trigger when you want a trigger to fire only after SQL Server completes all actions successfully. For example, if you insert a row in a table, the trigger associated with the insert event in this table will fire only after the row passes all the checks, such as primary key, rules, and constraints. If your insert fails, SQL Server will not fire the trigger. You can create any number of *AFTER* triggers on a table, although you cannot use an *AFTER* trigger on views.

You use an *INSTEAD OF* trigger when you want to perform a different operation from the statement that fires that trigger. An *INSTEAD OF* fires before SQL Server starts the execution of the action, providing you the possibility to change the operations in your database. For example, imagine that a user cannot update a client's data without your approval. So, you decide to create a table that will receive the proposed updates. To accomplish this task, you will then create an *INSTEAD OF* trigger on the *UPDATE* event of the client's table, telling SQL Server that it will perform an *INSERT* on the other table. You can create only one *INSTEAD OF* trigger for each *INSERT, UPDATE*, or *DELETE* statement for a view or a table. Also, you cannot create *INSTEAD OF DELETE* and *INSTEAD OF UPDATE* triggers on a table that has a cascading foreign key defined.

Head of the Class...

Triggers or Declarative Referential Integrity?

You can employ two ways to enforce referential integrity between tables: DML triggers and Declarative Referential Integrity (DRI). Although you can use both of them, specific situations govern the use of each.

When a *FOREIGN KEY* constraint is used, DRI is enforced when you modify data. This enforcement occurs before this change becomes part of the table, and it is much more efficient than executing trigger code. However, when you must enforce referential integrity across databases, you cannot define a *FOREIGN KEY*. So, in this case, you must use triggers to achieve integrity.

The routine within a DML trigger can be composed by any T-SQL statements, except *CREATE DATABASE, ALTER DATABASE, DROP DATABASE, LOAD DATABASE, LOAD LOG, RECONFIGURE, RESTORE DATABASE*, and *RESTORE LOG* statements. In addition, the following T-SQL commands are not allowed inside the body of your DML trigger when it is used against the table or view that is the target of the triggering action:

- CREATE INDEX
- CREATE SPATIAL INDEX
- CREATE XML INDEX
- ALTER INDEX
- DROP INDEX
- DBCC DBREINDEX
- ALTER PARTITION FUNCTION
- DROP TABLE
- ALTER TABLE (when managing columns, switching partitions; or managing keys)

Although DML triggers support many operations, you cannot create triggers against system tables or dynamic management views. Moreover, the *TRUNCATE TABLE* statement does not fire a trigger because this operation does not log individual row deletions. Nor does the *WRITETEXT* statement, whether logged or unlogged, activate a trigger.

The general Transact-SQL syntax for creating a DML trigger is as follows:

```
CREATE TRIGGER [ schema_name . ]trigger_name
ON { table | view }
[ WITH <dml_trigger_option> [,...n ] ]
{ FOR | AFTER | INSTEAD OF }
{ [ INSERT ] [, ] [ UPDATE ] [, ] [ DELETE ] }
[ WITH APPEND ]
[ NOT FOR REPLICATION ]
AS { sql_statement [ ; ] [,...n ] }

<dml_trigger_option> ::=
    [ ENCRYPTION ]
    [ EXECUTE AS Clause ]
```

Like other SQL Server objects, triggers must have a unique name that conforms to the rules of object identifiers. In the *CREATE TRIGGER* statement, you use the *ON* clause to specify the table or view to which the trigger will be attached. If you drop a table or a view, any triggers that are attached to that object will be dropped as well.

As in functions and procedures, the *WITH* clause of a trigger has the *ENCRYPTION* and *EXECUTE AS* options. You specify the *ENCRYPTION* option when you want to encrypt the trigger definition. The *EXECUTE AS* option specifies the security context under which the trigger is executed.

The *AFTER* and the *INSTEAD OF* clauses specify the fire mode of the trigger, as well as the event (or events) that will execute the trigger. You can define more than one event for a trigger. The *FOR* clause present in the syntax came from SQL Server 7.0 and older versions. It works in the same way as the *AFTER* clause, but you should use it only for compatibility. Another compatibility clause is the *WITH APPEND*, which is used to specify that an additional trigger of an existing type should be added. This works only in SQL Server 6.5 and below. You can use the *NOT FOR REPLICATION* clause if you want to indicate that your trigger should not be executed when a replication agent modifies the table to which the trigger is attached.

After the *AS* clause, you write the T-SQL routine that the trigger will perform when fired by the events specified earlier, on the *AFTER/INSTEAD OF* clause.

Configuring & Implementing...

Using Inserted and Deleted Tables

DML trigger statements can use two special tables that are dynamically created and managed by SQL Server: the *deleted* table and the *inserted* table. These temporary tables reside in memory, and they have the same column definition of the table on which the trigger was created. You can use them to test the effects of certain data modifications and to set conditions for DML trigger actions.

The *deleted table* stores copies of the affected rows when you run a *DELETE* or an *UPDATE* statement. During the execution of one of these statements, rows are deleted from the trigger table and transferred to the deleted table. The deleted table and the trigger table ordinarily have

Continued

no rows in common. The *inserted table* stores copies of the affected rows when you execute an *INSERT* or an *UPDATE* statement. During one of these transactions, new rows are added to both the inserted table and the trigger table. The rows in the inserted table are copies of the new rows in the trigger table. An update transaction is similar to a delete operation followed by an insert operation; the old rows are copied to the deleted table first; and then the new rows are copied to the trigger table and to the inserted table.

These dynamic tables can be used in many ways. For example, you can enforce business rules, extend referential integrity between tables, or manipulate this data in the way you want.

Example: Creating and Consuming a DML Trigger

Let's use the *Product* table from the *AdventureWorks2008* database. This table has two important columns responsible for the stock of a product: *SafetyStockLevel* and *ReorderPoint*. Your business requirements determine that the value of the *ReorderPoint* column will be 80 percent of the *SafetyStockLevel* column value.

As a database developer, you decide to create a DML trigger to enforce this business logic. With this object, you intend to automatically fill the *ReorderPoint* value every time that a user inserts or updates a row. Figure 3.14 shows how you can create a trigger that updates the *ReorderPoint* value after every insert or update operations in the table *Product*. When you create a DML trigger, it is stored in the active database, inside the folder **Triggers**, set under the table to which the trigger is attached.

Figure 3.14 The Creation Syntax of the DML Trigger

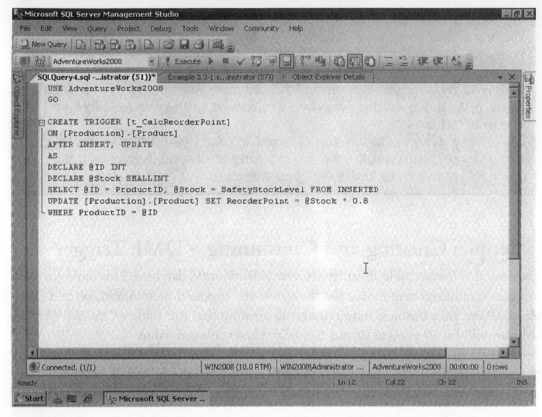

As you can see, the new trigger has the name *t_CalcReorderPoint*. It will be attached to the table *Product*, and it will fire on insert and update events. Once created, you can fire this trigger using *INSERT* or *UPDATE* against the table Product. Figure 3.15 shows an example of the column values before and after an update.

Figure 3.15 The DML Trigger in Action

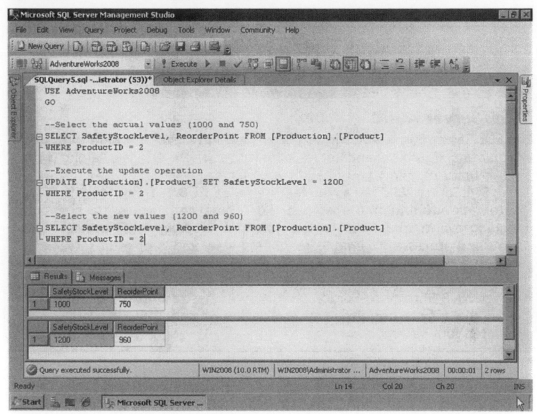

Creating DDL Triggers

Since version 2005, SQL Server has provided the ability to create triggers for DDL operations. These operations primarily correspond to T-SQL *CREATE, ALTER*, and *DROP* statements and certain system stored procedures that perform DDL-like operations. For example, if you use the *CREATE LOGIN* statement or the *sp_addlogin* stored procedure, they will both fire a DDL trigger that you created on a *CREATE_LOGIN* event. You can use *FOR/AFTER* clause in DDL triggers. However, *INSTEAD OF* cannot be used.

You can use this type of trigger to monitor and control actions performed on the server, and also audit these operations. DDL triggers can be used for administrative tasks such as auditing and regulating database operations.

New & Noteworthy...

SQL Server Audit

In SQL Server 2005, DDL triggers brought a new level of monitoring and regulating database and server operations. These triggers, along with other features, allow you to audit your server.

SQL Server 2008 has a new feature called *AUDIT*. This feature realizes automatic auditing on the server or a database, and involves tracking and logging events that occur on the system. SQL Server Audit provides the tools and processes to enable, store, and view audits on your server and database objects.

Although the audit feature is a great one, it is only available on SQL Server 2008 Enterprise Edition, and it consumes resources. So, you must verify the business requirements and decide which feature you will use to monitor your server.

The general Transact-SQL syntax for creating a DDL trigger is as follows:

```
CREATE TRIGGER trigger_name
ON { ALL SERVER | DATABASE }
[ WITH <ddl_trigger_option> [,...n ] ]
{ FOR | AFTER } { event_type | event_group } [,...n ]
AS { sql_statement [ ; ] [,...n ] }
<ddl_trigger_option> ::=
    [ ENCRYPTION ]
    [ EXECUTE AS Clause ]
```

Like DML triggers, DDL triggers must have a unique name that conforms to the rules of object identifiers. You use the *ON* clause to specify the scope of the trigger. If you use the *DATABASE* option, the scope of your DDL trigger will be the current database. If you use the *ALL SERVER* option, the scope of your DDL triggers to the current server.

The *WITH* clause of a trigger has the *ENCRYPTION* and *EXECUTE AS* options. You specify the *ENCRYPTION* option when you want to encrypt the trigger definition. The *EXECUTE AS* option specifies the security context under which the trigger is executed.

The *AFTER* clause specifies the event type and group that will fire the trigger. An *event type* is the name of the event that fires your DDL trigger. An *event group* is the name of a predefined grouping of T-SQL language events. You combine these two parts to define the firing event. For example, if you create a trigger that will fire when a user creates a table, the event type will be *CREATE* and the event group will be *TABLE*.

Exam Warning

DDL triggers fire only after SQL Server processes the event type and group defined in the *CREATE TRIGGER* statement. So, remember that if the execution of this event fails, the trigger will not fire.

After the *AS* clause, you write the T-SQL routine that the trigger will perform when fired by the events specified before, on the *AFTER* clause.

Example: Creating and Consuming a DDL Trigger

To protect the accidental dropping of tables in the *AdventureWorks2008* database, you decide to create a DDL trigger that will warn the user about table protection, and will roll back the operation. Figure 3.16 shows the code of the DDL trigger and a *DROP* statement that tries to drop a table.

Figure 3.16 The DDL Trigger Syntax
and the Execution of a DROP Statement

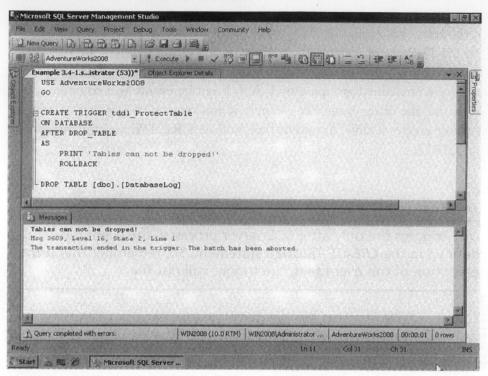

As the figure shows, the new trigger has the name *tddl_ProtectTable*, its scope will be the active database (*AdventureWorks2008*), and it will fire on *DROP_TABLE* events. You can also see that a *DROP TABLE* statement fails because of the created trigger.

When you create a DDL trigger, it is stored according to the scope defined in the trigger. If the scope is *DATABASE*, the trigger will be stored inside the folder **Triggers**, set under the **Programmability** folder inside the active database. If the scope is *ALL SERVER*, the trigger will be stored inside the folder **Triggers**, set under the **Server Objects** folder inside the server.

Creating Logon Triggers

Logon triggers fire in response to the *LOGON* event that is raised when a user session is being established with your server—after the authentication phase finishes, but before the user session is actually established. Therefore, all messages that you define inside the trigger to users, such as error messages, will be redirected to the SQL Server error log. Logon triggers do not fire if authentication fails. You can use logon triggers to audit and control server sessions, such as to track login activity or limit the number of sessions for a specific login.

The general T-SQL syntax for creating a logon trigger is as follows:

```
CREATE TRIGGER trigger_name
ON ALL SERVER
[ WITH <logon_trigger_option> [,...n ] ]
{ FOR | AFTER } LOGON
AS { sql_statement [ ; ] [,...n ] [ ; ] }
<logon_trigger_option> ::=
    [ ENCRYPTION ]
    [ EXECUTE AS Clause ]
```

Example: Creating and Consuming a Logon Trigger

In this example, you will protect your server from a logon of a specific login in your server. To accomplish that, you decide to create a logon trigger that will block the logon process after its authentication, executing a rollback in the operation. Figure 3.17 shows the code of the logon trigger that denies the logon process.

Figure 3.17 The Logon Trigger Syntax

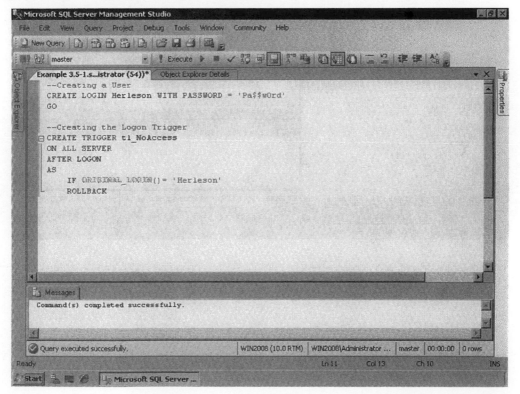

The figure shows that the new trigger has the name *tl_NoAccess*, its scope will be the whole server, and it will fire on *LOGON* events. You can also see that a *ROLLBACK* will be executed if the login is *Herleson*. All logon triggers are stored inside the folder **Triggers**, set under the **Server Objects** folder inside the server. You can fire this trigger trying to establish a new connection with the server. Figure 3.18 shows the error generated by SQL Server when you try to connect using the blocked login.

Figure 3.18 The Error Message
Generated by SQL Server for the Specific Login

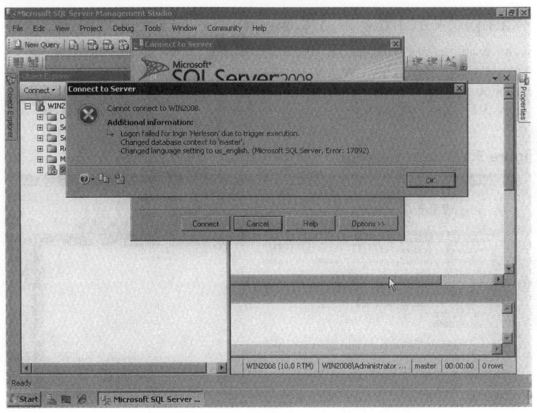

Logon Trigger Blocks All Login Attempts

Since Logon Triggers can block the access to an instance, sometimes you can face an unexpected trouble: you develop a Logon Trigger that should restrict the access for some logins. However, because of a mistake in the code, it blocks all logon attempts, including sysadmin logins. So, how can you regain the access to your SQL Server instance and disable this trigger? The solution relies on the DAC feature.

The Dedicated Administrator Connection (DAC) allows you to access a running instance of SQL Server Database Engine to troubleshoot problems on the server. Even when the server is unresponsive to other client connections or it's blocking the access, you can use DAC to connect and execute restoring operations. The DAC is available through the sqlcmd utility and SQL Server Management Studio.

So, in situations that a Logon Trigger works in an unexpected way, use DAC to connect to the instance and disable it. Then, connect to the instance normally and see what the problem of this trigger is.

Using Recursive and Nested Triggers

A trigger fires in response to an operation (DML, DDL, or Logon), and it can perform additional operations. Because of that, it can cause itself to fire, or it can fire additional triggers in a chain reaction.

A trigger that fires itself is called a *recursive trigger*. You can create two types of recursive triggers: direct and indirect recursion. A *direct recursion* occurs when your application updates table A. This operation fires a trigger that executes an update in table A. Because table A was updated, the trigger will fire again and again. An *indirect recursion* occurs when your application updates table A. This fires a trigger that updates table B. But table B has a trigger that updates table A. Then the trigger in table B will fire and update table A.

A trigger that fires additional triggers in a chain reaction is called a *nested trigger*. A nested trigger happens when your trigger changes a table on which there is another trigger. Then the second trigger is activated and calls a third trigger, and so on.

If any of your triggers in the chain set off an infinite loop, the nesting level is exceeded and the trigger is canceled. A trigger can be nested to a maximum of 32 levels. Also, an indirect recursion is a subset of a nested trigger.

You can enable or disable direct recursive triggers using the *RECURSIVE_ TRIGGERS* setting of a database. To enable or disable nested triggers and indirect recursive triggers, you can use the *nested triggers* option of *sp_configure* procedure.

Managing Triggers

As a database developer, you need to learn some basics about managing triggers, such as alter and drop them. Basically, there are two ways to manage these triggers: using the *SQL Server Management Studio (SSMS)* or using *Transact-SQL* statements.

In *SQL Server Management Studio*, you can alter the code of a DML trigger by right-clicking it and choosing **Modify** to open a new query tab. This tab shows the actual definition of the trigger and allows you to make changes at its code. After you have finished the changes, commit them by clicking on the **Execute** button. DDL and Logon triggers do not have the **Modify** option. Also, to drop a trigger, right-click the desired object and choose the **Delete** option. You can see the objects that depend on a function and the objects that a function depends on by right-clicking it and choosing the **View Dependencies** option.

You can also manage procedures using *Transact-SQL* statements. You can alter and remove a trigger using the *ALTER TRIGGER* and the *DROP TRIGGER* statements. The *ALTER TRIGGER* alters an existing trigger that you previously created. Its syntax and options are the same as the *CREATE TRIGGER* statement. The *DROP TRIGGER* removes one or more triggers from the current database.

You can also use *system stored procedures* and *catalog views* to provide information about triggers and their definitions. The following example shows you how to retrieve the definition and the information of the trigger *t_CalcReorderPoint* using *sp_help* and *sp_helptext*:

```
--View the definition
sp_helptext uspNewProductCategory

--View the information
sp_help uspNewProductCategory
```

You can also enable or disable a trigger. Disabling a trigger is useful in some scenarios, such as when you are executing a bulk operation. The following code shows the syntax of enabling or disabling a trigger.

```
DISABLE | ENABLE TRIGGER { [ schema_name . ] trigger_name [ ,…n ] | ALL }
ON { object_name | DATABASE | ALL SERVER } [ ; ]
```

Another important management task with triggers is to define their execution order, in scenarios that multiple triggers will fire with the same event. For example, you create four triggers against a table that will be executed at every update operation. When you set an order, you define which trigger will be fired first and which will be fired last. The other two triggers that are fired between the first and last triggers will be executed in undefined order. You can set the order only for the *AFTER* trigger. To specify the order of a trigger, you use the *sp_settriggerorder* procedure. The general syntax is as follows:

```
sp_settriggerorder [ @triggername = ] '[ triggerschema. ] triggername'
    , [ @order = ] 'value'
    , [ @stmttype = ] 'statement_type'
    [, [ @namespace = ] { 'DATABASE' | 'SERVER' | NULL } ]
```

After specifying the trigger's name, you define if this trigger will be the first or the last in the *@order* argument. Then, you state which event fires the trigger, at the *@stmttype* argument. When you specify a DDL trigger, you must inform the scope of this trigger, *DATABASE* or *SERVER* in the *@namespace* argument. If your trigger is a logon trigger, *SERVER* must be specified. DML triggers do not need this argument defined. The following two examples show how you can define the order of a DML and a DDL trigger:

```
--Seting the order of a DML trigger
sp_settriggerorder @triggername='dbo.t_CalcReorderPoint',
@order='Last', @stmttype='UPDATE';

--Seting the order of a DDL trigger
sp_settriggerorder @triggername='tddl_ProtectTable',
@order='First', @stmttype='DROP_TABLE', @namespace='DATABASE';
```

EXAM WARNING

If you create a trigger that fires with two or more events, you must execute the *sp_settriggerorder* for each event specified in the trigger.

EXERCISE 3.3

CREATING TRIGGERS

In this exercise, you will create a trigger that will block inserts and deletes operations in the table *ProductCategory*. You then will set its order.

1. Launch *SQL Server Management Studio (SSMS)*, connect to the instance, open a new query window, and change the context to the *AdventureWorks2008* database.

2. Execute the following statement to view the rows of the *ProductCategory* table.

```
SELECT * FROM [Production].[ProductCategory]
```

3. Create the trigger *t_ProtectTable* by executing the following code:

```
CREATE TRIGGER [dbo].[t_ProtectTable]

ON [Production].[ProductCategory]

AFTER INSERT, DELETE

AS

    PRINT 'This table only accepts update operations'

    ROLLBACK
```

4. Try to delete a product category using the *DELETE* statement, as follows:

```
DELETE FROM [Production].[ProductCategory]
```

5. Execute the following statement to see that no row of the *ProductCategory* table was deleted.

```
SELECT * FROM [Production].[ProductCategory]
```

6. Set the order of this trigger using the *sp_settriggerorder* procedure, as follows:

```
sp_settriggerorder @triggername='dbo.t_ProtectTable',
@order='First', @stmttype='INSERT';

sp_settriggerorder @triggername='dbo.t_ProtectTable',
@order='First', @stmttype='DELETE';
```

Summary of Exam Objectives

Functions, stored procedures, and triggers are objects used in SQL Server to construct programmability routines with T-SQL statements. You use functions to encapsulate selects and calculations, and return a scalar value or a table variable. Functions cannot make changes in data or objects. You use stored procedures to perform T-SQL routines on a server. They can return scalar values or result sets, and they allow the creation of an interface between your database and your application in a secure way. You use triggers to run statements as a response of events inside your server. You can create DML, DDL, or Logon triggers, according to the scope of it.

Exam Objectives Fast Track

Implementing Functions

- ☑ You use functions to encapsulate selects and calculations for reuse.
- ☑ Scalar functions return a scalar value.
- ☑ Table-valued functions return a table variable.
- ☑ Functions cannot make changes in data or objects.

Implementing Stored Procedures

- ☑ You use stored procedures to store and perform routines on a server.
- ☑ You can optionally return scalar value or result sets.
- ☑ You can create an interface between database and application with procedures.
- ☑ You can set the isolation levels for transactions inside stored procedures, to control locks.

Implementing Triggers

- ☑ SQL Server offers three types of triggers: DML, DDL, and Logon.
- ☑ DML triggers fire with insert, update or delete operations.
- ☑ DDL triggers are executed with DDL operations, such as create a table.
- ☑ Logon triggers fire when a login connects a SQL Server instance.

Exam Objectives
Frequently Asked Questions

Q: What are the types of functions, and how they are used?

A: Functions can be scalar or table-valued. A scalar function returns a single value, whereas a table-valued function returns a table variable.

Q: What is an Inline Function?

A: It's a special table-valued function that returns a table data type and can be used to achieve the functionality of parameterized views.

Q: When is a function deterministic?

A: A function is deterministic when it always returns the same value any time for a specific set of input values.

Q: What is the difference between functions and stored procedures?

A: Functions cannot alter data or objects in a server. Procedures can manipulate data and objects inside the database and server.

Q: Can a stored procedure execute a return?

A: Yes, a stored procedure can return a value or a result set, using the *OUTPUT* option.

Q: Which operations can a stored procedure not perform?

A: *USE, SET SHOWPLAN_TEXT,* and *SET SHOWPLAN_ALL* cannot be performed inside a procedure.

Q: Which are the transaction isolation levels that SQL Server offers?

A: READ UNCOMMITTED, READ COMMITTED, SNAPSHOT, REPEATABLE READ, and SERIALIZABLE.

Q: What are the types of triggers, and how are they used?

A: Triggers can be DML, DDL, or Logon types. DML triggers fire with insert, delete, and update operations. DDL triggers fire with DDL operations, such as *CREATE* and *GRANT.* Logon triggers fire when a login connects an instance.

Q: What are the types of DML triggers?

A: Triggers can be AFTER or INSTEAD OF types. You use an AFTER trigger when you want a trigger to fire only after SQL Server completes all actions successfully. You use an INSTEAD OF trigger when you want to perform a different operation from the statement that fires that trigger.

Self Test

1. You are creating a stored procedure that will execute a delete in the *Product* table in a database. The syntax of the stored procedure includes the following *T-SQL* statement.

```
CREATE PROCEDURE usp_DeleteProduct
(
     @ProductID INT
)
WITH ENCRYPTION
AS
BEGIN
BEGIN TRY
     BEGIN TRANSACTION
             USE AdventureWorks2008
             DELETE FROM [Production].[Product] WHERE ProductID =
             @ProductID
     COMMIT TRANSACTION
END TRY
BEGIN CATCH
    DECLARE @ErrorMessage NVARCHAR(250)
    DECLARE @ErrorSeverity INT
    DECLARE @ErrorState INT
    SELECT
        @ErrorMessage = ERROR_MESSAGE(),
        @ErrorSeverity = ERROR_SEVERITY(),
        @ErrorState = ERROR_STATE()
    RAISERROR (@ErrorMessage, @ErrorSeverity, @ErrorState)
    ROLLBACK TRANSACTION
END CATCH
END
```

You try to create the procedure and discover that it always returns an error. What should you do to solve this problem?

A. Add *SET* command to the *CATCH* block to set the value of parameters.

B. Remove the *COMMIT TRANSACTION* command from the *TRY* block.

C. Remove the *USE* command to the *TRY* block.

D. Add an *EXECUTE AS* option to the procedure.

E. Remove the *ENCRYPTION* option of the procedure.

2. You have a database that contains a trigger named *t_InsertOrder*, which fires when order data is inserted into the *Orders* table. You need to configure the trigger to prevent it from firing during a data import process. Which T-SQL statement should you use?

A. *DROP TRIGGER* t_InsertOrder

B. *DISABLE TRIGGER* t_InsertOrder *ON* Orders

C. *ALTER TRIGGER* t_InsertOrder *ON* Orders *NOT FOR REPLICATION*

D. *sp_settriggerorder* @triggername = t_InsertOrder, @order='None'

3. You discover that the table changes that were recently made in objects of your database have caused your site to stop functioning. It is unclear who made those changes. You decide that all changes to database objects will be tracked. You need to implement a mechanism that will track changes in your database. What should you do?

A. Implement a stored procedure that writes data about changes to a log table.

B. Implement *DDL AFTER* triggers that write user and changes to a log table.

C. Implement a *DML INSTEAD OF* trigger that writes data changes to a log table.

D. Implement a *DML AFTER* trigger that writes data about changes to a log table.

4. You decide to retrieve information about a user who is currently logged in, using a function that returns scalar information about the activity time for a particular user. How can you achieve this goal?

A. Create a function that returns a list of values that represent the login times for the given user.

B. Create a function that returns a list of values that represent the people who have logged more hours than the current user has logged.

C. Create a function that returns a numeric value that represents the number of hours that a user has logged for the current day.

D. Create a function that returns a numeric value that represents the people who have logged.

5. You have to import orders data from the *Orders* and *Region* table in your SQL Server 2005 database into your new SQL Server 2008 server. You must ensure that during the import process between servers, each value in the *RegionID* column of the *Orders* table will have a corresponding record in the *RegionID* column in the *Region* table of your new server. You also need to ensure that the import process won't fail if records are encountered that do not exist in the *Region* table. What should you do?

A. Drop the foreign key. Import the data by using the script. Re-create the foreign key.

B. Create a *CHECK* constraint.

C. Create a *DML INSTEAD OF* trigger that writes the failed records to a file or table.

D. Create a *DML AFTER* trigger that writes the failed records to a file or table.

6. The data from your partners is imported into the *Customer* table every weekend. You need to ensure that the customer record will be updated if it already exists in the *Customer* table. If the record does not exist, the data will be inserted into the *Customer* table. What should you do?

A. Create a *FOR* trigger.

B. Create an *INSTEAD OF* trigger.

C. Create an *AFTER* trigger.

D. Create a *DDL* trigger.

7. You are developing stored procedures as an interface for your database, and you decide that all procedures can only recognize changes in data before the start of the transaction or after the end of it. Which isolation level should you use in your procedure?

A. READ UNCOMMITTED

B. READ COMMITTED

C. REPEATABLE READ

D. SNAPSHOT

E. SERIALIZABLE

8. You have a stored procedure in your database that selects data from the *Customer* table. Users complain that the execution of this procedure is slow. You then decide to create an index at the *Customer* table. After you create the index, users report that the procedure is still slow. Which stored procedure option must you use to solve this problem?

   A. ENCRYPTION

   B. RECOMPILE

   C. OUTPUT

   D. EXECUTE AS

9. You have a database and decide to log the data modifications in tables. You need to ensure that changes came from stored procedures; otherwise direct commands will be logged. What should you do?

   A. Create a *Logon* trigger.

   B. Create an *INSTEAD OF* trigger.

   C. Create an *AFTER* trigger.

   D. Create a *DDL* trigger.

10. You have a stored procedure called *uspNewProductCategory* in your database. Developers who work with your database reported their inability to view the procedure definition. They have administrative rights inside the database. You decide to see the procedure properties to find out what the problem is. SQL Server shows the screen shown in Figure 3.19.

Figure 3.19 Stored Procedure Properties for
uspNewProductCategory : Problem Viewing Definition

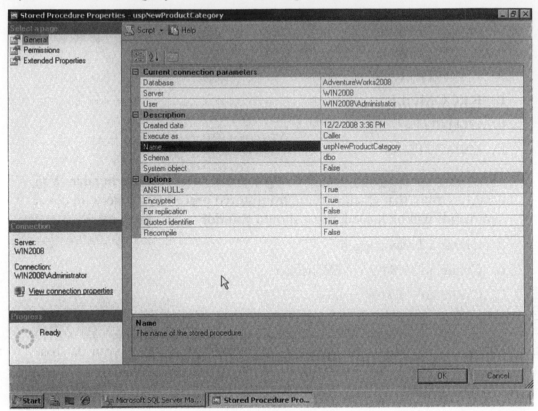

What should you do to solve this problem?

A. Drop and re-create the procedure with the same definition.

B. Set the *RECOMPILE* option with *ALTER PROCEDURE*.

C. Change the permissions of the procedure.

D. Remove the encryption with *ALTER PROCEDURE*.

11. An IT professional on your staff developed a DDL trigger that will prevent dropping tables in the *AdventureWorks2008* database in a server with multiple databases. He used the following T-SQL commands:

```
USE master
GO
CREATE TRIGGER tddl_ProtectTable
ON DATABASE
```

```
FOR DROP_TABLE
AS

       PRINT 'Tables can not be dropped!'
       ROLLBACK
```

After the creation, you realize that tables still can be dropped from the *AdventureWorks2008* database. What should you do?

A. Drop and re-create the trigger, changing its scope to *ALL SERVER*.

B. Change the event type of the trigger to *DELETE*.

C. Remove the *ROLLBACK* command.

D. Re-create the trigger, changing the active database.

12. You are developing a function that will return the clients whose orders are higher than a given value. The code used is as follows:

```
CREATE FUNCTION [dbo].[udfGetSales]
(
    @Amount MONEY
)
RETURN TABLE
AS

       RETURNS
       SELECT SalesOrderID, CustomerID, TotalDue
       FROM [Sales].[SalesOrderHeader]
       WHERE TotalDue > @Amount
```

When you execute the code, SQL Server returns an error. What should you do to create this function?

A. Add the variable *@tablename* and its definition in the *RETURN* clause.

B. Add the *BEGIN…END* clause in the function.

C. Change the places of the *RETURN* a *RETURNS* clause in the function.

D. Add an output parameter with the *OUTPUT* clause.

13. You need to create an object that will be called by the user and will select all the employees and return their names and salaries. If an employee is salaried, the object will count how many hours he or she worked and calculate the salary based on this count. If an employee is commissioned, the object will select his or her sales to calculate the salary. Which type of function will you use?

   A. Scalar-valued function

   B. Table-valued function

   C. Inline function

   D. DML trigger

   E. DDL trigger

14. You have a database that is set as read-only. Users always access it to execute *SELECT* statements. You must create procedures that will retrieve data from this database as fast as possible. Which isolation level should you set for your transactions inside your procedures?

   A. READ UNCOMMITTED

   B. READ COMMITTED

   C. REPEATABLE READ

   D. SNAPSHOT

   E. SERIALIZABLE

15. You are developing a procedure that updates data from the *Orders* table of your database. You must ensure that users will select data that is committed, although users can execute this procedure simultaneously. Which isolation level should you set for your transactions inside this procedure?

   A. READ UNCOMMITTED

   B. READ COMMITTED

   C. REPEATABLE READ

   D. SNAPSHOT

   E. SERIALIZABLE

16. You have to create a stored procedure in your database that will select data from the *Customer* table. Which stored procedure option must you use to return the selected data to the user?

   A. ENCRYPTION

   B. RECOMPILE

   C. OUTPUT

   D. EXECUTE AS

To solve the problem, you decide to enforce SQL Server to create a new plan and cache the plan each time it is executed. What should you do solve this problem?

A. Drop and re-create the procedure with the same definition.

B. Set the *RECOMPILE* option with *ALTER PROCEDURE*.

C. Change the permissions of the procedure.

D. Remove the encryption with *ALTER PROCEDURE*.

20. You are developing a function that will return the clients whose orders are higher than a given value. The code used is as follows:

```
CREATE FUNCTION [dbo].[udfGetSales]
(
    @Amount MONEY
)
RETURNS TABLE
AS
    RETURN
    BEGIN
      SELECT SalesOrderID, CustomerID, TotalDue
      FROM [Sales].[SalesOrderHeader]
      WHERE TotalDue > @Amount
    END
```

When you execute the code, SQL Server returns an error. What should you do to create this function?

A. Add the variable *@tablename* and its definition in the *RETURN* clause.

B. Remove the *BEGIN…END* clause in the function.

C. Change the places of the *RETURN* a *RETURNS* clause in the function.

D. Add an output parameter with the *OUTPUT* clause.

Self Test Quick Answer Key

1.	**C**	11.	**D**
2.	**B**	12.	**C**
3.	**B**	13.	**B**
4.	**C**	14.	**A**
5.	**C**	15.	**C**
6.	**B**	16.	**C**
7.	**D**	17.	**D**
8.	**B**	18.	**C**
9.	**C**	19.	**B**
10.	**D**	20.	**B**

Chapter 4

MCTS SQL Server 2008 Exam 433

Using the CLR

Exam objectives in this chapter:

- CLR and Managed Code Explained
- CLR Integration
- Languages Supported
- What Is the Base Class Library?
- Registering CLR Assemblies for Use with SQL Server
- Understanding Permission Sets
- Implementing SQL Server Objects Using Managed Code

Exam objectives review:

- ☑ Summary of Exam Objectives
- ☑ Exam Objectives Fast Track
- ☑ Exam Objectives Frequently Asked Questions
- ☑ Self Test
- ☑ Self Test Quick Answer Key

Introduction

Common Language Runtime (CLR) integration is a powerful feature of SQL Server. CLR integration was introduced in SQL Server 2005, and it has been extended in SQL Server 2008. Prior to SQL Server 2005, it was necessary to create extended stored procedures (XP) using C++ to take advantage of functionality beyond that provided by SQL Server natively. Today, CLR integration provides you with the flexibility to define stored procedures, functions, triggers, data types, and other database objects using either Transact-SQL or any .NET Framework language. The advantage of this approach is that you can choose the language more suited to the task at hand.

Transact-SQL is very powerful for querying data and working with native SQL Server data types. However, you may want to manipulate data in different ways or work with more complex data types that are not available in SQL Server. For example, you may want to use regular expressions to validate data, manipulate text using advanced string manipulation techniques, or store spatial coordinates in a single column. The CLR is well suited for these complex operations.

In some cases you may wish to offload certain processing from SQL Server, or access functionality outside the database server. You can call on this remote functionality using CLR–integrated objects. A good example of this would be accessing the latest currency exchange rates offered by a specialized provider over the Internet; you could use a CLR function or stored procedure to call a Web service and retrieve the information you need. CLR integration is also well suited to accessing resources like the Windows registry, file system, or Active Directory.

EXAM WARNING

Note that Transact-SQL must remain the primary method for implementing your database objects. Use the CLR only if your task cannot be performed using Transact-SQL or if implementing it using Transact-SQL is unnecessarily complicated. Do not choose to implement tasks using the CLR without first considering Transact-SQL alternatives.

You don't need to be a .NET programmer to be able to take advantage of CLR integration. Numerous tutorials and walkthroughs are available as part of SQL Server documentation and online sources. SQL Server applies additional security options to managed code running within it, which ensures that the managed code cannot compromise the server or affect its stability.

CLR and Managed Code Explained

The CLR is the execution environment provided by the Microsoft .NET Framework. It is likely that you had to install the .NET Framework at one time or another, usually as a prerequisite for installing an application. The .NET Framework is a new-generation application platform, and many modern applications, including SQL Server, use it as the execution environment. The .NET Framework provides developers with the ability to compile applications written in a .NET-compliant language. The .NET Framework serves as runtime for these applications. Figure 4.1 shows the key components of the .NET Framework.

Figure 4.1 The .NET Framework

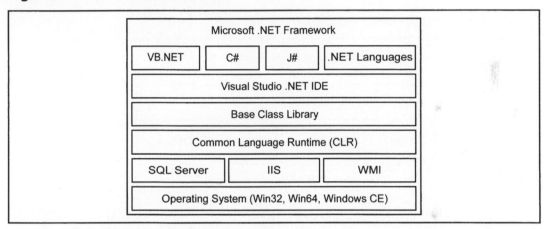

The .NET Framework is installed on an operating system and is used to access the operating system's services during runtime. There is a version of the .NET Framework for 32-bit and 64-bit Windows platforms, as well as some other operating systems like Windows CE and Windows Mobile. Application services exposed by applications like SQL Server, IIS, WMI, COM+, and many more are available to the developer through the .NET Framework. The Base Class Library provides commonly used functionality to developers in the form of classes and namespaces. We will examine the Base Class Library in more detail later in this chapter.

Developers usually use the Visual Studio .NET Integrated Development Environment (IDE) to create .NET applications. However, the IDE is not absolutely necessary, and it is possible to create simple text source code files and compile them using a .NET compiler. You can create .NET applications in any .NET-compliant language to suit the specific functionality you wish to implement. Over 60 major language families are available for the .NET Framework, each with many variants and branches. The most popular .NET languages are C# and Visual Basic .NET. Support for these languages is available out-of-the-box when you install Visual Studio .NET.

The .NET Framework includes a compiler component for each .NET-compliant language. This component compiles the source code written in the specific high-level language to the lower-level Microsoft Intermediate Language (MSIL). When the application is running, the CLR translates MSIL to native machine instructions. This is done by a component known as just-in-time (JIT) compilation. It is important to understand that no matter which .NET language you develop your application in, it will be compiled to the one common language—MSIL. This is from where the word *common* in Common Language Runtime originates.

The CLR is responsible for executing MSIL code. The CLR also manages the code that runs within it by providing the code with runtime services. Figure 4.2 outlines some of the services provided by the CLR.

Figure 4.2 Common Language Runtime Services

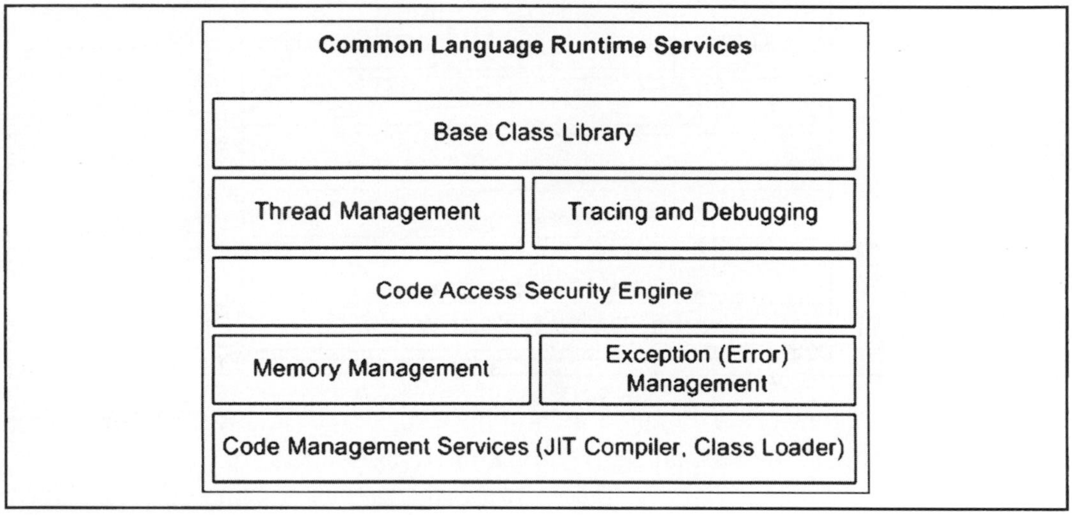

The CLR manages code execution by providing mandatory stability and security-checking engines, as well as resource management. For example, the Garbage Collection service provided by the CLR ensures optimal memory management. Thread management provides parallel processing capabilities. The Base Class Library support, error management, and debugging services create a consistent development environment for all .NET languages.

Code that runs within the CLR is known as *managed code*, as the CLR provides it with management services like those mentioned above. The term is often used to distinguish between .NET code and native code (for example, code written using Visual Basic 6 or C++). Native code runs outside the CLR and is referred to as *unmanaged code*. Unmanaged code is not subject to CLR services, like code access security. Within SQL Server, all objects that use CLR integration are written as managed code. Extended stored procedures (XPs) are unmanaged code and are written using C++.

EXAM WARNING

Remember that managed code is regarded as more stable and secure because it is subject to the mandatory code access security engine provided by the CLR. Unmanaged code implemented in XPs is not subject to CLR security services, and therefore it is up to the developers of the extended stored procedure to implement proper security and stability checking. Given the choice between a CLR stored procedure and an XP, always select the CLR stored procedure.

Additionally, XPs are deprecated, and support for this feature is likely to be removed in future versions of SQL Server.

The CLR abstracts essential services such as memory and security management away from developers, allowing them to concentrate on the specific functionality of their code.

New & Noteworthy...

Versions of the .NET Framework Supported by SQL Server 2008

SQL Server 2008 supports assemblies targeted at .NET Framework 2.0 or later. During installation of SQL Server 2008, .NET Framework 2.0 Service Pack 1 will be installed automatically. SQL Server 2008 does not support assemblies targeted at .NET Framework 1.0 and .NET Framework 1.1.

Visual Studio 2008 is the latest version of Visual Studio—the Microsoft IDE used to create .NET Framework applications. Visual Studio 2008 can be used to create a variety of applications, and one of the key new features is support for Language Integrated Query (LINQ). Both Visual Studio 2005 and Visual Studio 2008 can be used to create assemblies containing CLR objects for SQL Server 2008 CLR integration. Visual Studio 2003 and Visual Studio .NET 2001 cannot be used.

CLR Integration

As SQL Server became more widely used, database professionals and developers demanded the ability to incorporate advanced logic and functionality into their database objects. Transact-SQL remains the best language to perform set-based tasks as it was designed specifically for querying and manipulating large data sets efficiently. You should always choose Transact-SQL when querying data. As Transact-SQL is an immensely powerful query language, it is less well suited to complex operations. Consider how difficult it would be to implement the following tasks using Transact-SQL:

- Validate whether a phone number is valid for a specific city and country
- Store complex data types like GPS coordinates in a single column
- Read data from the Windows registry
- Split someone's full name into first name, last name, and middle initials
- Read a file from a network, and share and import its data and attributes
- Write to a file in the file system

CLR integration in SQL Server allows you to implement these tasks using only a few lines of code. This extended functionality can then be accessed in the same way as standard SQL Server database objects and as part of Transact-SQL queries.

Implementing advanced functionality using the CLR has many advantages. First of all, .NET languages are fully featured programming languages and offer elements like arrays, looping through collections, and object-oriented programming, just to name a few. Transact-SQL, being a query-oriented language, does not support those elements. Additionally, the Base Class Library is available through CLR integration. Using the Base Class Library you can access rich functionality for text manipulation, file and registry access, cryptography, and much more. Using managed code you can also define and manipulate complex data types like localized dates and times, currencies, and spatial coordinates. Finally, because managed code is compiled to native code, it may sometimes offer performance advantages over Transact-SQL, which is interpreted at runtime.

Configuring & Implementing…

Enabling CLR Integration

In SQL Server 2008, CLR integration is disabled by default, and you must explicitly enable this feature before you can use it. Only those accounts that have ALTER SETTINGS permissions to the SQL Server server can enable and disable CLR integration. By default, only members of sysadmin and serveradmin server roles have this permission. To enable CLR integration in SQL Server, use the *sp_configure* stored procedure with the *clr enabled* parameter set to the value of *1*, as shown in the following example:

```
sp_configure 'show advanced options', 1;

GO

RECONFIGURE;

GO

sp_configure 'clr enabled', 1;

GO

RECONFIGURE;

GO
```

The following output will be produced when the *sp_configure* succeeds:

```
Configuration option 'show advanced options' changed from 0 to 1. Run
the RECONFIGURE statement to install.

Configuration option 'clr enabled' changed from 0 to 1. Run the
RECONFIGURE statement to install.
```

To disable the CLR-integration feature, execute *sp_configure* with the *clr enabled* parameter set to *0*. When you disable CLR integration, all CLR object code executing within SQL Server is immediately interrupted. This may lead to data consistency issues, cause unexpected errors, and negatively impact users of the system. Ensure that no current activity is interrupted when you disable the functionality.

Note that the .NET Framework is available in many versions. Managed code is compiled for a specific version of the .NET Framework and cannot be executed by a different version. For example, code compiled for .NET Framework 1.1 will not execute in .NET Framework 1.0 and vice versa. SQL Server 2008 supports .NET Framework 2.0 and later. You can use Visual Studio 2005 or Visual Studio 2008 to write code targeting .NET Framework 2.0, but you cannot use Visual Studio 2003 or earlier.

Languages Supported

Over 60 languages are available for .NET Framework development. Some examples are Visual Basic .NET, C#, J#, IronRuby, Delphi.NET, CLISP, and many others. As part of the .NET Framework, the Common Language Specification (CLS) defines rules for all .NET-compliant languages. Many vendors have created new languages or adapted existing languages to run within the CLR by using this specification. As explained earlier, all .NET languages are compiled to MSIL, which is then executed by the CLR. This means that at runtime, no .NET language is inherently superior to another. It also means that there is full cross-language interoperability, and components created in one .NET language can be seamlessly used from within a different .NET language.

How should you choose a .NET language to develop your CLR-integrated SQL Server objects? Different languages suit different purposes. For example, the Perl family of languages has powerful regular expression capabilities, while Lisp-based languages can perform advanced mathematical calculations. However, most database developers choose the less exotic VB.NET or C# (pronounced *C Sharp*). These languages are installed as part of Visual Studio .NET, and a great wealth of sample code and guidance is available online. Corporate standards and language familiarity are usually the key factors in choosing a development language.

TEST DAY TIP

Don't worry if you are not familiar with a .NET programming language or with programming in general. In the exam you will be questioned about SQL Server CLR integration, not programming specifics. Focus on revising the specifics of registering CLR objects within SQL Server, and the general reasons for doing so, rather than programming language syntax.

What Is the Base Class Library?

The .NET Framework provides a rich library of commonly used functionality to developers creating applications using managed code. This library is known as the Base Class Library. For example, the Base Class Library allows developers to access the file system, use regular patterns, read and write to Active Directory, and much more. Usually a single, most granular logical entity providing specific functionality is known as a class. There are thousands of classes in the Base Class Library. Classes are divided into logical groups called namespaces and are physically stored as assemblies. An assembly is an EXE or DLL file containing managed code. Usually an assembly contains one or more namespaces, with each namespace containing related classes.

To get a feel for the richness of the ready-made functionality available to you when using the .NET Framework, let's take a look at some examples of namespaces and classes. Table 4.1 lists some of the namespaces available to us from the Base Class Library, and the functionality provided by classes in these namespaces. Note that Table 4.1 is not a complete list of classes in the Base Class Library; there are thousands of classes available.

Table 4.1 Base Class Library Class and Namespace Examples

Namespace	Class	Functionality
System.IO	File, Directory, FileStream	Manipulate files and directories; read and write to and from files in the file system
System.Data	DataSet, DataTable, DataRow	Manipulate tabular data in memory; the data can be populated from a variety of data sources
System.Xml	XMLDocument, XMLElement	Load and manipulate XML data
System.Security.Cryptography	CryptoStream, TripleDES, RSACryptoServiceProvider	Encrypting and decrypting data using a variety of industry-standard algorithms
System.Drawing	Brush, Font, Bitmap	Creating and manipulating on-screen graphics
System.Web.Services	WebService	Create and consume an XML Web service
System.Threading	Thread, Mutex, Semaphore	Create and synchronize multiple processor threads

Developers use classes from the Base Class Library to perform their desired functionality. The ability to access readily available functionality is one of the major advantages of the .NET Framework. When creating CLR objects for SQL Server, only a subset of the Base Class Library is available to you. CLR objects, such as CLR stored procedures, run within the context of SQL Server. Not all classes from the Base Class Library should be called within this context. For example, it makes no sense to create and launch visual forms or manipulate graphics from within a SQL Server stored procedure. Other classes, like those in the *System.Threading* namespace, could impact the stability of SQL Server if used. You can access any .NET class from within SQL Server, but not all are supported for use with SQL Server.

The namespaces that are listed as supported in SQL Server documentation have been tested for stability with SQL Server. Assemblies containing supported namespaces are loaded from the Global Assembly Cache (GAC) by default, and are always available to you when creating CLR-integrated objects. You don't need to do anything special to use classes from these namespaces. As of February 2009, the following namespaces and assemblies are listed as supported by SQL Server 2008:

- *CustomMarshalers*
- *Microsoft.VisualBasic*
- *Microsoft.VisualC*
- *mscorlib*
- *System*
- *System.Configuration*
- *System.Data*
- *System.Data.OracleClient*
- *System.Data.SqlXml*
- *System.Deployment*
- *System.Security*
- *System.Transactions*
- *System.Web.Services*
- *System.Xml*
- *System.Core.dll*
- *System.Xml.Linq.dll*

Even if the class you wish to call is in an unsupported assembly, it doesn't mean you cannot use it. Any custom assembly that you write yourself is unsupported, unless you can persuade the makers of SQL Server to test it for you. This unlikely event notwithstanding, you will have to use the unsupported library at your own risk. Unsupported libraries are not loaded by SQL Server by default, and therefore you have to register them explicitly. We will learn how to register assemblies with SQL Server later in this chapter. When using functionality from an unsupported assembly, you are responsible for testing it and ensuring it performs well, without affecting the stability of SQL Server.

Head of the Class...

Understanding Classes, Assemblies, Namespaces, and the GAC

For those among us who are not developers by profession, programming terms like class, namespace, and assembly can be confusing and intimidating. You will see these terms, possibly all of them, in the exam. To make matters worse, these terms can be used interchangeably in some situations, but in certain circumstances they cannot be exchanged for one another. First of all, it is worth mentioning that assemblies are purely a component of the .NET Framework, while the concept of classes and, to some extent, namespaces, can be found in other programming realms—for example, Java.

A class is a single logical programming entity and usually has methods (functionality) and properties (descriptors). For example, a *FileStream* class is used to read or write binary data to and from a file. It has properties like *Length*, which designates the size of a file in bytes. It has methods like *ReadByte* and *WriteByte* to read or write a single byte to the file. You could use a *FileStream* object to open a file from a file share and load its data into a SQL Server table.

A namespace is a logical group of classes. For example, the *FileStream* object belongs in the *System.IO* namespace, along with classes like *File*, *Path*, and *Directory*. These classes are all logically related and are grouped by their creator in the same namespace. On the other hand, a class like *XMLElement* doesn't belong in the **System.IO** namespace and therefore lives in a different namespace—*System.XML*.

Continued

An assembly is a physical EXE or DLL file containing MSIL code for one or more classes and namespaces. An assembly can also contain other resources beyond code, such as images, icons, or data. Developers write classes, group them in namespaces, and compile them into assemblies. Other developers can then load an assembly and use classes contained within it. When you come to create custom code for your CLR stored procedures and functions, you will both create and use assemblies.

The question is: When you use assemblies in your application, where do they come from? Some assemblies are stored with the application in their application folders—for example, C:\Program Files\MyApp\MyAssembly.dll. These are called local assemblies, because they are specific to the individual application. Other assemblies are used by many applications on your computer. These are shared assemblies. Shared assemblies are registered in the GAC. The GAC is a special repository for shared assemblies, and it stores information about them such as their versions. Assemblies that comprise the Base Class Library are stored in the GAC. You can see what's in the GAC by navigating to %Windir%\Assembly. If you delete an assembly out of the GAC or update it with a different version, this will affect all applications that use that assembly.

In summary, classes are grouped into namespaces and are contained within physical assemblies. These physical assemblies can be stored locally or in the GAC.

Registering CLR Assemblies for Use with SQL Server

Assemblies are physical units of deployment that contain managed code. This managed code can be called by CLR stored procedures, CLR functions, CLR triggers, CLR user-defined aggregates, and CLR user-defined data types. Assemblies are stored externally from SQL Server and thus can be used by other applications. When called by SQL Server, the code within the assembly is loaded into the SQL Server service process and is executed within its context.

Before you can use an assembly from SQL Server you must register it. When you register the assembly, it is imported into SQL Server and configured for use. Often assemblies depend on other assemblies, which in turn depend on others, and so on, forming a dependency tree. During registration, the entire chain of dependencies for your assembly must be imported into SQL Server. Assemblies are registered using the *CREATE ASSEMBLY* statement as shown in Example 4.1.

Example 4.1 Syntax—CREATE ASSEMBLY

```
CREATE ASSEMBLY assembly_name
[ AUTHORIZATION owner_name ]
FROM { <client_assembly_specifier> | <assembly_bits> [,…n ] }
[ WITH PERMISSION_SET = { SAFE | EXTERNAL_ACCESS | UNSAFE } ]
[ ; ]
```

The *assembly_name* is the unique name of the assembly within SQL Server. To avoid confusion, name your assemblies after their file names, unless there is a naming conflict with another registered assembly. For example, if you want to use the assembly MyAwesomeFunctions.dll, designate MyAwesomeFunctions as its name when registering it.

The *owner_name* is the role or user who will become the owner of the assembly. Registered assemblies have owners within SQL Server, much like tables, stored procedures, and other database objects. Note that when registering the assembly, you can only specify a role of which you are a member, or a user from whom you have permission to impersonate. If you don't specify the *owner_name* explicitly, you will be registered as the owner by default (again, the same principle as tables or stored procedures). Just like other objects, it is recommended to register all assemblies as owned by dbo. This will help avoid major interoperability problems that arise when assemblies that need to call each other are owned by different users.

EXAM WARNING

Be careful when choosing anything but dbo as the *AUTHORIZATION* parameter for *CREATE ASSEMBLY*. You must have a very specific reason not to use dbo, for example, if the calling user is not a member of *db_owner*. The best practice is to always use dbo for all assembly ownership.

The *client assembly specifier* is the local or network path of the physical assembly DLL file you wish to register. Alternatively, you can specify the actual bits of the assembly as the *assembly bits* instead of its network path. The bits are specified as either a literal varbinary value or an expression of a varbinary data type. You must first specify the bits for the root assembly and then all its dependencies.

EXAM WARNING

Remember that when SQL Server registers the assembly, it imports the assembly file as well as all its dependencies. If any dependency is not available, and it is not already registered with SQL Server, the registration statement will fail and report an error.

Also note that if a dependency is already registered, but under a different owner, your statement will also fail.

The *PERMISSION_SET* parameter specifies what security permissions are granted to the assembly code when it executes within SQL Server. We will discuss permission sets next in this chapter.

The following example registers the *MyAwesomeFunctions* assembly, owned by dbo;

```
CREATE ASSEMBLY MyAwesomeFunctions
AUTHORIZATION [dbo]
FROM 'C:\Valentine\MyAwesomeFunctions\bin\Debug\MyAwesomeFunctions.dll'
WITH PERMISSION_SET = SAFE;
```

For this statement to succeed, the calling user must be a member of *db_owner* role, and also have permission to access the MyAwesomeFunctions.dll file. All dependencies for the assembly must be available for SQL Server to import or must have been already registered with SQL Server. Remember, you don't need to register supported assemblies as they are registered by default.

EXAM WARNING

You cannot register an assembly if there is already another version of this assembly registered with the same name, public key, and culture (locale). The public key is used to generate a unique name for an assembly. For example, you cannot register MyAwesomeFunctions version 1.5.0 and MyAwesomeFunctions version 1.5.2.

Finally, you can unregister an assembly using the *DROP ASSEMBLY* statement and change the properties of an assembly using the *ALTER ASSEMBLY* statement. Supported assemblies that are loaded by default cannot be altered or dropped.

Understanding Permission Sets

When registering an assembly with SQL Server, code within that assembly may adversely affect or compromise the system. To help protect against these events, SQL Server allows you to restrict the operations the assembly is able to perform. This is done at assembly registration time, by using *permission sets*. *PERMISSION_SET* is a parameter supplied to the *CREATE ASSEMBLY* statement, and specifies what permission restrictions apply to the assembly. Note that these restrictions apply only when the assembly is accessed from within SQL Server—for example, when using a CLR stored procedure. If the assembly is called by some other means, these permission restrictions will not apply.

Three permission sets are available in SQL Server 2008:

- SAFE
- EXTERNAL_ACCESS
- UNSAFE

Let's examine the permission sets, and what effect they have on assembly execution. SAFE is the most restrictive permission set. SAFE is also the default permission set, which applies if you call *CREATE ASSEMBLY*, but do not specify the *PERMISSION_SET* parameter. When running with the SAFE permission set, assembly code is not able to access any external resources such as the network, files, or the Windows registry. The SAFE permission set is ideal for assemblies that perform computational tasks or store user-defined data types, and that don't require any external resource access. SAFE assemblies also have permission to access data within SQL Server using the execution context. If code within an assembly granted the SAFE permission set attempts to access external resources, the operation will fail and the code will receive a security exception.

EXTERNAL_ACCESS is the permission set you will assign to your assembly if you require it to access external resources. Assemblies registered with the EXTERNAL_ACCESS permission set can access and modify the file system, write to event logs, use network services like DNS and Active Directory, create outbound network connections including Web access (port 80 and 443) and SMTP mail access (port 25), and access HKEY_CLASSES_ROOT, HKEY_LOCAL_MACHINE, HKEY_CURRENT_USER, HKEY_CURRENT_CONFIG, and HKEY_USERS registry keys. When code from an assembly registered with the EXTERNAL_ACCESS permission set attempts to access resources outside SQL Server, it will do so under the SQL Server service account. Code with EXTERNAL_ACCESS permission can perform only those operations available as part of the .NET Framework Base Class Library. As mentioned earlier, the CLR performs extensive security and stability checks on code that executes within it. This means that managed code is inherently safer than unmanaged code, as it includes an extra layer of protection provided by the CLR. The EXTERNAL_ACCESS permission set does not allow you to call unmanaged code directly.

The UNSAFE permission set allows your code to perform all operations allowed under the EXTERNAL_ACCESS permission set. The difference between the two permission sets is that the UNSAFE permission set also allows code running under it to call unmanaged code directly. Unmanaged code is called using a mechanism known as Platform Invoke (P/Invoke). Because unmanaged code is not subject to CLR checks, it could potentially damage the stability of your server. In some cases, malicious unmanaged code can be used to subvert SQL Server security and even security of the server on which SQL Server is running. Assign the UNSAFE permission set with caution and only to assemblies that absolutely require it. You should be certain that any assemblies to which you assign the UNSAFE permission are trustworthy and stable.

Figure 4.3 explains a method you can use to select the required permission set for your assembly. Note that you must test all assemblies for stability regardless of the permission set you intend to assign to them. Untested assemblies may cause errors and make your application behave unexpectedly.

Figure 4.3 Selecting an Appropriate Permission Set

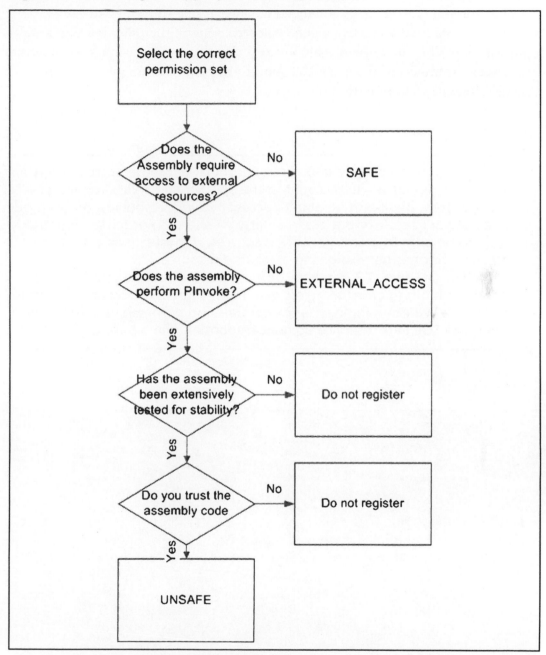

What account does the assembly code run as? The assembly code runs in the SQL Server service process. It runs as the SQL Server service account. This is another reason to configure the SQL Server service to run as a least-privileged service account, not the highly privileged Local System account. If the caller of the assembly is a SQL Server login, and the assembly is trying to access external resources, the external access call will not succeed. Only if the caller is a Windows login will the call be performed using the SQL Server service account credentials. It is possible to impersonate another account from within the assembly code, but normal Windows security restrictions apply.

TEST DAY TIP

Remember that any code that runs within CLR database objects will run as the SQL Server service account. If the SQL Server service account is Local System, it will not be able to access network resources. An example of a network resource is a file in a network share. In order for your CLR code to be able to access network resources, it must run as a domain account that has permissions to access the resource.

When calling a CLR database object, you must be authenticated as a Windows login in order to access external resources. If you are authenticated as a Windows login, your credentials and permissions *will not be used*. The SQL Server service account credentials will be used.

New & Noteworthy...

Understanding the *TRUSTWORTHY* Database Property

SQL Server 2008 databases have a *TRUSTWORTHY* property. This property indicates whether objects in your database, including user-defined functions and stored procedures, can access resources outside the database while running as the SQL Server service account. When the *TRUSTWORTHY* property is set to ON, your CLR integrated objects will be able to access external resources, subject to the permission set they have been assigned. When the *TRUSTWORTHY* property is set to OFF, your CLR objects will receive an error when attempting to access resources outside the database.

To check the current value of the *TRUSTWORTHY* property, query the *is_trustworthy_on* column in the sys.databases table as shown in the following example:

Continued

```
SELECT name, is_trustworthy_on AS IsTrustworthy

FROM sys.databases

WHERE name = 'DatabaseName'
```

To set the value of the *TRUSTWORTHY* property to either ON or OFF, run the following command:
ALTER DATABASE DatabaseName SET TRUSTWORTHY ON
By default, the *TRUSTWORTHY* property is off in databases to protect your system against malicious code. In order to change the *TRUSTWORTHY* property you must be a member of the sysadmin server role.

Implementing SQL Server Objects Using Managed Code

Let's examine how various SQL Server database objects can be implemented using managed code. You can use managed code to implement the following objects in SQL Server:

- Stored procedures
- Functions (scalar and table-valued)
- Aggregates
- Triggers
- User-defined data types

When creating stored procedures and functions you can accept input parameters and use output parameters to return data. You can also use return values for functions and stored procedures. When creating a CLR stored procedure, it can return nothing or return an integer representing the return code. Functions can return a single value of any type. When creating your CLR objects you can access SQL Server data from the calling context. This is known as using the *context connection*. The context connection provides you with access to the immediate execution environment, in other words, login credentials and selected database.

No matter what database object you choose to create, you are likely to use CLR integration *custom attributes*. What are custom attributes? In the context of .NET Framework development, custom attributes are keywords that mark a certain piece of code. The execution environment (in this case SQL Server) examines the attributes and provides services to your code based on these attributes. Although you don't need to know all the attributes that can be applied to each type of CLR object, it is worth understanding the concept of attributes. For example, the *SqlFunction* attribute indicates that the procedure marked with it is a SQL Server function. For the *SqlFunction* attribute you can specify multiple properties like *DataAccess*, *Name*, and *TableDefinition*. In this particular example, the *DataAccess* property specifies whether the function will read data from the SQL Server context connection, or will not access SQL Server data at all; the Name property is the name that will be used to register the function with SQL Server; and the *TableDefinition* property defines the columns in the table returned by a table-valued function.

TEST DAY TIP

You don't need to memorize the list of attributes and their available properties. The one key attribute to remember is *DataAccess.* This attribute can be set to *DataAccessKind.None* or *DataAccessKind.Read.* Remember that you must specify *DataAccess=DataAccessKind.Read* if your CLR object has to execute queries and read data from the context connection. Examples later in this chapter show how this is implemented.

Creating CLR Functions

As explained earlier in this book, user-defined functions are compiled routines that usually perform calculations and return a single value. Functions can be defined using Transact-SQL or any .NET language. Let's take a brief tour of creating functions using managed code. Note that while the examples will be presented in C# and Visual Basic .NET, you can create them using any .NET language.

When creating a function you should first determine whether it is a scalar or a table-valued function. Scalar functions return a single value of a SQL data type like bit or int. Table-valued functions return an expression that can be treated by the calling code as a SQL table comprising of columns and rows. All CLR-integrated user-defined functions are implemented as static methods of a class that is hosted by an assembly (see "Understanding Classes, Assemblies, Namespaces, and the GAC" earlier in this chapter). You can use the *SqlFunction* custom attribute to specify additional information about your function. Examples 4.2 and 4.3 show a very simple function named *SayHello* that returns the value "Hello world!"

Example 4.2 C#

```csharp
using System;
using System.Data;
using System.Data.SqlClient;
using System.Data.SqlTypes;
using Microsoft.SqlServer.Server;
public class UserDefinedFunctions
{
[Microsoft.SqlServer.Server.SqlFunction(DataAccess=DataAccessKind.None)]
    public static SqlString SayHello()
    {
        return new SqlString("Hello world!");
    }
}
```

Example 4.3 Visual Basic .NET

```vbnet
Imports System
Imports System.Data
Imports System.Data.SqlClient
Imports System.Data.SqlTypes
Imports Microsoft.SqlServer.Server
Public Class UserDefinedFunctions
    <Microsoft.SqlServer.Server.SqlFunction()> _
    Public Shared Function SayHello() As SqlString
        Return New SqlString("Hello world!")
    End Function
End Class
```

For those who are new to .NET programming, let's go through the elements of this code. It is worthy of mention that the two examples are absolutely equivalent, and do the same thing—return the value "Hello world!" when called. If you remember when we discussed managed code, both examples will compile to exactly the same set of MSIL statements.

The first set of lines are the *using* or *imports* directives. These directives tell the class that it will be using objects from the namespaces mentioned, including the *Microsoft.SqlServer.Server* namespace. This is true—we will be using the *SqlFunction* custom attribute that belongs in the *Microsoft.SqlServer.Server* namespace. We will also use the *SqlString* data type that belongs in the *System.Data.SqlTypes* namespace.

The second line declares the class. In this case, the class is called *UserDefined-Functions*. Note that the class doesn't have to be called *UserDefinedFunctions*; you could use any name—for example, *MyFunctions* or *SqlStuff*. Remember that classes are individual logical entities and have properties and methods. Notice that the class end needs to be specified by a close brace (}) in C# or the keywords *End Class* in Visual Basic .NET.

Once the class is declared, we implement the actual SQL function as a method of our class. To specify that the method should be registered as a SQL function we use the *SqlFunction* custom attribute. We also specify that the *SqlFunction* attribute has its *DataAccess* property set to *DataAccess.None*—our function will not be accessing SQL Server data.

The method that is marked as *SqlFunction* is called *SayHello*. It is marked as *public*, meaning that it can be accessed externally—for example, from SQL Server. It is also marked as *static* in C# or *Shared* in Visual Basic .NET. These keywords indicate that the method can be called directly, without creating an instance of the class. You must mark methods that will become SQL Server functions, stored procedures, and aggregates as *static/Shared* for them to work properly. Our method takes no parameters as it has two empty round brackets after it, and returns a value of type *SqlString* (text). Inside the body of the method we simply use the *return* keyword to return a new *SqlString* containing the value "Hello world!" When this function is called, it will return "Hello world!"

TEST DAY TIP

Remember that all SQL objects are written as methods of a class. They must be marked as *static* in C# or *Shared* in Visual Basic .NET. They must also be marked as *public*, or else the SQL Server execution environment will not be able to access them.

Table 4.2 lists all properties applicable to the *SqlFunction* custom attribute. You don't need to memorize all of these properties—the table is provided for you to get an idea of what type of control is available for your user-defined CLR functions.

Table 4.2 *SqlFunction* Custom Attribute Properties

Property	Explanation
IsDeterministic	True if the function will always return the same value, if called with the same parameters. False if the function can return different values when called with the same parameters. An example of a deterministic function is the *SayHello* function. An example of a nondeterministic function is a function that will use database data that varies.
DataAccess	Specifies whether the function will read data from the context SQL Server connection. Acceptable values are *DataAccessKind.None* and *DataAccessKind.Read*.
SystemDataAccess	Specifies whether the function will require access to system catalogs or system tables in SQL Server—for example, *sys.object*. Acceptable values are System *DataAccessKind.None* and *SystemDataAccessKind. Read*.
IsPrecise	Specifies whether the function will be performing imprecise computation, for example, float operations. True if the function does not involve these operations, false if it does. SQL Server uses this information for indexing.
FillRowMethodName	Used for table-valued functions. This is the name of a method in the same class that serves as the table-valued function contract.
TableDefinition	Used for table-valued functions. Defines the column list in the table returned.
Name	The name of the SQL function.

Here are a few examples of more complex user-defined functions. Look through these functions to understand how they are implemented. When looking through each function ask yourself if the function should be registered with the permission set of SAFE, EXTERNAL_ACCESS, or UNSAFE.

Registering CLR Functions

You must register CLR functions with a SQL Server database before they can be used. To do this, first register the assembly containing the function using *CREATE*

ASSEMBLY. Then, use the *CREATE FUNCTION* statement with *EXTERNAL NAME* parameter to register the function for use. Use the syntax shown in Example 4.4 to register the function.

Example 4.4 Syntax—Registering CLR Functions

```
CREATE FUNCTION dbo.function_name (@param1 as param1_data_type,
  @param2 as param2_data_type)
RETURNS return_data_type
AS EXTERNAL NAME assembly_name.class_name.function_name;
```

Note that parameters and return types must be specified when registering the user-defined CLR function. In Examples 4.5 and 4.6 we will register the *SayHello* function we have created earlier in this chapter. The *SayHello* function takes no parameters, and returns a value of type *SqlString.* The *SqlString* type is equivalent of the nvarchar SQL Server data type.

Example 4.5 Registering a Simple CLR Function

```
CREATE FUNCTION dbo.SayHello()
RETURNS nvarchar(max)
AS EXTERNAL NAME MyAwesomeFunctions.UserDefinedFunctions.SayHello;
```

Example 4.6 Calling a Simple CLR Function

```
Select dbo.SayHello()
--RESULTS:
-------------
Hello world!
(1 row(s) affected)
```

Creating CLR Aggregates

Aggregates are functions that operate on a set of values and return a single value. Examples of built-in aggregate functions are *SUM, AVG,* and *MAX.* In your query, you will usually pass a column to these aggregate functions and will be returned the total, average, or maximum value of all the rows in that column. Previously, SQL Server supported only built-in aggregates. Custom aggregate functionality was achieved using cursors, which was rather cumbersome. With CLR integration, you can now create your own custom aggregate functions. CLR integration is the only way to create custom aggregates in SQL Server. CLR aggregates are simpler, and offer better performance than cursors. Performance of custom aggregates compares to performance of built-in aggregates.

The ability to create custom aggregates is very powerful. For example, imagine being able to aggregate a list of binary photographs stored in the database as an image data type and determine which one has the most likeness to a specific photograph you pass to it. In the case of spatial data, you can determine the total length of a route around all those points, or the shortest route. You could also implement complex statistical analysis with functions unavailable in SQL Server out of the box, or you could simply concatenate string values from a varchar column.

In order to create a user-defined aggregate, your class must adhere to the *aggregation contract*. The aggregation contract consists of the following requirements:

- Mark your class with *SqlUserDefinedAggregate*.

- Create an instance method called *Init*. This method initializes the aggregation. Here, you will reset any variables that may have been set in a previous use, and instantiate any variables you will use during the aggregation.

- Create an instance method called *Accumulate*. It should accept one parameter: the value that is being accumulated. SQL Server calls this method for every value in the group being processed. You should use this method to update the state of your aggregate as the value is accumulated.

- Create an instance method called *Merge*. It should accept one parameter: another instance of your aggregate class. This method is used to merge multiple aggregations.

- Create an instance method called *Terminate*. This method should accept no parameters, but it should return the final result of your aggregation.

Table 4.3 lists all properties that apply to the *SqlUserDefinedAggregate* custom attribute.

Table 4.3 *SqlUserDefinedAggregate* Custom Attribute Properties

Property	Explanation
Format	Format of serializing the aggregate to a string. This can be either native or user-defined.
IsInvariantToDuplicates	Determines whether the function ignores duplicate values. For example, the MIN and MAX

Continued

Table 4.3 Continued. SqlUserDefinedAggregate Custom Attribute Properties

Property	Explanation
	aggregates ignore duplicate values. The *SUM* aggregate does not ignore duplicate values and will return a very different result when the same value is passed to it multiple times.
IsInvariantToNulls	Determines if the function ignores null values. For example, the *SUM* function will return the same value when null values are passed, while the *COUNT* function will not.
IsInvariantToOrder	This property is not used by SQL Server at this point. It is reserved for future use.
IsNullIfEmpty	Determines whether the aggregate will return null if no values have been passed to it.
MaxByteSize	The amount of memory in bytes your aggregate will consume during processing. The maximum value is 2GB. Specify between 1 to 8000 bytes, or –1 if your aggregate will consume over 8000 bytes (but less than 2GB).

Examples 4.7 and 4.8 show how we can list text values all on one line, separating them by a semicolon. This can be very useful when you have a column storing e-mail addresses and you want to list them all on one line with separators (and then perhaps send it to your e-mail system to send an e-mail to all those addresses).

Example 4.7 Implementing *ListWithSeparator*—C#

```
using System;
using System.Data;
using Microsoft.SqlServer.Server;
using System.Data.SqlTypes;
using System.Text;
using System.IO;

[Serializable]
[SqlUserDefinedAggregate(
    Format.UserDefined,
    IsInvariantToNulls = true,
    IsInvariantToDuplicates = true,
```

```
        IsInvariantToOrder = true,

    MaxByteSize = -1)

]
public class ListWithSeparator : IBinarySerialize

{
    // Comment: the tempStringBuilder variable holds the list while the
aggregation is being processed
    public StringBuilder tempStringBuilder;

    public void Init()

    {
        tempStringBuilder = new StringBuilder();

    }
    public void Accumulate(SqlString value)

    {
        if (!value.IsNull)

        {
            tempStringBuilder.Append(value.Value);

            tempStringBuilder.Append(";");

        }

    }
    public void Merge(ListWithSeparator anotherList)

    {
tempStringBuilder.Append(anotherList.tempStringBuilder.ToString());

    }
    public SqlString Terminate()

    {
        if (tempStringBuilder != null

            && tempStringBuilder.Length > 0)

        {
            return new SqlString(tempStringBuilder.ToString());

        }
        return new SqlString(string.Empty);

    }
    public void Read(BinaryReader reader)

    {
        tempStringBuilder = new StringBuilder(reader.ReadString());

    }
```

```
    public void Write(BinaryWriter writer)
    {
        writer.Write(tempStringBuilder.ToString());
    }
}
```

Example 4.8 Implementing *ListWithSeparator*—Visual Basic .NET

```
Imports System

Imports System.Data

Imports Microsoft.SqlServer.Server

Imports System.Data.SqlTypes

Imports System.Text

Imports System.IO

<Serializable(), SqlUserDefinedAggregate(Format.UserDefined,
IsInvariantToNulls:=True, IsInvariantToDuplicates:=True,
IsInvariantToOrder:=True, MaxByteSize:=-1)> _
Public Class ListWithSeparator

    Implements IBinarySerialize

    Private tempStringBuilder As StringBuilder

    Public Sub Init()

      tempStringBuilder = New StringBuilder()

    End Sub

    Public Sub Accumulate(ByVal value As SqlString)

        If value.IsNull Then

            Return

        End If

        tempStringBuilder.Append(value.Value).Append(","c)

    End Sub

    Public Sub Merge(ByVal anotherList As ListWithSeparator)

        tempStringBuilder.Append(anotherList.tempStringBuilder)

    End Sub

    Public Function Terminate() As SqlString

        If Not (tempStringBuilder Is Nothing) AndAlso tempStringBuilder.
Length > 0 Then

            return New SqlString(tempStringBuilder.ToString())

        End If
```

```
        Return New SqlString(String.Empty)
    End Function

    Public Sub Read(reader As BinaryReader)
        tempStringBuilder = New StringBuilder(reader.ReadString())
    End Sub
    Public Sub Write(writer As BinaryWriter)
        writer.Write(Me.intermediateResult.ToString())
    End Sub
End Class
```

Registering CLR Aggregates

Similarly to CLR functions, you must register your CLR aggregates with a SQL Server database. First register the assembly containing the aggregate using *CREATE ASSEMBLY.* Then, use the *CREATE AGGREGATE* statement with the *EXTERNAL NAME* parameter to register the aggregate. You must specify input parameter information and return type.

In Examples 4.9 and 4.10 we will register the *SayHello* function we have created earlier in this chapter. The *SayHello* function takes no parameters, and returns a value of type *SqlString.* The *SqlString* type is equivalent of the nvarchar SQL Server data type.

Example 4.9 Registering a Simple CLR Function

```
CREATE AGGREGATE ListWithSeparator
  (@value nvarchar(200))
  RETURNS nvarchar(max)
EXTERNAL NAME MyAwesomeFunctions.ListWithSeparator
```

Example 4.10 Calling a CLR Aggregate

```
USE AdventureWorks;
SELECT dbo.ListWithSeparator(Person.Contact.EmailAddress)
FROM Person.Contact
WHERE Person.Contact.FirstName like 'Val%'
--RESULTS (Truncated for brevity):
-------------------------------------------------------------------------
valerie0@adventure-works.com;mailto:valerie1@adventure-works.com;valerie2@ad…
(1 row(s) affected)
```

Creating CLR Stored Procedures

Stored procedures are similar to functions, except they are not used in single-valued expressions. Stored procedures can return multiple result sets, return error messages to the caller, and execute Data Manipulation Language (DML) and Data Definition Language (DDL) statements. In summary, stored procedures are designed to store compiled logic that may manipulate data. Stored procedures can be implemented using Transact-SQL and the CLR.

Creating a CLR stored procedure is very similar to creating a CLR function. Create a class, create a static/shared method, and mark it with the *SqlProcedure* attribute. The difference is that a CLR stored procedure must be either a void (in other words, return nothing) or return an integer value that represents the success or failure code.

You can also return tabular results and messages by using the *SqlContext.Pipe* object. This object represents the output to the SQL Server caller, and has the methods of *Send* and *Execute*. Use *Send* to send text, and *Execute* to send a query that will be executed by the SQL Server caller.

CLR stored procedures are registered with the database using the *CREATE PROCEDURE* statement with the *EXTERNAL NAME* clause. As with function and aggregate registration, you must specify the parameter definitions and return value, if any.

Examples 4.11 through 4.13 demonstrate how to create, register, and call a CLR stored procedure. In this stored procedure, we will write all scrap reasons from the Production.ScrapReason table to a text file. The stored procedure will accept the path to the text file as a parameter. We will call this stored procedure— *ExportComplaints*.

Example 4.11 Implementing the *ExportComplaints* Stored Procedure — C#

```csharp
using System;

using System.Data;

using System.Data.SqlClient;

using System.Data.SqlTypes;

using Microsoft.SqlServer.Server;

using System.IO;

public class StoredProcedures

{

    [Microsoft.SqlServer.Server.SqlProcedure()]

    public static void ExportComplaints(SqlString PathToLetter)

    {

        using(StreamWriter writer = new StreamWriter(PathToLetter.
ToString())){

        using(SqlConnection connection = new SqlConnection("context
connection=true"))

        {

            connection.Open();

            SqlCommand command = new SqlCommand("Select Name from Production.
ScrapReason", connection);

            using (SqlDataReader reader = command.ExecuteReader())

            {

                while (reader.Read())

                {

                    writer.WriteLine(reader[0].ToString());

                }

            }

        }

    }

SqlContext.Pipe.Send("Message from ExportComplaints CLR Stored Proc: Letter
created successfully!");

    }

}
```

Example 4.12 Implementing the Export Complaints Stored Procedure—Visual Basic .NET

```
Imports System

Imports System.Data

Imports System.Data.SqlClient

Imports System.Data.SqlTypes

Imports Microsoft.SqlServer.Server

Imports System.IO

Public Class StoredProcedures

<Microsoft.SqlServer.Server.SqlProcedure(DataAccess:=DataAccessKind.Read)> _

    Public Shared Sub ExportComplaints(ByVal PathToLetter As SqlString)

        Using writer As StreamWriter = New StreamWriter(PathToLetter.
ToString())

            Using connection As SqlConnection = New SqlConnection("context
connection=true")

                connection.Open()

                Dim command As SqlCommand = New SqlCommand("Select Name from
Production.ScrapReason", connection)

                Using reader As SqlDataReader = command.ExecuteReader()

                  Do While reader.Read()

                    writer.WriteLine(reader(0).ToString())

                  Loop

                End Using

            End Using

        End Using

        SqlContext.Pipe.Send("Message from ExportComplaints CLR Stored Proc:
Letter created successfully!")

    End Sub

End Class
```

Example 4.13 Registering the Export Complaints Stored Procedure with SQL Server

```
CREATE ASSEMBLY MyAwesomeFunctions

AUTHORIZATION [dbo]

FROM 'C:\Documents and Settings\Valentine\My Documents\MyAwesomeFunctions\bin\
MyAwesomeFunctions.dll'
```

```
WITH PERMISSION_SET = EXTERNAL_ACCESS;
Go
CREATE PROCEDURE dbo.ExportComplaints(@PathToLetter as nvarchar(1000))
AS EXTERNAL NAME MyAwesomeFunctions.StoredProcedures.ExportComplaints;
Go
```

Note that this time we had to register the assembly with the EXTERNAL_ ACCESS permission set; otherwise, we would not be able to write to the text file.

Example 4.14 shows the syntax for executing the *ExportComplaints* stored procedure.

Example 4.14 Executing the *ExportComplaints* Stored Procedure

```
EXECUTE dbo.ExportComplaints 'C:\Documents and Settings\Valentine\
My Documents\Complaint.txt'
```

After executing the stored procedure, a text file Complaint.txt will appear in My Documents. If you have time, try performing this example yourself—you will feel more comfortable with CLR integration and .NET Framework development as a whole.

Test Day Tip

You should understand what happens when an assembly that is registered with the SAFE permission set attempts to access external resources. The assembly code will receive an error. If we used the SAFE permission set with the preceding *ExportComplaints* example, we would receive an error that looks like this:

```
A .NET Framework error occurred during execution of user-defined routine
or aggregate "ExportComplaints": System.Security.SecurityException:
Request for the permission of type 'System.Security.Permissions.
FileIOPermission, mscorlib, Version=2.0.0.0, Culture=neutral,
PublicKeyToken=b77a5c561934e089' failed.
```

Creating CLR Triggers

A trigger is a statement that runs every time table data or the structure of a database is modified. Data Manipulation Language (DML) triggers run when someone runs an *INSERT*, *UPDATE*, or *DELETE* statement against a particular table. These triggers can be used to perform complex validation and roll back the operation if necessary. Data Definition Language (DDL) triggers run when someone modifies the structure of a database, usually by executing *CREATE*, *ALTER*, and *DROP* statements. These triggers can be used to audit modifications to the structure of the database.

CLR triggers have the same capabilities as Transact-SQL triggers. Specifically, CLR triggers can perform the following tasks:

- Determine which columns in a table have been updated
- Query the INSERTED and DELETED tables to find out what data is about to be inserted, deleted, or modified
- Determine which database objects were affected by a DDL statement

Most of these capabilities are accessed by using the *SqlContext.TriggerContext* object. Using this object is outside the scope of this exam. However, when you need to create a CLR trigger in real life, see SQL Server Books Online.

CLR triggers need to be registered with the specific table, just like regular Transact-SQL triggers. To do this, first register the assembly containing the trigger using *CREATE ASSEMBLY*, as explained earlier in this chapter. Then, use the *CREATE TRIGGER* statement to bind the trigger to the specific table, as shown in Example 4.15.

Example 4.15 Binding a CLR Trigger

```
CREATE TRIGGER dbo.ValidateCustomerEMailAddress
ON Customers
FOR INSERT, UPDATE
AS
EXTERNAL NAME MyAwesomeFunctions. Triggers.ValidateCustomerEMailAddress
```

EXAM WARNING

Although you don't need to remember the syntax of writing a trigger using C# or Visual Basic .NET, you should learn how the trigger is registered. Registering a CLR trigger is essentially the same as registering a regular trigger, except that you replace the Transact-SQL trigger definition with the keywords *EXTERNAL NAME*, followed by the full path to the trigger in the form *Assembly.Class.Method*.

Creating User-Defined Data Types Using the CLR

Ever since SQL Server 2005, we have had the ability to create custom data types and register them with SQL Server. These are known as User-Defined Types, or UDTs. UDTs are often used to represent complex data, such as spatial coordinates or currencies. Note that you should not use UDTs to represent logical structures like customers or orders. Complex structures are better implemented using traditional columns, rows, and relationships. Don't use UDTs just because you have the ability. Always consider traditional ways to store your data as this will deliver better performance. UDTs are created using managed code and can be used in place of any SQL Server data type—for example, to define columns in a table, to declare variables, and so on.

Creating a UDT in managed code is similar to creating a user-defined aggregate. Specifically, you create a class or a structure and mark it with the *SqlUserDefinedType* custom attribute. You must then implement a user-defined type contract, again, similar to creating a user-defined aggregate. Defining a CLR UDT is outside the scope of this exam. However, when you need to create a CLR UDT in real life, see SQL Server Books Online.

CLR user-defined data types need to be registered before they can be used. As with all CLR objects, you should first register the assembly with SQL Server using the *CREATE ASSEMBLY* statement. You can then use the *CREATE TYPE* statement to register the type with your database. The type is registered with a single database, not with the entire instance of SQL Server. This is another reason why you should consider alternatives to CLR UDTs—cross-database and cross-server operations may be difficult or even impossible. Similar to declaring a trigger, you should use the *EXTERNAL NAME* keywords to bind your UDT to the CLR object, as shown in Example 4.16.

Example 4.16 Registering a CLR User-Defined Data Type

```
CREATE TYPE dbo.RGBColor
EXTERNAL NAME MyAwesomeFunctions.[RGBColor];
```

EXAM WARNING

You are not expected to be able to write a CLR UDT using C# or Visual Basic .NET, but you should learn how the data type is registered. Use the *CREATE TYPE* statement with the *EXTERNAL NAME* parameter, followed by the full path to the class or structure representing your UDT in the form *Assembly.[Class]*.

EXERCISE 4.1

START TO FINISH: IMPLEMENTING A CLR FUNCTION IN SQL SERVER

In this exercise, we will create a simple CLR function to read data from the Windows registry. The function will accept a registry key name and a value name. The function will return the data held in the registry value. We will then register the function and call it from the SQL Server Management Studio.

Before you begin, you must have the following software installed on your computer:

- SQL Server 2008 (a free trial is available for download).
- Visual Studio 2005 or Visual Studio 2008.
- If you don't have Visual Studio, download and install the .NET Framework 2.0 SDK.
- AdventureWorks sample database.

First we will create the CLR function. To do this, use the following procedure:

1. If you have Visual Studio installed, open Visual Studio. To do this click **Start | All Programs | Microsoft Visual Studio 2005 | Microsoft Visual Studio 2005**.

2. In **Visual Studio**, on the menu bar, click **File | New | Project**.

3. In the **New Project** dialog, in the left pane, expand either **C#** or **Visual Basic** (choose which language you wish to use). Under your language of choice click **Database**.

4. In the **Templates** pane on the right, click **SQL Server Project**.

5. In the **Name** box type **MySQLLibrary**, and choose to save the project to an easy-to-remember location. In this example we will use **C:\Exercises**. Click **OK**.

6. In the **Add Database Reference** dialog, click **Cancel**.

7. In the **Solution Explorer** window on the left-hand side, right-click **MySQLLibrary**, then click **Add | User-Defined Function**.

8. In the **Name** box, type **ReadRegistryData**, then click **OK**.

The large code window in the middle of the screen shows a template for a user-defined function. You are ready to write the code for the function. Copy the code shown in Examples 4.17 and 4.18 into your template, according to the language you have chosen. If you do not use Visual Studio, simply open Notepad and copy the code into the blank text file.

Example 4.17 Exercise Code—C#

```
using System;
using System.Data;
using System.Data.SqlClient;
using System.Data.SqlTypes;
using Microsoft.SqlServer.Server;
using Microsoft.Win32;

public partial class UserDefinedFunctions
{
    [Microsoft.SqlServer.Server.SqlFunction]
    public static SqlString ReadRegistryData(SqlString Key, SqlString Value)
    {
        string hive = Key.ToString().ToUpper();
        hive = hive.Substring(0, hive.IndexOf('\\'));
        string subKey = Key.ToString().Remove(0, hive.Length + 1);
        if (hive == "HKEY_LOCAL_MACHINE")
        {
            RegistryKey registryKey = Registry.LocalMachine.
OpenSubKey(subKey, false);
            return (string)registryKey.GetValue(Value.ToString());
        }
        else if (hive == "HKEY_CURRENT_USER")
```

```
        {
            RegistryKey registryKey = Registry.CurrentUser.OpenSubKey(subKey,
false);

            return (string)registryKey.GetValue(Value.ToString());

        }
        return "Reading this key is not supported.";

    }

}
```

Example 4.18 Exercise Code—Visual Basic

```
Imports System

Imports System.Data

Imports System.Data.SqlClient

Imports System.Data.SqlTypes

Imports Microsoft.SqlServer.Server

Imports Microsoft.Win32

Partial Public Class UserDefinedFunctions

    <Microsoft.SqlServer.Server.SqlFunction()> _

    Public Shared Function ReadRegistryData(ByVal Key As SqlString, _
                            ByVal Value As SqlString) AsSqlString

        Dim hive As String = Key.ToString().ToUpper()

        hive = hive.Substring(0, hive.IndexOf("\"))

        Dim subKey As String = Key.ToString().Remove(0, hive.Length + 1)

        If hive = "HKEY_LOCAL_MACHINE" Then

            Dim keyToRead As RegistryKey = Registry.LocalMachine.
OpenSubKey(subKey, False)

            Return CType(keyToRead.GetValue(Value.ToString()), String)

        ElseIf hive = "HKEY_CURRENT_USER" Then

            Dim keyToRead As RegistryKey = Registry.CurrentUser.
OpenSubKey(subKey, False)

            Return CType(keyToRead.GetValue(Value.ToString()), String)

        End If

        Return "Reading this key is not supported."

    End Function

End Class
```

If you are not using Visual Studio and have entered the code into Notepad, save the file to the **C:\Exercises\MySQLLibrary** folder. Name the file **ReadRegistryData.vb** if you are using Visual Basic, or **ReadRegistryData.cs** if you are using C#. You can choose any other folder, but be consistent throughout the exercise.

Now we are ready to compile our code into an assembly. To do this, use the following procedure:

1. If you are using Visual Studio, on the menu bar click **Build | Build Solution**. The assembly called **MySQLLibrary.dll** will be output to **C:\Exercises\MySQLLibrary\MySQLLibrary\bin\Debug\ MySQLLibrary.dll**.

2. If you are not using Visual Studio, open the command prompt and navigate to the installation directory for .NET Framework (usually C:\WINDOWS\Microsoft.NET\Framework\v2.0.xxxxx). Execute the following command:

Compile—C#

```
csc /target:library /out:C:\Exercises\MySQLLibrary\MySQLLibrary.dll /debug
C:\Exercises\MySQLLibrary\ReadRegistryData.cs
```

Compile—Visual Basic .NET

```
vbc /target:library /out:C:\Exercises\MySQLLibrary\MySQLLibrary.dll /debug
C:\Exercises\MySQLLibrary\ReadRegistryData.vb
```

Now that our code has been compiled to an assembly, we can register it with SQL Server. Open SQL Management Studio, and execute the query shown in Example 4.19 against the AdventureWorks database.

Example 4.19 Creating the Assembly and Registering the *ReadRegistryData* Function in SQL Server

```
-- COMMENT: ENABLE CLR ON THE SERVER
sp_configure 'show advanced options', 1;
GO
RECONFIGURE;
GO
sp_configure 'clr enabled', 1;
GO
```

```
RECONFIGURE;
GO

-- COMMENT: SET THE TRUSTWORTHY PROPERTY
ALTER DATABASE AdventureWorks
SET TRUSTWORTHY ON
GO

-- COMMENT: REGISTER THE ASSEMBLY
CREATE ASSEMBLY MySQLLibrary
AUTHORIZATION [dbo]
FROM 'C:\Exercises\MySQLLibrary\MySQLLibrary.dll'
WITH PERMISSION_SET = EXTERNAL_ACCESS;
GO

-- COMMENT: REGISTER THE FUNCTION
CREATE FUNCTION dbo.ReadRegistryData(@Key as nvarchar(1000), @Value as
nvarchar(200))
RETURNS nvarchar(max)
AS EXTERNAL NAME MySQLLibrary.UserDefinedFunctions.ReadRegistryData;
go
```

Finally, we are ready to test the function execution. Run the following statements and observe the results:

```
SELECT dbo.ReadRegistryData(
'HKEY_LOCAL_MACHINE\SOFTWARE\Microsoft\Windows\CurrentVersion',
'ProgramFilesDir')
SELECT dbo.ReadRegistryData(
'HKEY_CURRENT_USER\Control Panel\Desktop', 'Wallpaper')
SELECT dbo.ReadRegistryData(
'HKEY_CURRENT_USER\Control Panel\Current', 'Color Schemes')
```

Summary of Exam Objectives

In this chapter we have introduced CLR integration, a powerful capability of SQL Server 2008. CLR can be used to implement custom functionality in SQL Server that cannot be easily implemented using Transact-SQL. The ability to understand *when* implementing a CLR object is appropriate, and how to go about doing it, is an exam objective. Implementing simple CLR objects is covered by the exam. The following types of SQL Server objects can be implemented using the CLR:

- User-defined functions (UDFs)
- Stored procedures
- User-defined aggregates
- Triggers
- User-defined data types (UDTs)

To implement the CLR object, you must write its definition as a .NET class (for user-defined aggregates and user-defined data types), or a .NET method (for user-defined functions, stored procedures, and triggers). You can write your object in any .NET language, with C# and Visual Basic .NET being the most popular. Once you have created your object, you will compile it. Compiling your code will create a .NET assembly.

The assembly is a physical DLL file that you will register with SQL Server. Installing a .NET assembly for SQL Server to use is another area covered within the exam. This task is performed using the *CREATE ASSEMBLY* statement. This statement is key to understanding how to install a CLR object. In Example 4.20, the *CREATE ASSEMBLY* statement is used to register the Utilities.dll assembly with the EXTERNAL_ACCESS permission set.

Example 4.20 Registering an Assembly

```
CREATE ASSEMBLY Utilities
AUTHORIZATION [dbo]
FROM 'C:\Documents and Settings\valentine\My Documents\Utilities\
\Utilities.dll'
WITH PERMISSION_SET = EXTERNAL_ACCESS;
```

Permission sets are crucial to proper assembly registration. The default permission set is SAFE, which does not allow assembly code to access any external resources, locally or on the network. Always mark assemblies that do not require access to external resources as SAFE, as it will help protect the system from malicious or accidental damage. If the assembly requires access to external resources, mark it as EXTERNAL_ACCESS. This allows access to external resources in the most stable manner, using managed code calls only. Finally, if your assembly needs to call unmanaged code, it must be marked as UNSAFE. It is possible for code in assemblies marked as UNSAFE to damage SQL Server and the system it is running on, and even compromise system security. You should therefore avoid using UNSAFE, unless absolutely necessary.

When assemblies are marked as EXTERNAL_ACCESS or UNSAFE, they access external resources running as a SQL Server service account. You can only call EXTERNAL_ACCESS or UNSAFE assembly code as a Windows login. If a SQL Server login is used, the resource access call will fail. When registering assemblies, mark them for dbo ownership (AUTHORIZATION), to avoid assembly chaining issues.

Once you have registered the assembly using the *CREATE ASSEMBLY* statement, you are ready to consume the CLR objects within it. The technique for doing this depends on the type of object you wish to consume. User-defined functions, aggregates, stored procedures, and triggers must be registered with a specific table or database using the *CREATE OBJECT* statement with the *EXTERNAL NAME* parameter. User-defined data types need to be made available to the database by using the *CREATE TYPE* statement with the *EXTERNAL NAME* parameter.

Exam Objectives Fast Track

CLR and Managed Code Explained

- ☑ The .NET Framework is an application platform allowing developers to create standardized applications using a variety of languages.

- ☑ The Common Language Runtime (CLR) is the execution environment of the .NET Framework. The CLR manages code execution by providing services to the code such as memory management and security checking.

- ☑ .NET code is known as managed code, which is regarded as more stable and secure than unmanaged code, because the CLR enforces security and stability checking on all managed code.

CLR Integration

- ☑ SQL Server can call .NET Framework code through CLR objects.

- ☑ CLR objects are SQL Server functions, stored procedures, aggregates, triggers, and user-defined data types that are created using managed code.

CLR objects offer richer functionality than Transact-SQL. For example, you can access files, the Windows registry, and network resources using the CLR, and perform advanced logical operations.

☑ Always consider implementing objects in Transact-SQL first, and only use CLR if the required functionality is unavailable, or impractical to implement using Transact-SQL.

☑ CLR objects must be registered with SQL Server. Once the assembly is registered, you can call CLR user-defined functions, stored procedures, and aggregates as you would Transact-SQL objects.

Languages Supported

☑ Code for the .NET Framework must be written using a .NET language.

☑ Over 60 .NET languages are available, and new languages can be created. C# and Visual Basic .NET are popular and are included by default with the Visual Studio .NET IDE.

☑ Regardless of what .NET language was used to create your source code, the source code will be compiled to MSIL, which will be executed at runtime.

What Is the Base Class Library?

☑ The Base Class Library is an extensive library of functionality that can be used by developers writing .NET code.

☑ The Base Class Library contains thousands of classes to perform various tasks. For example, there are classes used to access the file system, classes to work with data, classes to show graphics on the screen, classes for text manipulation, and many more.

☑ You can use classes from the Base Class Library in your CLR objects. For example, you can use classes from the *System.Security.Cryptography* namespace, if your CLR object needs to encrypt and decrypt data.

Registering CLR Assemblies for Use with SQL Server

☑ *CREATE ASSEMBLY* is used to register an assembly with SQL Server. *CREATE ASSEMBLY* specifies the assembly location, authorization, and permission set.

- ☑ *AUTHORIZATION* defines who owns the registered assembly. In most cases this should be specified as dbo.

- ☑ *PERMISSION_SET* defines the code-access security permissions granted to your code.

- ☑ Use the *CREATE TRIGGER, CREATE PROCEDURE, CREATE FUNCTION*, or *CREATE AGGREGATE* statement with the *EXTERNAL NAME* parameter to bind a CLR trigger to a table, or register a CLR object with the database.

- ☑ Use the *CREATE TYPE* statement with the *EXTERNAL NAME* parameter to register a CLR data type within a database.

Understanding Permission Sets

- ☑ *PERMISSION_SET* is either *SAFE, EXTERNAL_ACCESS*, or *UNSAFE*.

- ☑ SAFE is the default permission set.

- ☑ If your code is accessing external resources, use *EXTERNAL_ACCESS*, otherwise use *SAFE*.

- ☑ The *UNSAFE* permission set should be avoided, except in extreme circumstances when you must call unmanaged/native code. *UNSAFE* code could compromise the system.

Implementing SQL Server Objects Using Managed Code

- ☑ CLR objects are created using managed code written in any .NET language.

- ☑ The code is compiled into an assembly (DLL) file.

- ☑ Custom attributes are used to mark parts of the code as a SQL object.

- ☑ Use the Database Project template installed with Visual Studio to easily create SQL Server CLR integrated objects. Although this is optional, using the template saves time and makes it easier to create the objects correctly.

Exam Objectives
Frequently Asked Questions

Q: When should I choose to use the CLR over Transact-SQL to implement database objects?

A: You should use the CLR only when the functionality you are trying to implement is very difficult or impossible to write using Transact-SQL. For example, you simply cannot use Transact-SQL to read files or the registry. Also, if your functionality requires a cursor in Transact-SQL, you may get more simplicity and better performance out of a CLR aggregate.

Q: Do I need to obtain and install Visual Studio to develop CLR integrated objects?

A: No, you can create source files in Notepad and compile them using a command-line compiler found in the .NET Framework SDK. However, Visual Studio offers an integrated development environment with visual feedback and intelligence suggestions. If you are undertaking a large-scale commercial development, you will benefit greatly from Visual Studio features.

Q: What is the difference between managed and unmanaged code?

A: Managed code is written in a .NET language, and when it executes it is serviced by the CLR. The CLR ensures that the code is stable (that the code does not attempt any illegal operations) and applies code access security. Managed code accesses system resources using the Base Class Library. Unmanaged code, also known as native code, is written in a language like C or C++. This code accesses low-level resources such as memory and the disk directly. It is not subject to safety or security checking. It is possible to severely damage the system using unmanaged code, cause a Blue Screen of Death, or compromise security in some unlikely cases. Basically, managed code is more likely to be a good citizen on the system.

Q: Why is it a best practice that I use *AUTHORIZATION dbo* when registering assemblies using CREATE ASSEMBLY?

A: The *AUTHORIZATION* parameter specifies the owner of the assembly. An assembly cannot call another assembly that is owned by a different person. The one exception is that any assembly can call assemblies owned by dbo.

As you cannot register an assembly twice, specifying a variety of owners for your assemblies will cause ownership chaining issues. Therefore, it is a best practice to register your assemblies as *AUTHORIZATION dbo.*

Q: How do I know whether an assembly is calling external resources using P/Invoke, and therefore needs to be registered as UNSAFE?

A: To find P/Invoke calls, look in the assembly source code for functions declared as *extern* and marked with the *DllImport* attribute. The easiest way is simply to look for the keywords *extern* and *DllImport* using the Find feature of Visual Studio. If found, the assembly is performing P/Invoke and must be registered as UNSAFE.

Q: For the exam, do I need to learn the syntax of a .NET language like Visual Basic and C#?

A: No, you will not be required to write .NET code or find deliberate mistakes in .NET code. You should be able to read the code, and understand what it is trying to do. Focus your efforts on understanding SQL statements, and concepts related to CLR integration, like *CREATE ASSEMBLY*, *PERMISSION_SET*, and *EXTERNAL NAME.*

Self Test

A Quick Answer Key follows the Self Test questions. For complete questions, answers, and explanations to the Self Test questions in this chapter, as well as the other chapters in this book, see the **Self Test Appendix**.

1. You need to register a custom assembly created by a contract C# developer, to use functions within it. None of the functions require access to anything other than the data in the Inventory database. You are under instruction to minimize the risk of a possible security breach. What is the best way to register this assembly?

   A. `WITH PERMISSION_SET = UNSAFE`

   B. `WITH PERMISSION_SET = SAFE`

   C. `WITH PERMISSION_SET = EXTERNAL_ACCESS`

   D. `AUTHORIZATION SAFE`

2. You are connected to the SQL Server with the login name Keith, and you are a member of the db_owner database role for the Inventory database. You need to register a .NET assembly called StockAnalysis in the Inventory database. Database users will be calling CLR user-defined functions, and stored procedures defined in the assembly. Other assemblies running within SQL Server will also use functionality of the StockAnalysis assembly. How should you register the assembly?

   A.
   ```
   CREATE ASSEMBLY StockAnalysis FROM 'D:\StockAnalysis.dll' WITH
   PERMISSION_SET = SAFE
   ```

   B.
   ```
   CREATE ASSEMBLY StockAnalysis AUTHORIZATION [Keith] FROM
   'D:\StockAnalysis.dll' WITH PERMISSION_SET = SAFE
   ```

   C.
   ```
   CREATE ASSEMBLY StockAnalysis AUTHORIZATION [dbo] FROM
   'D:\StockAnalysis.dll' WITH PERMISSION_SET = SAFE
   ```

   D.
   ```
   CREATE ASSEMBLY StockAnalysis AUTHORIZATION [public] FROM
   'D:\StockAnalysis.dll' WITH PERMISSION_SET = SAFE
   ```

3. Your organization has recently hired a consultant to lock down your SQL Server for tighter security. You have noticed that after the security tightening,

some of your applications have stopped working. Upon further investigation you realize that it is the CLR user-defined functions and triggers that are not executing. You suspect that the consultant has disabled CLR integration on the server. How should you re-enable the CLR integration?

A. Execute the "sp_configure 'clr enabled', 1" command on the server.

B. Execute the "sp_configure 'set_trustworthy', 1" command on the server.

C. Execute "*ALTER DATABASE* DatabaseName *SET TRUSTWORTHY ON*" command for every database on the server.

D. Use the SQL Server Configuration Manager tool to enable CLR integration.

4. You are asked to create two custom functions to be used in SQL Server. The functions must encrypt and decrypt data using an encryption algorithm based on the Local Security Authority (LSA) key. What is the best technology to use for creating these functions?

A. `.NET assembly written in C# or Visual Basic .NET`

B. `Extended stored procedure written in C++`

C. `Transact-SQL statement`

D. `COM component written in Visual Basic`

5. You have registered an assembly called FacialRecognition with SQL Server, using the EXTERNAL_ACCESS permission set. The assembly accesses photographs in a network share and compares them with photograph data stored in the database. The assembly is written in C#, and uses only managed code to perform its functionality. You are connected to SQL Server as a Windows login Valentine. You are calling a function from the FacialRecognition assembly, but are receiving an access-denied exception. What should you do to resolve the error (select all choices that apply)?

A. Grant Valentine Read permission to the network share.

B. Ensure that the database is marked as TRUSTWORTHY.

C. Grant the SQL Server service account permission to the network share.

D. Ensure that the SQL Server service account is running as a domain account.

E. Ensure that the SQL Server service account is running as a Local System.

6. Your organization maintains a legacy ERP system written in unmanaged C++. You create a .NET assembly and write a SQL CLR function that uses P/Invoke functionality to call into the ERP system's DLLs. How should you register the assembly?

   A. WITH PERMISSION_SET = SAFE

   B. WITH PERMISSION_SET = UNSAFE

   C. WITH PERMISSION_SET = EXTERNAL_ACCESS

   D. You cannot call unmanaged code from CLR functions registered in SQL Server for security reasons.

7. You are designing a database system that stores coordinates in space and time. You wish to store these space-time coordinates in a single column, as you will be performing special operations with them. What is the best way to store this information?

   A. Create a CLR function that has two *bigint* parameters for longitude and latitude, and one *DateTime* parameter for the time coordinates.

   B. Create a table with three columns: DateTime, Longitude, Latitude; create foreign key relationships to other tables.

   C. Create a computed column.

   D. Create a CLR user-defined type (UDT).

8. You have created an assembly named DiskAccess that defines a CLR trigger. This trigger stores contents of an image type column as a file on the local file system, every time a row is inserted or updated in a certain table. How should you register this assembly without granting it unnecessary permissions?

   A. WITH PERMISSION_SET = UNSAFE

   B. WITH PERMISSION_SET = SAFE

   C. WITH PERMISSION_SET = EXTERNAL_ACCESS

   D. With the default permission set

9. You have registered an assembly called FunctionLibrary using this statement: *CREATE ASSEMBLY FunctionLibrary FROM 'C:\FunctionLibrary.dll'*. What actions can the code in your assembly perform? Select all that apply.

   A. Perform calculations.

   B. Access SQL Server table data in the current database.

C. Access the registry on the local server.

D. Access network shares.

E. Call unmanaged code.

10. You are writing a CLR-integrated function in C#. The function is named *GetFullName* and returns a person's full name given first name, last name, and middle initials. The function declaration in managed code is as follows:

```
[Microsoft.SqlServer.Server.SqlFunction]
public static SqlString GetFullName(SqlString FirstName, SqlString
LastName, SqlString MiddleInitial)
{
// code goes here
}
```

How should you register the function with SQL Server, assuming the assembly has already been registered?

A.

```
CREATE FUNCTION dbo.GetFullName(@FirstName as nvarchar(200), @LastName
as nvarchar(200), @MiddleInitial as nvarchar(10))
RETURNS nvarchar(410)
AS EXECUTE FunctionLibrary.UserDefinedFunctions.GetFullName(@FirstName,
@LastName, @MiddleInitial);
```

B.

```
CREATE FUNCTION dbo.GetFullName(@FirstName as nvarchar(200), @LastName
as nvarchar(200), @MiddleInitial as nvarchar(10))
RETURNS nvarchar(410)
AS EXTERNAL NAME FunctionLibrary.UserDefinedFunctions.GetFullName;
```

C.

```
CREATE FUNCTION dbo.GetFullName
OUTPUT nvarchar(410)
INPUT (@FirstName as nvarchar(200), @LastName as nvarchar(200),
@MiddleInitial as nvarchar(10)
AS EXTERNAL NAME FunctionLibrary.UserDefinedFunctions.GetFullName;
```

D.

```
CREATE FUNCTION dbo.GetFullName(@FirstName as nvarchar(200), @LastName
as nvarchar(200), @MiddleInitial as nvarchar(10))
```

```
RETURNS nvarchar(410)
WITH PERMISSION_SET = SAFE
```

11. You have created a CLR-integrated trigger in C#. This trigger is named *OutputInvoiceFile*. Its functionality is to create an invoice file every time an Order record is added to the Sales.SalesOrderHeader table. The assembly containing the trigger, FunctionLibrary.dll, has already been registered. How should you register the trigger?

    A. CREATE TRIGGER dbo. OutputInvoiceFile

       ON Sales.SalesOrderHeader

       FOR INSERT

       AS

       EXTERNAL NAME FunctionLibrary.Triggers. OutputInvoiceFile

    B. CREATE TRIGGER dbo. OutputInvoiceFile

       EXTERNAL NAME FunctionLibrary.Triggers. OutputInvoiceFile

    C. CREATE TRIGGER dbo. OutputInvoiceFile

       ON Sales.SalesOrderHeader

       FOR INSERT

       AS

       EXECUTE OutputInvoiceFile(@@IDENTITY)

    D. CREATE ASSEMBLY dbo. OutputInvoiceFile

       ON Sales.SalesOrderHeader

       FOR INSERT

       AS

       EXTERNAL NAME FunctionLibrary. Triggers. OutputInvoiceFile

12. You obtained some C# source code for a CLR-integrated function on a Web site. You would like to try this code in your SQL Server environment. What must you do before you can use the function?

    A. Compile the source code into an EXE assembly file. Register the assembly by running the executable file.

    B. Compile the source code into a DLL assembly file. Install the assembly into the Global Assembly Cache.

    C. Save the source code as a CS file. Register the assembly using *CREATE ASSEMBLY*.

    D. Compile the source code into a DLL assembly file. Register the assembly using *CREATE ASSEMBLY*.

13. You have created a SQL Server aggregate using C#. The aggregate is named Deviation, and it operates on integer values. The aggregate declaration in managed code is as follows:

```
[Serializable]
[SqlUserDefinedAggregate(
   Format.UserDefined,
   IsInvariantToNulls = true,
   IsInvariantToDuplicates = true,
   IsInvariantToOrder = true,
   MaxByteSize = -1)
]
public class Deviation : IBinarySerialize
{
   // aggregate code here

}
```

How should you register the aggregate with SQL Server, assuming the assembly has already been registered?

A.
```
CREATE AGGREGATE Deviation
   (@value int)
RETURNS int
EXTERNAL NAME FunctionLibrary.Deviation
```

B.
```
CREATE AGGREGATE FunctionLibrary.Deviation
   (@value int)
RETURNS int
```

C.

```
CREATE AGGREGATE Deviation
EXTERNAL NAME FunctionLibrary.Deviation
```

D.

```
CREATE FUNCTION Deviation
   (@value int)
   RETURNS int

EXTERNAL NAME FunctionLibrary.Deviation
```

14. Your database contains many CLR functions and stored procedures, some of which access external resources. The database was working well until you backed it up and restored it onto a different server. Now CLR objects that require external access have stopped working. The CLR objects that do not require external access continue to function properly. What is the most likely reason for this issue?

A. The new server does not have CLR integration enabled.

B. You need to re-register all assemblies after backup and restore.

C. Your backup was corrupt.

D. The restored database does not have its *TRUSTWORTHY* property set to 1.

15. You are creating a CLR integrated user-defined aggregate. As part of writing the aggregate you must implement the aggregation contract. What methods should you implement to adhere to the aggregation contract?

A. *Merge*

B. *Accumulate*

C. *Finalize*

D. *Terminate*

E. *Init*

16. You wish to implement the following functionality: attempt to access a network share; if access is denied, or the share is unavailable, output an error message to the caller; otherwise read a comma-delimited file and insert its contents into a SQL Server table; and finally, empty and save the file you have just read. What type of object is best to implement this functionality in SQL Server?

A. A CLR trigger

B. A CLR function

C. A Transact-SQL stored procedure

D. A CLR stored procedure

17. You are executing a CLR stored procedure, and are receiving the following error message: *System.Security.SecurityException: Request for the permission of type 'System.Security.Permissions.FileIOPermission, mscorlib, Version=2.0.0.0, Culture=neutral, PublicKeyToken=b77a5c561934e089' failed.* What could be causing the error (select all that apply)?

A. The assembly is registered with the SAFE permission set, and is attempting to access external resources.

B. The assembly is registered with the EXTERNAL_ACCESS permission set, and is attempting to call native code.

C. The assembly is registered with AUTHORIZATION UserA, where UserA is a low-privileged user.

D. The caller is a SQL Server login.

18. You have created a CLR user-defined data type that stores coordinates in space and time. The UDT is called *PointInSpaceTime.* How should you register the data type, provided that the assembly containing it has already been registered?

A.
```
CREATE TYPE dbo. PointInSpaceTime
EXTERNAL NAME FunctionLibrary.[ PointInSpaceTime]
```

B.
```
CREATE TYPE dbo. PointInSpaceTime
EXTERNAL NAME FunctionLibrary.UserDefinedTypes.[PointInSpaceTime]
```

C.
```
CREATE TYPE dbo. PointInSpaceTime(@Latitude int, @Longitude int,
@Time DateTime)
EXTERNAL NAME FunctionLibrary.UserDefinedTypes.[PointInSpaceTime]
```

D.
```
CREATE TYPE dbo. PointInSpaceTime
RETURNS (@Latitude int, @Longitude int, @Time DateTime)
EXTERNAL NAME FunctionLibrary.UserDefinedTypes.[PointInSpaceTime]
```

19. What are the steps for creating a CLR stored procedure and using it within SQL Server (select all that apply)?

    A. Install the assembly into the Global Assembly Cache (GAC).

    B. Register the assembly using the *CREATE ASSEMBLY* statement.

    C. Write the procedure source code and compile it into an assembly.

    D. Register the function using the *CREATE FUNCTION* statement with the *EXTERNAL NAME* parameter.

20. You have downloaded a .dll assembly file from the Internet. The file is called SUPERSQLFUNCTIONS.DLL. The file is unsigned, but its makers state that it contains some very useful SQL Server CLR functions. The site tells you that in order to perform some of the powerful functionality, this assembly must use P/Invoke to call Windows platform code. How should you register this assembly?

    A. `WITH PERMISSION_SET = UNSAFE`

    B. `WITH PERMISSION_SET = EXTERNAL_ACCESS`

    C. Do not register the assembly—unmanaged code calls within it could severely damage the system, and the assembly does not originate from a trusted source

    D. `WITH AUTHORIZATION dbo`

Self Test Quick Answer Key

1. **B**

2. **C**

3. **A**

4. **A**

5. **B, C, D**

6. **B**

7. **D**

8. **C**

9. **A, B**

10. **B**

11. **A**

12. **D**

13. **A**

14. **D**

15. **A, B, D, E**

16. **D**

17. **A, D**

18. **A**

19. **B, C, D**

20. **C**

Chapter 5

MCTS SQL Server 2008 Exam 433

Implementing Error Handling

Exam objectives in this chapter:

- Understanding Errors
- Managing and Raising User-Defined Errors
- Handling Errors

Exam objectives review:

- ☑ Summary of Exam Objectives
- ☑ Exam Objectives Fast Track
- ☑ Exam Objectives Frequently Asked Questions
- ☑ Self Test
- ☑ Self Test Quick Answer Key

Introduction

As a database developer, one of the most important tasks you must realize in your database is to ensure that your data is in a consistent state. Your data is in a consistent state when it is correct at all times. When incorrect data appears, you must remove it from your database or block its insertion. To programmatically enforce data consistency in your database, you can use the transaction mechanism. The main advantage of using transactions for this purpose is that any changes you realize are visible only to your connection. Other users don't see changes until the transaction is committed or rolled back. When you commit a transaction, the changes you make are saved. When you roll back a transaction, the changes are removed and the previous state of data is restored.

Although transactions give you significant control of data consistency, this feature alone is not enough to deal effectively with problems when they arise. Also, returning and managing customized errors that inform users about the success or failure of a command can be painful if these errors are inserted within the code of your procedures, functions, or other programming objects.

To control the flow of code in case of problems and standardize your database messages, SQL Server gives you the ability to handle and manage errors. Also, it lets you create customized errors and raise them according to your needs. So, it's essential that you understand how error handling works and how to use it in your code. This knowledge will allow you to develop better code and control the flow of scripts.

Error handling plays an essential role in your database environment. Error handling allows you to take care of SQL Server and business requirement errors, including errors in queries and scripts against your database. However, many professionals don't know how to work with these errors or implement them in the application. This situation often results in the redevelopment of features that are already implemented and increased work in the development of the application.

Error handling in versions 2005 and 2008 of SQL Server is quite different from that of version 2000 and prior. While in the 2000 version you must monitor for specific conditions within your code and then decide what to do at the point you detect an error, versions 2005 and 2008 provide genuine error handling with a *TRY…CATCH* block. This new feature allows you to develop more flexible and consistent code.

This chapter covers information about both ways of handling errors, the statements involved, and their features and uses. Also, you will learn how to create your own errors and how to raise them whenever you need. We'll focus on the creation and management of these codes as well as best practices when handling errors and messages in the real world.

Understanding Errors

Basically, SQL Server returns two types of messages: *information* and *error*. An *information* message is a return of some information to users. This type of message is informational in nature and doesn't create errors at runtime. For example, when you execute a check in your database with a *DBCC CHECKDB* statement, an informational message related to the database is returned. This type of message might also be returned as output from *PRINT* and *DBCC* statements, as a message citing an error from *sys.messages* catalog view, or as a *RAISERROR* statement.

An *error* message is a return of a warning message that informs you about problems that affect the execution of your statement. For example, when your statement calls an object that doesn't exist, SQL Server generates and returns an error message then terminates execution of the statement. These error messages are returned only as messages citing errors from *sys.messages* catalog view or as a *RAISERROR* statement. You can use these messages to handle various types of errors: errors that stop your code from proceeding further; errors that raise warnings, but continue the execution of your code; and errors that belong to the business logic of your application and are not SQL Server errors.

Although information messages are not exactly error messages, they are handled and managed the same way as error messages. The only difference between them is severity, which is further discussed later in this chapter.

Error Types

There are two types of errors in SQL Server: *system* and *user-defined*. *System* errors arise when the Database Engine service encounters an error in code execution. This service provides objects and structures that allow the return of system errors or messages according to executed code. The Database Engine verifies the code of each operation and returns a status indicating the success or failure of its execution. When an operation fails, the service picks the error information from the *sys. messages* catalog view and shows it to the user. SQL Server raises system errors automatically when executing an operation. However, you can handle these errors using T-SQL commands.

Although SQL Server provides a significant set of error messages, you may face situations when SQL Server doesn't recognize parts of your code as errors but you wish to raise them as errors. These customized errors are called *user-defined* errors, and they must be raised manually. For example, you create a procedure that inserts a product name and stock inside a table. Although the stock column can accept any *INT* value, your business requirement specifies that a product must be added with a minimum stock level of 100. So, your procedure checks the stock input parameter, and, if the value is less than the required minimum, it will return an error. In this case, you define the error and write code that raises it every time a validation fails.

sys.messages Catalog View

SQL Server stores system and user-defined errors inside a catalog view called *sys.messages*. This catalog contains all system error messages, which are available in many languages. Each message has five properties arranged in columns:

- **message_id:** This column stores the ID of a message and its value. Together with *language_id,* this is unique across the instance. Messages with IDs less than 50000 are system error messages.

- **language_id:** This column indicates the language used in the message text, for example English or Spanish, as defined in the name column of the *sys.syslanguages* system table. This is unique for a specified *message_id*.

- **severity:** This column contains the severity level of the message. When you are creating errors, keep in mind that the severity must be the same for all message languages within the same *message_id*.

- **is_event_logged:** When you want to log the event when an error is raised, set the value of this column equal to1. Like severity, this column must be the same for all message languages within the same *message_id*.

- **text:** This column stores the text of the message. This text is written in the language indicated by the *language_id* property.

Severity Level

The *severity* level of an error indicates how critical the impact of this error is on the execution of your operation. The level indicated also helps you understand the scope of the problem. The severity levels for SQL Server range from information message to system and server level problems and are distributed into four major groups:

- **Information Messages (Levels 1–10):** Errors in this group are purely informational and are not severe. Status information or error reports are returned with a specific error code. SQL Server doesn't use levels 1–9: these levels are available for user-defined errors.

- **User Errors (Levels 11–16):** Errors in this group are quite simple and can be corrected by you or the user. They don't impact service or terminate connection with the database.

- **Software Errors (Levels 17–19):** Errors in this group are severe and require system administrator attention as well as yours. They are related to problems in the Database Engine service and can't be solved by users.

- **System Errors (Levels 20–25):** Errors in this group are critical since they indicate system problems. They are fatal errors that force the end of the statement or batch in the Database Engine. Errors in this group record information about what occurred and then terminates. You must be aware that these errors can close the application connection to the instance of SQL Server. Error messages in this severity level group are written to the error log.

Severity levels are important not only to help you diagnosis the impact of a problem but also to help you to organize and manage user-defined errors according to database needs.

Scenarios of Use

Error handling provides efficient ways of controlling flow and debugging code, making the execution of operations more predictable and providing proactive solutions. For example, you can handle an error that arises from a transaction dead-lock by returning a message and logging the error in a table of your database for posterior analysis. Also, you can debug a long string of transaction code without the application being available by programming the code to raise errors and show the line and statement where the code fails. Another advantage of handling errors inside SQL Server is that you reduce the application's workload by distributing it among servers, thereby letting developers focus on business requirements instead of SQL Server commands and transactions.

In addition to system errors, you can also create and handle user-defined errors to customize and standardize the return of procedures, functions, and other programmable objects in your database. This gives you a centralized, organized, and effective way to attend to business requirements. For example, you can create a customized error message about the failure of a business validation. After the message is created, you can raise the error whenever you want. Also, when you make changes to the error, your modifications are applied to all codes that call it. Another great advantage of user-defined errors inside SQL Server is that they are independent from the programming language of your application. If you have an application that was developed with language A and you decide to develop a new one using language B, you won't need to recreate new error messages. Because the messages are stored inside SQL Server, they are available to both applications. You can further enhance this scenario by creating a library of user-defined errors that are shared among multiple SQL Server databases in the same environment, providing efficient management across multiple applications.

Managing and Raising User-Defined Errors

As mentioned, SQL Server allows you to create customized error messages and raise them inside your code. As a database developer, you should create a set list of additional messages for use by your application so you can reuse them inside your programmable objects. Also, user-defined errors can significantly improve readability of operations and problems that occur in your application. Remember that these user-defined error messages help you customize and standardize messages returned from the procedures, functions, and other programmable objects in your database. This feature also provides you with an efficient way to develop code with the reuse of the same messages.

System Procedures and Parameters

User-defined error messages can be managed with the use of three system procedures: *sp_addmessage*, *sp_altermessage,* and *sp_dropmessage.* The *sp_addmessage* procedure lets you store a user-defined error message in an instance. Remember that these messages can be viewed using the *sys.messages* catalog view. The syntax of this procedure is as follows:

```
sp_addmessage [ @msgnum = ] msg_id, [ @severity = ] severity,
[ @msgtext = ] 'msg'
    [, [ @lang = ] 'language' ]
    [, [ @with_log = ] { 'TRUE' | 'FALSE' } ]
    [, [ @replace = ] 'replace' ]
```

When you compare the syntax of this procedure with the structure of the *sys.messages* catalog view, you can easily understand how to use it. The first parameter is the message ID number. For user-defined error messages, you can define an ID number as an integer between 50,001 and 2,147,483,647. As you saw in the *sys.messages* structure, the combination of this number and language must be unique. This parameter is mandatory.

The second parameter is severity level. The severity value must be an integer between 1 and 25. Keep in mind that you should choose the severity level of this customized error message according to SQL Server severity levels, easing maintenance, organization, and usability. This parameter is also mandatory.

The last mandatory input parameter is the text of the error message. This parameter accepts text in *NVARCHAR(255)* and supports arguments passed by *RAISERROR* statements. This ability to utilize arguments provides a flexible and rich use of user-defined error messages, including ways to show important information such as the login that executed the code that raised the error message.

One of the most interesting parameters of the *sp_addmessage* procedure is language. This optional input allows you to add the same message in different languages. SQL Server offers support for 33 languages, whose information is stored in the *sys.syslanguages* table. Languages supported by SQL Server include English (British and American), Portuguese, Spanish, Italian, and Japanese. Because multiple languages may be installed on the same server, this parameter specifies the language in which the message is written. If you don't inform the input, the default language of the session is the assumed value of this parameter.

If you need to create an error that must write to the Windows application log, the *@with_log* parameter is the key. This parameter accepts *TRUE* or *FALSE* values. If you inform *TRUE*, your error will always be written to the Windows application log. If you inform *FALSE*, your user-defined error may still be written to the log depending on how the error is raised. An important feature of this parameter is that only members of the *sysadmin* server role can use it. Also, when an error is written to the Windows application log, it is also written to the Database Engine error log file.

The last parameter, replace, is used to update the message text, severity level, and log option of an existing error message. An interesting feature useful in multiple language environments is that when you replace a U.S. English message, the severity level is replicated for all messages in all other languages with the same ID number.

Another way to change the log option of a user-defined error is with the *sp_altermessage* procedure. Contrary to what the name suggests, this procedure doesn't alter error messages: it just changes their log option value. The syntax of this procedure is as follows:

```
sp_altermessage [ @message_id = ] message_number, 'WITH_LOG', { 'TRUE'
| 'FALSE' }
```

This procedure is a straightforward statement: you only need to inform the message ID number and the *WITH_LOG* parameter value, which can be *TRUE* or *FALSE*. Like the WITH_LOG parameter in the *sp_addmessage*, this procedure can only be executed by members of the *sysadmin* server role.

You can drop a user-defined error using the *sp_dropmessage* procedure. The syntax of this procedure is as follows:

```
sp_dropmessage [ @msgnum = ] message_number
   [, [ @lang = ] 'language' ]
```

By default, you only need to inform the ID number of the error message you want to drop. One cool thing about this procedure is the optional language parameter. You can drop a language version of an error message, while keeping the other languages versions intact. If you want to drop all language versions of a message, you need to specify the *ALL* value for the language parameter.

Configuring & Implementing...

Database Documentation

As a database developer, you should always document your database. Documentation describes all aspects of your solution and provides information that helps you manage, control, and update objects created such as tables, procedures, and functions. Also, documentation is essential for troubleshooting, since it gives you a history of your database and the changes realized.

It is especially convenient that your library of user-defined error messages allows you to develop this documentation faster and with more consistency.

Example: Creating User-Defined Error Messages

In this example, we will create an error message in three languages and see how to manage them in SQL Server. The first part is creating the message in English, Portuguese, and Spanish using the *sp_addmessage* procedure. Figure 5.1 shows the syntax of this process.

Figure 5.1 Creating an Error Message in Three Languages

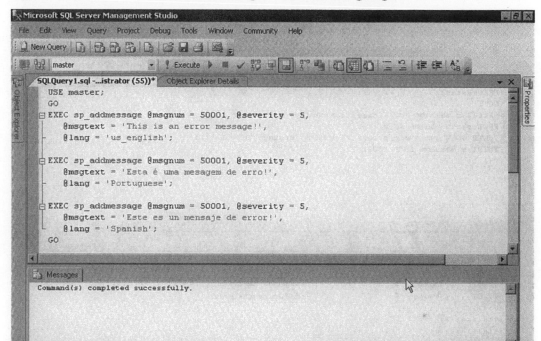

Let's take a better look at the code in the figure. You can see that we used the *sp_addmessage* procedure three times, using the same error number but a different language each time. Observe that the severity is the same for all three procedures: the severity level of one language version of a particular error message must be the same as the severity level of the other language versions.

The next step is to see these messages stored inside SQL Server using the *sys.messages* catalog view. Figure 5.2 shows a *SELECT* statement that returns your new message and its language versions.

Figure 5.2 New Error Message in SQL Server

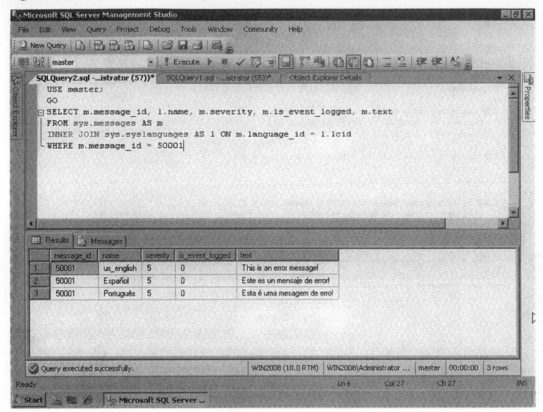

We used an *INNER JOIN* statement with the *sys.syslanguages* system table to retrieve the language name, giving us a better look at the result set. You can see that all three versions of the error message are stored inside SQL Server with the same number and severity. Also, this error message isn't logged, as the *is_event_logged* column has the value 0.

Now we will change the severity value of this message from 5 to 7. Remember that *sp_addmessage* is also capable of making changes to the message using the *@replace* parameter. Figure 5.3 shows the code that executes the desired change and the appearance of our error message inside SQL Server after the modification.

Figure 5.3 *@replace* Parameter
and Result in *sys.messages* Catalog View

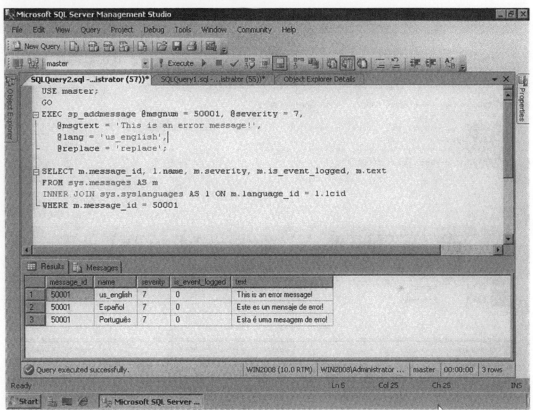

As you've seen before, when you change the severity of the English version of a message, this modification is replicated to the other language versions of the same message. Now all versions have a severity level of 7.

Now, let's say that you wish to log this error when it arises. You could use the *sp_addmessage* with the *@replace* parameter to change this property, but let's use an easier way: the *sp_altermessage* procedure. Figure 5.4 shows the syntax of *sp_altermessage* and its result in SQL Server.

Figure 5.4 Using *sp_altermessage* to Log an Error

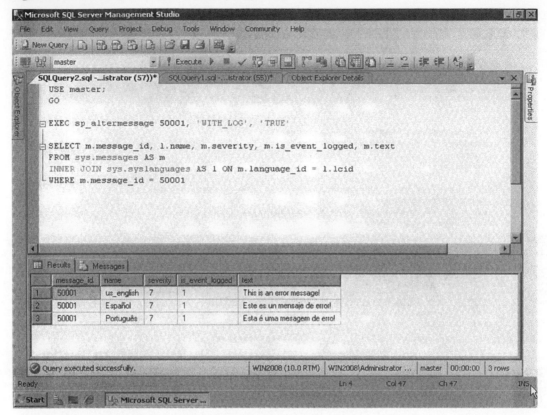

As you can see, all versions now have the *is_event_logged* column with the value 1, indicating that this error will log when it arises. Now, let's finish this example using the *sp_dropmessage* procedure to remove this error. First, we will remove the Spanish version of this message. Figure 5.5 shows how to drop one version of your message.

Figure 5.5 Using *sp_dropmessage* to Remove a Message Version

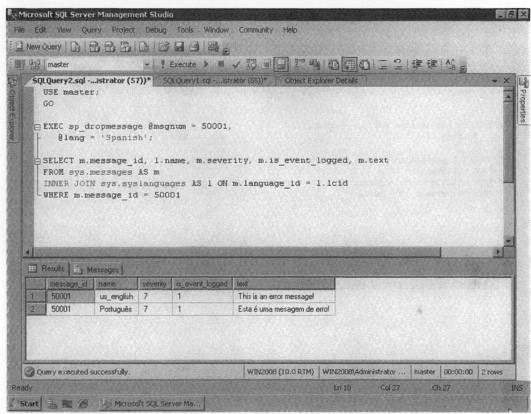

You can see that the Spanish version was removed from the *sys.messages* catalog view. Now, we will remove all language versions of this error message using the *ALL* value for the *@language* parameter. See the result in SQL Server in Figure 5.6.

Figure 5.6 Removing a Message with *sp_dropmessage* Using the *ALL* Value

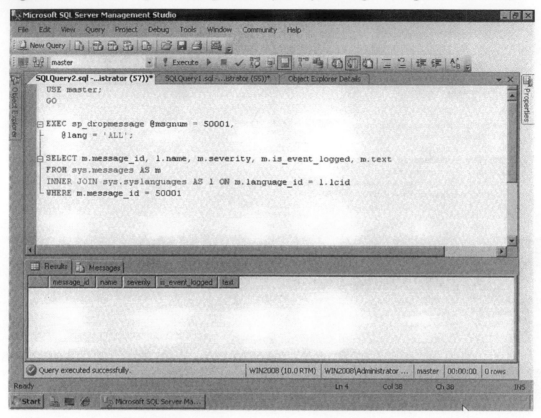

Raising User-Defined Error Messages

Once your custom error messages are created, the next step is to understand how to return them to applications and users when they are executing your T-SQL codes. As mentioned before, SQL Server does not understand a user-defined error as an error until you tell it to raise a custom message as one. To manually raise a user-defined error message in SQL Server, you must use a *RAISERROR* statement. The general syntax of this statement is as follows:

```
RAISERROR ( { msg_id | msg_str | @local_variable }
    {,severity,state }
    [,argument [,...n ] ] )
    [ WITH option [,...n ] ]
```

The *RAISERROR* statement is really easy to understand when you already know how to manage user-defined error messages. The statement is divided in four parts, plus a WITH clause. The first part is where you inform SQL Server which error you want to raise. If the error message that you wish to raise is already included in the *sys.messages* catalog view, you only need to indicate its ID number. That's why you should standardize your messages and add them in SQL Server: you can reuse them inside your programmable objects and transactions.

A *RAISERROR* statement can also inform a customized text or a local variable of your script that stores a text as the error message. The customized text can have a maximum of 2,047 characters and the associated error number is 50000. If your message contains 2,048 or more characters, SQL Server will only display the first 2,044, and three ellipsis points will indicate that the message has been truncated.

Configuring & Implementing...

Avoid Using Customized Text Directly in the *RAISERROR* Statement

Although the *RAISERROR* statement allows you to customize text directly, the management of these messages becomes difficult if you use the same message many times across your database. Keep in mind that the best way to standardize, control, and manage error messages is by using the *sys.messages* catalog view, and you, as the database developer, should always use this method.

One of the most interesting things that customized text supports is the use of *arguments*. Arguments allow you to show important information, such as the database that the user was connected to when he executed the code that raised the error message. An argument can be a string or a value, and it's placed inside the customized text. The general syntax of an argument is as follows:

```
% [[flag] [width] [. precision] [{h | l}]] type
```

The items between the percent symbol (%) and *type* are responsible for formatting the argument and are optional. The *flag* determines spacing and justification for your argument. Table 5.1 shows a list of flags supported by SQL Server:

Table 5.1 Flags Supported by SQL Server

Flag	Description
- (dash or minus sign)	Left-justify the argument value. Only makes a difference when you supply a fixed width.
+ (plus sign)	Indicates the positive or negative nature if the parameter is a signed numeric type.
0 (zero)	Tells SQL Server to pad the left side of a numeric value with zeros until the minimum width is reached.
# (pound sign)	Tells SQL Server to use the appropriate prefix (0 or 0x) depending on whether it is octal or hexadecimal. Applies only to octal and hexadecimal values.
' ' (blank)	Pads the left of a numeric value with spaces if positive

The *width* part of an argument sets the amount of space you want to hold for the argument value. This is an integer value. You can also specify an asterisk (*) to let SQL Server automatically determine the width according to the value you set for precision. The *precision* part determines the maximum number of digits or characters that will be outputted. For example, if a string has 10 characters and precision is set at 5, only the first 5 characters of the string value are used. On the other hand, the precision will be the minimum number of digits printed if your argument is an integer. Following precision, you can indicate if a value is an *h* (*shortint*) or *l* (*longint*) when the type parameter is set as an integer, octal, or hexadecimal value.

The last step is informing the value type for the argument. Table 5.2 shows the supported value types and their respective symbols.

Table 5.2 Argument Types Supported by SQL Server

Type of Argument	Symbol
Signed integer	*d*
Unsigned integer	*u*
String	*s*
Unsigned octal	*o*
Unsigned hexadecimal	*x*

You can use a maximum of 20 arguments in a customized text. Their values are passed after the *state* part of the *RAISERROR* statement in the same sequence that they are placed inside the text. Arguments are also supported within the text of the *sp_addmessage* procedure, providing you great flexibility.

EXAM WARNING

Argument types are based on the *printf* function of the C standard library. Be careful about types that aren't supported by *RAISERROR*, because SQL Server may not have a data type similar to the associated C data type. For example, the *%p* specification for pointers is not supported by *RAISERROR* because there is no pointer data type in SQL Server.

The next part of the *RAISERROR* statement is *severity*, where you inform the severity level associated with your error message. If you use the message ID number to raise your error, the severity specified here will override the severity specified in the *sys.messages* catalog view. Severity levels from 0 through 18 can be specified by any user. However, severity levels from 19 through 25 can only be specified by members of the *sysadmin* fixed server role. Also, messages with severity levels from 19 through 25 require logging.

After severity, the next part is to define the *state* of the error. The state is an integer value from 0 through 255 that helps you find the section of code raising the error, when same user-defined error can rise at multiple locations. To accomplish this, you only need to define a unique state number for each location that can raise the message. The state part is really useful when you are dealing with complex and long strings of code.

The *argument* is the last part and it's optional. Here you provide values for the arguments defined in the text of your error message. The order of argument values must correspond to their respective arguments as defined in the text of the message. Remember that you can use 20 arguments at maximum. Each argument can be any of these data types: *tinyint, smallint, int, char, varchar, nchar, nvarchar, binary*, or *varbinary*. No other data types are supported.

Finally, the *WITH* clause makes three more options available: *LOG, NOWAIT*, and *SETERROR*. The *LOG* option logs the raised error in the error log and the application log for the instance. To use this option, the user executing the *RAISERROR* statement must be a member of the *sysadmin* fixed server role. The *NOWAIT* option forces the message to be delivered to the client immediately instead of waiting until everything is done. This option is really useful when dealing with long reports and debugging your code, since it displays all of the prints and selects ahead of it.

The *SETERROR* option allows you to set the value of the *@@ERROR* function to be equal to the last error ID number raised. By default, a *RAISERROR* statement doesn't set *@@ERROR* to the value of the error ID you raised. Instead, it reflects the success or failure of your actual *RAISERROR* statement. The *SETERROR* option overrides this and sets the value of the *@@ERROR* variable to equal the last error ID number raised. Look for more about *@@ERROR* later in this chapter.

Example: Raising Messages Using the *RAISERROR* Statement

In this example, we will raise some error messages using the *RAISERROR* statement and some options. First, let's raise a basic custom text. Figure 5.7 shows the code of the *RAISERROR* statement and its return to the user.

Figure 5.7 Raising a Basic Error Message Using *RAISERROR*

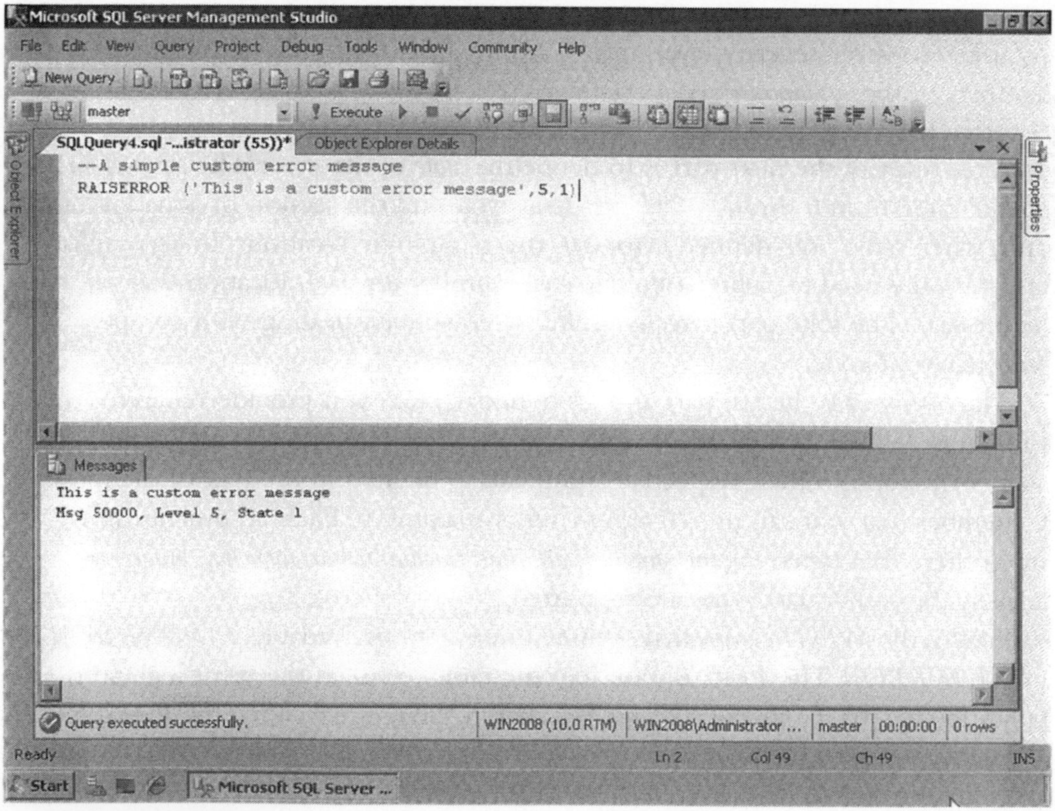

Let's look at the return from SQL Server. First, it shows the text of the error message raised. Then, it shows the error number of this message. In this example, the error number is 50000 because we used a custom text. Remember that when you raise a user-defined error stored in SQL Server, the error ID number is from the *message_id* column of the *sys.messages* catalog view. SQL Server also exhibits the severity level and the state of the message. In this example, the severity level is 5 and the state is 1.

Now, let's raise a more complex error message using arguments. Figure 5.8 shows a *RAISERROR* statement with four interesting arguments and the return to the user.

Figure 5.8 Raising an Error Message with Arguments

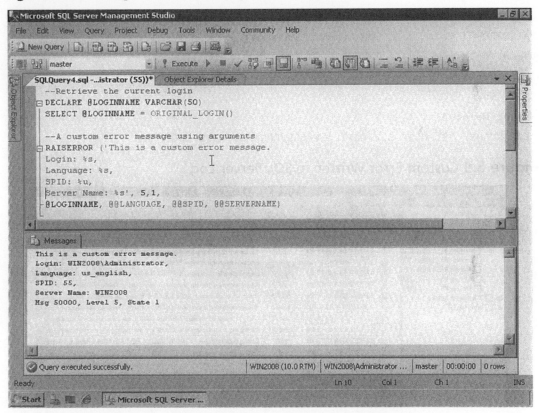

Now, your error message is more dynamic and informational. In the text of the message, you defined four arguments: three strings *(%s)* and one unsigned integer *(%u)*. You can see that these arguments show the user some important information such as the number of his process inside SQL Server. After the message text, severity, and state, you inform the value of the four arguments. The argument values must be in the same order as their respective arguments in the text of the message.

Also, you can see that these arguments can be local variables of your script or global variables and functions of your instance. This property gives you great flexibility to develop your custom messages as your business requires.

Now, let's assume that your error message is so important that it must be logged. To log this error, you only need to add *WITH LOG* at the end of the *RAISERROR* statement. The following code shows how to use *WITH LOG* and Figure 5.9 displays your error in the SQL Server log.

```
--Retrieve the current login
DECLARE @LOGINNAME VARCHAR(50)
SELECT @LOGINNAME = ORIGINAL_LOGIN()
--A custom error message using arguments
RAISERROR ('This is a custom error message.
Login: %s,
Language: %s,
SPID: %u,
Server Name: %s', 5,1,
@LOGINNAME, @@LANGUAGE, @@SPID, @@SERVERNAME) WITH LOG
```

Figure 5.9 Custom Error Written in SQL Server Log

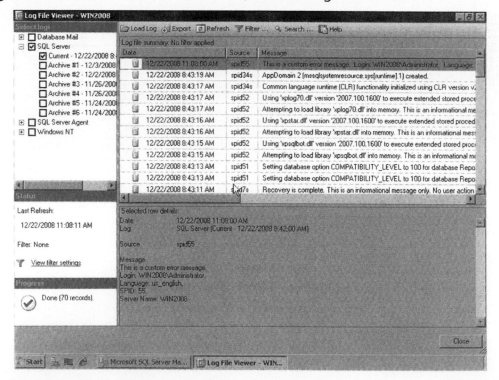

Although this *RAISERROR* statement is great, you decide that this error message will be reused many times inside your database. So, to standardize this error message, you decide to use the *sp_addmessage* procedure and add it to SQL Server. Figure 5.10 shows the code to add the error message and the *RAISERROR* statement that raises it.

Figure 5.10 Using *RAISERROR* to Return User-Defined Error Messages

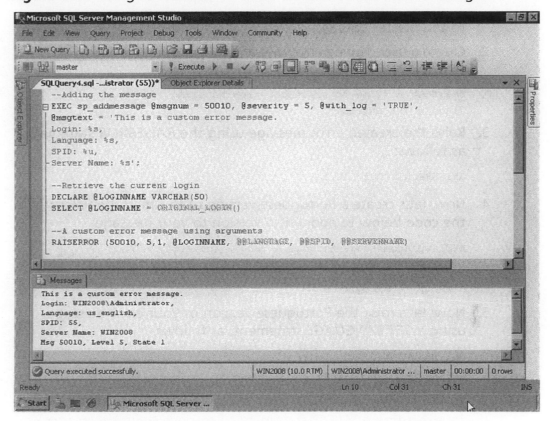

There is no need to indicate the text of the message and the log option in the *RAISERROR* statement. These were defined in the *sp_addmessage* procedure and will be retrieved at execution time. Also, observe that the *RAISERROR* statement is much smaller when you use a previously defined error message, easing the management of your code throughout your database.

EXERCISE 5.1

CREATING AND RAISING USER-DEFINED ERRORS

In this exercise, you will create a customized error message and raise it. You then will create a new language version and raise it. At the end, you will review the information in the message.

1. Launch SQL Server Management Studio (SSMS), connect to the instance, open a new query window, and change the context to the master database.

2. Create a user-defined error message by executing the following code:

```
EXEC sp_addmessage @msgnum = 50005, @severity = 7,
@msgtext = 'Time to practice error handling.',
@lang = 'us_english';
```

3. Raise the created error message using the *RAISERROR* statement, as follows:

```
RAISERROR(50005, 7, 1)
```

4. Now, let's create a Portuguese version of this message. Execute the code below to add a new version to your message:

```
EXEC sp_addmessage @msgnum = 50005, @severity = 7,
  @msgtext = 'Hora de praticar manipulação de erros.',
  @lang = 'Portuguese';
```

5. Now, let's raise the Portuguese version of your error message using a *SET LANGUAGE* statement, as follows:

```
SET LANGUAGE 'Portuguese'
RAISERROR(50005, 7, 1)
```

6. To finish, view the information and versions of this error message by executing a *SELECT* statement to retrieve the *sys.messages* catalog view with the following code:

```
SELECT * FROM sys.messages WHERE message_id = 50005
```

Handling Errors

In versions prior to SQL Server 2005, error-handling options were limited to the *@@ERROR* function. In these versions, you had to check for error conditions in a proactive way, meaning you had to monitor for error conditions within your own code and then decide what to do at the point you detected the error. In short, for every statement that could raise an error, you had to create code to handle it. As a result, codes that handled errors in SQL Server 2000 and previous versions are long, complex, and hard to maintain.

However, since the development of SQL Server 2005, you can use a *TRY… CATCH* block to handle errors. This block tries to run your code, and, if an error occurs, SQL Server begins execution of code that handles this error. This feature offers database developers great control of the flow of code and also lets you retrieve customizable information about the raised error.

@@ERROR Function

The *@@ERROR* function returns the error ID number generated by the most recent statement executed by a user. If the value returned is zero, then no error occurred. This function is available in all versions of SQL Server, and it's the only way to handle errors in version 2000 and previous of SQL Server.

For each statement of your code that SQL Server executes, the value of *@@ERROR* is cleared and reset. This means that you must check the value of this function immediately following each statement that is verified or save its value to a local variable that can be checked later.

Exam Warning

The *SETERROR* option of the *RAISERROR* statement allows you to raise an error without resetting its value. It means that SQL Server doesn't change the *@@ERROR* return, although it executed a statement after the statement that raised the error.

Because of this behavior, codes developed using *@@ERROR* are generally complex and full of verifications using *IF* statements. Also, there are some errors that terminate execution when raised, which *@@ERROR* can't handle, since the code that refers to this function isn't executed. The following code shows the use of *@@ERROR* in a transaction in the AdventureWorks2008 database.

```
--Executing a defective INSERT
INSERT INTO [Production].[ProductCategory](Name, ModifiedDate)
VALUES ('Custom Category 1', '2008-20-20');

--Print the @@ERROR value
RAISERROR('The number of the error is: %u', 16, 1, @@ERROR)
```

An error should be returned since the date informed in the *INSERT* statement doesn't exist. The following code shows the output of the execution:

```
Msg 242, Level 16, State 3, Line 1
The conversion of a varchar data type to a datetime data type resulted in an
out-of-range value.
The statement has been terminated.
Msg 50000, Level 16, State 1, Line 6
The number of the error is: 242
```

Let's take a look at the last line of this output. SQL Server shows the message that we defined in the *RAISERROR* statement, plus the number 242. That value is the error number that was raised, and it can be manipulated in your code. Also, you should have noticed that the example calls the *@@ERROR* function immediately after the statement that can raise the error to retrieve its value before it's reset. Let's now change the code to see what will happen if there are two statements to be executed. See the following code:

```
--Executing two INSERT statements
INSERT INTO [Production].[ProductCategory](Name, ModifiedDate)
VALUES ('Custom Category 1', '2008-20-20');
INSERT INTO [Production].[ProductCategory](Name, ModifiedDate)

--Print the @@ERROR value
RAISERROR('The number of the error is: %u', 16, 1, @@ERROR)
```

Now, SQL Server will return interesting information. First, SQL Server will return the error of the first *INSERT* statement caused by the date value. Then, SQL Server will execute the second *INSERT* without problems. The output is as follows:

```
Msg 242, Level 16, State 3, Line 2
The conversion of a varchar data type to a datetime data type resulted in an
out-of-range value.
The statement has been terminated.

(1 row(s) affected)
Msg 50000, Level 16, State 1, Line 7
The number of the error is: 0
```

@@ERROR has some tricky behavior: although there was an error in the first statement of your code, the second statement executes correctly. Because of the last successful statement, SQL Server clears the previous value of *@@ERROR* and sets its value to 0. To solve this situation, you should use a local variable to store the error number and *IF* statements to verify the possible errors that may arise.

Another important thing that you must be aware of is the retrieval of information about the error. The *@@ERROR* function doesn't provide direct access to properties like the severity level or the text of a message. In this case, you have two options: you can define your own custom error message for each possible error that can arise in the code, or you can select the error information in the *sys.messages* catalog view and store it in local variables. Although the last option may sound nice, most of these messages will be useless to you, especially when system errors are involved. The following code shows why retrieving error information with an *@@ERROR* value and then raising it as an error might be useless for your application:

```
--Creating the local variables
DECLARE @num INT
DECLARE @text VARCHAR(255)
DECLARE @severity INT

--Executing a defective INSERT
INSERT INTO [Production].[ProductCategory](Name, ModifiedDate)
VALUES ('Custom Category 2', '2008-20-20');

--Setting the local variable value with the @@ERROR value
SET @num = @@ERROR

--Retrieving the error data
SELECT @text = text, @severity = severity FROM [master].[sys].[messages]
WHERE message_id = @num and language_id = '1033'

--Raise the custom error message
RAISERROR(@text, @severity, 1)
```

You can see that the last error raised by the code shows two *NULL* values in the text. Those are arguments that belong to the message and were not replaced with their values when the first error arose. As a result, this error message becomes useless to the application if you don't know which parts are the arguments and inform them in the *RAISERROR* statement. In short, it's too much work for too little a result.

Keep in mind that the best way to handle errors with the *@@ERROR* function is to use an *IF* statement and define custom messages according to the error ID number that you store in a local variable.

New & Noteworthy...

@@ERROR: Just Say NO!

Although SQL Server 2008 still supports the @@ERROR function, avoid using it in new database development. This function requires a lot more work when developing code. Only if your database is to be installed on an SQL Server version 2000 or earlier should you consider using the @@ERROR function.

Example: Handling Errors with @@ERROR Function

In this example, we will develop a stored procedure that inserts a new credit card in the AdventureWorks2008 database and handle its output with an @@ERROR function and some user-defined error messages. Figure 5.11 shows the structure of the CreditCard table.

Figure 5.11 Structure of CreditCard Table

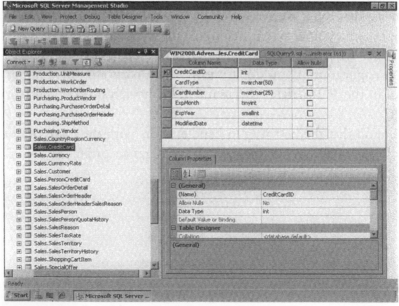

To standardize your database messages and make management efficient, you decide to create two user-defined messages: one for the successful insertion of a credit card and the other for an error that arises in case of failure. Figure 5.12 shows the syntax of these messages.

Figure 5.12 Creating User-Defined Error Messages Using *sp_addmessage*

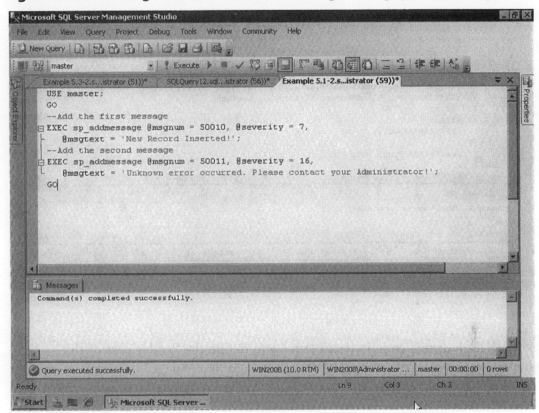

You can see that the severity level of these messages follows the SQL Server standard for system messages, providing organization for them. After you add the messages, the next step is the creation of your new procedure. Based on the *CreditCard* table structure, you can create a procedure that receives four input parameters. Figure 5.13 shows the syntax of a new *uspInsertValidatedCreditCard* procedure.

Figure 5.13 Creating the *uspInsertValidatedCreditCard* Procedure

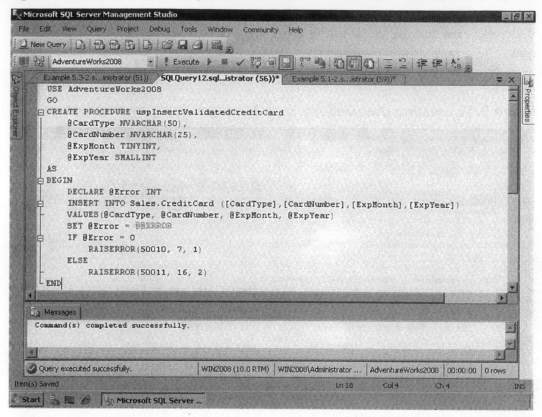

Let's look at this code in detail. After you define the header part of the procedure, you start the routine of the procedure declaring a local variable called *@Error*. This local variable will store the *@@ERROR* value. Then, after the *INSERT* statement, you retrieve the *@@ERROR* value and set it as the *@Error* value. With the variable value defined, you can now analyze it using an *IF* statement. If the value of the variable is 0, then there is no error and the success message will be raised. Otherwise, an error will arise and your custom error message will be shown.

Figure 5.14 shows the *uspInsertValidatedCreditCard* procedure being called twice and the last three *CreditCard* table rows. The first call will return the successful message, while the second will raise an error caused by a duplicate key violation in the credit card number column.

Figure 5.14 Testing the *uspInsertValidatedCreditCard* Procedure

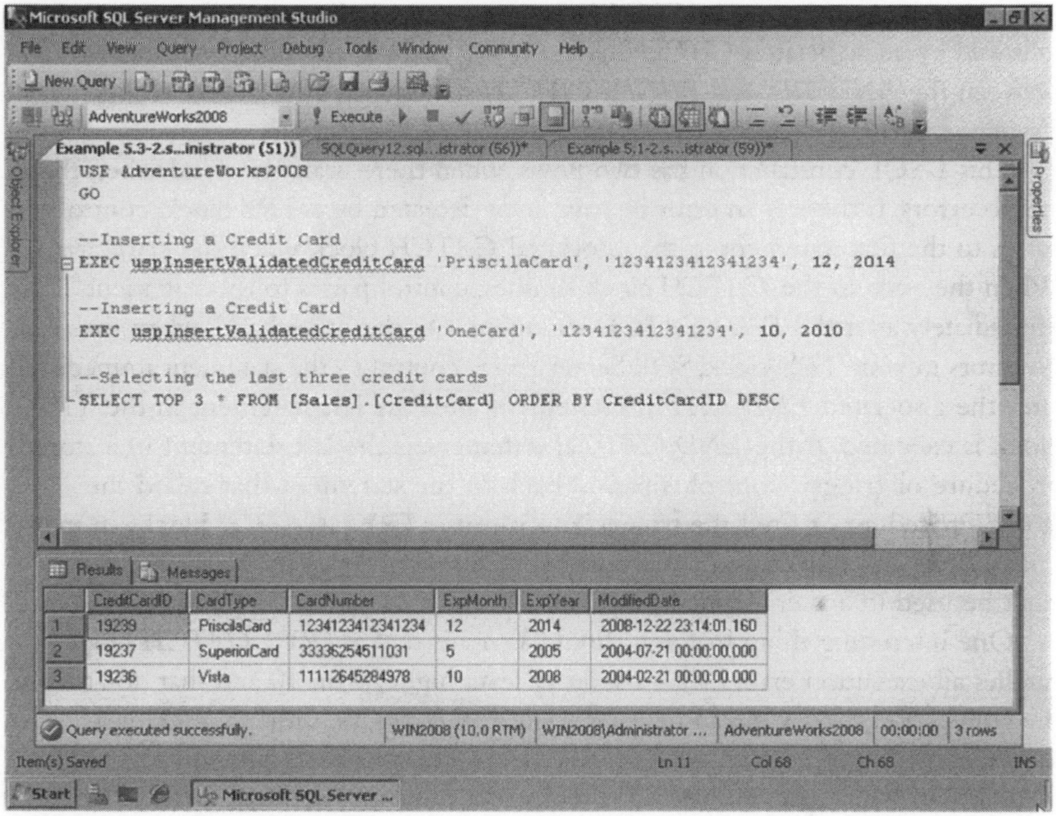

TRY...CATCH Block

SQL Server 2005 and 2008 provide you with a powerful error handling feature in your T-SQL code: a *TRY* and *CATCH* control of flow statement. This error handling technique is similar to exception handling, which exists in programmability languages. *TRY* defines a block of code that might raise an error. If any statement in this block generates an error, execution immediately stops, and the code in the *CATCH* block is run. The syntax of the *TRY...CATCH* block is as follows:

```
BEGIN TRY
    { sql_statement | statement_block }
END TRY
BEGIN CATCH
    [ { sql_statement | statement_block } ]
END CATCH
[ ; ]
```

In both blocks, you can place a single statement or a group of statements in a batch or enclosed in a *BEGIN…END* block. A *TRY* block must be immediately followed by an associated *CATCH* block. If you include any other statements between the *END TRY* and *BEGIN CATCH* statements, SQL Server will generate a syntax error.

This T-SQL construction has two flows: when there is an error and when there are no errors. If there is an error in your code detected by a *TRY* block, control passes to the first statement in the associated *CATCH* block when the error arises. When the code in the *CATCH* block finishes, control passes to the statement immediately after the *END CATCH* statement. On the other hand, when there are no errors in your *TRY* block, SQL Server passes control to the statement immediately after the associated *END CATCH* statement after the last statement in the *TRY* block is executed. If the *END CATCH* statement is the last statement in a stored procedure or trigger, control is passed back to the statement that called the stored procedure or fired the trigger. You can use *TRY…CATCH* blocks in many transactions and objects such as stored procedures and triggers. However, they can't be used in a user-defined function.

One interesting thing that you should know is that a *TRY…CATCH* block catches all execution errors with a severity level higher than 10 and that don't close the connection. Also, you can nest *TRY…CATCH* blocks. Either a *TRY* or a *CATCH* block can contain nested *TRY…CATCH* constructs, providing great flexibility to your code. However, this construct can't span multiple batches or multiple blocks of statements. For example, you can't use two *BEGIN…END* blocks inside a *TRY…CATCH* block.

The *TRY…CATCH* block allows you to handle errors that occur during compilation or statement-level recompilation of your code such as when calling an object that doesn't exist. In these situations, you can handle these errors by executing the code that generates the error in a separate batch within the TRY block. For example, you can place the code in a stored procedure or use the *sp_executesql* system procedure to dynamically create your statement. These two methods allow *TRY…CATCH* to catch the error at a higher level of execution than the error occurrence. Within the *CATCH* block, you can determine what caused the problem and get information about the error using special T-SQL error handling functions. These functions retrieve data from the *sys.messages* catalog view. The following list shows system functions you can use to obtain information about the error that caused the *CATCH* block to be executed:

- **ERROR_NUMBER():** Returns the error ID number.
- **ERROR_SEVERITY():** Returns the severity level of an error.

- **ERROR_STATE():** Returns the error state number.

- **ERROR_PROCEDURE():** Returns the name of the stored procedure or trigger where the error occurred. This is very handy information when you have nested programmability objects, as the procedures or triggers that cause an error may not be the ones to actually handleit.

- **ERROR_LINE():** Returns the line number inside the routine that caused the error.

- **ERROR_MESSAGE():** Returns the complete text of the error message. The great thing about this function is that the text includes the values supplied for any arguments.

By using these functions, you can determine whether you need to use *ROLLBACK* in your *CATCH* block to roll back your transaction.

TEST DAY TIP

It's important to you review these SQL Server system functions and understand their returns. There will be questions on the exam where knowledge of these functions makes a difference.

Example: Handling Errors with a *TRY…CATCH* Block

In this example, we will develop a stored procedure that inserts a new credit card in the AdventureWorks2008 database. We will handle its output using a *TRY…CATCH* block. Figure 5.15 shows the code used to create the *uspInsertValidated-CreditCard_2* procedure.

Figure 5.15 Creating the *uspInsertValidatedCreditCard_2* Procedure

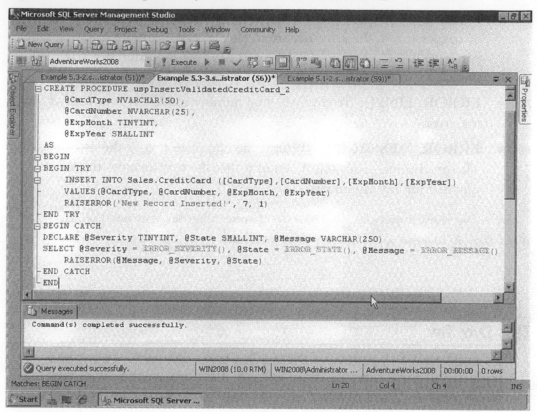

You can see that this code has some important differences from the previous example, which used the *@@ERROR* function. After the header of the procedure, there is a *TRY* block with the main code of the procedure composed of *INSERT* and *RAISERROR* statements. The normal flow of this procedure would be the insertion of credit card information and the exhibition of a message stating that it completed successfully.

However, an error may arise when a user executes this procedure, and that is when the *CATCH* block enters. You can see that the code creates three local variables: *@Severity*, *@State*, and *@Message*. These variables are designed to receive values from the error handling functions *ERROR_SEVERITY()*, *ERROR_STATE()*, and *ERROR_MESSAGE()* via a SELECT statement. Then, after the local variable values are set, a custom error message is created using a *RAISERROR* statement.

To test this new procedure and see how it handles errors, let's try to insert the same credit card number twice. Figure 5.16 shows a script that tries to violate the unique constraint of this table.

Figure 5.16 Inserting Two Credit Cards with the Same Number

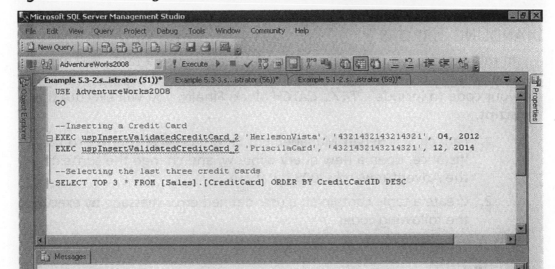

The output when you execute the two procedures is really interesting. The first credit card is inserted without any error, and SQL Server shows the successful completion message after its execution. The second credit card has the same number as the first one, so it will raise an error. However, instead of SQL Server showing the message and stopping execution when the error arose, SQL Server stops execution of the *INSERT* statement and starts to execute the *CATCH* block. You can see that the error message raised is exactly what was defined in the *CATCH* block. This means that you can create custom messages as outputs of your code and control SQL Server error messages in an easy and efficient way. Also, observe that the text of the error message brings the arguments filled, avoiding having to inform them in the *RAISERROR* statement.

EXERCISE 5.2

HANDLING ERRORS

In this exercise, you will develop a script that creates a table and handles any possible errors using the @@ERROR function. You will then change your code to include a TRY...CATCH block. Finally, you will execute the script.

1. Launch SQL Server Management Studio (SSMS), connect to the instance, open a new query window, and change the context to the AdventureWorks2008 database.

2. Create a table containing a user-defined error message by executing the following code:

```
CREATE TABLE [dbo].[TestTable]
(
   ID INT NOT NULL PRIMARY KEY
)
IF @@ERROR != 0
   RAISERROR('There was a problem!', 16, 1)
ELSE
   RAISERROR('Everything is OK!', 5, 1)
```

3. Verify that the table was created by executing the *sp_help* system procedure, as follows:

```
sp_help TestTable
```

4. Now, let's execute the code that creates the *TestTable* table again. We know that SQL Server will return an error message since the table already exists. But, a strange thing should happen. The output of SQL Server should be the following:

```
Msg 2714, Level 16, State 6, Line 1
There is already an object named 'TestTable' in the database.
```

5. You may be asking: Why didn't SQL Server show my custom error message? The answer is that the @@ERROR function handled the error in the analyze step. To solve this problem, let's rewrite the code using a TRY...CATCH block, as follows:

```
BEGIN TRY
   CREATE TABLE [dbo].[TestTable]
   (
           ID INT NOT NULL PRIMARY KEY
   )
   RAISERROR('Everything is OK!', 5, 1)
END TRY
BEGIN CATCH
   RAISERROR('There was a problem!', 16, 1)
END CATCH
```

6. Execute the code again. Now SQL Server should display your
    custom message.

Summary of Exam Objectives

SQL Server gives you ways to control the flow of code in case of problems. You can standardize your database messages as well as handle and manage errors. Also, it lets you create customized error messages and raise them according to your needs. You can add custom error messages to SQL Server using *sp_addmessage* and see all the stored messages by selecting the *sys.messages* catalog view. To raise errors, you use the *RAISERROR* statement, which provides many ways to customize and organize output. To handle errors, you can use the *@@ERROR* function or a *TRY... CATCH* block. While *@@ERROR* is limited and works in previous versions of SQL Server, the *TRY...CATCH* block provides a powerful way to handle errors in versions 2005 and 2008 of SQL Server.

Exam Objectives Fast Track

Understanding Errors

☑ SQL Server has two types of error messages: *information* and *error*.

☑ All messages are stored inside the *sys.messages* catalog view.

☑ Severity level helps you determine the nature of errors.

Managing and Raising User-Defined Errors

☑ You can manage custom messages using the *sp_addmessage*, *sp_altermessage,* and *sp_dropmessage* procedures.

☑ Each message has an ID number, a text, and a severity level. You can also create different language versions of the same message.

☑ You can use a *RAISERROR* statement to raise errors in your code.

☑ You can raise stored or custom error messages.

Handling Errors

☑ SQL Server offers two ways to handle errors: *@@ERROR* function and *TRY...CATCH* block.

☑ *@@ERROR* function is a limited way of handling errors, but it works in previous versions of SQL Server.

☑ *TRY...CATCH* block provides more flexible error handling capabilities, but it works only in versions 2005 and 2008 of SQL Server.

☑ You can retrieve error information with system error handling functions using the *TRY...CATCH* block.

Exam Objectives
Frequently Asked Questions

Q: What types of errors does SQL Server have, and what are their differences?

A: SQL Server has two types of error messages: *information* and *error*. They differ in severity level: information messages have a severity level from 0 to 10; error messages have a severity from 11 to 25.

Q: Where does SQL Server store the messages that I add?

A: All messages are stored inside the *sys.messages* catalog view.

Q: What information tells me the seriousness of an error?

A: The severity level helps you to determine how critical an error is.

Q: How do I add custom error messages to SQL Server?

A: You can add custom messages to SQL Server using the *sp_addmessage* procedure.

Q: Can I make changes to SQL Server system error messages?

A: No, only user-defined error messages can be modified.

Q: Does SQL Server only support English error messages?

A: No, SQL Server has native support for 33 languages, and you can create different language versions for user-defined error messages.

Q: What data types does a *RAISERROR* statement support in the text of a message?

A: Only the following data types are supported: *tinyint, smallint, int, char, varchar, nchar, nvarchar, binary,* and *varbinary*.

Q: Can I use a date value as an argument for a *RAISERROR* statement?

A: Yes, if you convert the date to an *(N)CHAR* or *(N)VARCHAR* before.

Q: What are the differences between the *@@ERROR* function and a *TRY…
CATCH* block?

A: The *@@ERROR* function provides a limited way to handle errors, and it works
in previous versions of SQL Server. *TRY…CATCH* blocks provide better error
handling capabilities, but they only work in versions 2005 and 2008 of SQL
Server.

Self Test

1. You are creating a stored procedure that will execute a delete in the *Product* table in a database. The routine inside the stored procedure includes the following T-SQL statement to handle any errors that might occur:

```
BEGIN TRY
  BEGIN TRANSACTION
    DELETE FROM [Production].[Product] WHERE ProductID = @ProductID
  COMMIT TRANSACTION
END TRY
BEGIN CATCH
  DECLARE @ErrorMessage NVARCHAR(250)
  DECLARE @ErrorSeverity INT
  DECLARE @ErrorState INT
  SELECT
    @ErrorMessage = ERROR_MESSAGE(),
    @ErrorSeverity = ERROR_SEVERITY(),
    @ErrorState = ERROR_STATE()
  RAISERROR (@ErrorMessage, @ErrorSeverity, @ErrorState)
END CATCH
```

You test the procedure and discover that it leaves open transactions. You need to modify the stored procedure so that it properly handles the open transactions. What should you do to solve this problem?

A. Add a *COMMIT TRANSACTION* command to the *CATCH* block.

B. Remove the *COMMIT TRANSACTION* command from the *TRY* block.

C. Add a *ROLLBACK TRANSACTION* command to the *CATCH* block.

D. Add a *ROLLBACK TRANSACTION* command to the *TRY* block.

2. You are creating a stored procedure that will execute an insert in the *Product* table in a database. The routine inside the stored procedure includes the following T-SQL statement to handle any errors that occur:

```
INSERT INTO [Production].[Product] VALUES (@ProductID)
PRINT 'The ID of the new product will be: ' + @ProductID
IF @@ERROR <> 0
  PRINT 'Error! Try Again!'
ELSE
  PRINT 'Record Inserted!'
```

You test the procedure and discover that it shows the success message even when the *INSERT* statement raises an error. You need to modify the stored procedure so that it properly handles the error. What should you do to solve this problem?

A. Change the *PRINT* statement to a *RAISERROR* statement.
B. Set a local variable to store the error number after the *INSERT* statement.
C. Verify if this procedure is being created in SQL Server 2000.
D. Place this routine inside a *BEGIN...END* block.

3. You are developing code that will execute an insert in the *CreditCard* table in a database. The routine has the following T-SQL statement:

```
BEGIN TRY
  BEGIN TRANSACTION
    INSERT INTO [Sales].[CreditCard] VALUES (@CreditCardID)
END TRY
  COMMIT TRANSACTION
BEGIN CATCH
  ROLLBACK TRANSACTION
END CATCH
```

You try to execute the routine and discover that SQL Server is returning an error. You need to modify the routine so that it properly executes the update. What should you do to solve this problem?

A. Add a *COMMIT TRANSACTION* command to the *CATCH* block and remove the *COMMIT TRANSACTION* command after the *TRY* block.
B. Move the *COMMIT TRANSACTION* command to the *TRY* block and remove the *ROLLBACK TRANSACTION* command from the *CATCH* block.
C. Remove the *COMMIT TRANSACTION* command from between the *END TRY* and the *BEGIN CATCH* and add it to the *TRY* block.
D. Remove the *COMMIT TRANSACTION* command and move the *ROLLBACK TRANSACTION* command to the *TRY* block.

4. You are developing procedures that will manipulate some data from a database. This database was created in SQL Server 2000, SQL Server 2005, and SQL Server 2008 instances. You wish to handle the possible errors that your procedure may create. Which error handling feature should you use in your code?

A. *TRY...CATCH* statements
B. *sp_addmessage* procedure

    C. *RAISERROR* statement

    D. *@@ERROR* function

5. You created some user-defined messages that are stored in the *sys.messages* catalog view. You noticed that some of them must have their text changed. Which procedure or statement will allow you to change the text of your custom messages?

    A. sp_altermessage procedure

    B. sp_addmessage procedure

    C. ALTER MESSAGE statement

    D. UPDATE statement

6. You created some user-defined messages for an English application that uses a database in SQL Server. Now you will develop the same application in three other languages: Portuguese, Spanish, and French. You have to avail the messages in these new languages with minimum impact to the application. What should you do?

    A. Translate all the messages into the three new languages. Add each translated message as a new message with an *sp_addmessage* procedure.

    B. Translate all the messages into the three new languages. Install three SQL Server instances, one for each language, then add each translated message as a new message with an *sp_addmessage* procedure using the same error ID number.

    C. Buy three new servers, each one with Windows Server and SQL Server installed in the desired language. Translate all the messages into the three new languages. Then add each translated message as a new message with an *sp_addmessage* procedure using the same error ID number.

    D. Translate all the messages into the three new languages. Add each translated message as a new language version of the English message with an *sp_addmessage* procedure.

7. You need to create a user-defined message that will show a business requirement error of your database. This error can arise in many parts of your code. You need to ensure that it is logged every time it arises with the minimum effort possible. What should you do to ensure that?

    A. Add messages using an *sp_addmessage* procedure with the *@with_log* parameter and raise them using *RAISERROR*.

    B. Add messages using an *sp_addmessage* procedure and raise them using *RAISERROR* with the *WITH LOG* option.

    C. Add messages using an *sp_addmessage* procedure with the *@lang* parameter and raise them using *RAISERROR*.

    D. Add messages using an *sp_addmessage* procedure and raise them using *RAISERROR* with the *WITH SETERROR* option.

8. You are creating a user-defined error message in a new SQL Server instance. The following T-SQL statement shows the syntax of this message:

```
EXEC sp_addmessage @msgnum = 50005, @severity = 21,
  @msgtext = 'System crashed!',
  @lang = 'us_english';
```

You try to create this user-defined error message, but SQL Server returns an error. You need to add this message. What should you do to solve this problem?

    A. Change the number of the error to 50000.

    B. Add the *@with_log* parameter and set it to *TRUE*.

    C. Change the severity level to 30.

    D. Add the *@replace* parameter and set it to *NONE*.

9. You are creating a user-defined function in a new SQL Server instance. The following T-SQL statement shows the syntax of this function:

```
CREATE FUNCTION [dbo].[udfGetAvgCustomer]
(
  @CustomerID INT
)
RETURNS MONEY
AS
BEGIN
BEGIN TRY
  DECLARE @Amount MONEY
  SELECT @Amount = AVG(TotalDue)
  FROM [Sales].[SalesOrderHeader]
  WHERE CustomerID = @CustomerID
  RETURN @Amount
END TRY
BEGIN CATCH
  RAISERROR ('There is a problem!', 16, 1)
END CATCH
END
```

You try to create this user-defined function, but SQL Server returns an error. What should you do to solve this problem?

A. Change the severity level of the *RAISERROR* statement to 10.

B. Add the *WITH LOG* option to the *RAISERROR* statement.

C. Remove the *TRY…CATCH* block and the *RAISERROR* statement.

D. Add *COMMIT TRANSACTION* and *ROLLBACK TRANSACTION* statements in the *TRY…CATCH* block.

10. You need to create a procedure that retrieves data from four other procedures and generates a report. Also, you decide to handle errors that may arise when executing this object. Which error handling functions should you use to know exactly where the error is when it arises?

A. ERROR_NUMBER( ) and ERROR_SEVERITY( )

B. ERROR_STATE( ) and ERROR_NUMBER( )

C. ERROR_PROCEDURE( ) and ERROR_LINE( )

D. ERROR_PROCEDURE( ) and ERROR_MESSAGE( )

11. You need to create a procedure that inserts data into a table of your database. You decide to handle the errors that may arise, retrieve all information about the errors, and guarantee that the insert will be undone if an error rises. Which error handling feature should you use in your code?

A. *TRY…CATCH* statements

B. *sp_addmessage* procedure

C. *RAISERROR* statement

D. *@@ERROR* function

12. You need to generate customized messages for error handling that may arise in your database. You wish to discard the SQL Server error messages and return only your own customized messages to users. Which error handling feature should you use in your code?

A. *TRY…CATCH* statements

B. *sp_addmessage* procedure

C. *RAISERROR* statement

D. *@@ERROR* function

13. You need to develop a procedure that executes a *DROP TABLE* in your database. You want to handle possible errors that may arise in your database. Which error handling feature should you use in your code?

A. *TRY…CATCH* statements

B. *sp_addmessage* procedure

C. *RAISERROR* statement

D. *@@ERROR* function

14. You are developing a code that will try to select data from a table. The following code shows the syntax used:

```
BEGIN TRY
  SELECT * FROM @Table;
END TRY
BEGIN CATCH
  SELECT
    ERROR_NUMBER() AS ErrorNumber,
    ERROR_MESSAGE() AS ErrorMessage;
END CATCH;
```

You plan to reuse this code many times, so you set the *@Table* value in a *SELECT* statement. After some tests, you realize that SQL Server isn't handling errors that arise when you inform a table that doesn't exist. You need to handle all possible errors that may arise in this code. What should you do?

A. Remove the *TRY…CATCH* statements.

B. Create a procedure that executes the *SELECT* statement.

C. Add a *RAISERROR* statement inside the *CATCH* block.

D. Use a *@@ERROR* function to handle this error.

15. You are developing a procedure that will dynamically create code that will be executed using an *sp_executesql* system procedure. You need to handle all possible errors that may arise in this dynamic statement. What should you do?

A. Add a *TRY…CATCH* block in your procedure.

B. You can't create a procedure that executes the *sp_executesql* system procedure within it.

C. Add a *RAISERROR* statement inside a *CATCH* block.

D. Use the *@@ERROR* function to handle any errors.

16. You are developing a transaction that will decide if a statement will be committed or rolled back by using an *XACT_STATE()* system function and an *IF* statement. You need to decide it according to possible errors that may arise in your statement. You need to accomplish this using the least effort possible. Which error handling feature should you use in your code?

A. *TRY…CATCH* statements

B. *sp_addmessage* procedure

C. *RAISERROR* statement

D. *@@ERROR* function

17. You are creating a user-defined error message in a new SQL Server instance. The following T-SQL statement shows the syntax of this message:

```
EXEC sp_addmessage @msgnum = 50000, @severity = 10,
  @msgtext = 'A customized message',
  @lang = 'us_english';
```

You try to create this user-defined error message, but SQL Server returns an error. You need to add this message. What should you do to solve this problem?

A. Change the ID number of the error.

B. Add the *@with_log* parameter and set it to *TRUE*.

C. Change the severity level to 30.

D. Add the *@replace* parameter and set it to *NONE*.

18. You created some user-defined messages that are stored in the *sys.messages* catalog view. You noticed that some of them aren't logged when raised. Which statement will allow you to change the log option text of your custom messages with the least effort possible?

A. sp_altermessage procedure

B. sp_addmessage procedure

C. ALTER MESSAGE statement

D. UPDATE statement

19. You need to create a procedure that retrieves data from other procedures and generates a report. Also, you decide to handle any errors that may arise when executing this object. Which error handling functions should you use to know exactly what the error is and its gravity?

A. ERROR_SEVERITY( ) and ERROR_NUMBER( )

B. ERROR_STATE( ) and ERROR_NUMBER( )

C. ERROR_PROCEDURE( ) and ERROR_MESSAGE( )

D. ERROR_MESSAGE( ) and ERROR_SEVERITY( )

20. You need to create user-defined messages that will show custom messages for your database. These messages must be displayed in English, Portuguese, Spanish, and French, according to the user's location. What should you do to ensure that?

A. Add messages using an *sp_addmessage* procedure with the *@with_log* parameter and raise them using *RAISERROR*.

B. Add messages using an *sp_addmessage* procedure and raise them using *RAISERROR* with the *WITH LOG* option.

C. Add messages using an *sp_addmessage* procedure with the *@lang* parameter and raise them using *RAISERROR*.

D. Add messages using an *sp_addmessage* procedure and raise them using *RAISERROR* with the *WITH SETERROR* option.

Self Test Quick Answer Key

1. C
2. B
3. C
4. D
5. B
6. D
7. A
8. B
9. C
10. C
11. A
12. A
13. A
14. B
15. A
16. A
17. A
18. A
19. D
20. C

Chapter 6

MCTS SQL Server 2008 Exam 433

Implementing Transactions

Exam objectives in this chapter:

- **Transactions Explained**
- **ACID**
- **Isolation Level Explained**
- **Locking**
- **Deadlocking**
- **Transaction Traps**
- **Troubleshooting Transactions**

Exam objectives review:

- ☑ **Summary of Exam Objectives**
- ☑ **Exam Objectives Fast Track**
- ☑ **Exam Objectives Frequently Asked Questions**
- ☑ **Self Test**
- ☑ **Self Test Quick Answer Key**

Introduction

Transactions are an extremely important aspect when it comes to working with databases. Transactions ensure that everything happens to and is stored in the database all at once. If any action statement within the transaction fails and the transaction is rolled back, the entire sequence of events is not stored in the database. In this chapter, we'll cover transactions in depth, focusing on the practical aspects.

We'll also cover isolation level and how it relates to transactions.

Transactions Explained

Transactions are logical groups of commands that are committed to the database or rolled back in the database at the same time. This allows you to insert, update, and delete several different tables and revert those changes if a single command within the transaction fails, or commit all the work if there are no errors. You can control the locking that SQL Server takes on the tables used within the transaction by changing the transaction isolation level. There are a few myths about transactions that are important to know are not true:

1. *If a single command within your transaction fails then none of the data will be written.* This is incorrect. If you don't have any error catching that causes the transaction to be rolled back then the statements that were successful will be committed when the *COMMIT* statement is issued.

2. *A stored procedure is automatically a transaction.* This is also incorrect. Each statement within the stored procedure is executed within its own autocommitted transaction, but the stored procedure as a whole is not an autocommitted transaction. If you want the entire context of the stored procedure to be executed within a single transaction then you will need to explicitly define a transaction within the stored procedure.

3. *If a statement fails then the transaction will roll back.* That isn't going to happen either. If a command fails and there is no logic to roll back the transaction then the transaction will continue and commit the data when it gets to the *COMMIT* statement.

4. *If I create a transaction and run a select statement no one else can access the rows.* This is sort of true. Depending on the transaction isolation (read on for more information) of the person running the select statement this may or may not be true. If you are using the default isolation level of READ_COMMITED then this statement is true. If the *SELECT* statement has been issued under the READ_UNCOMMITED isolation level then this statement is not true.

There are two kinds of transactions available to you as a programmer. There are local transactions that are defined with the *BEGIN TRANSACTION* statement. These local transactions are used for statements that are going to be within the scope of the local database instance. The *BEGIN TRANSACTION* statement can be abbreviated as *BEGIN TRAN*.

There are also distributed transactions that are defined with the *BEGIN DISTRIBUTED TRANSACTION* statement. These distributed transactions are used when statements within the transaction must go beyond the scope of the instance. This is most often done via a query or stored procedure execution between instances of SQL Server through a linked server. This can also be done via an *OPENROWSET* call. In order for distributed transactions to work a transaction is created on all the servers that are involved in the transaction and are kept in sync by the use of the distributed transaction coordinators (MSDTC in the case of SQL Server) that must be installed on all the servers involved in the transaction. The *BEGIN DISTRIBUTED TRANSACTION* statement can be abbreviated as *BEGIN DISTRIBUTED TRAN*.

Distributed transactions can be created against database platforms other than Microsoft SQL Server. Both Oracle and DB2 have distributed transaction coordinators that can be configured and work with the MSDTC service that SQL Server uses.

MSDTC does not come configured for server to server distributed transactions on Windows 2003 or Windows 2008. Although the configuration of MSDTC is beyond the scope of this book, knowledge of the fact that it needs to be configured is necessary.

There are three kinds of transactions within SQL Server. There are explicit transactions, which are transactions where the *BEGIN TRANSACTION, ROLLBACK,* and *COMMIT* statements are explicitly used within the T/SQL code. There are autocommit transactions, which are what each T/SQL statement is by default. An autocommit transaction does not require the use of *BEGIN TRANSACTION, ROLLBACK,* or *COMMIT* statements. The third kind of transaction is the implicit transaction. Implicit transactions are enabled by using the *SET IMPLICIT_ TRANSACTIONS* statement and setting it to ON. The transaction will then be started when the next statement is executed. The transaction will continue until a *COMMIT* or *ROLLBACK* statement is issued. After the transaction is committed or rolled back when the next statement is executed a new transaction will be started.

Named Transactions

Named transactions are transactions that have a specific name assigned to them. Transactions are typically named so that you can more easily identify which transaction you are rolling forward or backward within the T/SQL code. Naming transactions also makes it easier to know which transactions within a stored procedure are causing locking and blocking.

All transactions within Microsoft SQL Server are technically named transactions. By default each transaction that does not have a name assigned to it is given the name *user_transaction*. Transactions are named within the *BEGIN TRANSACTION* command by simply specifying the name of the transaction on the same line.

```
BEGIN TRANSACTION YourTransactionName

...

COMMIT TRNASACTION YourTransactionName
```

The name of the transaction must conform to the normal SQL Server naming convention, but be no longer than 32 characters in length. The transaction name can be a variable, but the variable must be declared as a char, varchar, nchar, or nvarchar data type.

EXERCISE 6.1

CREATE A NAMED TRANSACTION

1. Use the *BEGIN TRANSACTION* command to create a transaction named SampleUpdate, and update some data in the AdventureWorks database.

2. Roll the transaction back and see that the data was not updated.

3. Rerun the command this time committing the transaction again, and viewing that the data has been changed. A sample update statement has been provided.

```
UPDATE Person.Contact
  SET LastName = 'Jones'
WHERE ContactID = 8
```

In addition to naming your transaction, you can also place a mark in the transaction log with a description. This is done by adding the *WITH MARK* option to the *BEGIN TRANSACTION* statement. This allows you to place a description of the transaction within SQL Server transaction log. This allows you to restore the database to a specific transaction mark. The transaction mark is stored in the logmarkhistory table of the MSDB database.

```
BEGIN TRNASACTION YourTransactionName WITH MARK 'Doing something in a
transaction'

...

COMMIT TRANSACTION YourTransactionName
```

The description of the mark can be any valid string of characters up to 255 characters when using a Unicode string. If you are using a non-Unicode string then the mark can be up to 510 characters.

Nesting

Transaction nesting is a technique where you can control within a single parent transaction several smaller groups of commands that are committed or rolled back independently. Each nested or inner transaction must be committed independently of the parent or outer transaction. The parent transaction must also be committed in order for the data to be committed to the database. If the inner transactions are committed and the outer transaction is rolled back, then the inner transaction will be rolled back. If the inner transactions are rolled back and the outer transaction is committed, then the inner transactions are rolled back and any commands within the outer transaction that are not within the inner transactions are committed and written to the database.

```
BEGIN TRANSACTION Parent1

     UPDATE …

     BEGIN TRNASACTION Child1

          …

     COMMIT TRANSACTION Child1

     UPDATE …

     BEGIN TRANSACTION Child2

          …

     COMMIT TRANSACTION Child2

     IF @SomeVariable = 0

          ROLLBACK TRANSACTION Parent1

     ELSE

          COMMIT TRANSACTION Parent1
```

COMMIT and ROLLBACK

COMMIT and *ROLLBACK* are the statements used to tell SQL Server engine that the transaction has been completed and whether the transaction has been completed successfully or not. If the transaction was successful and the data should be written to disk then the *COMMIT* statement should be used. If there was a problem and the data should not be written to the database then the *ROLLBACK* statement should be used.

You have to be careful when rolling back transactions. If you have a failed transaction and you write error data to an error table, then roll back your transaction, the writing of the error data to that error table will also be rolled back. Temporary tables are also controlled by your transaction, so writing your error data to a temporary table will not get you past this; however, data in a table variable will persist through a rollback allowing you to write the data from the table variable to the error table after the rollback has been completed.

```
DECLARE @ErrorData TABLE (ErrorNumber INT, ErrorMessage NVARCHAR(MAX))

BEGIN TRANSACTION Test1

        BEGIN TRY

        …

        END TRY

        BEGIN CATCH

                INSERT INTO @ErrorData

                SELECT ERROR_NUMBER(), ERROR_MESSAGE()

        END CATCH

        IF EXISTS (SELECT * FROM @ErrorData)

                ROLLBACK TRANSACTION Test1

        ELSE

                COMMIT TRANSACTION Test1

INSERT INTO ActualErrorTable

SELECT ErrorNumber, ErrorMessage

FROM @ErrorData
```

You can use the *XACT_STATE* system function to determine the state of the current transaction. This function returns three possible values: 1, 0, and −1. A value of 1 means that a healthy committable transaction is in process. A value of 0 means that there is no transaction running. A value of −1 means that the transaction is in such a state that it must be completely rolled back. A value of −1 tells you that the transaction cannot be committed, nor can it be rolled back to any transaction save point.

Normally if a single statement within the transactions fails, the transactions continue, unless the state of the failure is critical enough that the entire batch is killed. This normal process of continuing the transaction can be overridden by setting the *XACT_ABORT* setting to ON. This setting tells SQL Server that if any statement fails then the database engine should roll back the entire transaction. This setting defaults to OFF.

When writing to another database server over a linked server against an OLE DB provider the *XACT_ABORT* needs to be set to ON. The exception to this is if the OLE DB provider supports nested transactions. If the provider supports nested transactions you can set the *XACT_ABORT* to either ON or OFF.

Save Points

Save points are special optional markers within a transaction. These markers allow you to roll back from the current location to the named save point, leaving the commands prior to the save point committed to the database. All save points are named, and duplicate names are allowed, but if you reuse the save point name within the transaction and the transaction is rolled back, the transaction is rolled back to the latest save point of that name.

```
BEGIN TRANSACTION
     UPDATE Table1 …
     SAVE TRANSACTION Point1
     UPDATE Table2 …
     SAVE TRANSACTION Point2
COMMIT
```

An important note with save points is that save points cannot be used in distributed transactions. This includes explicit transactions that are started with the *BEGIN DISTRIBUTED TRANSACTION* or explicit distributed transactions, which are escalated automatically from a local transaction to a distributed transaction.

ACID

ACID (Atomicity, Consistency, Isolation, and Durability) is the basic foundation upon which transactions are built. In order to be considered a transaction, the statement must fulfill these foundations.

Atomicity

Transactions are atomic units of work. This means that either all the work within the transaction is completed or none of the work is completed. Think of an update statement, which is unto itself an autocommit transaction. When you run an update statement either all rows affected by the update statement are changed, or all the rows are left unchanged. There is no way for a single update statement to commit half of the changes and roll back the other half.

Consistency

When a transaction is consistent it means that the data within the transaction remains through the committing of the transaction, at which point it is available for other processes to change it. Within a relational database with foreign keys this means that all the rules that maintain the data integrity of the database must be enforced. This includes the internal structures of the database such as the B-Tree lists that make up the physical table.

Isolation

The isolation of a transaction tells us that no other transaction can change the data that we have locked for reading or writing. When two transactions are running and working with the same table a single transaction recognizes the data from the state it was in before the other transaction works with the data, or after that transaction works with the data, but it does not recognize that the data is available while the other transaction is working with that data. This is known as serializing access to the data as only a single statement at any one time can access the data. SQL Server controls this isolation by taking locks of the row, page, or table before data modification and releasing those locks after the statement has completed in the case of an autocommit transaction, or when the transaction is completed or rolled back in the case of the explicit transaction.

Durability

A transaction is durable when the data that has been modified by the transaction remains in the state that the transaction left it in. This data must also survive the event of a system failure. When it is said that the data must remain in that state, this does not preclude another transaction from making changes to this data after the initial transaction has been completed.

Isolation Level Explained

Isolation levels are how SQL Server decides what level of locking to take when working with data. There are five isolation levels available for your transactions in SQL Server 2008: READ UNCOMMITED, READ COMMITED, REPEATABLE READ, SNAPSHOT, and SERIALIZABLE. Only one isolation level can be set for your connection, and that isolation level persists until the connection to SQL Server is broken or the isolation level is explicitly changed by using the *SET TRANSACTION ISOLATION LEVEL* statement.

If a stored procedure has a *SET TRANSACTION ISOLATION LEVEL* statement within it and the calling code uses a different isolation level, then the isolation level will be changed, and will revert back to the calling code isolation level upon completion of the stored procedure. If table locking hints are included within a query, those locking hints will override the default locking hints of the isolation level.

The READ UNCOMMITTED isolation level is similar to the WITH (NOLOCK) hint in that it allows you to perform dirty reads of the tables and pages that you are reading even if other transactions have modified those records. This is the least restrictive of the isolation levels. You can protect yourself from locking contention while preventing dirty reads by setting the *READ_COMMITTED_SNAPSHOT* option of the database to true, and using the READ COMMITTED isolation level, or by using the SNAPSHOT isolation level.

The READ COMMITTED isolation level protects the transactions from dirty reads. This is the default isolation level of SQL Server. The behavior of this isolation level will depend on the value of the *READ_COMMITTED_SNAPSHOT* setting of the database. If this setting is disabled then this isolation level will not allow statements to read pages that are locked for update by other transactions. If this setting is enabled then this isolation level will allow statements to read the prior version of the pages that are locked since backup pages will be written to the TEMPDB database while they are locked for update. If the setting is enabled and you wish to revert to the disabled locking behavior then you can use the *WITH(READCOMMITTEDLOCK)* table hint within your command.

The REPEATABLE READ isolation level is the next restrictive isolation level within SQL Server. When using this isolation level statements cannot read data that has been modified but not committed by other transactions. It also prevents data that has been selected by other transactions from being updated. The prevention of other transactions' reading data is controlled by shared locks on the rows or data pages that are read, which prevents an update statement from being able to take its locks on those rows or data pages.

The SNAPSHOT that is the newest isolation level in SQL Server requires that all data used by the transaction will be the same version of the transaction at the beginning of the transaction as it is at the end of the transaction. This is done by SQL Server taking copies of the data it needs to work with and placing those copies of the data into the TEMPDB database so that other transactions using the READ COMMITTED isolation level can read them instead of the original data pages from within the user database. Before you can use the SNAPSHOT isolation level you must enable the *ALLOW_SNAPSHOT_ISOLATION* setting on the database. If your transaction will span more than one database, then this setting must be enabled on all the databases within the transaction or the transaction will return an error message. This isolation level was introduced with Microsoft SQL Server 2005 and cannot be used on SQL Server 2000 and below.

New & Noteworthy...

A New Isolation Level

The snapshot isolation isn't new in SQL Server 2008, but it was new in SQL Server 2005. The addition of a new isolation level is a very large event. Microsoft has had only four transaction isolation levels since the Microsoft code base broke from the Sybase code base back in SQL Server 4.2 days. To this day Sybase still has only four transaction isolation levels.

The SERIALIZABLE isolation level is the most restrictive of the isolation levels. When using this isolation level no access to the data being used by this transaction is allowed, no matter the isolation level of the other transaction. No transaction may insert a value into the table that falls within the key range of the values being locked by the SERIALIZABLE transaction. This guarantees that any select statements that are performed within the database will return the exact same data every time they are run within the context of the transaction.

EXAM TIP

Use the *SET TRANSACTION ISOLATION LEVEL* statement to change the isolation level between the various isolation levels.

It is important to note that user-defined functions (UDFs) and CLR user-defined types (UDTs) cannot change the isolation of the current session via the *SET TRANSACTION ISOLATION LEVEL* command. In order to change the isolation level for the scope of these commands you must set the isolation level, then call the UDF or UDT, and then set the isolation level back.

If you are using the *BULK INSERT* statement, the BCP command-line command, and you are using the .NET bulk data loading methods, these commands will block and be blocked by transactions that are using SNAPSHOT, READ UNCOMMITTED, and READ COMMITTED (when row versioning is being used).

In addition to changing the isolation level through *SET TRANSACTION ISOLATION LEVEL* you can edit the query options within SQL Server Management Studio. You can do this by right-clicking on the white space in the query window and selecting **Query Options** from the context menu. On the Execution | Advanced page you can adjust the Transaction Isolation Level as shown in Figure 6.1.

Figure 6.1 Query Options

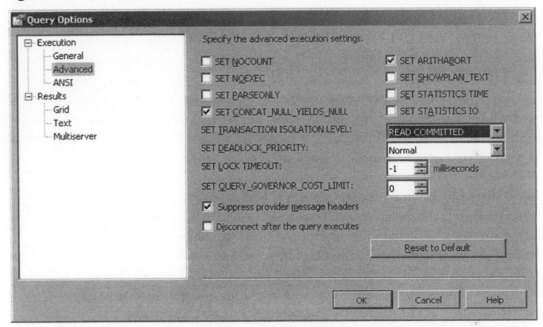

You should be very careful when adjusting this setting. When you change this setting it affects only the current session, which could change the way the locks are done when running the statements in this state, and in other states.

Locking

Locking is the method by which SQL Server controls who has what access to what data within the table. Every command that is run in the database takes some sort of lock against SQL Server. There are seven basic kinds of locks that can be taken and four different levels. These levels are at the row level, page level, table level, or database level. SQL Server will automatically escalate locks from row to page to table as it becomes more efficient to take the lock at the higher level. SQL Server will never escalate a lock from the table level to the database level.

Locks at the database level are taken only when specific database options are changed via the *ALTER DATABASE* command.

The kinds of locks that can be taken are the same for the row, page, and table levels. They fall into two groups: basic locks and extended locks. The basic locks are shared (S), update (U), and exclusive (X). These three locks can then be modified as needed by the extended locks, which are intent (I), schema (Sch), bulk update (BU), and key-range (KR). How these extended locks are combined with the basic locks is described a little later in this section.

The shared lock is taken when reading a table with a select statement. This lock allows other shared locks to be taken by other transactions attempting to read the data. No transaction can update data that is locked by a shared lock until the shared lock has been released.

The update lock is taken when updating the rows of a table. This update lock is used while SQL Server is reading the rows that will be modified. When the rows are being modified this update lock is converted to an exclusive lock. This is done to prevent two transactions, both using update statements to cause a deadlock. Without the update lock when an update statement is issued SQL Server would take a shared lock while reading the table, then convert that to an exclusive lock when changing the data. The problem would occur when two update commands were running against the same set of data. Both would take a shared lock while reading the table, and then neither would be able to convert that shared lock to an exclusive lock because of the other shared lock.

The exclusive lock is used to prevent any other process from accessing the locked resource. Read operations can take place against an exclusive lock only when a NOLOCK hint is used or the reading transaction is using the READ UNCOMMITTED isolation level. All other operations against a resource with an exclusive lock will be blocked until the exclusive lock is released.

There are six different types of intent locks that can be taken against a resource. These intent locks are used for a variety of things.

The intent shared (IS) lock protects requested or acquired shared locks on some lower level resources. If a shared lock is taken on a record, an intent shared lock could be taken on the database page that holds that record.

The intent exclusive (IX) locks required or acquired exclusive locks on some lower level resources. The intent exclusive lock is a superset of the intent shared lock. If an exclusive lock is placed on a record an intent exclusive lock could be taken on the page that holds that record.

The shared with intent exclusive (SIX) lock protects shared locks on the resources lower in the locking hierarchy and intent exclusive locks on some resources that are lower in the locking hierarchy. Acquiring a shared with intent exclusive lock on a table also takes intent exclusive locks on the pages being modified, or exclusive locks on the rows being modified. Although there can only be one shared with intent exclusive lock per table at a time, preventing changes by other transactions, while allowing other transactions to read the rows and pages in the table by obtaining intent shared locks at the table level.

The intent update (IU) lock protects shared or requested lock pages in the table being updated. Intent update locks are converted to intent exclusive locks when the update operation takes place.

The shared intent update lock is a combination of shared and intent update locks. This lock is taken when a transaction first takes a shared lock by reading the table from one statement, then by performing an update through a second statement. This is done most often by using the PAGLOCK table hint within the select statement that takes the shared lock. The update statement then takes an intent update lock, which is then escalated to a shared intent update lock as it is more efficient for SQL Server to manage a single lock than multiple locks.

EXERCISE 6.2

VIEWING LOCKS

1. Open two query windows in SQL Server Management Studio.

2. In the first use the *BEGIN TRANSACTION* statement and an update statement. This will begin the transaction and hold the locks on the objects.

3. In the second window use the sys.dm_tran_locks dynamic management view. Use this dynamic management view to see what locks were taken.

4. Roll back the query in the first window, and run other statements.

5. Change the isolation level of the transaction in the first window, and rerun the statements.

6. Rerun the *sp_lock* procedure and see how the locks have changed.

The update intent exclusive lock is a combination of update and intent exclusive locks being taken at different times but held at the same time. Like the shared intent update lock it is more efficient to hold one lock than two locks.

When DDL statements are run against the objects in the database, they use schema modification locks (Sch-M) to prevent access to the object in which the DDL statement is run. This schema modification lock prevents all access to the object by any other statements until the schema modification lock is released. When a *TRUNCATE TABLE* command is issued against a table a schema modification lock is taken against the table for the duration of the time it takes for the truncate statement to be completed.

When SQL Server is compiling and executing statements it takes a schema stability lock against the objects in question. The schema stability lock does not block any object level locks, including the exclusive lock. It does block the schema modification lock, however, from being taken until after the schema stability lock has been released.

The database engine uses bulk update locks (BU) when bulk copying data into a table through bcp, bulk insert, Integration Services, and so on, and either the TABLOCK table hint is used, or the "table lock on bulk load" table option is set using the *sp_tableoption* system stored procedure. The bulk update lock allows multiple threads to bulk load data into the table, while blocking other processes from accessing the table. When using bcp you can force the BU lock to be taken by specifying the *−h* switch in the command line and adding the TABLOCK hint. When using the *BULK INSERT* statement, simply specify the *TABLOCK* switch in the command. When using SQL Server Integration Services to bulk load data, check the **Table lock** check box as shown in Figure 6.2.

Figure 6.2 SQL Server Integration Services Table Lock Check box

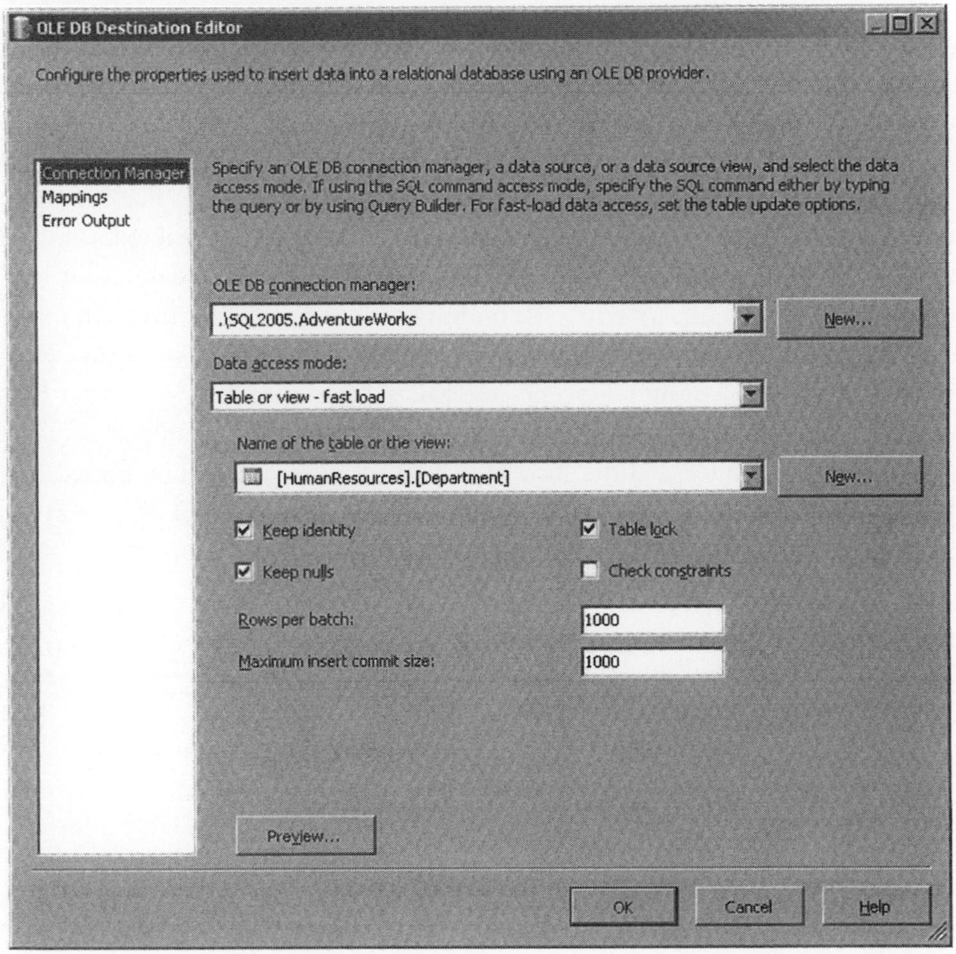

Key range locks protect a set of rows included within a record set being read by a T/SQL statement while using the serializable transaction isolation level. By protecting the range of rows being worked with it prevents phantom inserts, deletes, or reads against the protected rows.

If you wish to manually take locks against the database objects you can use the system stored procedure *sp_getapplock*. This procedure allows you to specify the object you wish to lock, the lock type you wish to take, the owner of the lock, and the length of time that the lock will last. If a lock taken with *sp_getapplock* doesn't time out, or you take the lock without a timeout, you can use the *sp_releaseapplock* system stored procedure to release the lock that you took. This procedure takes the same basic parameters, asking for the object name and lock owner. When you use these procedures they must be used within an explicit transaction.

Deadlocking

Deadlocks are a terminal locking issue that involves two transactions. When the deadlock occurs one of the transactions is killed and rolled back. A deadlock occurs when you have multiple threads running against the same object at the same time, but the transactions lock the same resources and then try to access the resources locked by the other transaction. This can be shown most easily with a diagram like the one in Figure 6.3. As you can see in the figure, Transaction 1 begins and makes an update. Transaction 2 begins at the same time, and attempts to make an update but is blocked because of locks that Transaction 1 took on the table. Transaction 1 then attempts to make another update to the table, but is blocked because Transaction 2 now has a lock on the table. A deadlock now has occurred because there is no way for either transaction to ever complete no matter how long they wait. When the deadlock occurs one of the transactions is killed and the second is allowed to complete. The transaction that has been killed will be rolled back and the session disconnected. An error is also logged to SQL Server ERRORLOG when a deadlock occurs.

Figure 6.3 Visual Diagram of a Deadlock

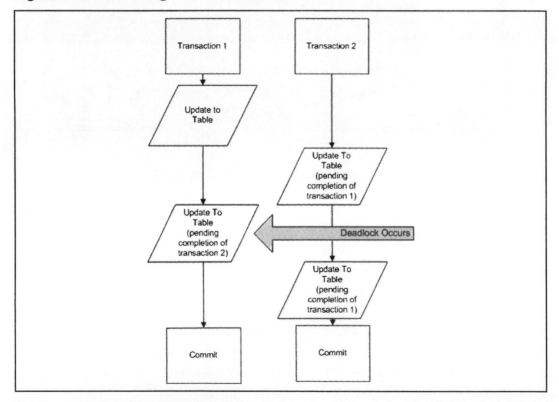

If your application is suffering from deadlocks you have a few options to resolve the issue. You can start by reducing the length of time for which your transactions are held. As the transactions complete more quickly your deadlocks should be reduced as the length of time that the locks are held for is reduced. Another option is to combine your commands into a single command as this will stop Transaction 1 from needing to wait for Transaction 2 to complete.

Head of the Class...

Deadlocks Are Tough to Deal With

A system that has lots of deadlocks can be very difficult to handle, especially if your transactions are already short. If your system load is high enough and your transactions are already as short as they can be, you may not be able to do anything.

At one finance company that I worked for our OLTP load origination system was having a large number of deadlocks on a daily basis. We reviewed our system, and found that our transactions were as short as they could be. Because of the extremely high load on our system it turned out that a hardware upgrade was the only way to get the system to process the transactions any faster.

If you are getting a lot of deadlocks are you are not sure which statements are causing the deadlocks you can enable trace flags 1204 and 1222. These trace flags will output information about the deadlock to the ERRORLOG file, which will enable you to find the statements that are causing the deadlocks as well as which statement is being killed.

Transaction Traps

Transaction traps are *BEGIN TRANSACTION, COMMIT, ROLLBACK*, and *SET TRANSACTION ISOLATION LEVEL*.

When working with explicit transactions there are a few statements you can use to control the transaction. The *BEGIN TRANSACTION* statement is what tells SQL Server that you are starting a new explicit transaction. All commands after the

BEGIN TRANSACTION statement are included within the transaction. The transaction can be named or not, marked or not, and will function the same either way. The transaction will survive through multiple batches and multiple stored procedures.

All statements will continue to be kept in the transaction until either the *COMMIT* or *ROLLBACK* statement is issued. The *COMMIT* statement tells SQL Server to write the completed statements to the database file. The *ROLLBACK* statement tells SQL Server to roll back the statements, which leaves the data in the same state it was before the transaction was started.

If you wish to change the transaction isolation level that SQL Server uses then you use the *SET TRANSACTION ISOLATION LEVEL* statement. This will allow you to change the isolation level that the connection is using. It will not affect any other transactions or sessions on the instance, nor will it affect the default transaction isolation level, since the default transaction isolation level cannot be changed from READ COMMITTED.

Although explicit transactions are started and stopped with the *BEGIN TRANSACTION*, *COMMIT*, and *ROLLBACK* commands, autocommit transactions do not require these statements. Because each statement you execute against the database is contained within its own autocommit transaction, these autocommit transactions are affected by changing the transaction isolation level in the same way that explicit transactions are.

As the processes are blocked, and therefore cannot issue new commands to the engine, checking for deadlocks is left to an outside process. The process that checks for deadlocks runs only every 5 seconds. Because of this your processes could be hung for several seconds before the deadlock is identified and killed. In the event that a deadlock is found, the interval that the deadlock detection process is run is reduced, to as often as 100 milliseconds. Once no more deadlocks are detected the interval is increased back up to 5 seconds.

When SQL Server detects that a deadlock has occurred it must pick one of the transactions to roll back. It does this by calculating the cost of rolling back both transactions, and then rolling back the transaction that costs the least to roll back. You can overwrite the logic by setting the deadlock priority of the transaction with the *SET DEADLOCK_PRIORITY* statement. This value can be set to any whole value from −10 to 10, LOW (−5), MEDIUM (0), or HIGH (5). The transaction with the lower deadlock priority will be killed no matter the rollback cost. The value of MEDIUM (0) is the default deadlock priority.

Troubleshooting Transactions

When you start working with explicit database transactions you may start seeing some slowdown within the database. This is because where you had locks being taken and released as soon as the statement had been completed you now have locks being taken and held until other statements are completed. This can cause other processes within the database to appear to take longer as they are being blocked by these locks on the database resources.

One way to see what process is blocking the other process or processes is to query the sys.dm_exec_requests dynamic management view. By looking at the blocking_session_id column you can identify which database process id (spid) is blocking the database in question. You can then get the SQL Handle for that session from the sys.dm_exec_requests dynamic management view, and use that SQL Handle along with the sys.dm_exec_sql_text dynamic management function, which will give you the text of the command that is causing the blocking. If the command comprises multiple statements use the statement_start_offset and statement_end_offset values from the sys.dm_exec_requests to select the correct statement.

EXERCISE 6.3

QUERY THE DMV

1. Query the sys.dm_exec_requests dynamic management view. You can manually create a block by opening two query windows.

2. In the first window begin a transaction and run an update against a table.

3. In the second window select those rows.

4. In another window query the sys.dm_exec_requests DMV to view the block.

5. After you have identified the offending spids, use the sys.dm_exec_sql_text dynamic management function to view the commands that are being run.

When you are working with transactions you will want to check and see whether all the transactions have been committed or not. This is done by checking the value of the @@TRANCOUNT system function. This system function tells you the number of open transactions on the current session. If you have open transactions after all the transactions should have been closed you can either *ROLLBACK or COMMIT* the transactions based on the output of the *@@TRANCOUNT* system function.

Transaction Examples

The most common time you will commonly want to use transactions when you need to modify data in several tables and have the ability to roll back the changes if there is a problem. A common example would be that of the customer tables in an order entry database. You have a Customer table, an Address table, and a Person table, and you wish to put records in all tables or no tables. Your transaction to do this might look something like this:

```
CREATE PROCEDURE InsertCustomer
...
AS
BEGIN TRANSACTION CustomerEntry
      BEGIN TRY
      INSERT INTO Customer

      ...

      INSERT INTO Person

      ...

      INSERT INTO Address

      ...

      END TRY
      BEGIN CATCH
            ROLLBACK
      END CATCH
IF @@TRANCOUNT <> 0
      COMMIT
```

Summary of Exam Objectives

Successful statements are rolled back only if the transaction is explicitly rolled back, or if the *XACT_ABORT* setting is enabled. Distributed transactions are used only if the transaction crosses instances. MSDTC is used to coordinate the transaction between the servers. Named transactions are used to make it easier to identify and control which transaction you are committing and rolling back. Marked transactions are used to put a mark in the transaction log, which can be used as an identification point when rolling the transaction log forward. Nested transactions are used to allow smaller parts within the transaction to be rolled back while the bulk of the transaction is rolled forward. Transactions must be atomic units of work.

Data must be consistent both before and after the transaction is complete. Transactions must be isolated from each other. After a transaction is complete the changes must be able to survive a system restart or system failure. The isolation level of the transaction can be adjusted via the *SET TRANSACTION ISOLATION LEVEL* statement. Locks are taken by the database engine when data is accessed or written in order to ensure that the data remains consistent. As operations change from read to write the locks are changed. As operations require the use of more resources the locks are escalated from rows, to pages, to the entire table.

Deadlocks occur when two transactions end up waiting for each other to complete. Deadlock rollbacks are done based on the transaction that takes the fewest resources to roll back. Deadlock rollback calculations can be overwritten by using the *DEADLOCK_PRIORITY* setting within the batch. Locking information can be viewed by the sys.dm_tran_locks system procedure. Blocking information can be viewed by the sys.dm_exec_requests dynamic management view.

Exam Objectives Fast Track

Transactions Explained

☑ Marked transactions place a mark in the transaction log so that the transaction log can be rolled forward to that mark when restoring the database and log.

☑ Every statement that is executed against the database is contained within a transaction.

ACID

- ☑ ACID stands for the four basic foundations that define a transaction: Atomicity, Consistency, Isolation, and Durability.

- ☑ To be a transaction the statement must fulfill all four foundations.

Isolation Level Explained

- ☑ Each transaction isolation level has different locking, which will be taken by default.

- ☑ The isolation level can be changed with the *SET TRANSACTION ISOLATION LEVEL* statement.

- ☑ The default isolation level for the instance cannot be changed.

Locking

- ☑ As the database takes more locks on rows, those locks will be escalated by page locks, then to table locks. This lowers the amount of memory needed to manage the locks.

- ☑ Locks are always taken, even against temporary tables.

- ☑ Locks are taken when the statement starts and are held until the transaction that contains the statement has been completed.

Deadlocking

- ☑ Deadlock roll back priority can be configured by setting the *DEADLOCK_PRIORITY* setting.

- ☑ Deadlocks typically occur when transactions are kept open too long.

- ☑ Transactions should be as short as possible to help prevent deadlocks.

Transaction Traps

- ☑ *BEGIN TRAN* or *BEGIN TRANSACTION* is used to begin an explicit transaction.

- ☑ *COMMIT, COMMIT TRAN*, or *COMMIT TRANSACTION* is used to commit the changes made within an explicit transaction.

☑ *ROLLBACK, ROLLBACK TRAN*, or *ROLLBACK TRANSACTION* is used to *roll back* the changes made within an explicit transaction.

Troubleshooting Transactions

☑ Ensure that all transactions that are started are either committed or rolled back.

☑ To protect from excessive locking the lower level of transaction isolation should be used.

☑ When nesting transactions use named transactions to provide easier identification of which transactions are left open.

Exam Objectives
Frequently Asked Questions

Q: What is the default transaction isolation level that SQL Server uses?

A: Microsoft SQL Server uses the READ COMMITED transaction isolation level as the default isolation level.

Q: If a stored procedure throws an error message will the statements all be rolled back?

A: No, a stored procedure is not necessarily a single transaction. The only time a stored procedure is a single transaction is when the *BEGIN TRANSACTION* and *COMMIT* statements are explicitly within the procedure.

Q: If I want to run select statements without using table locking hints what transaction isolation level should I use?

A: You will want to use the READ UNCOMMITED transaction isolation level as this will allow *SELECT* statements to run without taking any locks and without requiring table locking hints.

Q: I'm getting deadlocks on a server; how can I get more information about the deadlocks?

A: You will want to enable trace flags 1204 and 1222. These flags will output information about both statements that are involved in the deadlock to the ERRORLOG file.

Q: What option is used to control the rollback priority when dealing with deadlocks?

A: You will want to use the *SET DEADLOCK_PRIORITY* switch. You can either use LOW, MEDIUM, and HIGH, or for more control use any whole value from −10 to 10, giving you a total of 21 settings.

Q: What needs to be configured in order to allow a transaction to go between servers?

A: You will need to configure the MSDTC service in order for transactions to be escalated from local transactions to distributed transactions.

Self Test

1. You are writing a stored procedure that will be used to modify a lot of data in a table within your database. You must select data from the table, then do several calculations on the data, then update the rows. You need to ensure that no one else can query the data in the table from the time that you start the process until the time that you finish the process. You need to ensure that other tables that are accessed during the process are not locked because other users will need to access those tables during your process. What technique should you use?

   A. Set the transaction isolation level to READ UNCOMMITED before beginning your process.

   B. Set the transaction isolation level to SERIALIZABLE before beginning your process.

   C. Set the transaction isolation level to READ UNCOMMITED before beginning your process. Use *sp_getapplock* to take an exclusive lock on the table before beginning your process.

   D. Do not adjust the transaction isolation level. Use the sp_getapplock to take an exclusive lock on the table before beginning your process.

2. You are writing a stored procedure that you want to ensure that you can roll back to in the event that the end result isn't what is desired. What code should you use?

   A.

   ```
   BEGIN TRANSACTION MARK 'Maintenance Transaction'
       UPDATE Table …
       COMMIT
   ```

   B.

   ```
   BEGIN TRANSACTION MaintenanceTransaction
       UPDATE Table …
       COMMIT MaintenanceTransaction
   ```

   C.

   ```
   BEGIN TRANSACTION
       UPDATE Table …
       COMMIT
   ```

D.
```
BEGIN TRANSACTION
    SAVE TRANSACTION MaintenanceTransaction
    UPDATE Table …
    COMMIT
```

3. You are working with your database application and you need to add a query over a linked server within an existing transaction. Because of the way that the work must be done you cannot remove the explicit transaction. When you first run the procedure you get an error that the distributed transaction cannot begin. What service needs to be configured to get distributed transactions working correctly?

    A. MsDtsServer Service

    B. MSDTC Service

    C. SQL Server Service

    D. SQL Server Agent Service

4. You are working with a stored procedure that has a transaction within it on a legacy system running on SQL Server 2000. When there is an error not all the statements are rolling back. Which stored procedure code should you be using?

    A.
    ```
    CREATE PROCEDURE YourProcedure @UserId INT, @ProductId INT AS
    BEGIN TRANSACTION
          UPDATE Users
                SET NumberOfOrders=NumberOfOrders+1
          WHERE UserId = @UserId

          INSERT INTO Orders
          (UserId, ProductId)
          VALUES
          (@UserId, @ProductId)
    COMMIT
    GO
    ```

    B.
    ```
    CREATE PROCEDURE YourProcedure @UserId INT, @ProductId INT AS
    BEGIN TRANSACTION
          UPDATE Users
                SET NumberOfOrders=NumberOfOrders+1
    ```

```
      WHERE UserId = @UserId

      INSERT INTO Orders

      (UserId, ProductId)

      VALUES

      (@UserId, @ProductId)

      IF @@ERROR <> 0

      ROLLBACK

COMMIT
GO
```

C.

```
CREATE PROCEDURE YourProcedure @UserId INT, @ProductId INT AS
BEGIN TRANSACTION

      UPDATE Users

            SET NumberOfOrders=NumberOfOrders+1

      WHERE UserId = @UserId

      INSERT INTO Orders

      (UserId, ProductId)

      VALUES

      (@UserId, @ProductId)

      IF @@ROWCOUNT <> 0

          ROLLBACK

COMMIT
GO
```

D.

```
CREATE PROCEDURE YourProcedure @UserId INT, @ProductId INT AS
BEGIN TRANSACTION

      UPDATE Users

            SET NumberOfOrders=NumberOfOrders+1

      WHERE UserId = @UserId

      IF @@ERROR <> 0

      BEGIN

          ROLLBACK

          BREAK

              END

      INSERT INTO Orders

      (UserId, ProductId)
```

```
                VALUES

                (@UserId, @ProductId)

                IF @@ERROR <> 0

                BEGIN

                        ROLLBACK

                        BREAK

                END

        COMMIT

        GO
```

5. You are troubleshooting a stored procedure that has several transactions defined within it. You run the procedure in SQL Server Management Studio with no problem. When you close the window you get an error telling you that there is an open transaction, and asking you if you would like to Commit the transaction. Which syntax should you change the stored procedure to?

    A.

```
CREATE PROCEDURE …

BEGIN TRANSACTION

        UPDATE …

        BEGIN TRANSACTION

                UPDATE …

        BEGIN TRANSACTION

                UPDATE …

COMMIT

GO
```

    B.

```
CREATE PROCEDURE …

BEGIN TRANSACTION

        UPDATE …

        BEGIN TRANSACTION

                UPDATE …

        COMMIT

        BEGIN TRANSACTION

                UPDATE …

COMMIT

GO
```

C.

```
CREATE PROCEDURE ...
BEGIN TRANSACTION
        UPDATE ...
        BEGIN TRANSACTION
                UPDATE ...
        COMMIT
        BEGIN TRANSACTION
                UPDATE ...
COMMIT
GO
```

D.

```
CREATE PROCEDURE ...
BEGIN TRANSACTION
        UPDATE ...
        BEGIN TRANSACTION
                UPDATE ...
        COMMIT
        BEGIN TRANSACTION
                UPDATE ...
        COMMIT
COMMIT
GO
```

6. You are writing a stored procedure, and you have noticed that at times your query is being blocked. You would prefer not to change the transaction isolation level for the entire transaction. Normally you would change the transaction isolation level to READ UNCOMMITTED. What table locking hint will give you the same result?

A. TABLOCK

B. NOLOCK

C. NOWAIT

D. ROWLOCK

7. Your application is taking different locks than when you run the same T/SQL statements on your workstation's SQL Server Management Studio compared to the client application. You realize that this is because you have changed the transaction isolation level that your Management Studio uses when connecting to the SQL Server. The application uses the default transaction isolation level. What transaction isolation level should you set Management Studio to?

   A. READ UNCOMMITTED

   B. READ COMMITTED

   C. REPEATABLE READ

   D. SERIALIZABLE

   E. SNAPSHOT

8. Which of the follow statements is valid syntax for creating a transaction?

   A.

   ```
   BEGIN TRANS
   ...
                   COMMIT
   ```

   B.

   ```
   BEGIN TRANSCT
   ...
                   COMMIT
   ```

   C.

   ```
   BEGIN TRAN
   ...
                   COMMIT
   ```

   D.

   ```
   BGN TRN
   ...
                   COMMIT
   ```

9. You are writing a SQL stored procedure that has a single large transaction. You want to ensure that the transaction is healthy before you attempt to commit the transaction. What function should you query?

   A. XACT_STATE

   B. XACT_ABORT

   C. @@TOTAL_ERRORS

   D. @@TRANCOUNT

10. When DDL is run against a table, all access to that table is blocked. What kind of lock is taken against that object when the DDL is executed until the transaction is committed?

    A. Exclusive

    B. Intent exclusive

    C. Schema modification

    D. Schema stability

11. You wish to examine the current blocking that is happening with the database server. What DMV should you query to see which sessions are blocking which sessions?

    A. sys.dm_exec_requests

    B. sys.dm_exec_sessions

    C. sys.dm_exec_procedure_stats

    D. sys.dm_exec_connections

12. You are writing a large T/SQL script. You want to ensure that if any statement within the transaction fails, all statements are rolled back. What setting should you set to ON?

    A. XACT_STATE

    B. XACT_ABORT

    C. @@TOTAL_ERRORS

    D. @@TRANCOUNT

13. You are using the *XACT_STATE* function to ensure that the transaction is healthy before you commit the transaction. What value from the *XACT_STATE* function indicates that the transaction is no longer healthy?

    A. 1

    B. 0

    C. −1

14. You are writing a complex stored procedure with several layers of nested transactions. This is causing problems as sometimes the stored procedure exists with transactions still open. What function can you use to determine if there are transactions that are still open?

    A. `XACT_STATE`

    B. `XACT_ABORT`

    C. `@@TOTAL_ERRORS`

    D. `@@TRANCOUNT`

15. You are writing a maintenance stored procedure and you need to ensure that no other transactions are able to access some tables in the database while the maintenance is being performed. You do not want to change the isolation level of the transaction. What is the most efficient method to use?

    A. Write *SELECT* statements against the tables you wish to lock, then perform your maintenance.

    B. Write *UPDATE* statements against the tables you wish to lock, then perform your maintenance.

    C. Use the *sp_getapplock* procedure to take exclusive locks against the tables in question, then perform your maintenance. After your maintenance use *sp_releaseapplock* to release the locks.

16. Which statement is used to create multistatement transactions without requiring the use of the *BEGIN TRANSACTION* statement?

    A. `SET TRANSACTION ISOLATION LEVEL`

    B. `SET IMPLICIT_TRANSACTIONS`

    C. `SET XACT_ABORT`

    D. `SET XACT_STATE`

17. The *TRUNCATE TABLE* statement is a minimally logged operation, but it still takes a lock on the table being truncated. What type of lock does it take?

    A. Exclusive

    B. Update

    C. Bulk update

    D. Schema modification

18. You are looking to set the *DEADLOCK_PRIORITY* of a transaction, so that if it is involved in a deadlock with another transaction this transaction is the losing transaction. What setting should you use to ensure that this transaction is the one which is killed?

    A. `SET DEADLOCK PRIORITY LOW`

    B. `SET DEADLOCK PRIORITY MEDIUM`

    C. `SET DEADLOCK PRIORITY HIGH`

    D. `SET DEADLOCK PRIORITY 0`

19. When you execute an update statement against a SQL Server table, what locks are taken?

    A. An update lock is taken.

    B. An intent update lock is taken, and then an intent exclusive lock is taken.

    C. A shared lock is taken, and then an update lock is taken.

    D. An exclusive lock is taken.

20. What lock is taken against objects while statements are being compiled?

    A. Shared

    B. Intent shared

    C. Schema stability

    D. Schema modification

Self Test Quick Answer Key

1. **C**

2. **A**

3. **B**

4. **D**

5. **D**

6. **B**

7. **B**

8. **C**

9. **A**

10. **C**

11. **A**

12. **B**

13. **C**

14. **D**

15. **C**

16. **B**

17. **D**

18. **A**

19. **B**

20. **C**

Chapter 7

MCTS SQL Server 2008 Exam 433

Working with DML Queries

Exam objectives in this chapter:

- Using the *INSERT* Statement
- Using the *UPDATE* Statement
- Using the *DELETE* Statement
- Using the *MERGE* Statement

Exam objectives review:

- ☑ Summary of Exam Objectives
- ☑ Exam Objectives Fast Track
- ☑ Exam Objectives Frequently Asked Questions
- ☑ Self Test
- ☑ Self Test Quick Answer Key

Introduction

As part of developing and using SQL Server databases, you will often need to insert, modify, and delete data in SQL Server tables. Data Manipulation Language, or DML, is the part of the Transact-SQL language that allows you to perform these operations. In this chapter we will examine the core statements that comprise DML, and the best practices to apply when using them.

To correctly modify table data, you must be familiar with *INSERT*, *UPDATE*, *DELETE*, and *MERGE* DML statements. We will examine these statements in depth as they are mapped directly to the exam objectives. The *MERGE* statement is new in SQL Server 2008. It allows you to insert, update, and delete data in a table, based on a comparison with a source set of rows. You could replace the *MERGE* statement functionality by individual *INSERT*, *UPDATE*, and *DELETE* statements. However, the single *MERGE* statement is more efficient. We will examine the syntax and capabilities of the *MERGE* statement in detail.

DML statements always succeed or fail as a whole. For example, if you were inserting 1,000 records into a table, but one violated a *PRIMARY KEY* or *UNIQUE constraint*, all 1,000 rows would roll back and nothing would be inserted. If a *DELETE* statement violated a *FOREIGN KEY constraint*, even on one row, the entire *DELETE* statement would fail and nothing would be deleted. You will never have a partial result set from a DML statement.

TEST DAY TIP

Remember that DML statements commit as a whole, or not at all.

When preparing for the exam, ensure that you have practiced using all DML statements, and have achieved a good understanding of the DML syntax. The AdventureWorks sample database is a great tool for learning Transact-SQL without the risk of damaging your live databases. Exercises in this chapter are based on the AdventureWorks database. Perform all exercises to get hands-on experience in writing and executing DML queries.

Using the *INSERT* Statement

The *INSERT* statement adds new rows into a table. The following variations of the *INSERT* statement are most commonly used:

- **INSERT...VALUES** Insert a list of data values into an existing table.

- **INSERT...SELECT** Insert the result of an inline query into an existing table.

- **INSERT...EXECUTE** Insert the results of a stored procedure into a new table.

- **INSERT TOP** Insert a specified number, or percent of rows from a query using the *TOP* clause.

- **SELECT...INTO** Use this statement to create a new table based on query results. Although this is not technically an *INSERT* statement, we will learn about the *SELECT...INTO* statement, as it often is confused with the *SELECT* statement.

You can use the flowchart in Figure 7.1 to select the most appropriate *INSERT* statement syntax.

Figure 7.1 Writing an *INSERT* Statement

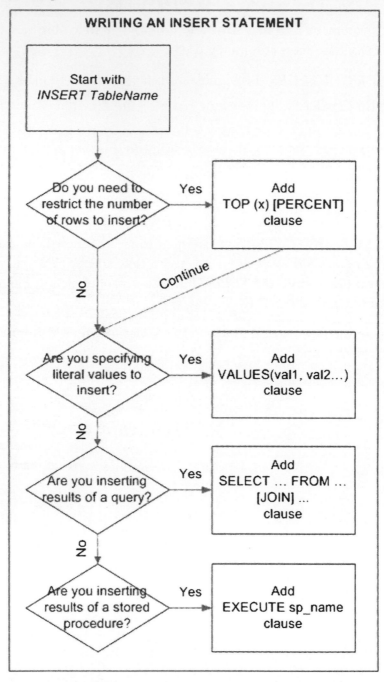

Using the *INSERT* Statement with the *VALUES* Clause

Let's examine the basic syntax of the *INSERT…VALUES* statement. The following elements are required for a properly constructed *INSERT* statement.

INSERT…VALUES Statement—Core Elements

```
INSERT [INTO] table_or_view [(comma separated list of column names)]
VALUES ({data_value | DEFAULT | NULL | Scalar Expression}, …n), [...n]
```

In this statement, the *INSERT* keyword is required. The *INTO* keyword is optional, and it makes no difference whether it is specified or not. The *INTO* keyword is considered a "noise" word.

The *table_or_view* is the name of the table or view into which you wish to insert the data. As well as tables and views, you can also use a table-valued variable. If you are using a view for your *INSERT* statement, it must be updateable. Updateable views are based upon a single table. You could insert data into a multitable view, as long as you specify columns from only one base table as the *column_list*.

The *column_list* is the list of columns from the table or view into which you will be inserting values. You can completely omit the *column_list* if you want, but SQL Server will assume that you will provide values for all columns in the table, and in the order they are defined in the table. Using the column list, you can provide values for a subset of columns only. The columns you do not include in the list will receive their default values. You can specify columns in a different order as they are defined in the table, as long as the order of the values you are inserting matches the order of the columns you are inserting into.

VALUES is a keyword that specifies the list of literal values to insert. The *VALUES* clause essentially creates an in-memory set of rows out of the listed values. You can use a single *VALUES* clause to insert up to 1,000 rows of values. Within the actual list of values you can specify the following:

- **Data_value** A literal data value of the type corresponding to a column type; for example, a varchar or an integer value. The value must be of the same data type as the column you are inserting into, or be a data type that can be implicitly converted to the column's data type.

- **DEFAULT** Tells the INSERT statement to insert the default value for that column. If the column does not have a default associated with it, a null value is inserted.

- **NULL** Tells the *INSERT* statement to explicitly insert a NULL value into the column, regardless of the default.

- **Scalar_Expression** A single-valued variable, subquery, function, or another expression. Results of the expression will be inserted. The resultant value must be of the same data type as the column you are inserting into, or be a data type that can be implicitly converted to the column's data type.

Sometimes, the *INSERT* statement needs to be modified to accommodate certain types of columns, like IDENTITY columns and GUID columns that may use NEWID as the default value. When these types of columns are configured with default values, it is recommended that the *INSERT* statement simply omits the columns, and does not specify a value for these columns. We will discuss these special cases later in this chapter. Under no circumstances can you insert values into computed columns. If you attempt to insert values into a computed column, an error will be raised.

In Example 7.1 we will insert a single row into the Sales.Currency table using the *VALUES* clause. This example does not specify column names, so all the columns in the Currency table are used, and column values are specified by the *VALUES* clause in the same order as they are defined in the table.

Example 7.1 Inserting a Single Row Using *VALUES* Clause

```
USE AdventureWorks
GO
INSERT Sales.Currency
VALUES ('ZZZ', 'Unspecified Currency', GETDATE())
GO
```

Note that this statement would have failed, if the Currency table had more than three columns. This is why it is a best practice to specify the column list explicitly. This is useful maintainability. You are able to add an extra column to the table, without affecting your stored procedures that use the *INSERT* statement.

EXAM WARNING

Always choose to specify column names, as this helps avoid issues in the future when the column structure changes.

In Example 7.2 we will insert three rows of values into the HumanResources. Departments table, specifying the list of columns. The Departments table contains DepartmentID, Name, GroupName, and ModifiedDate columns, in that order. The example *INSERT* statement omits the DepartmentID column, so the next *IDENTITY* value for the table is used. The example also lists GroupName, Name, and ModifiedDate columns. The order of columns is different from the column order in the table, but the *INSERT* statement will still work, because we have explicitly listed the columns, and specified column values in the correct order.

Example 7.2 Inserting Multiple Rows Using *VALUES* Clause

```
INSERT HumanResources.Department (GroupName, Name, ModifiedDate)
VALUES
('Executive General and Administration', 'Database Administration',
GETDATE()),
('Inventory Management', 'Stock Control', GETDATE()),
('Executive General and Administration', 'Legal', GETDATE())
```

EXAM WARNING

When dealing with an IDENTITY column, it is best to omit it from the column list altogether. Omitting the column will ensure that the next *IDENTITY* value is inserted into the column. This helps avoid the *error* "Cannot insert explicit value for identity column in table 'Department' when *IDENTITY_INSERT* is set to OFF." We will discuss the IDENTITY_INSERT option in the next chapter.

Using the *INSERT...SELECT* Statement to Insert Query Results into a Table

Sometimes, instead of the list of values, you may wish to insert results of a subquery into your existing table. In this case, you will not use the *VALUES* clause. Instead of the *VALUES* clause you will use the *INSERT* statement with the *SELECT* clause. Here are the core elements of the *INSERT...SELECT* statement.

```
INSERT [INTO] table_or_view [(comma separated list of column names)]
derived_table
```

The *derived_table* is a result of a *SELECT* statement that returns a list of rows. The list of rows returned must have the same structure as the columns specified in the *INSERT* statement. There must be the same number of columns returned, and they must have the same data types. The following example demonstrates the use of the *INSERT* statement with a *SELECT* subquery.

In Example 7.3, we will create a Colors table to store color values. We will then use a *SELECT* statement to select all individual colors from the Production.Product table. We will restrict the result set for non-null values and sort them in alphabetical order. The entire *SELECT* statement will evaluate first, and the resultant set of rows will be inserted into the Colors table. If the *SELECT* statement returned more than one column, or the column returned by the query was of a different data type, the *INSERT* statement will fail.

Example 7.3 Inserting Rows Using a *SELECT* Subquery

```
CREATE TABLE dbo.Colors
(ColorID int IDENTITY NOT NULL PRIMARY KEY,
Color nvarchar(15))
GO
INSERT Colors
SELECT DISTINCT Color
FROM
Production.Product
WHERE Color is not NULL
ORDER BY Color
GO
SELECT * FROM Colors
```

Using the *INSERT* Statement with the *EXECUTE* Clause

The *EXECUTE* keyword allows you to execute a stored procedure, or to interpret a string as a Transact-SQL command, and execute the resultant command. If you wish to insert results of a stored procedure into a table, you must use the *EXECUTE* clause. Two correct uses of the *INSERT…EXECUTE* statement are shown in Examples 7.4 and 7.5. Both examples use the Colors table we created in an earlier example.

Example 7.4 *INSERT* Statement with the *EXECUTE* Clause (Stored Procedure)

```
CREATE PROC GetMostPopularColors
AS
SELECT Color
FROM Production.Product
JOIN Sales.SalesOrderDetail
ON Production.Product.ProductID = Sales.SalesOrderDetail.ProductID
WHERE Color is not null
GROUP BY Color Having COUNT(*) > 10000
GO
INSERT Colors (Color)
EXECUTE GetMostPopularColors
GO
```

Example 7.5 *INSERT* Statement with the *EXECUTE* Clause (Inline Command)

```
INSERT Colors (Color)
EXECUTE ('SELECT "Orange" as Color')
GO
```

In Example 7.4, we have created a stored procedure named *GetMostPopularColors*. This procedure returns colors of products that have been ordered more than 10,000 times. We will then use the results to populate the Colors table using *INSERT... EXECUTE*. In Example 7.5 we have created an inline string statement that simply selects the color Orange in the color column. Use the *INSERT...EXECUTE (inline_statement)* to treat the text as a command and execute it, and then insert the execution results into the Colors table.

Test Day Tip

Remember to use parentheses (round brackets) with the *EXECUTE* statement around the inline command text. If you forget the parentheses, you will get an error similar to this: *Msg 102, Level 15, State 1, Line 2. Incorrect syntax near 'SELECT 'Orange' as Color'.*

Using the *INSERT* Statement with the *TOP* Expression

Sometimes you may wish to restrict the number of rows inserted into a table using the *INSERT* statement. Usually you would use the *TOP* (*n*) or the *TOP* (*n*) *PERCENT* clause to achieve this. The *TOP* (*n*) clause specifies that only the first *n* number of rows returned from the query result should be inserted using the *INSERT* statement. *TOP* (*n*) *PERCENT* is similar, except instead of specifying a numeric value you specify a percentage of the rows to be inserted. Often the *ORDER BY* clause is included in the *SELECT* query, so the rows are sorted before the top rows are identified.

TEST DAY TIP

You can use the *TOP* expression in exactly the same way with all DML statements: *INSERT, UPDATE, DELETE,* and *MERGE.* You can also use it with the *SELECT* statement. However, you can only use the *WITH TIES* expression with the *SELECT* statement.

The syntax for using the *TOP* expression with the *INSERT* statement is shown in Example 7.6.

Example 7.6 *INSERT TOP...SELECT* Statement—Core Elements

```
INSERT table_name
TOP (n) [PERCENT]
[WITH TIES]
SELECT ... FROM ... [JOIN...][WHERE...]
```

Here, *n* is the numeric value that specifies the number of rows to be returned. You must surround this value in parentheses when using the *TOP* expression with the *INSERT* statement. For backward compatibility, you can still use the *TOP* expression without parentheses, but in *SELECT* statements only. It is not recommended to call the *TOP* expression without the parentheses. If you specify an *ORDER BY* clause for your query, the top *n* rows are returned in that order. If your query does not use *ORDER BY*, the order of the rows is arbitrary.

If you specify the optional *PERCENT* keyword, the numeric value *n* will be treated as a percentage.

The *WITH TIES* keyword can be used only in *SELECT* statements. When specified, if there are rows that have the same values as the rows included in the top *n* set, they will be included also. Consequently, your result set may contain more rows than the actual *n* specified.

In Example 7.7 we will create a table called SickLeave containing EmployeeID, FullName, and SickLeaveHours columns. We will insert the information about the top 10 percent of employees with the most sick leave hours into this table. We will also insert 20 employees who have taken the least number of sick leave hours into this table (see Example 7.8).

Example 7.7 Using the *INSERT TOP (n) PERCENT* Statement

```
CREATE TABLE dbo.SickLeave
(EmployeeID int, FullName nvarchar(100), SickLeaveHours int)
GO
INSERT TOP (10) PERCENT
SickLeave
SELECT
EmployeeID, FirstName + ' ' + LastName, SickLeaveHours
FROM Person.Contact JOIN HumanResources.Employee
ON Person.Contact.ContactID = HumanResources.Employee.ContactID
ORDER BY SickLeaveHours DESC
-- Comment: 29 rows affected
```

Example 7.8 Using the *INSERT TOP (n)* Statement

```
INSERT TOP (20)
SickLeave
SELECT
EmployeeID, FirstName + ' ' + LastName, SickLeaveHours
FROM Person.Contact JOIN HumanResources.Employee
ON Person.Contact.ContactID = HumanResources.Employee.ContactID
ORDER BY SickLeaveHours ASC
-- Comment: 20 rows affected
```

Configuring & Implementing…

Generating a Random Sample

Sometimes we are asked to produce a random sample of rows from a particular table, and insert them into another table. One way to do this is to use the *TOP* (n) [PERCENT] expression, along with the *NEWID()* function. The *NEWID()* function produces a globally unique identifier (GUID) that is so close to random it can be treated as such. Sorting by the *NEWID()* function generates a GUID for each row. You can then use the *TOP* clause to take a certain number or percentage of rows.

In Example 7.9 we will create a table named SurveySample, which has a FullName column. We will then use the technique described here to insert 10 random employee names into the SurveySample table.

This method should not be used with large tables (millions of rows), as the results will take a very long time to return, and the query will consume a large amount of memory. In these cases you should use an expression like *ABS(CAST((BINARY_CHECKSUM(key_column, NEWID())) as int)) % 100) < n* in the *WHERE* clause. This expression generates a random number between 0 and 99 for each row, then selects only those rows whose random number is under a specified percentage.

Example 7.9 Generating a Random Sample of 10 Employees

```
CREATE TABLE SurveySample (FullName nvarchar(200))
GO
INSERT TOP(10)
SurveySample
SELECT
FirstName + ' ' + LastName
FROM Person.Contact JOIN HumanResources.Employee
ON Person.Contact.ContactID = HumanResources.Employee.ContactID
ORDER BY NEWID()
```

Head of the Class…

Using *SELECT… INTO* vs. *INSERT INTO…SELECT*

Many confuse *SELECT…INTO* with *INSERT INTO…SELECT*. These statements are not equivalent. You have learned that *INSERT INTO…SELECT* is a form of the *INSERT* statement that allows you to run a query, and insert rows returned by this query into an existing table. The row structure, specifically the number, and data types of columns, must be the same for the *INSERT INTO…SELECT*. Remember that the *INTO* keyword is an optional keyword that has no impact. It can be omitted. Here is an example of *INSERT INTO…SELECT*.

```
INSERT INTO dbo.Table1

SELECT * FROM dbo.Table2
```

The *SELECT…INTO* statement may look similar, but it performs an entirely different function. This statement executes the query specified in the *SELECT* statement, and then creates a *new table* with the table name specified in the *INTO* clause. The new table will have the same number of columns as those returned by the query, and the columns will have the same data types. The new table will not have any constraints or defaults associated with it. The *SELECT…INTO* statement is a quick way to generate a new table with a subset of rows from a query. Don't try to use it, however, to insert rows into an existing table—you will get an error. Here is an example of *SELECT…INTO*.

```
SELECT * FROM dbo.Table2

INTO dbo.NewTable
```

In summary, use the *SELECT…INTO* statement to produce a *new table* based on results of a query. Use the *INSERT INTO…SELECT* (or simply *INSERT…SELECT*) to insert rows returned by a query into an *existing table*.

EXERCISE 7.1

USING THE *INSERT* STATEMENT

In this exercise, we will practice using the *INSERT* statement in various scenarios.

Before you begin, you must have the following software installed on your computer:

- SQL Server 2008 (a free trial is available for download)
- AdventureWorks sample database

We will be adding rows to the Purchasing.ShipMethod table in the AdventureWorks database.

1. Open SQL Server Management Studio. Click *Start | All Programs | Microsoft SQL Server 2008 | SQL Server Management Studio*.

2. Create a new query against the AdventureWorks database.

3. Create an *INSERT* statement to insert two rows into Purchasing.ShipMethod with the values listed in Table 7.1.

Table 7.1 Values for Purchasing.ShipMethod Table

	Name	ShipBase	ShipRate
Row1	INTERNATIONAL EXPRESS	25.00	2.50
Row2	INTERNATIONAL VALUE SHIPPING	15.00	2.00

4. Write and execute your statement.

Use the *INSERT* statement to add two extra rows to Purchasing.ShipMethod:

```
- View the data and structure of Purchasing.ShipMethod
SELECT * From Purchasing.ShipMethod
GO

-- Insert two rows into Purchasing.ShipMethod
INSERT Purchasing.ShipMethod(Name, ShipBase, ShipRate)
VALUES
('INTERNATIONAL EXPRESS', 25.00, 2.50),
```

```
('INTERNATIONAL VALUE SHIPPING', 15.00, 2.00)
GO

-- View the new rows in Purchasing.ShipMethod. Note that the
ShipMethodID, rowguid and ModifiedDate columns receive their default
values
SELECT * From Purchasing.ShipMethod
GO
```

Next, we will be using the Production.ProductReview table from the AdventureWorks database. Familiarize yourself with the table structure.

1. Find out the relationships between Person.Contact, Sales. SalesOrderDetail, and Sales.SalesOrderHeader. You may find it helpful to create a diagram, mapping these relationships.

2. Create an *INSERT* statement to insert reviews from customers who have placed the top 10 order lines by their LineTotal.

3. Use Table 7.2 to obtain the necessary column values.

Table 7.2 Column Values for Production.ProductReview Table

ProductReview Column	Value to Insert	Originating Table
ProductID	*ProductID*	SalesOrderDetail
ReviewerName	*FirstName + ' ' + LastName*	Contact
ReviewDate	*Today's date*	None
EmailAddress	*EmailAddress*	Contact
Rating	*5*	None
Comment	*'Great product!!!'*	None

Use the *INSERT...SELECT* statement to add 10 rows to the Production. ProductReview table based on results of a query:

```
-- View the data and structure of Production.ProductReview
SELECT * From Production.ProductReview
GO

-- Select ProductID, Full Name (First Name + ' ' + LastName) as
ReviewerName, today's date as ReviewDate, EMailAddress, 5 as rating and
'Great Product!!!' as comment. Insert the top 10 records, with highest
LineTotal into Production.ProductReview.
```

```
INSERT

TOP (10)

Production.ProductReview(ProductID, ReviewerName, ReviewDate,
EmailAddress, Rating, Comments)

SELECT SalesOrderDetail.ProductID, Contact.FirstName + ' ' + Contact.
LastName, GETDATE(), Contact.EmailAddress, 5, 'Great Product!!!'

FROM Sales.SalesOrderDetail JOIN Sales.SalesOrderHeader

ON SalesOrderDetail.SalesOrderID = SalesOrderHeader.SalesOrderID

JOIN Person.Contact ON Contact.ContactID = SalesOrderHeader.ContactID

ORDER BY SalesOrderDetail.LineTotal DESC

GO

-- View the data and structure of Production.ProductReview

SELECT * From Production.ProductReview

GO
```

Using the *UPDATE* Statement

The *UPDATE* statement updates existing rows in an existing table or updateable
view. Let's examine the syntax of the *UPDATE* statement. The elements shown in
Example 7.10 appear most commonly in the *UPDATE* statement.

Example 7.10 *UPDATE* Statement—Core Elements

```
UPDATE
    [ TOP (n) [PERCENT] ]
table_or_view
SET
{ column_to_update = { new_value | DEFAULT | NULL }
| column_to_update { .WRITE (new_value, @Offset, @Length ) }
| @variable = new_value
| @variable = column_to_update = new_value
| column_to_update { += | -= | *= | /= | %= | &= | ^= | |= } new_value
| @variable { += | -= | *= | /= | %= | &= | ^= | |= } new_value
| @variable = column_to_update { += | -= | *= | /= | %= | &= | ^= | |= } new_
value }
[FROM ...
WHERE ... ]
```

The *table_or_view* is the name of the table or view in which you are updating rows. If you are using a view for your *UPDATE* statement, this view must be updateable. Updateable views are based upon a single source table. You could also substitute a table-valued variable as the *table_or_view*.

The *TOP (n) [PERCENT]* clause serves the same purpose as it does in the *INSERT* statement. Only the top *n*, or top *n* percent of rows will be updated, if this clause is specified. For a detailed description of the *TOP* expression, see "Using the *INSERT* Statement with the *TOP* Expression" earlier in this chapter.

The *SET* keyword specifies the list of columns or variables that will be updated. The *column_to_update* is the name of the column containing the data that should be changed. *Column_to_update* must be a column from the *table_or_view*. Identity columns cannot be updated.

The *new_value* is a literal value, a variable, a subselect statement (enclosed within parentheses), or any scalar expression. When the *UPDATE* statement completes, the *column_to_update* or *@variable* value will be set to the *new_value*.

The *FROM* is essentially the filter criteria for defining what data should be updated, and what it should be updated to. If this part of the *UPDATE* statement is omitted, all data in the table or view will be updated. Ensure that you specify an alias if the table or view you are trying to update is mentioned more than once in the *FROM* clause.

The *WHERE* clause specifies an additional filter for data that should be updated.

Exam Warning

Always include a *WHERE* clause in the *UPDATE* statement. Otherwise, data in the entire table will be updated indiscriminately.

The column can be set to its new value using not just the familiar equals to (=) operator, but also a variety of other assignment operators. Table 7.3 lists assignment operators available. Use these operators with the *SET* clause of the *UPDATE* statement.

Table 7.3 Assignment Operators

Operator Sign	Use
=	Assign
+=	Add and assign
−=	Subtract and assign
*=	Multiply and assign
/=	Divide and assign
%=	Modulo and assign
&=	Bitwise AND and assign
ˆ=	Bitwise XOR and assign
|=	Bitwise OR and assign

UPDATE Statement Examples

Examples 7.11 through 7.13 demonstrate the most common uses of the *UPDATE* statement. Feel free to run these examples against the AdventureWorks database. Performing the examples yourself will give you a better understanding of how the *UPDATE* statement is used.

Exam Warning

When a view has an *INSTEAD OF UPDATE* trigger registered with it, you cannot use the *UPDATE* statement with the *FROM* clause on this view.

Example 7.11 Using the *UPDATE...SET...WHERE* Statement

```
SELECT DISTINCT Color from Production.Product
GO

--Change all product with NULL color to show 'N/A'
USE AdventureWorks
GO
```

```
UPDATE Production.Product

SET Color = 'N/A'

WHERE

Color is NULL

GO

SELECT DISTINCT Color from Production.Product

GO
```

Example 7.12 Using the
UPDATE...SET...FROM...WHERE Statement with Ambiguous Table Names

```
-- List all employees managed by David Bradley, along with their vacation
hours

SELECT Employee.VacationHours, Person.Contact.FirstName + ' ' + Person.
Contact.LastName as EmployeeName,

ManagerContact.FirstName + ' ' + ManagerContact.LastName as ManagerName

FROM HumanResources.Employee

join Person.Contact ON HumanResources.Employee.ContactID = Person.Contact.
ContactID

join HumanResources.Employee as Manager ON HumanResources.Employee.ManagerID =
Manager.EmployeeID

join Person.Contact as ManagerContact ON Manager.ContactID = ManagerContact.
ContactID

WHERE ManagerContact.FirstName = 'David' AND ManagerContact.LastName =
'Bradley'

GO

-- Add 10 vacation hours to all employees managed by David Bradley

UPDATE Humanresources.Employee

SET VacationHours += 10

FROM HumanResources.Employee

join Person.Contact ON HumanResources.Employee.ContactID = Person.Contact.
ContactID

join HumanResources.Employee as Manager ON HumanResources.Employee.ManagerID =
Manager.EmployeeID

join Person.Contact as ManagerContact ON Manager.ContactID = ManagerContact.
ContactID

WHERE ManagerContact.FirstName = 'David' AND ManagerContact.LastName =
'Bradley'

GO
```

```
-- List all employees managed by David Bradley, along with their vacation
hours
-- Ensure that the hours have been updated by the previous statement
SELECT Employee.VacationHours, Person.Contact.FirstName + ' ' + Person.
Contact.LastName as EmployeeName,
ManagerContact.FirstName + ' ' + ManagerContact.LastName as ManagerName
FROM HumanResources.Employee
join Person.Contact ON HumanResources.Employee.ContactID = Person.Contact.
ContactID
join HumanResources.Employee as Manager ON HumanResources.Employee.ManagerID =
Manager.EmployeeID
join Person.Contact as ManagerContact ON Manager.ContactID = ManagerContact.
ContactID
WHERE ManagerContact.FirstName = 'David' AND ManagerContact.LastName =
'Bradley'
GO
```

Example 7.13 Using the
UPDATE...SET...FROM...WHERE Statement with Ambiguous Table Names

```
-- Show all products by cost, only from subcategies that contains 'Bikes'
-- Show the ListPrice for each Product
SELECT Product.Name, Product.StandardCost, Product.ListPrice,
ProductSubcategory.Name
FROM Production.Product JOIN Production.ProductSubcategory
ON ProductSubcategory.ProductSubcategoryID = Product.ProductSubcategoryID
WHERE ProductSubcategory.Name like '%Bikes%'
ORDER BY Product.StandardCost DESC
GO

-- Increase the ListPrice by 20% for the 10 highest-cost products, from
subcategies that contains 'Bikes'
UPDATE Production.Product
SET Product.ListPrice *= 1.15
WHERE Product.ProductID in
(SELECT TOP (10) ProductID
FROM Production.Product JOIN Production.ProductSubcategory
ON ProductSubcategory.ProductSubcategoryID = Product.ProductSubcategoryID
WHERE ProductSubcategory.Name like '%Bikes%'
```

```
ORDER BY Product.StandardCost DESC)

GO

-- Show the ListPrice for each Product after the Increase

SELECT Product.Name, Product.StandardCost, Product.ListPrice,
ProductSubcategory.Name

FROM Production.Product JOIN Production.ProductSubcategory

ON ProductSubcategory.ProductSubcategoryID = Product.ProductSubcategoryID

WHERE ProductSubcategory.Name like '%Bikes%'

ORDER BY Product.StandardCost DESC

GO
```

EXAM WARNING

Remember that you cannot use the *ORDER BY* clause directly with the *UPDATE* statement. Instead use the *WHERE ID_Column in (SELECT TOP (n) ID_Column FROM ...)* statement.

Understanding the *Column.WRITE* Expression

SQL Server 2008 provides a capability to append or insert text into existing text columns as part of the *UPDATE* statement. This is achieved using the *column. WRITE* expression. Let's examine the *column.WRITE* expression in more detail. The elements of the *column.WRITE* statement are shown in Example 7.14.

Example 7.14 *UPDATE...SET Column.WRITE(...)* Statement—Core Elements

```
UPDATE table_or_view
column_to_update { .WRITE (new_value, @Offset, @Length ) }
[FROM ...
WHERE ... ]
```

The *column.WRITE* statement tells SQL Server to append, remove, or insert text into the existing text value in *column_name* (see Example 7.15). The *@Length* characters starting from *@Offset* of *column_name* are replaced with the *new_value*. If the *new_value* is set to *NULL*, *@Length* is ignored, and the value in *column_name* is truncated at the specified *@Offset*. Only columns of varchar(max), nvarchar(max), or varbinary(max) can be specified with this clause. When using the *.WRITE* method, you cannot qualify the *column_name* with a table name or table alias.

@Offset is the number of characters after which the *new_value* replaces the existing characters. If *@Offset* is *NULL*, the *new_value* will be appended to the end of the column, regardless of the *@Length* parameter. If *@Offset* is larger than the length of the column value, the operation will fail, and an error will be reported.

@Length is the number of characters to be replaced by the *new_value*. If *@Length* is *NULL*, the update operation removes all data from *@Offset* to the end of the *column_name* value.

Example 7.15 Using the *Column.WRITE* Statement

```
USE AdventureWorks
GO
-- Create a new table to hold advertising copy
CREATE TABLE AdvertisingCopy (AdvertisementName nvarchar(100),
AdvertisementText varchar(max))
GO

INSERT AdvertisingCopy VALUES
('Reflector', 'Be seen at night.')
GO
SELECT * FROM AdvertisingCopy
GO
-- AdvertisementText is 'Be seen at night.'

UPDATE AdvertisingCopy
SET AdvertisementText .WRITE(' by traffic coming behind you.', 16, 30)
WHERE AdvertisementName = 'Reflector'
SELECT * FROM AdvertisingCopy
GO
-- AdvertisementText is 'Be seen at night by traffic coming behind you.'

UPDATE AdvertisingCopy
SET AdvertisementText .WRITE('The most advanced reflector ever. ', 0, 0)
WHERE AdvertisementName = 'Reflector'
SELECT * FROM AdvertisingCopy
GO
-- AdvertisementText is 'The most advanced reflector ever. Be seen at night
by traffic coming behind you.'

UPDATE AdvertisingCopy
SET AdvertisementText .WRITE(Null, 34, NULL)
```

```
WHERE AdvertisementName = 'Reflector'

SELECT * FROM AdvertisingCopy

GO

-- AdvertisementText is 'The most advanced reflector ever.'

UPDATE AdvertisingCopy

SET AdvertisementText .WRITE('(Well, sort of...).', 28, NULL)

WHERE AdvertisementName = 'Reflector'

SELECT * FROM AdvertisingCopy

GO

-- AdvertisementText is 'The most advanced reflector (Well, sort of...).'
```

EXAM WARNING

Remember that only columns of varchar(max), nvarchar(max), or varbinary(max) can be specified with this clause. When using the *.WRITE* method, you cannot qualify the *column_name* with a table name or table alias.

EXERCISE 7.2

USING THE *UPDATE* STATEMENT

In this exercise, we will practice using the *UPDATE* statement.

Before you begin, you must have the following software installed on your computer:

- SQL Server 2008 (a free trial is available for download)
- AdventureWorks sample database

This exercise does not depend on you completing any previous exercises. We will be modifying rows in the Production.Product table in the AdventureWorks database.

1. Open SQL Server Management Studio. Click **Start | All Programs | Microsoft SQL Server 2008 | SQL Server Management Studio**.

2. Create a new query against the AdventureWorks database.

3. Examine and execute the following *SELECT* statement. This statement shows all rows with Road-350-W as the product model.

```
SELECT Product.Name, DiscontinuedDate, ProductModel.Name as Model
FROM Production.Product JOIN Production.ProductModel
ON Product.ProductModelID = ProductModel.ProductModelID
WHERE ProductModel.Name = 'Road-350-W'
ORDER BY DiscontinuedDate DESC
GO
```

4. Create and execute an *UPDATE* statement that will set *DiscontinuedDate* to today's date for all products with Road-350-W as the product model.

5. Use the *UPDATE* statement to discontinue all products of model Road-350-W:

```
UPDATE Production.Product
SET DiscontinuedDate = GETDATE()
FROM Production.Product JOIN Production.ProductModel
ON Product.ProductModelID = ProductModel.ProductModelID
WHERE ProductModel.Name = 'Road-350-W'
GO
```

6. Execute the *SELECT* statement again. Notice that the *DiscontinuedDate* has changed from NULL to today's date value.

TEST DAY TIP

To quickly memorize the syntax of the *UPDATE* statement, think "UPDATE table SET column = value FROM table WHERE condition." The verbs are UPDATE...SET...FROM...WHERE.

Using the *DELETE* Statement

The *DELETE* statement deletes existing rows from an existing table or updateable view based on a given criteria. Let's examine the syntax of the *DELETE* statement. The elements shown in Example 7.16 appear most commonly in the *DELETE* statement.

Example 7.16 *DELETE* Statement—Core Elements

```
DELETE
    [ TOP (n) [PERCENT] ]
[FROM ]table_or_view
[FROM …
WHERE … ]
```

The *table_or_view* is the name of the table or view from which you are deleting rows. If you are using a view for your *DELETE* statement, this view must be updateable. Updateable views are based upon a single source table. You could also substitute a table-valued variable like *table_or_view*.

The *TOP (n) [PERCENT]* clause serves the same purpose as it does in the *INSERT* and *UPDATE* statements. Only the top *n*, or top *n* percent of rows will be deleted if this clause is specified. For a detailed description of the *TOP* expression, see "Using the *INSERT* Statement with the TOP Expression" earlier in this chapter.

The *FROM* is the filter criteria for what data should be deleted. Ensure that you specify an alias if the table or view from which you are trying to delete is mentioned more than once in the *FROM* clause.

The *WHERE* clause specifies an additional filter for data that should be deleted.

EXAM WARNING

Always include a *WHERE* clause in the *DELETE* statement, even if it is arbitrary. Otherwise, all rows in the source table will be deleted.

DELETE Statement Examples

Example 7.17 demonstrates the most common uses of the *DELETE* statement. Feel free to run this example against the AdventureWorks database. Performing the example yourself will give you a better understanding of how the *DELETE* statement is used.

Example 7.17 Using the *DELETE* Statement

```
USE AdventureWorks
GO
-- Create a new table holding Product Name, SubcategoryID, SubCategory, Price
and Color
SELECT Production.Product.Name as ProductName,
```

```
Production.ProductSubcategory.ProductSubcategoryID as ProductSubCategoryID,

Production.ProductSubcategory.Name as ProductSubCategory,

Production.Product.ListPrice as Price,

Production.Product.Color as Color
INTO dbo.ProductAnalysis
FROM Production.Product JOIN Production.ProductSubcategory
ON Production.Product.ProductSubcategoryID = Production.ProductSubcategory.
ProductSubcategoryID
JOIN Production.ProductCategory
ON Production.ProductSubcategory.ProductCategoryID = Production.
ProductCategory.ProductCategoryID
GO

-- List the products in the ProductAnalysis table
SELECT * FROM ProductAnalysis
ORDER BY PRICE
GO

-- Delete all Products priced under $50
DELETE ProductAnalysis
WHERE Price < 50
-- List the products in the ProductAnalysis table
SELECT * FROM ProductAnalysis
ORDER BY PRICE
GO

-- List all products along with Category of Components
SELECT ProductAnalysis.ProductName, ProductCategory.Name as CategoryName,
ProductAnalysis.ProductSubCategory
FROM
ProductAnalysis JOIN Production.ProductSubcategory
ON ProductAnalysis.ProductSubcategoryID = Production.ProductSubcategory.
ProductSubcategoryID
JOIN Production.ProductCategory
ON Production.ProductSubcategory.ProductCategoryID = Production.
ProductCategory.ProductCategoryID
WHERE ProductCategory.Name = 'Components'
GO

-- Delete all products in the Category 'Components' from ProductAnalysis by
joinin ProductAnalysis table with Production.ProductCategory table via the
Production.ProductSubcategory table
```

```
DELETE ProductAnalysis

FROM

ProductAnalysis JOIN Production.ProductSubcategory

ON ProductAnalysis.ProductSubcategoryID = Production.ProductSubcategory.
ProductSubcategoryID

JOIN Production.ProductCategory

ON Production.ProductSubcategory.ProductCategoryID = Production.
ProductCategory.ProductCategoryID

WHERE ProductCategory.Name = 'Components'

GO

-- List all products along with Category of Components

SELECT ProductAnalysis.ProductName, ProductCategory.Name as CategoryName,
ProductAnalysis.ProductSubCategory

FROM

ProductAnalysis JOIN Production.ProductSubcategory

ON ProductAnalysis.ProductSubcategoryID = Production.ProductSubcategory.
ProductSubcategoryID

JOIN Production.ProductCategory

ON Production.ProductSubcategory.ProductCategoryID = Production.
ProductCategory.ProductCategoryID

WHERE ProductCategory.Name = 'Components'

GO
```

EXERCISE 7.3

USING THE *DELETE* STATEMENT

In this exercise, we will practice using the *DELETE* statement.

Before you begin, you must have the following software installed on your computer:

- SQL Server 2008 (a free trial is available for download)
- AdventureWorks sample database

This exercise does not depend on you completing any previous exercises. First, we will be deleting rows in the ProductionProductReview table in the AdventureWorks database.

1. Open SQL Server Management Studio. Click **Start | All Programs | Microsoft SQL Server 2008 | SQL Server Management Studio**.

2. Create a new query against the AdventureWorks database.

3. Execute the following *SELECT* statement. View the data and structure of the Production.ProductReview table. Take note of the number of rows in the table.

```
SELECT * From Production.ProductReview
GO
```

4. Create and execute a *DELETE* statement to delete all reviews from reviewers whose e-mail addresses end in "@fourthcoffee.com".

5. Use the *DELETE* statement to delete all reviews from people whose e-mail addresses end in "fourthcoffee.com".

```
DELETE Production.ProductReview
WHERE EmailAddress like '%@fourthcoffee.com'
```

6. Execute the *SELECT* statement from step 3 again. Have records been deleted?

Next, we will be using a *DELETE…FROM* statement to delete rows in the Production.ProductReview table based on results of a query.

1. Create a new query against the AdventureWorks database.

2. Find out the relationships between Production.ProductReview and Production.Product. You may find it helpful to create a diagram, mapping these relationships.

3. Create and execute a *DELETE* statement to delete all reviews for the product named HL Mountain Pedal. How many rows were affected?

4. Use the *DELETE* statement to delete all reviews for the HL Mountain Pedal Product.

```
DELETE Production.ProductReview
FROM Production.ProductReview JOIN Production.Product
ON ProductReview.ProductID = Product.ProductID
WHERE Product.Name = 'HL Mountain
```

Using the *MERGE* Statement

The *MERGE* statement is new in SQL Server 2008. It allows you to synchronize one table with another. This is achieved by performing *INSERT*, *UPDATE*, and *DELETE* operations on a target table based on the results of a join with a source table. Expect to be asked about the *MERGE* statement in the exam because it is a new feature of SQL Server 2008. The syntax elements shown in Example 7.18 appear most commonly in the *MERGE* statement.

Example 7.18 *MERGE* Statement—Core Elements

```
MERGE
     [ TOP (n) [PERCENT] ]
[INTO] target_table
USING source_table ON merge_search_condition
[WHEN MATCHED [AND search_condition] THEN
     matched_action]
[WHEN NOT MATCHED [BY TARGET] [AND search_condition] THEN
     Not_matched_by_target_action]
[WHEN NOT MATCHED BY SOURCE [AND search_condition] THEN
     Not_matched_by_source_action]
```

The *MERGE* keyword specifies that a *MERGE* operation is to be performed. The *target_table* is the table into which you will be merging the data. The *USING source_table* clause specifies the table or query from which you will be merging the data. You can also specify a *VALUES* expression as the source table. For more information about the *VALUES* expression see "Using the *INSERT* Statement with the *VALUES* Clause" earlier in this chapter. You must be able to join this table or query to the target table. This join between the source and target tables is how data matches will be established. You can alias both the source and destination tables using the *as* keyword. Although doing this is optional, this practice greatly helps the readability of your statement. Consider aliasing the target table as *tgt*, and the source table or query as *src*.

The *ON merge_search_condition* clause specifies the criteria of the join between the source and target tables. This join is how SQL Server determines whether the data in the destination table has been matched by the source table.

The *TOP (n) [PERCENT]* clause serves the same purpose as it does in the *INSERT*, *UPDATE*, and *DELETE* statements. If this clause is specified, only the top *n*, or top *n* percent of rows will be processed by the *MERGE* operation. For a detailed description of the *TOP* expression, see "Using the *INSERT* Statement with the *TOP* Expression" earlier in this chapter.

WHEN MATCHED, WHEN NOT MATCHED BY SOURCE, and *WHEN NOT MATCHED BY TARGET* specify the actions to be carried out when a match is established, or when data is found in one table that is not found in another. Valid actions are *UPDATE*, *INSERT*, and *DELETE* statements.

MERGE Statement Examples

Examples 7.19 through 7.21 demonstrate uses of the *MERGE* statement. We will start with a simpler example, then work our way through to more advanced examples. You can run any of these examples against the AdventureWorks database. Performing the examples yourself will give you a better understanding of how to use the *MERGE* statement.

Example 7.19 Using the *MERGE*
Statement to Insert, Update, and Delete Data

```
USE AdventureWorks

GO

-- Create two tables, Produce and Fruit. Insert values into the tables.
CREATE TABLE Produce (Name nvarchar(20), Price smallmoney)

GO

CREATE TABLE Fruit (Name nvarchar(20), Price smallmoney)

GO

INSERT Produce VALUES ('Milk', 2.4), ('Honey', 4.99), ('Apples', 3.99),
('Bread', 2.45), ('Pears', 4.00)

GO

INSERT Fruit VALUES ('Apples', 6.00), ('Pears', 7.00), ('Bananas', 4.95),
('Mandarins', 3.95), ('Oranges', 2.50)

GO

-- Show records in both tables. Note that some records (Apples and Pears) are
in Produce and in Fruit, but prices differ. There are some records in Produce
that are not in Fruit, and some in Fruit that are not in Produce.
SELECT * FROM Produce

GO

SELECT * FROM Fruit

GO

-- Use MERGE to update prices in Produce for those records that exist in
Fruit. Insert records from Fruit that are not in Produce. Delete any records
that are not in Fruit from Produce.
MERGE INTO Produce

USING Fruit

ON (Produce.Name = Fruit.Name)

WHEN MATCHED THEN

      UPDATE SET Price = Fruit.Price
```

```
WHEN NOT MATCHED BY TARGET THEN

        INSERT (Name, Price) VALUES(Fruit.Name, Fruit.Price)

WHEN NOT MATCHED BY SOURCE THEN

        DELETE;

GO

-- Show records in Produce. Note that prices for Apples and Pears have been
updated; Bananas, Oranges and Mandarins have been inserted; and all non-fruit
i.e. Milk, Honey etc. is deleted

SELECT * FROM Produce

GO
```

Example 7.20 Using the *MERGE* Statement with the *VALUES* Clause

```
USE AdventureWorks

GO

-- Show Data in HumanResources.Department table. Note that the Production
Control department is in the Manufacturing group. Note the number of
departments.

SELECT * FROM HumanResources.Department

GO

-- Use MERGE to update prices in Produce for those records that exist in
Fruit. Insert records from Fruit that are not in Produce. Delete any records
that are not in Fruit from Produce.

MERGE INTO HumanResources.Department as Target

USING (VALUES('Production Control', 'Inventory Management'), ('Building
Security', 'Maintenance Services'))

        AS Source (DepartmentName, NewGroupName)

ON Target.Name = Source.DepartmentName

WHEN MATCHED THEN

        UPDATE SET GroupName = Source.NewGroupName

WHEN NOT MATCHED BY TARGET THEN

        INSERT (Name, GroupName) VALUES(Source.DepartmentName, Source.
          NewGroupName);

GO

-- Show Data in HumanResources.Department again. Note that the Production
Control department is now in the Inventory Management group. Note that the
Building Security department was added.

SELECT * FROM HumanResources.Department

GO
```

Example 7.21 Using the *MERGE* Statement to Insert and Update Data

```
USE AdventureWorks
GO

-- Use the SELECT…INTO statement to create a new table named ScrapAudit, and
insert two values from the Production.ScrapReason table into it
SELECT Name
INTO dbo.ScrapAudit
FROM Production.ScrapReason
WHERE Name = 'Wheel misaligned' OR Name = 'Color incorrect'
GO

-- Add two new values to the ScrapAudit table
INSERT ScrapAudit Values ('Glue not set'), ('Item falling apart')
GO

-- Show values in ScrapAudit and Production.ScrapReason. Note that ScrapAudit
has two values that are also in the ScrapReason table, and two values that
are not.
SELECT * FROM ScrapAudit
GO
SELECT * FROM Production.ScrapReason
GO

-- Use the merge statement to insert values that don't exist in Production.
ScrapReason from ScrapAudit. Where values exist in both tables, update the
ModifiedDate in ScrapReason to be today's date
MERGE
  INTO Production.ScrapReason
USING ScrapAudit
ON (ScrapReason.Name = ScrapAudit.Name)
WHEN MATCHED THEN
    UPDATE SET ModifiedDate = GETDATE()
WHEN NOT MATCHED BY TARGET THEN
    INSERT (Name, ModifiedDate) VALUES (ScrapAudit.Name, GETDATE());
GO

-- Show values in Production.ScrapReason. Note that the two new values are
added, and two existing values show ModifiedDate as today.
SELECT * FROM Production.ScrapReason
GO
```

EXAM WARNING

Ensure that you understand the *MERGE* statement, and have extensively practiced using it to update, insert, and delete data. This is a new statement and you are likely to be asked about it in the exam.

EXERCISE 7.4

USING THE *MERGE* STATEMENT

In this exercise, we will practice using the *MERGE* statement in various scenarios.

Before you begin, you must have the following software installed on your computer:

- SQL Server 2008 (a free trial is available for download)
- AdventureWorks sample database

This exercise does not depend on you completing any previous exercises.

1. Open SQL Server Management Studio. Click **Start | All Programs | Microsoft SQL Server 2008 | SQL Server Management Studio**.

2. Create a new query against the AdventureWorks database.

3. Create a table named ProductAudit containing the columns ProductID, ProductName, and ListPrice by executing the following statement.

   ```
   CREATE TABLE ProductAudit

   (ProductID int PRIMARY KEY, ProductName nvarchar(255),
   ListPrice money)
   ```

4. Insert all products priced over 1,000 from Production.Product into ProductAudit. To do this, execute the following statement:

   ```
   INSERT INTO ProductAudit

   SELECT ProductID, Product.Name as ProductName, ListPrice

   FROM Production.Product

   WHERE ListPrice > 1000
   ```

5. In the ProductAudit table, reduce the price for all products containing 'Yellow' in the name, to 80% of the original. To do this, execute the following statement:

```
UPDATE ProductAudit SET ListPrice *= 0.8
WHERE ProductName like '%Yellow%'
```

6. Write and execute a *MERGE* statement targeting Production. Product performing the following actions:

   ■ Find all products that exist in both tables, but with different prices. Set the *ListPrice* for these products to be the value from ProductAudit.

   ■ Where products are not listed at all in ProductAudit, discontinue them by setting the *DiscontinuedDate* to today's date. Your statement should look like this:

```
MERGE INTO Production.Product
USING ProductAudit ON Product.ProductID = ProductAudit.ProductID
WHEN MATCHED AND Product.ListPrice <> ProductAudit.ListPrice THEN
        UPDATE SET ListPrice = ProductAudit.ListPrice
WHEN NOT MATCHED BY SOURCE THEN
        UPDATE SET DiscontinuedDate = GETDATE();
```

   How many rows were updated by this MERGE statement? What would happen if you reran the statement?

7. Write and execute a *MERGE* statement targeting ProductAudit performing the following actions:

   ■ Find all products that exist in both ProductAudit and Product, and add 20 to the list price of these products.

   ■ Find all products that exist in Product, but not in ProductAudit, and add them to the ProductAudit table. Your statement should look like this:

```
MERGE INTO ProductAudit
USING Production.Product ON ProductAudit.ProductID = Product.
ProductID
WHEN MATCHED THEN
        UPDATE SET ListPrice += 20.00
WHEN NOT MATCHED BY TARGET THEN
        INSERT VALUES(Product.ProductID, Product.Name,
Product.ListPrice)
```

   How many rows were updated by this *MERGE* statement? What would happen if you reran the statement?

Summary of Exam Objectives

In this chapter we have learned to use Data Modification Language (DML) statements to modify data in tables and views. DML is a subset of Transact-SQL that deals with modifying data. Do not confuse DML with Data Definition Language (DDL), which deals with creating and modifying the structure of tables and other objects. Five core DML statements are available:

- ***INSERT*** Inserts new rows into an existing table
- ***UPDATE*** Updates existing data in an existing table
- ***DELETE*** Deletes rows in a table based on a search condition
- ***SELECT...INTO*** Creates a ne w table based on the results of a *SELECT* query
- ***MERGE*** A new statement that allows you to insert, update, and delete data in a table based on the join with another table

Using the *INSERT* statement, you can insert values or query results into another table. As a best practice you should specify the list of columns that will be affected by the *INSERT* statement. The *VALUES* expression can be used to insert literal values, as opposed to query results. For example, you can use the *VALUES* expression to insert two new departments into the HumanResources.Department table as follows:

```
INSERT HumanResources.Department (Name, GroupName)
VALUES
('Database Administration', 'Executive General and Administration'),
('Inventory Management', 'Stock Control')
```

The *SELECT...INTO* statement simply executes a *SELECT* query, and inserts its results into a brand-new table. Do not confuse the *SELECT...INTO* statement with the *INSERT* statement (which can also have an optional *INTO* keyword). The *INSERT* statement inserts into an existing table, whereas the *SELECT...INTO* statement creates a new table.

The *UPDATE* statement is used to update existing rows in a table. It is used with the *SET* expression (*SET table1.ColumnX = table2.ColumnY*). The *SET* expression can be used with an equals assignment operator (=) or any other assignment operator; for example, += (add value and assign).

The *DELETE* statement is used to delete data in a table. Use the *DELETE* statement with a *WHERE* clause to restrict rows to be deleted. The *DELETE* statement deletes entire rows. Use a *FROM* clause to specify a join between your target table and another table. In this case, only those rows included in the join are deleted.

Use the *MERGE* statement to synchronize data between tables. In the *MERGE* statement, you must specify the source and target tables, as well as a join expression. When there is a match between the tables, or when rows from either the source or destination are unmatched, you can choose to perform certain actions. The valid actions to perform are *INSERT*, *UPDATE*, and *DELETE*. These actions are performed against the target table.

All DML statements can be used with the *TOP* keyword, which directs the statement to operate only on a given number of rows. The *TOP* keyword can also be used with the *PERCENT* keyword, which tells the statement to use a percentage of source rows, rather than a set number. The *TOP* keyword usually is used together with the *ORDER BY* clause. For example, you may wish to update the top 10 percent of sales personnel records in order of their sales figures (*ORDER BY … DESC*).

Exam Objectives Fast Track

Using the *INSERT* Statement

☑ The *INSERT* statement is used to insert rows into an existing table. A good example is *INSERT TableX(ColumnA, ColumnB) VALUES ('Value 1', 'Value 2'), ('Value 3', 'Value 4')*.

☑ Always specify a column list with the *INSERT* statement. This makes your statements future-proof, allowing for table structure changes.

☑ The *SELECT…INTO* statement executes a *SELECT* query and inserts its results into a new table.

☑ Do not confuse the *SELECT … INTO* and *INSERT INTO … SELECT* statements. The former creates a new table; the latter inserts records into an existing table.

Using the *UPDATE* Statement

☑ The *UPDATE* statement can update existing rows based on a search condition and/or a join. An example of an *UPDATE* statement is *UPDATE TableA SET ColumnA = 'Value' WHERE ColumnB = 'Search Value'*.

☑ The *UPDATE* statement can be used with a *FROM* clause. The *FROM* clause can specify that only rows that are returned by a join are affected by the *UPDATE* operation. The *FROM* clause can also specify the source data set containing new values to be used in the *UPDATE* operation.

☑ You cannot use the *ORDER BY* clause directly with the *UPDATE* statement. Instead, use the WHERE ID_Column in (*SELECT TOP (n) ID_Column FROM ...)* statement.

Using the *DELETE* Statement

☑ The *DELETE* statement deletes rows, and can be used with a *WHERE* clause or a *FROM* clause specifying a join.

☑ You can use the *FROM* clause to specify a join that will filter the rows you want to delete. This sometimes is referred to as a *DELETE FROM... FROM* statement. In this case your statement will look like this: *DELETE [FROM] TableX FROM TableX join TableY on TableX.ColumnA = TableY. ColumnA*.

☑ Always specify a *WHERE* clause, or a join with the *DELETE* statement, and the *UPDATE* statement. The only exception is when your intention is to affect all data in a table.

☑ If you are using a view for your *DELETE* statement, this view must be updateable.

Using the *MERGE* Statement

☑ The *MERGE* statement is new in SQL Server 2008.

☑ The *MERGE* statement merges data from one table into another. An example is *MERGE INTO TableX USING TableY ON TableX.ColumnA = TableY. ColumnA WHEN MATCHED THEN UPDATE SET (ColumnB) = TableY. ColumnB WHEN NOT MATCHED BY TARGET INSERT (ColumnA, ColumnB) VALUES(TableY.ColumnA, TableY.ColumnB);*.

☑ Use the *MERGE* statement in place of multiple *INSERT*, *UPDATE*, and *DELETE* statements if you can, as this is more efficient.

☑ You must specify the *ON merge_search_condition* clause. This clause defines the criteria of the join between the source and target tables. This join is how SQL Server determines whether the data in the destination table has been matched by the source table.

☑ Actions that can be used with the *MERGE* statement are *INSERT*, *UPDATE*, and *DELETE*.

Exam Objectives
Frequently Asked Questions

Q: When I use the *INSERT* statement with values or a query, what happens if one of the values already exists in the table, and the *INSERT* operation violates a *PRIMARY KEY* or *UNIQUE* constraint?

A: The entire *INSERT* operation will fail and you will receive an error message like *"Violation of UNIQUE KEY constraint…Cannot insert duplicate key in object 'dbo.TableY'"*. *The entire INSERT operation will be terminated, so no records will be inserted, even if only one violates the constraint. If this is not the behavior you intend, use the MERGE statement instead.*

Q: When should I use a *FROM* clause with my *UPDATE* statements versus a *WHERE* clause?

A: The *WHERE* clause simply restricts the rows to be updated. Use it when you want to update the filtered rows to a single static value or expression. Use the FROM clause when you are updating rows to values stored in another table's column, or calculated by a subquery.

Q: Can I use a function or a subquery with an *UPDATE…SET* statement?

A: Absolutely. For example, you could use *Update TableX SET ColumnA = HOST_ NAME( ) WHERE ColumnA = 'UNKNOWN'*. You could also use a subquery enclosed in parentheses, for example, *Update TableX SET ColumnA = (SELECT TOP (1) ColumnA from TableY) WHERE ColumnA = 'UNKNOWN'*.

Q: Sometimes I see *DELETE FROM…FROM* statements, which look like *DELETE FROM TableX FROM TableX join TableY on TableX.ColumnA = TableY. ColumnA*. Why are there two *FROM* keywords?

A: The first *FROM* is an optional "noise" or "filler" word. The second *FROM* specifies that the delete operation will delete results of a join. You could write this statement as *DELETE TableX FROM TableX join TableY on TableX.ColumnA = TableY.ColumnA*.

Q: Does the *MERGE* statement always have to end with a semicolon?

A: Yes, the *MERGE* statement must always end with a semicolon, or it will not execute.

Q: Why should I use the *MERGE* statement, when I can write the same functionality with individual *INSERT*, *UPDATE*, and *DELETE* statements?

A: The *MERGE* statement is especially optimized, and results in better performance, mainly due to locking optimizations. Also, a well-written *MERGE* statement will be simpler to read and write than the equivalent expressed by the individual *INSERT*, *UPDATE*, and *DELETE* statements.

Self Test

1. You have a Customers table containing current customer details, and a CustomerHistory table containing historical data about customers. Some records in CustomerHistory are in Customers, but data in Customers is more up to date. Some records in Customers are new, and don't exist in the CustomerHistory table. What is the most efficient way to update CustomerHistory with the most recent data?

   A. Use the *DELETE* statement to delete all rows in CustomerHistory that don't exist in Customers. Then insert all rows from Customers into CustomerHistory.

   B. First, use an *UPDATE…SET…FROM* statement to update all rows in CustomerHistory to equivalent values in Customers based on a join. Then, use the *INSERT…SELECT* statement to find all rows that exist in Customers, but not in CustomerHistory, and insert them into CustomerHistory.

   C. Use a *MERGE* statement with CustomerHistory as the target table and Customers as the source table. Use the *WHEN MATCHED* clause with the *UPDATE* merge action, and *WHEN NOT MATCHED BY TARGET* with an *INSERT* merge action.

   D. First, use the *INSERT…SELECT* statement to find all rows that exist in Customers, but not in CustomerHistory, and insert them into CustomerHistory. Then, use an *UPDATE…SET…FROM* statement to update all rows in CustomerHistory to equivalent values in Customers based on a join.

2. You have a table named Sales.SalesPerson with SalesPersonID and Bonus columns. You also have a Sales.SalesOrderHeader table containing a TotalDue column and a foreign key SalesPersonID. What is the best way to double the bonus for the top five salespeople by their total orders due?

   A.

```
UPDATE TOP (5 ) Sales.SalesPerson
SET Bonus *= 2
FROM (Select SalesPersonID FROM Sales.SalesPerson
join Sales.SalesOrderHeader on SalesOrderHeader.SalesPersonID =
SalesPerson.SalesPersonID
```

```
ORDER BY SUM(SalesOrderHeader.TotalDue)DESC)) as T1
JOIN Sales.SalesPerson on T1.SalesPersonID = SalesPerson.SalesPersonID
```

B.

```
UPDATE TOP (5 ) Sales.SalesPerson
SET Bonus *= 2
FROM Sales.SalesPerson
join Sales.SalesOrderHeader on SalesOrderHeader.SalesPersonID =
SalesPerson.SalesPersonID
```

C.

```
UPDATE TOP (5 ) Sales.SalesPerson
SET Bonus *= 2
from (Sales.SalesPerson
join Sales.SalesOrderHeader on SalesOrderHeader.SalesPersonID =
SalesPerson.SalesPersonID
GROUP BY SalesPerson.SalesPersonID, SalesPerson.Bonus
ORDER BY SUM(SalesOrderHeader.TotalDue)DESC)
```

D.

```
UPDATE Sales.SalesPerson
SET Bonus *= 2
WHERE SalesPersonID IN (SELECT TOP (5 ) SalesPerson.SalesPersonID
FROM Sales.SalesPerson JOIN Sales.SalesOrderHeader on SalesOrderHeader.
SalesPersonID = SalesPerson.SalesPersonID
GROUP BY SalesPerson.SalesPersonID, SalesPerson.Bonus
ORDER BY SUM(SalesOrderHeader.TotalDue) DESC)
```

3. You wish to delete 'orphaned' departments from the HumanResources. Department table. These are departments that no employees have ever worked in. The HumanResources.EmployeeDepartmentHistory table contains records of employees linked to departments by DepartmentID. Select all possible ways to perform this operation (select all that apply).

A.

```
DELETE FROM HumanResources.Department
FROM HumanResources.Department left join HumanResources.
EmployeeDepartmentHistory
ON Department.DepartmentID = EmployeeDepartmentHistory.DepartmentID
WHERE EmployeeDepartmentHistory.DepartmentID is NULL
```

B.

```
MERGE INTO HumanResources.Department
USING HumanResources.EmployeeDepartmentHistory
ON (Department.DepartmentID = EmployeeDepartmentHistory.DepartmentID)
WHEN NOT MATCHED BY TARGET THEN
DELETE;
```

C.

```
DELETE FROM HumanResources.Department
WHERE DepartmentID not in
(SELECT DepartmentID FROM HumanResources.EmployeeDepartmentHistory)
```

D.

```
MERGE INTO HumanResources.Department
USING HumanResources.EmployeeDepartmentHistory
ON (Department.DepartmentID = EmployeeDepartmentHistory.DepartmentID)
WHEN NOT MATCHED BY SOURCE THEN
DELETE;
```

4. Your customer is a restaurant, and has a WinterMenu and a more recent
    SpringMenu table. These tables are shown in Figure 7.2. What is the best way
    to merge the data from the SpringMenu into the WinterMenu, and update
    prices for those items that appear in both menus to the SpringMenu prices?

Figure 7.2 WinterMenu and SpringMenu Tables

WinterMenu Table	
Item	Price
Triple Cheese and Macaroni	29.00
Ricciolini with Bacon and Olives	35.00
Apricot Stuffed Lamb Chops	32.00
Broiled Lobster	45.00

SpringMenu Table	
Item	Price
Vegetarian Lasagne	29.00
Blackened Red Snapper	37.00
Broiled Lobster	49.00
Ricciolini with Bacon and Olives	30.00
Free-range organic goat sausages	28.00

A.

```
MERGE INTO WinterMenu

USING SpringMenu

ON (WinterMenu.Item = SpringMenu.Item)

WHEN MATCHED THEN

      UPDATE SET Price = SpringMenu.Price

WHEN NOT MATCHED BY SOURCE THEN

      INSERT (Item, Price) VALUES(SpringMenu.Item, SpringMenu.Price);
```

B.

```
MERGE INTO WinterMenu

USING SpringMenu

ON (WinterMenu.Price <> SpringMenu.Price)

WHEN MATCHED THEN

      UPDATE SET Price = SpringMenu.Price

WHEN NOT MATCHED BY TARGET THEN

      INSERT (Item, Price) VALUES(SpringMenu.Item, SpringMenu.Price)
```

C.

```
MERGE INTO WinterMenu

USING SpringMenu

ON (WinterMenu.Item = SpringMenu.Item)

WHEN MATCHED THEN

      UPDATE SET Price = SpringMenu.Price

WHEN NOT MATCHED BY TARGET THEN

      INSERT (Item, Price) VALUES(SpringMenu.Item, SpringMenu.Price);
```

D.

```
MERGE INTO WinterMenu

USING SpringMenu

ON (WinterMenu.Price <> SpringMenu.Price)

WHEN MATCHED THEN

      UPDATE SET Price = SpringMenu.Price

WHEN NOT MATCHED BY TARGET THEN

      INSERT (Item, Price) VALUES(SpringMenu.Item, SpringMenu.Price);
```

5. You have a HumanResources.Department table defined as follows.

```
CREATE TABLE HumanResources.Department
        (DepartmentID smallint IDENTITY(1,1) NOT NULL,
        Name nvarchar(200) NOT NULL,
        GroupName nvarchar(200) NOT NULL,
        ModifiedDate datetime NOT NULL DEFAULT GETDATE())
```

You must add two new departments: Legal and Catering, both in the "Executive General and Administration" group. How can you insert these two rows into this table (select all that apply)?

A.

```
INSERT HumanResources.Department (Name, GroupName)
VALUES ('Legal', 'Executive General and Administration'),
('Catering', 'Executive General and Administration')
```

B.

```
INSERT INTO HumanResources.Department
(ModifiedDate, Name, GroupName)
VALUES (DEFAULT, 'Legal', 'Executive General and Administration'),
(GETDATE(), 'Catering', 'Executive General and Administration')
```

C.

```
SELECT INTO HumanResources.Department
(ModifiedDate, Name, GroupName)
VALUES (DEFAULT, 'Legal', 'Executive General and Administration'),
(GETDATE(), 'Catering', 'Executive General and Administration')
```

D.

```
INSERT INTO HumanResources.Department
VALUES ('Legal', 'Executive General and Administration'),
('Catering', 'Executive General and Administration')
```

E.

```
INSERT INTO HumanResources.Department
VALUES (100, 'Legal', 'Executive General and Administration', GETDATE()),
(101, 'Catering', 'Executive General and Administration', GETDATE())
```

6. You have three related tables: Product, ProductSubCategory, and ProductCategory. You wish to create a new table called ProductDetails that will contain columns Product, SubCategory, and Category, and insert all data from the three tables into this new table. How would you do this?

A.

```
INSERT INTO ProductDetails

SELECT Product.Name as Product, ProductSubcategory.Name as Subcategory,
ProductCategory.Name as Category

FROM Production.Product JOIN

Production.ProductSubcategory ON Product.ProductSubcategoryID =
ProductSubcategory.ProductSubcategoryID

JOIN Production.ProductCategory ON ProductSubcategory.ProductCategoryID =
ProductCategory.ProductCategoryID
```

B.

```
MERGE INTO ProductDetails

USING (SELECT Product.Name as Product, ProductSubcategory.Name as
Subcategory, ProductCategory.Name as Category

FROM Production.Product JOIN

Production.ProductSubcategory ON Product.ProductSubcategoryID =
ProductSubcategory.ProductSubcategoryID

JOIN Production.ProductCategory ON ProductSubcategory.ProductCategoryID =
ProductCategory.ProductCategoryID) as tgt

ON ProductDetails.Product = tgt.Product

WHEN NOT MATCHED BY TARGET THEN

INSERT (Product, Subcategory, Category) values (tgt.Product, tgt.
Subcategory, tgt.Category);
```

C.

```
SELECT Product.Name as Product, ProductSubcategory.Name as Subcategory,
ProductCategory.Name as Category

INTO ProductDetails

FROM Production.Product JOIN

Production.ProductSubcategory ON Product.ProductSubcategoryID =
ProductSubcategory.ProductSubcategoryID

JOIN Production.ProductCategory ON ProductSubcategory.ProductCategoryID =
ProductCategory.ProductCategoryID
```

D.

```
SELECT INTO ProductDetails
Product.Name as Product, ProductSubcategory.Name as Subcategory,
ProductCategory.Name as Category
FROM Production.Product JOIN
Production.ProductSubcategory ON Product.ProductSubcategoryID =
ProductSubcategory.ProductSubcategoryID
JOIN Production.ProductCategory ON ProductSubcategory.ProductCategoryID =
ProductCategory.ProductCategoryID
```

7. You have a table that holds survey results as shown in Figure 7.3. The Rating column is the product rating between 1 (lowest) and 5 (highest). You wish to use the *column.WRITE* expression to update the Comment column and prepend the text "PLEASE REFUND: " to the beginning of the text contained in the Comment column, for reviews with rating 3 or lower. How can you achieve this?

Figure 7.3 SurveyResults Table

SurveyResults Table		
SurveyID (int)	Rating (int)	Comment (varchar(max))
1	5	Excellent product!
2	5	The best in it's class :-)
3	4	Would gladly buy again.
4	3	The product left me cold.
5	2	The product was disappointing, the shipping slow...
6	2	Not happy with product.
7	1	The product was damaged, and no refund was offered :-(

A.

```
UPDATE SurveyResults
SET Comment .WRITE('PLEASE REFUND. ', 0, 0)
WHERE Rating <= 3
```

B.

```
UPDATE SurveyResults
SET Comment .WRITE('PLEASE REFUND. ', 15, 0)
WHERE Rating <= 3
```

C.

```
UPDATE SurveyResults
SET Comment .WRITE('PLEASE REFUND. ', 0, 15)
WHERE Rating <= 3
```

D.

```
UPDATE SurveyResults
SET Comment .WRITE('PLEASE REFUND. ', NULL, NULL)
WHERE Rating <= 3
```

8. Which of the following statements will add 30 percent onto the value in the SalesQuota column for all salespeople who have a bonus over 3,000?

A.

```
UPDATE Sales.SalesPerson
SET SalesQuota += 1.3
WHERE Bonus > 3000
```

B.

```
UPDATE Sales.SalesPerson
SET SalesQuota *= 1.3
WHERE Bonus > 3000
```

C.

```
UPDATE Sales.SalesPerson
SET SalesQuota *= 1.3
```

D.

```
UPDATE Sales.SalesPerson
SET SalesQuota += 30 PERCENT
WHERE Bonus > 3000
```

9. You have a Sales.SpecialOffer table that contains a column Description of type nvarchar(255). You wish to add the words "Christmas Promotion" on to the end of the Description column for the row with a SpecialOfferID of 15. How can you achieve this (select all that apply)?

A.

```
UPDATE Sales.SpecialOffer
SET Description.Write('Christmas Promotion', NULL, NULL)
WHERE SpecialOfferID = 15
```

B.

```
UPDATE Sales.SpecialOffer
SET Description += 'Christmas Promotion'
WHERE SpecialOfferID = 15
```

C.

```
UPDATE Sales.SpecialOffer
SET Description.Write('Christmas Promotion', 0, 0)
WHERE SpecialOfferID = 15
```

D.

```
UPDATE Sales.SpecialOffer
SET Description = Description + ' ' + 'Christmas Promotion'
WHERE SpecialOfferID = 15
```

10. Your customer is a restaurant, and has a WinterMenu and a more recent SpringMenu. These tables are shown in Figure 7.4. What is the best way to delete the items from the SpringMenu that have already appeared on the WinterMenu, except the lobster dish, and increase prices for other items on the SpringMenu by 10 percent?

Figure 7.4 WinterMenu and SpringMenu Tables

WinterMenu Table	
Item	Price
Triple Cheese and Macaroni	29.00
Ricciolini with Bacon and Olives	35.00
Apricot Stuffed Lamb Chops	32.00
Broiled Lobster	45.00

SpringMenu Table	
Item	Price
Vegetarian Lasagne	29.00
Blackened Red Snapper	37.00
Broiled Lobster	49.00
Ricciolini with Bacon and Olives	30.00
Free-range organic goat sausages	28.00

A.

```
MERGE INTO WinterMenu

USING SpringMenu ON (SpringMenu.Item = WinterMenu.Item )

WHEN MATCHED AND WinterMenu.Item not like '%Lobster%' THEN
      DELETE

WHEN NOT MATCHED BY SOURCE THEN.UPDATE SET Price*=1.1;
```

B.

```
MERGE INTO SpringMenu

USING WinterMenu ON (SpringMenu.Item = WinterMenu.Item )

WHEN MATCHED AND SpringMenu.Item not like '%Lobster%' THEN
      DELETE

WHEN NOT MATCHED BY SOURCE THEN UPDATE SET Price*=1.1;
```

C.

```
MERGE INTO SpringMenu

USING WinterMenu ON (SpringMenu.Item = WinterMenu.Item )

WHEN MATCHED AND SpringMenu.Item not like '%Lobster%' THEN
      DELETE

WHEN NOT MATCHED BY TARGET THEN UPDATE SET Price*=1.1;
```

D.

```
MERGE INTO SpringMenu

USING WinterMenu ON (SpringMenu.Item = WinterMenu.Item )

WHEN MATCHED THEN
      DELETE

WHEN NOT MATCHED BY TARGET AND SpringMenu.Item not like '%Lobster%'

THEN UPDATE SET Price*=1.1;
```

11. What would the following statement do, assuming that "Customer" is a table, that is not referenced by any FOREIGN KEY constraints?

```
DELETE Customer
```

A. The statement will delete the table object from the database.

B. The statement will delete all data from the Customer table.

C. The statement will report an error, as no *FROM* keyword is specified.

D. The statement will delete no data from the Customer table, as no *WHERE* clause is specified.

12.   Your development team has asked you to justify why they should update the flagship database application to use *MERGE* statements. They are arguing that the same functionality is working well currently with individual *INSERT*, *DELETE*, and *UPDATE* statements. What are the advantages of the *MERGE* statement? Select all that apply.

A.   Because the *MERGE* statement can detect whether data is present, and update the data instead of insert, it may lead to fewer *PRIMARY KEY* and *UNIQUE* constraint violations.

B.   The *MERGE* statement will deliver better performance than the individual *INSERT*, *UPDATE*, and *DELETE* queries.

C.   The *MERGE* statement is simpler to read, modify, and debug.

D.   The *MERGE* statement is is a logged operation and can be rolled back; the *INSERT*, *UPDATE*, and *DELETE* statements are not.

13.   You have a stored procedure named *Get_NewProducts* defined as shown:

```
CREATE PROCEDURE Get_NewProducts
AS Select Name, ProductNumber, Color
FROM CandidateProducts
WHERE ApprovedFlag = 1
```

You wish to insert the results of this stored procedure into the Production. Product table. What is the best way to do this?

A.

```
INSERT Production.Product (Name, ProductNumber, Color)
EXECUTE Get_NewProducts
```

B.

```
INSERT Production.Product
EXECUTE Get_NewProducts
```

C.

```
INSERT Production.Product (Name, ProductNumber, Color)
VALUES (EXECUTE Get_NewProducts)
```

D.

```
INSERT Production.Product (Name, ProductNumber, Color)
VALUES (Get_NewProducts.Name, Get_NewProducts.ProductNumber,
Get_NewProducts.Color)
```

14. You have a table-valued user-defined function named *ufn_GetNewProducts* defined as shown:

```
CREATE FUNCTION ufn_GetNewProducts()
RETURNS @newProducts TABLE
(Name nvarchar(255), ProductNumber nvarchar(10), ListPrice money)
AS BEGIN
INSERT @newProducts
SELECT Name, ProductNumber, ListPrice FROM Production.ProductCandidate
WHERE ApprovedFlag = 1
RETURN END
```

What is the best way to merge the results of this function with the Production. Product table? Insert the rows that don't exist in the Production.Product table, and update *Name* and *ListPrice* for those that do.

A.

```
MERGE INTO Production.Product
USING ufn_GetNewProducts()as src ON
Product.ProductNumber = src.ProductNumber
WHEN MATCHED THEN
     UPDATE SET Name = src.Name, ListPrice = src.ListPrice
WHEN NOT MATCHED BY SOURCE THEN
     INSERT (Name, ProductNumber, ListPrice) VALUES(src.Name,
src.ProductNumber, src.ListPrice);
```

B.

```
MERGE INTO Production.Product
USING ufn_GetNewProducts() as src ON
Product.ProductNumber = src.ProductNumber
WHEN NOT MATCHED BY TARGET THEN
     UPDATE SET Name = src.Name, ListPrice = src.ListPrice
WHEN MATCHED THEN
     INSERT (Name, ProductNumber, ListPrice) VALUES(src.Name,
src.ProductNumber, src.ListPrice);
```

C.

```
MERGE INTO ufn_GetNewProducts()
USING Production.Product as src ON
Product.ProductNumber = src.ProductNumber
```

```
WHEN MATCHED THEN
      UPDATE SET Name = src.Name, ListPrice = src.ListPrice
WHEN NOT MATCHED BY TARGET THEN
       INSERT (Name, ProductNumber, ListPrice) VALUES(src.Name,
src.ProductNumber, src.ListPrice);
```

D.

```
MERGE INTO Production.Product
USING ufn_GetNewProducts()as src ON
Product.ProductNumber = src.ProductNumber
WHEN MATCHED THEN
      UPDATE SET Name = src.Name, ListPrice = src.ListPrice
WHEN NOT MATCHED BY TARGET THEN
       INSERT (Name, ProductNumber, ListPrice) VALUES(src.Name,
src.ProductNumber, src.ListPrice);
```

15. You have a table named TeamMembers containing the data shown in Table 7.4.

Table 7.4 TeamMembers Table

MemberName varchar(50) PRIMARY KEY
Valentine
Hayden
Matthew

MemberName is the PRIMARY KEY for the table. You execute the following statement:

```
INSERT TeamMembers Values ('Todd'), ('Valentine'), ('Peter')
```

Which team members will be present in the TeamMembers table after the statement executes?

A. Valentine, Hayden, Matthew, Todd

B. Valentine, Hayden, Matthew, Todd, Peter

C. Valentine, Hayden, Matthew, Todd, Valentine, Peter

D. Valentine, Hayden, Matthew

16. You have a table named TeamMembers containing the data shown in Table 7.5.

Table 7.5 TeamMembers Table

MemberName varchar(50) PRIMARY KEY
Valentine
Hayden
Matthew

MemberName is the PRIMARY KEY for the table. You execute the following statement:

```
MERGE INTO TeamMembers
Using (Values ('Todd'), ('Valentine'), ('Peter')) as src(MemberName)
ON TeamMembers.MemberName = src.MemberName
WHEN NOT MATCHED BY TARGET THEN
    INSERT (MemberName) Values (SRC.MemberName);
```

What team members will be present in the TeamMembers table after the statement executes?

A. Valentine, Hayden, Matthew, Todd

B. Valentine, Hayden, Matthew, Todd, Peter

C. Valentine, Hayden, Matthew, Todd, Valentine, Peter

D. Valentine, Hayden, Matthew

17. You are using a single *DELETE* statement to delete three rows from the Production.Product table. One of the rows has a related row in Sales. SalesOrderDetail and a FOREIGN KEY constraint with default options exists between the two tables. How many rows will be deleted from the Production. Product table?

A. The *DELETE* statement will delete the two rows from the Production.Product table that don't have any related rows in the Sales.SalesOrderDetail table.

B. The *DELETE* statement will not delete any rows from the Production. Product table nor the Sales.SalesOrderDetail table.

C. The *DELETE* statement will delete three rows in the Production.Product table and all related rows in the Sales.SalesOrderDetail table.

D. The *DELETE* statement will delete three rows in the Production.Product table and no rows in the Sales.SalesOrderDetail table.

18. You have created a CLR user-defined data type that stores coordinates in space and time. The UDT is called *PointInSpaceTime*. How should you register the data type, provided that the assembly containing it has already been registered?

A.

```
CREATE TYPE dbo. PointInSpaceTime
EXTERNAL NAME FunctionLibrary.[ PointInSpaceTime]
```

B.

```
CREATE TYPE dbo. PointInSpaceTime
EXTERNAL NAME FunctionLibrary.UserDefinedTypes.[PointInSpaceTime]
```

C.

```
CREATE TYPE dbo. PointInSpaceTime(@Latitude int, @Longitude int,
@Time DateTime)
EXTERNAL NAME FunctionLibrary.UserDefinedTypes.[PointInSpaceTime]
```

D.

```
CREATE TYPE dbo. PointInSpaceTime
RETURNS (@Latitude int, @Longitude int, @Time DateTime)
EXTERNAL NAME FunctionLibrary.UserDefinedTypes.[PointInSpaceTime]
```

19. You work with very large data sets and need only to affect a percentage of rows when modifying data. You have decided that you will use the *TOP* expression to achieve this. What statements are available for you to use with the *TOP* expression? Select all that apply.

A. *UPDATE*

B. *INSERT*

C. *MERGE*

D. *DELETE*

20. In the Production.Product table, a product with *ProductNumber* 'BK-T79Y-46' is listed with the color Blue. You execute the following statements:

```
DECLARE @Color nvarchar(15);
SET @Color = 'Red';
UPDATE Production.Product
SET @Color = Color = 'Blue'
WHERE ProductNumber = 'BK-T79Y-46';
SELECT @Color;
```

What is the value of the *@Color* variable selected?

A. Yellow

B. Red

C. Blue

D. None. The statement fails with an error stating that you cannot use two = assignment operators on the same line.

Self Test Quick Answer Key

1.	C	11.	B
2.	D	12.	A, B, C
3.	A, C, D	13.	A
4.	C	14.	D
5.	A, B	15.	D
6.	C	16.	B
7.	A	17.	B
8.	B	18.	A
9.	B, D	19.	A, B, C, D
10.	B	20.	C

Chapter 8

MCTS SQL Server 2008 Exam 433

Using Advanced Functionality with DML

Exam objectives in this chapter:

- Using @@IDENTITY and NEWID Functions in DML Statements
- Returning Data from DML Operations Using the OUTPUT Clause
- Using the OUTPUT Clause with the MERGE Statement
- Performing Nonlogged DML Operations

Exam objectives review:

- ☑ Summary of Exam Objectives
- ☑ Exam Objectives Fast Track
- ☑ Exam Objectives Frequently Asked Questions
- ☑ Self Test
- ☑ Self Test Quick Answer Key

Introduction

The use of DML is not limited to DML queries. Usually, database developers create stored procedures that encapsulate DML statements. These stored procedures can accept parameters. The stored procedure's behavior will vary depending on the parameter values passed to it. Stored procedures can return multiple result sets and messages. Often it is useful to include information about what data was affected by the DML statement.

In this chapter we will examine the aspects of creating and executing DML. As this functionality is key to creating SQL Server applications, expect to be asked about the *OUTPUT* clause and nonlogged DML operations in the exam. This chapter assumes that you are familiar with writing DML statements (covered in the previous chapter) as well as creating stored procedures and user-defined functions (covered in Chapter 2).

As a best practice, ensure that the performance of statements and stored procedures containing DML is adequate. DML carries the overhead of data locking. Sometimes DML statements are called simultaneously by multiple users, and could affect large result sets. This could result in poor performance, blocking, or even deadlocks. When you are using DML statements, always try to access data in the same order, to avoid locking and blocking issues. Locking is covered in Chapter 6.

Let's take a look at an example of a stored procedure containing DML. This stored procedure will accept a product ID and a price as parameters. It will then update the price for the product with the given product ID. But how do we know what product was affected? What was the old price? The *OUTPUT* clause serves this purpose. It returns data affected by the DML statement. View the execution results produced by Examples 8.1 and 8.2 to see what the *OUTPUT* statement can do.

Example 8.1 *sp_UpdateProductPrice* DML Stored Procedure

```
CREATE PROCEDURE sp_UpdateProductPrice(@ProductID int, @ListPrice money)
AS
UPDATE Production.Product SET ListPrice = @ListPrice
OUTPUT inserted.ProductID as ProductIDAffected, inserted.Name as
ProductNameAffected, deleted.ListPrice as OldPrice, inserted.ListPrice
as NewPrice
WHERE ProductID = @ProductID
```

Example 8.2 *sp_UpdateProductPrice* Execution Results

```
EXECUTE sp_UpdateProductPrice 316, 40
--Results:
--ProductIDAffected   ProductNameAffected   OldPrice   NewPrice
-------------------   -------------------   --------   --------
--316                 Blade                 00.00      40.00
--(1 row(s) affected)
```

As you can see, this stored procedure not only executes the DML statement and updates the data but also returns information about the data affected using the *OUTPUT* statement. In this chapter, we will examine how data returned by DML statement execution can be passed back to the caller. This includes the use of the *OUTPUT* statement, the *NEWID* function, the *@@IDENTITY* variable, and others. Finally, we will examine nonlogged DML operations, like the *TRUNCATE TABLE* statement. As with the previous chapter, ensure that you practice all these statements using exercises in this chapter, as your ability to use these statements is important for the exam.

Using @@IDENTITY and NEWID Functions in DML Statements

Using automatically incrementing IDENTITY columns is very popular with database developers. You don't need to explicitly calculate unique surrogate keys when inserting new data; the IDENTITY column functionality does that for you. The IDENTITY feature also allows you to specify useful *Seed* and *Increment* properties. When you use an *INSERT* statement to insert data into a table with an IDENTITY column defined, SQL Server will generate a new IDENTITY value. You can use the *@@IDENTITY* variable and the *SCOPE_IDENTITY* and *IDENT_CURRENT* functions to return the last *IDENTITY* value that has been generated by SQL Server. This is very useful when you need to return the key for the row that has just been inserted, back to the caller. In Example 8.3 a stored procedure inserts a new row into the Person.Contact table, and returns the IDENTITY value of the new record. This value can then be used in other statements.

Example 8.3 Using @@*IDENTITY* to
Return the Last IDENTITY Value Generated

```
USE AdventureWorks;
GO
CREATE PROCEDURE sp_InsertPerson
@FirstName nvarchar(50), @LastName nvarchar(50), @PersonKey int OUT
AS
INSERT Person.Contact(FirstName, LastName, PasswordHash, PasswordSalt)
VALUES (@FirstName, @LastName, 'NO PASSWORD', 'NONE')
SET @PersonKey = @@IDENTITY
GO

DECLARE @NewKey int;
EXECUTE sp_InsertPerson 'Valentine', 'Boiarkine', @NewKey OUT
SELECT @NewKey
GO
-- Results:
-- (1 row(s) affected)
-- -----------
-- 19990
```

We could have used *SCOPE_IDENTITY* and *IDENT_CURRENT* in this
stored procedure with the same results. The difference between these functions is
scope. The *@@IDENTITY* variable holds the last IDENTITY value generated by
SQL Server for the current session. The *SCOPE_IDENTITY* function returns
the last IDENTITY value generated by SQL Server limited to the current session
and scope only. This is useful when you are inserting into a table with a trigger
bound to it, and the trigger itself causes the generation of another IDENTITY
value. The *IDENT_CURRENT* function is not restricted by session or scope. This
function returns the value of the last IDENTITY generated for a specific table.
IDENT_CURRENT requires a table name parameter.

Example 8.4 shows the correct use of the *SCOPE_IDENTITY* and
IDENT_CURRENT functions.

Example 8.4 Using @@IDENTITY, IDENT_CURRENT, and SCOPE_IDENTITY

```
USE AdventureWorks;
GO
INSERT Production.ScrapReason(Name)
VALUES ('Glue too weak')
SELECT @@IDENTITY as IDENTITY_VALUE,
IDENT_CURRENT('Production.ScrapReason') as IDENT_CURRENT_VALUE,
SCOPE_IDENTITY() as SCOPE_IDENTITY_VALUE
GO
-- Results:
-- (1 row(s) affected)
-- IDENTITY_VALUE    IDENT_CURRENT_VALUE    SCOPE_IDENTITY_VALUE
-- ---------------   -------------------    --------------------
-- 23                23                     23
-- (1 row(s) affected)
```

How do you decide when to use *SCOPE_IDENTITY* versus *@@IDENTITY* versus *IDENT_CURRENT*? When your DML statement has affected only one table, and you are querying the IDENTITY value from the same connection that made the modifications, all three will return the same value. This is the case in the previous example. However, if you query *@@IDENTITY* and *SCOPE_IDENTITY* from a new connection, they will return *NULL*. This is because *@@IDENTITY* and *SCOPE_IDENTITY* values are specific to the connection that executed the DML statement that changed the IDENTITY values. When would *@@IDENTITY* and *IDENT_CURRENT* functions return different values? The *@@IDENTITY* function returns the last IDENTITY value created in any scope within the connection, whereas *IDENT_CURRENT* is specific to the current scope. These functions will return different values if an IDENTITY value for a second table is changed in a nested scope—for example, by a trigger.

In Example 8.5, we will work with two tables: Fruit and FruitAudit; both containing IDENTITY columns named FruitID. The Fruit table contains three rows, and FruitAudit contains five. A trigger is defined on the Fruit table that will insert the new value into the FruitAudit table. When we insert a new row into Fruit, two *IDENTITY* values will be produced: one for the Fruit table and one for the FruitAudit table, which was modified by the trigger. The *@@IDENTITY* will return the last IDENTITY value regardless of scope (i.e., the IDENTITY value for the FruitAudit table). SCOPE_IDENTITY will return the IDENTITY value from the current scope, not the nested scope of the trigger. SCOPE_IDENTITY will return the IDENTITY value for the Fruit table. Try going through the following example yourself—it will give you a closer understanding of the various IDENTITY functions.

Example 8.5 Demonstrating the Use of Different IDENTITY Functions

```
CREATE TABLE dbo.Fruit (FruitID int IDENTITY PRIMARY KEY, FruitName
varchar(50))
GO

CREATE TABLE dbo.FruitAudit (FruitID int IDENTITY PRIMARY KEY, FruitName
varchar(50))
GO

CREATE TRIGGER Fruit_Inserted ON dbo.Fruit AFTER INSERT
AS
INSERT FruitAudit(FruitName) SELECT FruitName FROM INSERTED
GO

INSERT FruitAudit(FruitName) Values ('Mango'), ('Watermelon')
GO

INSERT Fruit(FruitName) Values ('Apple'), ('Banana'), ('Apricot')
GO

INSERT Fruit Values ('Pear')
- Execute the following statement from the same connection
SELECT @@IDENTITY as [@@IDENTITY], SCOPE_IDENTITY() as [SCOPE_IDENTITY],
IDENT_CURRENT('Fruit') as [IDENT_CURRENT_FRUIT],
IDENT_CURRENT('FruitAudit') as [IDENT_CURRENT_FRUITAUDIT]
-- Results (same connection):
-- @@IDENTITY  SCOPE_IDENTITY IDENT_CURRENT_FRUIT IDENT_CURRENT_FRUITAUDIT
-- ----------  -------------- ------------------- ------------------------
-- 6          4              4                   6

-Execute the following statement from a new connection
SELECT @@IDENTITY as [@@IDENTITY], SCOPE_IDENTITY() as [SCOPE_IDENTITY],
IDENT_CURRENT('Fruit') as [IDENT_CURRENT_FRUIT],
IDENT_CURRENT('FruitAudit') as [IDENT_CURRENT_FRUITAUDIT]
-- Results (different connection):
-- @@IDENTITY  SCOPE_IDENTITY  IDENT_CURRENT_FRUIT IDENT_CURRENT_FRUITAUDIT
-- ----------  --------------  ------------------- ------------------------
-- NULL        NULL            4                   6
```

EXAM WARNING

Remember that @@*IDENTITY* is specific to the local server. When executing the *INSERT* statement against a remote table on a linked server, the last IDENTITY value generated for that table will not be held in @@*IDENTITY*. To obtain the remote @@*IDENTITY* value, execute a stored procedure in the context of the remote server, assigning the @@*IDENTITY* value to an output parameter.

Using IDENTITY_INSERT to Insert Explicit Values into IDENTITY Columns

You may wish to override the auto-generating behavior of *IDENTITY* columns; for example, if you have a table with an *IDENTITY* column defined, but you have deleted many rows in this table. The *IDENTITY* value will never decrement itself, and therefore you will experience gaps in your key values. If this behavior is undesirable, you can use the *SET IDENTITY_INSERT [database_name].[schema_name].table_name ON | OFF* statement to enable *IDENTITY_INSERT* functionality. Example 8.6 demonstrates the proper use of *IDENTITY_INSERT*.

Example 8.6 Using *IDENTITY_INSERT*

```
CREATE TABLE Fruit (FruitID int IDENTITY PRIMARY KEY, FruitName nvarchar(50))
GO

INSERT Fruit (FruitName) VALUES ('Apple'), ('Pomegranate'), ('Kiwifruit')
SELECT * FROM Fruit
GO
-- Results:
-- FruitID      FruitName
-- ----------- -------------
-- 1            Apple
-- 2            Pomegranate
-- 3            Kiwifruit

DELETE Fruit WHERE FruitID = 1 OR FruitID = 3
INSERT Fruit (FruitName) VALUES ('Jackfruit'), ('Mango')
SELECT * FROM Fruit
```

```
GO
-- Results (Note that we now have gaps in key values):
-- FruitID      FruitName
-- ----------- -----------
-- 2            Pomegranate
-- 4            Jackfruit
-- 5            Mango

INSERT Fruit (FruitID, FruitName) VALUES (1, 'Seaberry'), (3, 'Durian')
GO
-- Results:
-- Msg 544, Level 16, State 1, Line 1
-- Cannot insert explicit value for identity column in table 'Fruit' when
IDENTITY_INSERT is set to OFF.

SET IDENTITY_INSERT Fruit ON
INSERT Fruit (FruitID, FruitName) VALUES (1, 'Seaberry'), (3, 'Durian')
SET IDENTITY_INSERT Fruit OFF
SELECT * FROM Fruit
GO
-- Results:
-- FruitID      FruitName
-- ----------- -----------
-- 1            Seaberry
-- 2            Pomegranate
-- 3            Durian
-- 4            Jackfruit
-- 5            Mango
```

TEST DAY TIP

Remember that the IDENTITY value for a table is incremented even if an *INSERT* statement fails. This means failed DML statements and transactions will cause gaps in the IDENTITY column. You can correct the gaps by setting *IDENTITY_INSERT* to ON, and manually inserting new data with explicitly specified IDENTITY values.

Configuring & Implementing...

Using the DBCC CHECKIDENT Statement to View and Modify IDENTITY Values

SQL Server automatically maintains IDENTITY values for tables with IDENTITY columns defined. However, you may wish to reset the IDENTITY value back to its initial value, or to a specified value. You may also wish to view the current IDENTITY value for a table. These tasks are performed using the *DBCC CHECKIDENT* statement. The statement is used as follows:

```
DBCC CHECKIDENT (table_name, NORESEED | RESEED, [new_reseed_value])
```

When *NORESEED* is specified, the IDENTITY value for the table is not reset. The current IDENTITY value and the maximum value contained in the IDENTITY column are returned. If the two values are not the same, you may wish to reset the IDENTITY value to avoid gaps in IDENTITY column values.

When *RESEED* is specified, the identity value for the table is reset to either the maximum value contained in the IDENTITY column, or a value you specified for *new_reseed_value*. If the table contains no data, the identity value for the table is reset to its initial value.

The *DBCC CHECKIDENT* statement is especially useful after you have used *IDENTITY_INSERT*. For example, you may have just inserted a number of explicit IDENTITY values into a table. You can now use *IDENTITY_INSERT* to reset the IDENTITY value to the next logical value, so that the next record receives the correct IDENTITY value.

You may want to use the *DBCC CHECKIDENT* statement when you have emptied a table. Although the table is empty, the IDENTITY value remains at what it was when the table had data. You can now use the *DBCC CHECKIDENT* statement to reset the IDENTITY back to its initial value (usually 1).

Using the NEWID Function

Columns of type *uniqueidentifier* store globally *unique identifier* (GUID) data. Sometimes you need to insert values into these columns. The *NEWID* function can be used to generate a new value of type *uniqueidentifier*. This value is guaranteed to be globally unique. Example 8.7 demonstrates the use of the *NEWID* function.

Example 8.7 Using the *NEWID* Function

```
CREATE TABLE SpareParts (PartID uniqueidentifier PRIMARY KEY,
PartName nvarchar(50))
GO

INSERT SpareParts(PartID, PartName)
VALUES
(NEWID(), 'Fibre Channel Card'),
(NEWID(), 'Diagnostics Card')

SELECT * FROM SpareParts
-- Results:
-- PartID                               PartName
-- -----------------------------------  --------------------
-- AD4A4B10-A62B-4322-905A-9A5C51EB6010  Fibre Channel Card
-- 8750D92A-9FAC-4DC2-AB92-FB7A9C76E333  Diagnostics Card
```

EXAM WARNING

Do not confuse the *@@IDENTITY* and NEWID functions. The *@@IDENTITY* function holds the value of the last IDENTITY value generated by the server for the current user session. The NEWID() function generates and returns a new GUID.

EXERCISE 8.1

WORKING WITH IDENTITY AND UNIQUEIDENTIFIER COLUMNS

In this exercise, we will practice working with *IDENTITY* and *UNIQUEIDENTIFIER* data.

Before you begin, you must have the following software installed on your computer:

- SQL Server 2008 (a free trial is available for download)
- AdventureWorks sample database

We will be adding rows to the Purchasing.ShipMethod table in the AdventureWorks database.

1. Open SQL Server Management Studio. **Click Start | All Programs | Microsoft SQL Server 2008 | SQL Server Management Studio**.

2. Create a new query against the AdventureWorks database.

3. Create a table named Stars by executing the following statement:

```
CREATE TABLE Stars
(StarID uniqueidentifier PRIMARY KEY,
StarName nvarchar(50))
```

4. Use the *NEWID* function to insert two rows into the Stars table with star names 'Deneb' and 'Pollux'. Write and execute your statement as follows:

```
INSERT Stars (StarID, StarName)
VALUES (NEWID(), 'Deneb'),
(NEWID(), 'Pollux')
```

5. Use the *SELECT* statement to view the data contained in a table. Yours statement and results should look as follows.

```
SELECT * FROM Stars
-- Results:
-- StarID                                StarName
-- ------------------------------------  ---------
-- 57559159-5B56-4346-9871-0ED3A228D6C1  Pollux
-- 1861C6D2-AB79-431B-A5D9-8E42FDE1F4B5  Deneb
```

6. Create a new query against the AdventureWorks database.

7. Create a table named Planets by executing the following statement:

```
CREATE TABLE Planets
(PlanetID int IDENTITY PRIMARY KEY,
PlanetName nvarchar(50))
```

8. Use the *INSERT* statement with PlanetName only in the ColumnList to insert three rows into the Planets table: 'Mars', 'Earth', and 'Jupiter'. Examine the data contained in the table, and the value of the *@@IDENTITY* variable. Write and execute your statement as follows:

```
INSERT Planets (PlanetName)
VALUES('Mars'), ('Earth'), ('Jupiter')
SELECT * FROM Planets
```

```
SELECT @@IDENTITY as [Last IDENTITY]
-- Results:
-- PlanetID      PlanetName
-- ----------    ----------
-- 1             Mars
-- 2             Earth
-- 3             Jupiter
-- Last          IDENTITY
```

9. Delete the record with *PlanetID = 2*. Examine the data contained in the Planets table. Write and execute your statement as follows:

```
DELETE Planets WHERE PlanetID = 2
SELECT * FROM Planets
-- Results:
-- PlanetID      PlanetName
-- ----------    ----------
-- 1             Mars
-- 3             Jupiter
```

10. Using *IDENTITY_INSERT*, insert the planet Venus with a PlanetID of 2. Write and execute your statement as follows:

```
SET IDENTITY_INSERT Planets ON
INSERT Planets (PlanetID, PlanetName)
VALUES(2, 'Venus')
SET IDENTITY_INSERT Planets OFF
SELECT * FROM Planets
-- Results:
-- PlanetID      PlanetName
-- ----------    ----------
-- 1             Mars
-- 2             Venus
-- 3             Jupiter
```

Returning Data from DML Operations Using the OUTPUT Clause

The *OUTPUT* clause is a very powerful feature of *INSERT*, *UPDATE*, *DELETE*, and *MERGE* DML statements. This clause allows you to return information about the data affected by a DML statement. For example, when you update a table, you can return the affected rows and their values before and after modification. You can insert the rows returned by the *OUTPUT* statement into a table, or a table-valued variable using the *OUTPUT INTO* statement. Examples 8.8 and 8.9 show the syntax of the *OUTPUT* and *OUTPUT INTO* clauses.

Example 8.8 *OUTPUT* Clause—Syntax

```
OUTPUT [INSERTED.Column_name, …][DELETED.Column_name,…][Scalar_expression |
Variable | From_clause_table.Column_name]
```

Example 8.9 *OUTPUT INTO* Clause—Syntax

```
OUTPUT [INSERTED.Column_name, …][DELETED.Column_name,…][Scalar_expression |
Variable | From_clause_table.Column_name] INTO output_table | @table_variable
[(Column_list)]
```

How do you reference values that are old and new? These values are stored in special tables: INSERTED and DELETED. These are the same INSERTED and DELETED tables you used when learning about triggers. The INSERTED table contains new values for the rows that have been affected by the *UPDATE* statement. It also contains values of rows that have been added by the *INSERT* statement. The DELETED table contains old values for the rows that have been affected by an *UPDATE* statement. It also contains values of rows that have been deleted by the *DELETE* statement. You cannot use the INSERTED table with the *OUTPUT* clause of a *DELETE* statement. Likewise, you cannot use the DELETED table with the *OUTPUT* clause of an *INSERT* statement. You can use both tables with the *OUTPUT* clause on an *UPDATE* statement.

You can specify *INSERTED.Column_name*, *DELETED.Column_name*, *INSERTED.**, and *DELETED.** in the *OUTPUT* clause. You can also specify *From_clause_table.Column_name*. This is any column from a table mentioned in the *FROM* clause, except the table affected by the DML statement. Finally, you can specify a variable or a scalar expression. When you use variables in the *OUTPUT* clause, and these variables were modified by the DML statement, the clause will always return the original variable values.

When using the *OUTPUT INTO* clause you can specify a table or table-valued variable. This table will accept the results returned by the *OUTPUT* clause.

This table or variable must have the same column structure as values returned by the *OUTPUT INTO* clause. You cannot use the following types of tables with the *OUTPUT INTO* clause:

- Remote tables
- Views
- Common table expressions
- Tables with triggers
- Tables participating in FOREIGN KEY constraints
- Tables participating in merge replication, or transactional replication with updateable subscribers

Let's examine some examples of using the *OUTPUT* clause with *INSERT*, *UPDATE*, and *DELETE* DML statements. Performing these examples yourself will familiarize you with the *OUTPUT* clause (see Examples 8.10 through 8.14).

Example 8.10 Using the *INSERT* Statement with the *OUTPUT* Clause

```
CREATE TABLE FarmAnimals
(AnimalID int IDENTITY PRIMARY KEY,
AnimalName nvarchar(50),
Price money)
GO
INSERT FarmAnimals (AnimalName, Price)
OUTPUT inserted.AnimalID as ins_animal_ID, inserted.AnimalName as ins_animal_
name, inserted.Price ins_price
VALUES ('Goat', 250),('Sheep', 300)
GO
-- Results:
-- ins_animal_ID    ins_animal_name   ins_price
-- -------------    ---------------   ---------
-- 1                Goat              250.00
-- 2                Sheep             300.00
```

Example 8.11 Using the *UPDATE* Statement with the *OUTPUT* Clause

```
UPDATE FarmAnimals
SET AnimalName = 'Llama', Price = 3000
OUTPUT
inserted.AnimalID as ins_animal_ID, inserted.AnimalName as ins_animal_name,
inserted.Price ins_price,
deleted.AnimalID as del_animal_ID, deleted.AnimalName as del_animal_name,
deleted.Price del_price
WHERE AnimalID = 2
GO
-- Results:
-- ins_animal_ID    ins_animal_name   ins_price
-- -------------    ---------------   ---------
-- 2                Llama             3000.00
-- Results (CONTINUED):
-- del_animal_ID    del_animal_name   del_price
-- -------------    ---------------   ---------
-- 2                Sheep             300.00
```

Example 8.12 Using the *DELETE* Statement with the *OUTPUT* Clause

```
DELETE FarmAnimals
OUTPUT
deleted.AnimalID as del_animal_ID, deleted.AnimalName as del_animal_name,
deleted.Price del_price
WHERE AnimalID = 1
GO
-- Results:
-- del_animal_ID    del_animal_name   del_price
-- -------------    ---------------   ---------
-- 1                Goat              250.00
```

Example 8.13 Using the *UPDATE* Statement with the *OUTPUT INTO* Clause

```
DECLARE @ResultTable TABLE
(LocationName nvarchar(50),
NewRate smallmoney,
OldRate smallmoney,
RateChange smallmoney)

UPDATE Production.Location
SET CostRate = 25.00
OUTPUT inserted.Name,
inserted.CostRate,
deleted.CostRate,
deleted.CostRate - inserted.CostRate
INTO @ResultTable
WHERE LocationID = 1
SELECT * FROM @ResultTable
GO
-- Results:
-- LocationName  NewRate  OldRate  RateChange
-- ------------  -------  -------  ----------
-- Tool Crib     25.00    0.00     -25.00
```

Example 8.14 Using the *OUTPUT INTO*
Clause with an Existing Table and a *FROM* Join

```
CREATE TABLE DeprecatedProducts (ProductID int, ProductName varchar(50),
OriginalPrice money, OrderDate datetime)
GO

UPDATE TOP (2) Production.Product SET DiscontinuedDate = GETDATE(),
ListPrice = 0
OUTPUT inserted.ProductID, inserted.Name, deleted.ListPrice, SalesOrderHeader.
OrderDate INTO DeprecatedProducts
FROM Production.Product join Sales.SalesOrderDetail
ON Product.ProductID = SalesOrderDetail.ProductID
join Sales.SalesOrderHeader ON
SalesOrderDetail.SalesOrderID = SalesOrderHeader.SalesOrderID
```

```
SELECT * from DeprecatedProducts
GO

-- Results:
-- ProductID    ProductName        OriginalPrice    OrderDate
-- ---------    -----------        -------------    ---------
-- 749          Road-150 Red,  62  3578.27          2001-07-06 00:00:00.000
-- 751          Road-150 Red,  48  3578.27          2001-07-07 00:00:00.000
```

EXAM WARNING

Remember that if the DML statement fails, for example, due to a constraint violation, the *OUTPUT* clause would still return the rows that would have been inserted or deleted. Therefore, you should never rely on the *OUTPUT* statement to indicate that the statement was successful. Your database application should check for errors from DML statements. If the application encounters an error, the *OUTPUT* results should not be used.

Using the OUTPUT Clause with the MERGE Statement

The *OUTPUT* clause is of great value when used with the *MERGE* statement. Because the *MERGE* statement can perform multiple actions depending on the results of a join, it is hard to tell what data was updated, what data was inserted, and what data was deleted. The *OUTPUT* clause can return this information. The *OUTPUT* clause is specified for the entire *MERGE* statement, not each individual action.

Additionally, you can output the *$action* value. This value is available only for the *MERGE* statement. It stores the action performed on a particular row. The *$action* value is of nvarchar(10) type, and can hold only the following values:

- *INSERT*
- *UPDATE*
- *DELETE*

Let's examine some examples of using the *OUTPUT* clause with the *MERGE* statement. Again, be sure to perform these examples yourself against the AdventureWorks database (see Example 8.15).

Example 8.15 Using the *MERGE* Statement with the *OUTPUT* Clause

```
CREATE TABLE FarmAnimals
(AnimalID int IDENTITY PRIMARY KEY,
AnimalName nvarchar(50),
Price money)
GO

CREATE TABLE Pets
(AnimalID int IDENTITY PRIMARY KEY,
AnimalName nvarchar(50),
Price money)
GO

INSERT FarmAnimals (AnimalName, Price)
VALUES ('Goat', 250),('Sheep', 300)
GO

INSERT Pets (AnimalName, Price)
VALUES ('Kitten', 75),('Puppy', 120), ('Goat', 350)
GO

MERGE INTO Pets
USING FarmAnimals ON Pets.AnimalName = FarmAnimals.AnimalName
WHEN MATCHED THEN
UPDATE SET Price = FarmAnimals.Price
WHEN NOT MATCHED BY TARGET THEN
INSERT (AnimalName, Price) VALUES (FarmAnimals.AnimalName, FarmAnimals.Price)
OUTPUT $action, inserted.AnimalName as ins_name, deleted.AnimalName as del_
name, deleted.Price as old_price;
--Results:
-- $action    ins_name   del_name   old_price
-- -------    --------   --------   ---------
-- INSERT     Sheep      NULL       NULL
-- UPDATE     Goat       Goat       350.00
```

TEST DAY TIP

Practice using the *OUTPUT* clause with the *MERGE* statement until you can use it confidently. Because the *MERGE* statement is new in SQL Server 2008, you are likely to be asked about its use in the exam. The use of the *OUTPUT* clause with all DML statements is one of the exam objectives.

Performing Nonlogged DML Operations

Most DML operations are logged operations. When an operation is logged, data about the operation is stored in the SQL Server transaction log. The transaction log files can be backed up and replayed into an earlier database backup. Although the log replay functionality is slow, it allows you to restore the database to the point in time when the database file itself was lost.

For performance reasons, some operations that affect SQL Server data are nonlogged, or minimally logged. This means that the information about these operations is not fully recorded in the SQL Server transaction log. Nonlogged operations offer much better performance than logged operations. However, if a nonlogged operation occurred after the database has been backed up, you will not be able to replay the logs into the database after you have restored the database from backup.

EXAM WARNING

Remember that it is highly recommended to back up the database after performing any nonlogged operations. This will ensure that you are able to recover as much database data as possible.

The following DML operations are either nonlogged or minimally logged:

- *TRUNCATE TABLE*.
- *WRITETEXT* and *UPDATETEXT*. These statements are deprecated and should not be used. Use *column.Write* instead. You learned about the *column. Write* statement in the previous chapter.
- *SELECT INTO*. You learned about the *SELECT…INTO* statement in the previous chapter.

Configuring & Implementing...

Effect of the Database Recovery Model on Bulk-Logged Operations

The database recovery model determines how transaction logs are used by SQL Server for a specified database. Your choice of recovery model affects which operations are performed as nonlogged, and whether the database can be recovered to a point in time. Three recovery models are available for SQL Server 2008 databases:

- Simple recovery model
- Full recovery model
- Bulk-Logged recovery model

When the database recovery model is set to Simple, log files are reused as soon as they become full. This means that very little space is consumed by the transaction logs, and you don't need to worry about log file management. However, when a database is set to a Simple recovery model, and the database file is lost, you will not be able to recover any changes made after the last full backup. You will also not be able to recover to a point in time, as transaction details are stored in transaction logs that have been overwritten in this case.

The Full recovery model could be said to be the opposite of the Simple recovery model. Transaction logs are kept and all transactions without exception are written to the logs. This includes nonlogged operations like *TRUNCATE TABLE*, *SELECT...INTO*, and so on. Although you lose performance advantages of nonlogged operations with this recovery model, all data is recoverable provided transaction logs are intact. You can also restore to a point-in-time if necessary.

The Bulk-Logged recovery model is similar to the Full recovery model, except that nonlogged operations are performed as nonlogged. This provides a performance advantage for Bulk-Logged operations. However, if a Bulk-Logged operation has occurred since the last full backup, you will not be able to recover any changes made since the last full backup. The Bulk-Logged recovery model does not support point-in-time recovery.

Continued

In production environments the full database recovery model generally is used, because it ensures maximum recoverability. However, if the administrator wishes to perform a high performance nonlogged operation, he would temporarily switch the recovery model to Bulk-Logged, perform the operation, switch the recovery model back to Full, and perform a full backup. The Full recovery model is the default when creating databases in SQL Server.

Let's examine the *TRUNCATE TABLE* statement. The *TRUNCATE TABLE* statement deletes all data in a given table. Its result is equivalent to a *DELETE* statement with no *WHERE* or *FROM* clause. The syntax for this statement is simple, as follows:

```
TRUNCATE TABLE [database_name].[schema_name].table_name
```

The *TRUNCATE TABLE* statement cannot be used on tables that are referenced by a FOREIGN KEY constraint, unless the FOREIGN KEY constraint is self-referencing. The *TRUNCATE TABLE* statement cannot be used on a table that is a part of an indexed view. You cannot use the *TRUNCATE TABLE* statement on tables that are published by transactional or merge replication. The *TRUNCATE TABLE* statement will not activate triggers, as triggers rely on transaction logs, and *TRUNCATE TABLE* is a nonlogged operation.

Head of the Class...

TRUNCATE TABLE vs DELETE statements

Why should you use a *TRUNCATE TABLE* statement at all, if you can accomplish the same task using the DELETE statement? The *TRUNCATE TABLE* statement is nonlogged, and therefore offers much better performance than using the DELETE statement. Additionally, *TRUNCATE TABLE* has the following advantages:

- The *TRUNCATE TABLE* statement uses much less transaction log space. The DELETE statement logs information about every row that is affected in the transaction log. When deleting from a table with millions of rows, this is both time- and disk-space-consuming.

Continued

> ■ The DELETE statement holds a lock on each individual row it is
>   deleting. The *TRUNCATE TABLE* statement locks only the table
>   and each data page. This offers better performance, as locking
>   is one of the most time-consuming SQL Server activities.
>
> ■ The DELETE statement will leave empty data pages for the
>   table and its indexes. If you wish to shrink the database by
>   deleting data in a large table, the DELETE statement may
>   prove counterproductive. The *TRUNCATE TABLE* statement, on
>   the other hand, is guaranteed to leave zero data pages behind.
>
> In summary, *TRUNCATE TABLE* is a more efficient statement. However,
> in a production database you must back up the database as soon as you
> have committed a nonlogged operation like the *TRUNCATE TABLE*
> statement, to reduce the risk of data loss due to a disaster.

In Example 8.16 we will use *SELECT…INTO* and *TRUNCATE TABLE* nonlogged operations. In Table 8.1 we will compare the time consumed by the *INSERT, SELECT…INTO, DELETE,* and *TRUNCATE TABLE* statements.

Example 8.16 Using Nonlogged Operations

```
USE AdventureWorks
GO

DECLARE @StartTime datetime = GetDate()
        SELECT * INTO AllPersonalRecords
            FROM Person.Contact
SELECT DATEDIFF(millisecond, @StartTime, GetDate()) as [Time consumed by
SELECT INTO]
GO
-- Results:
-- Time consumed by SELECT INTO
-- ---------------------------
-- 610
```

```
SELECT COUNT(*) FROM AllPersonalRecords
--Results: 19982 rows
DECLARE @StartTime datetime = GetDate()
        TRUNCATE TABLE AllPersonalRecords
SELECT DATEDIFF(millisecond, @StartTime, GetDate()) as [Time consumed by
Truncate]
GO
-- Results:
-- Time consumed by Truncate
-- ------------------------
-- 0

SET IDENTITY_INSERT dbo.AllPersonalRecords ON
GO
DECLARE @StartTime datetime = GetDate()
      INSERT AllPersonalRecords (ContactID, NameStyle, Title, FirstName,
MiddleName, LastName, Suffix, EmailAddress, EmailPromotion, Phone,
PasswordHash, PasswordSalt, AdditionalContactInfo, rowguid, ModifiedDate)
            SELECT * FROM Person.Contact
    SELECT DATEDIFF(millisecond, @StartTime, GetDate()) as [Time consumed
    by INSERT]
    GO
-- Results:
-- Time consumed by INSERT
-- -----------------------
-- 893

DECLARE @StartTime datetime = GetDate()
      DELETE AllPersonalRecords
SELECT DATEDIFF(millisecond, @StartTime, GetDate()) as [Time consumed
by DELETE]
--Results:
-- Time consumed by DELETE
-- -----------------------
-- 1376
```

Table 8.1 Time Consumed by DML Statements Comparison (19,982 Rows)

	SELECT INTO	INSERT	TRUNCATE TABLE	DELETE
Milliseconds	610	893	0	1376

TEST DAY TIP

Remember that the *TRUNCATE TABLE* statement is the most efficient way to empty a table. However, the *TRUNCATE TABLE* statement will not work if a table is a target of a FOREIGN KEY constraint.

Summary of Exam Objectives

In this chapter we have learned about advanced DML functionality. We have examined the specifics of working with *IDENTITY* columns. Often we need to return the last *IDENTITY* value generated by SQL Server to the caller. For example, you may need to return the key value for the record you have just inserted into the table, so that it can be used in subsequent manipulations. To obtain the latest *IDENTITY* value generated by SQL Server, use the *@@IDENTITY, IDENT_CURRENT*, or *SCOPE_IDENTITY* functions. These functions vary by scope and session. If you need to insert explicit values into an *IDENTITY* column, you can use the *SET IDENTITY_INSERT table_name ON* statement. This is useful if you would like to eliminate the gaps that may have appeared in key values due to deletions. Use the *NEWID* function when you need to generate a new *GUID* value, and insert this value into a *uniqueidentifier* column.

One of the key elements of DML is the ability to return and manipulate data affected by the DML statement. This is performed by using the *OUTPUT* clause. The *OUTPUT* clause can reference the INSERTED and DELETED special tables. It is used with the following syntax:

```
OUTPUT [INSERTED.Column_name, …][DELETED.Column_name,…][Scalar_expression |
Variable | From_clause_table.Column_name] [INTO output_table | @table_variable
[(Column_list)]]
```

Values from the INSERTED and DELETED tables, as well as other scalar expressions, can be returned by the *OUTPUT* statement. You can also insert the results of the *OUTPUT* statement into a table or a table-valued variable. To do this, use the *OUTPUT INTO* clause. The *OUTPUT* and *OUTPUT INTO* clauses are especially useful with the *MERGE* DML statement. When used with the *MERGE* statement, we can specify the *$action* expression in the *OUTPUT* clause. The *$action* expression will tell us whether a particular row has been inserted, modified, or deleted by the *MERGE* statement.

We have also learned about nonlogged DML operations, like the *SELECT INTO* and *TRUNCATE TABLE* statements. These operations accomplish the equivalent of *INSERT* and *DELETE* statements, but offer much better performance. However, you must always back up a production database after using a nonlogged operation. This is because details of records affected by nonlogged operations are not recorded in the SQL Server transaction logs. Should the database be lost due to a disaster, you will not be able to replay the log files into an earlier database backup.

Exam Objectives Fast Track

Using @@IDENTITY and NEWID Functions in DML Statements

☑ To return the last *IDENTITY* value that has been generated by SQL Server, use the *@@IDENTITY*, *IDENT_CURRENT*, and *SCOPE_IDENTITY* functions.

☑ The *@@IDENTITY* variable stores the last IDENTITY value generated for any table by the current connection.

☑ The *SCOPE_IDENTITY()* function will return the last IDENTITY value generated for the current scope. It ignores nested scopes like those created by triggers.

☑ The *IDENT_CURRENT*(table_name) function returns the last IDENTITY value inserted into a specified table regardless of the connection or scope from which it is called.

☑ IDENTITY columns are maintained automatically by SQL Server. However, sometimes you may wish to insert an explicit value into an IDENTITY column. To enable the insert of explicit IDENTITY values into IDENTITY columns use the *SET IDENTITY_INSERT* [database_name].[schema_name]. table_name ON statement.

☑ The *NEWID* function returns a new value of type uniqueidentifier.

Returning Data from DML Operations Using the OUTPUT Clause

☑ The OUTPUT clause allows you to return rows affected by the DML statement, or to insert these results into a table or table-valued variable.

☑ Use the OUTPUT clause to find out what data was affected by your *INSERT*, *UPDATE*, *DELETE*, and *MERGE* statements.

☑ The Special tables *INSERTED* and *DELETED* are accessible from within the *OUTPUT* clause. The *INSERTED* table contains new values that have been inserted or updated. The *DELETED* table contains old values for the rows that have been deleted or updated. The structure of these special tables is the same as the structure of the table that has been affected by the DML statement.

Using the OUTPUT Clause with the MERGE Statement

☑ When the *OUTPUT* clause is used with the *MERGE* statement, the *$action* expression becomes available. This expression is not available with other DML statements.

☑ The *$action* expression will store the value *INSERT*, *UPDATE*, or *DELETE* for each target table record affected by the *MERGE* statement.

☑ Only one *OUTPUT* clause can be specified for a MERGE statement.

☑ The *OUTPUT* clause should be the last clause in the *MERGE* statement.

Performing Nonlogged DML Operations

☑ The *SELECT INTO* and *TRUNCATE TABLE* statements are nonlogged operations.

☑ Nonlogged operations perform better than logged DML statements like *INSERT* and *DELETE*, when Bulk-Logged recovery model is used.

☑ You must back up a production database after using nonlogged operations.

☑ You cannot use a *TRUNCATE TABLE* statement on a table that is the target of a FOREIGN KEY constraint.

Exam Objectives
Frequently Asked Questions

Q: What is the difference between *IDENTITY* and uniqueidentifier columns?

A: *IDENTITY* is a special property that makes a numeric column automatically increment its new values. You can specify a seed and an increment value for an *IDENTITY* column. *IDENTITY* columns are usually of the integer data type. Uniqueidentifier is a special data type that holds GUID type values; for example, 6F9619FF-8B86-D011-B42D-152C04FC964FF.

Q: Can I use *@@IDENTITY* without an *INSERT* statement?

A: Yes, but it will return *NULL*. *@@IDENTITY* holds the last value of any IDENTITY column generated by SQL Server for your session.

Q: Can I reference *INSERTED* and *DELETED* tables outside the *OUTPUT* clause?

A: No, these tables are available only to the *OUTPUT* clause. They are also available to DML triggers discussed earlier in this book.

Q: In a *MERGE* statement can I specify an *OUTPUT* clause for each *MERGE* action?

A: No, there can be only one *OUTPUT* clause for the entire *MERGE* statement. However, you can filter by the $action value.

Q: If I perform a nonlogged operation like *TRUNCATE TABLE*, and then replay the logs into an earlier backup of the database, will the *TRUNCATE* table operation be rolled back?

A: No, SQL Server will not allow you to replay the logs if a nonlogged operation has occurred since the last database backup.

Q: Does the *TRUNCATE TABLE* statement delete the table object as well as the data?

A: *TRUNCATE TABLE* deletes only the data contained in the table; the table definition and structure remain intact. To remove the table object, use the *DROP TABLE* statement.

Self Test

1. You have a Products table that contains a ProductID column defined as *IDENTITY*. You have created a stored procedure that creates a new product record and inserts it into the Products table based on parameters passed to the stored procedure. How should you return the ProductID value for the new product record to the caller?

   A. Use the *NEWID()* function.

   B. Use the *@@IDENTITY* function.

   C. After your *INSERT* statement is complete, locate the record using the values passed and extract its ProductID.

   D. Enable the *IDENTITY_INSERT* setting. Use the *MAX* function to find the last IDENTITY value and add 1. Insert this value into the ProductID column and return it to the caller.

2. You have a very large table containing documents stored as a column of the varbinary data type. The table is named Documents and is not referenced by FOREIGN KEY constraints. What is the most efficient way of removing all records from this table, while leaving the table ready for inserting new records?

   A. `TRUNCATE TABLE Documents`

   B. `DELETE Documents`

   C. `DELETE FROM Documents`

   D. `DROP TABLE Documents`

3. You have two tables, FarmAnimals and Pets, with data as shown.

FarmAnimals Table

AnimalID	AnimalName	Price
1	Llama	2600.00
2	Piglet	400.00

Pets Table

AnimalID	AnimalName	Price
1	Kitten	75.00
2	Puppy	120.00
3	Piglet	350.00

You wish to use the *MERGE* statement against the Pets table to delete all records that exist in the FarmAnimals table. For those records in Pets that are not also in FarmAnimals, you wish to add 30% to the Price. You want to output the action, animal_name, and price_change into a table-valued variable named @result. What is the best way to achieve this?

A.

```
DECLARE @Result TABLE (action nvarchar(10), animal_name nvarchar(50),
price_change money)

MERGE INTO FarmAnimals

USING Pets ON Pets.AnimalName = FarmAnimals.AnimalName

WHEN MATCHED THEN DELETE

WHEN NOT MATCHED BY SOURCE THEN UPDATE SET Price *=1.3

OUTPUT $action, deleted.AnimalName, inserted.Price - deleted.Price
into @Result;
```

B.

```
DECLARE @Result TABLE (action nvarchar(10), animal_name nvarchar(50),
price_change money)

MERGE INTO Pets

USING FarmAnimals ON Pets.AnimalName = FarmAnimals.AnimalName

WHEN MATCHED THEN DELETE

WHEN NOT MATCHED BY SOURCE THEN UPDATE SET Price *=1.3

OUTPUT $action, deleted.AnimalName, inserted.Price - deleted.Price
into @Result;
```

C.

```
DECLARE @Result TABLE (action int, animal_name nvarchar(50), price_change
money)

MERGE INTO Pets
```

```
USING FarmAnimals ON Pets.AnimalName = FarmAnimals.AnimalName
WHEN MATCHED THEN DELETE
WHEN NOT MATCHED BY SOURCE THEN UPDATE SET Price *=1.3
OUTPUT $action, deleted.AnimalName, inserted.Price - deleted.Price
into @Result;
```

D.

```
DECLARE @Result TABLE (action nvarchar(10), animal_name nvarchar(50),
price_change money)
MERGE INTO @Result
USING FarmAnimals ON Pets.AnimalName = FarmAnimals.AnimalName
WHEN MATCHED THEN DELETE
WHEN NOT MATCHED BY SOURCE THEN UPDATE SET Price *=1.3;
```

4. You have a very large database several terabytes in size. The database is backed up over the weekend, with transaction logs backed up daily. You are asked to empty one of the unnecessary historical tables to free space in the database. You must do this in the most efficient way with the least risk to business continuity. What is the best way to do this?

   A. Use the *TRUNCATE TABLE* statement. Do not deviate from the backup schedule.

   B. Use the *DELETE* statement. Do not deviate from the backup schedule.

   C. Use the *TRUNCATE TABLE* statement. Perform a full backup of the database as soon as the statement completes.

   D. Use the *DELETE* statement. Perform a full backup of the database as soon as the statement completes.

5. You have a stored procedure that uses the *TRUNCATE TABLE* statement to empty the table named Pets. You would like to return all rows that were deleted to the caller. What is the best way to do this?

   A. Use the *OUTPUT* clause to return *TRUNCATED.**

   B. Use a DML ON *DELETE* trigger to return the row values from the *DELETED* table.

   C. Use the *OUTPUT* clause to return *DELETED.**

   D. Rewrite your statement to use *DELETE* instead of *TRUNCATE TABLE*.

6. You have a stored procedure named Get_NewProducts. You wish to insert the results of this stored procedure into the Production.Product table and output the inserted.* values using the *OUTPUT* clause. What is the best way to do this?

   A.
   ```
   INSERT Production.Product (Name, ProductNumber, Color)

   OUTPUT Inserted.*

   EXECUTE Get_NewProducts
   ```

   B.
   ```
   INSERT Production.Product (Name, ProductNumber, Color)

   OUTPUT Inserted.*

   SELECT * FROM Get_NewProducts
   ```

   C.
   ```
   INSERT Production.Product (Name, ProductNumber, Color)

   VALUES (EXECUTE Get_NewProducts) OUTPUT Inserted.*
   ```

   D. Rewrite the stored procedure as a table-valued function.

7. You have a table named Contact with an *IDENTITY* column ContactID. You also have a table named Address with an *IDENTITY* column AddressID. You have an *INSERT DML* trigger on table Contact that creates a new record in the Address table. You successfully use the *INSERT* statement to add a new Contact record. You then query the value of *@@IDENTITY*. What will the *@@IDENTITY* variable contain?

   A. *@@IDENTITY* will contain the last IDENTITY value from ContactID.

   B. *@@IDENTITY* will contain the last IDENTITY value from AddressID.

   C. *@@IDENTITY* will contain NULL.

   D. *@@IDENTITY* will contain the success code of 0.

8. You have a table defined as follows.
   ```
   CREATE TABLE Components
   (ComponentID uniqueidentifier PRIMARY KEY,
   ComponentName nvarchar(50))
   ```

   What is the best way to insert two rows into this table, with Component Names 'Fibre Switch', 'NAS Head'?

   A.
   ```
   DECLARE @id uniqueidentifier;
   SET @id = NEWID()
   INSERT Components Values (@id, 'Fibre Switch'), (@id, 'NAS Head')
   ```

B.

```
INSERT Components Values (NEWID(), 'Fibre Switch'), (NEWID(), 'NAS Head')
```

C.

```
INSERT Components Values (@@IDENTITY, 'Fibre Switch'),
(@@IDENTITY, 'NAS Head')
```

D.

```
INSERT Components Values (CURRENT_IDENT(), 'Fibre Switch'),
CURRENT_IDENT(), 'NAS Head')
```

9. You have a FarmAnimals table containing data as shown.

FarmAnimals Table

AnimalID	AnimalName	Price
1	Llama	2600.00
2	Piglet	400.00

You wish to delete the animal with ID of 1, and output its ID, Name, and Price into a table named Pets. The table Pets has the same structure as the FarmAnimals table. What is the best way to achieve this?

A.

```
DELETE FarmAnimals
WHERE AnimalID = 1
OUTPUT
deleted.AnimalID, deleted.AnimalName, deleted.Price into Pets (AnimalID,
AnimalName, Price)
```

B.

```
DELETE FarmAnimals
OUTPUT
deleted.AnimalName, deleted.Price, deleted.AnimalID into Pets
(AnimalID, AnimalName, Price)
WHERE AnimalID = 1
```

C.

```
DELETE FarmAnimals
OUTPUT
deleted.AnimalID, deleted.AnimalName, deleted.Price into Pets
(AnimalID, AnimalName, Price)
WHERE AnimalID = 1
```

D.

```
DELETE FarmAnimals
OUTPUT
inserted.AnimalID, inserted.AnimalName, inserted.Price into Pets
(AnimalID, AnimalName, Price)
WHERE AnimalID = 1
```

10. You have a table named EmployeePhoto. This table is not referenced by any *FOREIGN KEY* constraints. What is the most efficient way of deleting the EmployeePhoto table entirely, including data and structure?

A.

```
TRUNCATE TABLE EmployeePhoto
```

B.

```
DELETE EmployeePhoto
```

C.

```
DELETE FROM EmployeePhoto
```

D.

```
DROP TABLE EmployeePhoto
```

11. You have created an updateable view called DeletedLocations in the AdventureWorks database. You execute the following statement.

```
DELETE Production.Location
OUTPUT deleted.* INTO DeletedLocations
WHERE LocationID = 1
```

What data will be contained in DeletedLocations view?

A. The row for Location number 1.

B. None, but the *DELETE* statement will succeed.

C. None, but the *DELETE* statement will fail.

D. The row for Location number 1, but only the LocationID column will be populated.

12. You have a table named Pets with an AnimalID *IDENTITY* column as follows.

Pets Table

AnimalID int PRIMARY KEY	AnimalName nvarchar(50)
1	Kitten
3	Piglet
4	Puppy

You would like to insert Llama with AnimalID of 2 into the table. What is the best way to achieve this?

A.

```
SET IDENTITY_INSERT PETS ON;
  INSERT PETS (AnimalID, AnimalName) VALUES (2, 'Llama')
```

B.

```
SET IDENTITY_INSERT PETS ON;
  INSERT PETS VALUES (2, 'Llama')
```

C.

```
SET IDENTITY_INSERT PETS OFF;
  INSERT PETS (AnimalID, AnimalName) VALUES (2, 'Llama')
```

D.

```
SET IDENTITY_INSERT PETS OFF;
  INSERT PETS VALUES (2, 'Llama')
```

13. You have three tables: FarmAnimals, Pets, and AllAnimals, with data.

FarmAnimals Table

AnimalID	AnimalName
1	Llama
2	Piglet

Pets Table

AnimalID	AnimalName
1	Kitten
2	Piglet
3	Puppy

AllAnimals Table

AnimalID	AnimalName
3	Puppy

You wish to use the *MERGE* statement against the AllAnimals table to insert rows from both Pets and FarmAnimals, and delete rows that don't exist in Pets or FarmAnimals. You want to output the action and inserted_animal_name, deleted_animal_name into a table-valued variable named @result. What is the best way to achieve this?

A.

```
DECLARE @Result TABLE (action nvarchar(10), inserted_animal_name
nvarchar(50)

MERGE INTO AllAnimals

USING (SELECT * FROM FarmAnimals UNION SELECT * FROM PETS) as src ON
AllAnimals.AnimalName = src.AnimalName

WHEN NOT MATCHED BY TARGET THEN INSERT (AnimalName, Price) VALUES
(SRC.AnimalName, SRC.Price)

WHEN NOT MATCHED BY SOURCE THEN DELETE

OUTPUT $action, inserted.AnimalName, deleted.AnimalName INTO @Result;

SELECT * FROM @Result;
```

B.

```
DECLARE @Result TABLE (action nvarchar(10), inserted_animal_name
nvarchar(50), deleted_animal_name nvarchar(50))

MERGE INTO AllAnimals

USING (SELECT * FROM FarmAnimals UNION SELECT * FROM PETS) as src ON
AllAnimals.AnimalName = src.AnimalName
```

```
WHEN NOT MATCHED BY TARGET THEN INSERT (AnimalName, Price) VALUES
(SRC.AnimalName, SRC.Price)

WHEN NOT MATCHED BY SOURCE THEN DELETE

OUTPUT $action, inserted.AnimalName, deleted.AnimalName INTO @Result;

SELECT * FROM @Result;
```

C.

```
DECLARE @Result TABLE (action nvarchar(10), inserted_animal_name
nvarchar(50), deleted_animal_name nvarchar(50))

MERGE INTO AllAnimals

USING (SELECT * FROM FarmAnimals UNION SELECT * FROM PETS) as src ON
AllAnimals.AnimalName = src.AnimalName

WHEN NOT MATCHED BY TARGET THEN INSERT (AnimalName, Price) VALUES
(SRC.AnimalName, SRC.Price)

WHEN NOT MATCHED BY SOURCE THEN DELETE

OUTPUT @@action, inserted.AnimalName, deleted.AnimalName INTO @Result;

SELECT * FROM @Result;
```

D.

```
DECLARE @Result TABLE (action nvarchar(10), inserted_animal_name
nvarchar(50), deleted_animal_name nvarchar(50))

MERGE INTO AllAnimals

OUTPUT $action, inserted.AnimalName, deleted.AnimalName INTO @Result

USING (SELECT * FROM FarmAnimals UNION SELECT * FROM PETS) as src ON
AllAnimals.AnimalName = src.AnimalName

WHEN NOT MATCHED BY TARGET THEN INSERT (AnimalName, Price) VALUES
(SRC.AnimalName, SRC.Price)

WHEN NOT MATCHED BY SOURCE THEN DELETE;
```

14. You are connected to SQL Server running on ServerX. You have registered a linked server named ServerY. You have created an empty new table called Production.DeletedLocations in the AdventureWorks database on ServerY. You execute the following statement against ServerX.

```
DELETE Production.Location

OUTPUT deleted.* INTO ServerY.AdventureWorks.Production.DeletedLocations

WHERE LocationID = 1
```

What data will be contained in DeletedLocations table on ServerY?

A. The row for Location number 1.

B. None, but the *DELETE* statement will succeed.

C. None, but the *DELETE* statement will fail.

D. The row for Location number 1, but only if it was previously deleted from ServerY.

15. You are using a *DELETE* statement with an *OUTPUT* clause to output the deleted values into a history table. Your *DELETE* statement fails with a *FOREIGN KEY* constraint violation. What values will be inserted by the *OUTPUT* clause into the history table?

A. No values will be inserted into the history table, as no values have been deleted.

B. A row of *NULL* values will be inserted into the history table, as no values have been deleted.

C. An error message will be inserted into the history table.

D. A row of values that would have been deleted will be inserted into the history table.

16. You have a table named Contact with an *IDENTITY* column ContactID. You also have a table named Address with an *IDENTITY* column AddressID. You have an *INSERT DML* trigger on table Contact that creates a new record in the Address table. You successfully use the *INSERT* statement to add a new Contact record. You then examine the value returned by the *SCOPE_ IDENTITY* function. What will the *SCOPE_IDENTITY* function return?

A. The *SCOPE_IDENTITY* function will return the last IDENTITY value from ContactID.

B. The *SCOPE_IDENTITY* function will return the last IDENTITY value from AddressID.

C. The *SCOPE_IDENTITY* function will return *NULL*.

D. The *SCOPE_IDENTITY* function will return the success code of 0.

17. You have a table named Orders that is referenced by a *FOREIGN KEY* constraint from the OrderDetails table. The OrderDetails table is empty. What is "the" most efficient way of deleting all data in the the Orders table?

A.
```
TRUNCATE TABLE Orders
```
B.
```
DELETE Orders
```
C.
```
TRUNCATE TABLE Orders, OrderDetails
```

D.

```
DROP TABLE Orders
```

18. You have a table named Sales.SalesPerson. You are using the following statement to double the bonus for the top five salespeople by their total orders due.

```
UPDATE Sales.SalesPerson
SET Bonus *= 2
WHERE SalesPersonID IN (SELECT TOP (5) SalesPerson.SalesPersonID
FROM Sales.SalesPerson JOIN Sales.SalesOrderHeader on SalesOrderHeader.
SalesPersonID = SalesPerson.SalesPersonID
GROUP BY SalesPerson.SalesPersonID, SalesPerson.Bonus
ORDER BY SUM(SalesOrderHeader.TotalDue) DESC)
```

What is the best way to return the ID of the sales persons affected, along with the original value of their bonus?

A.

```
OUTPUT INSERTED.SalesPersonID, INSERTED.Bonus
```

B.

```
OUTPUT INSERTED.SalesPersonID, DELETED.Bonus
```

C.

```
OUTPUT @@Identity, DELETED.Bonus
```

D.

```
OUTPUT SalesPerson.SalesPersonID, DELETED.Bonus
```

19. The following statement returns approved new products from the ProductCandidate table, then merges them into the Product table.

```
1) DECLARE @newProducts TABLE
(Action nvarchar(10), Name nvarchar(255), ProductNumber nvarchar(10),
ListPrice money)
2) MERGE INTO Production.Product
3) USING (SELECT Name, ProductNumber, ListPrice FROM Production.
ProductCandidate WHERE ApprovedFlag = 1) as src ON
Product.ProductNumber = src.ProductNumber
4) WHEN MATCHED THEN
5) UPDATE SET Name = src.Name, ListPrice = src.ListPrice
WHEN NOT MATCHED BY TARGET THEN
6) INSERT (Name, ProductNumber, ListPrice) VALUES(src.Name, src.
ProductNumber, src.ListPrice)
7);
```

What is the best way to insert the newly inserted products into a table-level variable named @NewProducts?

What is the best way to store the new and updated products in the @newProducts variable, along with the operation performed on the product (*INSERT* or *UPDATE*)?

A.

Add this statement between lines 2 and 3:

```
OUTPUT $action, inserted.Name, inserted.ProductNumber,
inserted.ListPrice INTO @newProducts
```

B.

Add this statement between lines line 6 and 7:

```
OUTPUT $action, inserted.Name, inserted.ProductNumber,
inserted.ListPrice INTO @newProducts;
```

C.

Add this statement between lines 5 and 6:

```
OUTPUT $action, inserted.Name, inserted.ProductNumber,
inserted.ListPrice INTO @newProducts
```

D.

Add this statement after line 7:

```
OUTPUT $action, inserted.Name, inserted.ProductNumber,
inserted.ListPrice INTO @newProducts
```

20. You have two tables, FarmAnimals and Pets, with data.

Pets Table

AnimalID	AnimalName	Price
1	Kitten	75.00
2	Puppy	120.00
3	Piglet	350.00

FarmAnimals Table

AnimalID	AnimalName	Price
1	Llama	2600.00
2	Piglet	400.00

You execute the following statement against these tables.

```
MERGE INTO Pets
USING FarmAnimals ON Pets.AnimalName = FarmAnimals.AnimalName
WHEN MATCHED THEN
    UPDATE SET Price = FarmAnimals.Price
WHEN NOT MATCHED BY TARGET THEN
    INSERT (AnimalName, Price) VALUES (FarmAnimals.AnimalName,
FarmAnimals.Price)
OUTPUT $action, inserted.AnimalName as ins_name, deleted.AnimalName as
del_name, deleted.Price as old_price;
```

What are the results of the statement?

A.

$action	ins_name	del_name	old_price
UPDATE	Piglet	Piglet	350.00

B.

$action	ins_name	del_name	old_price
UPDATE	Llama	Llama	2600.00
UPDATE	Piglet	Piglet	350.00

C.

$action	ins_name	del_name	old_price
INSERT	Llama	NULL	NULL
UPDATE	Piglet	Piglet	350.00

D.

$action	ins_name	del_name	old_price
INSERT	Llama	NULL	NULL
DELETE	Piglet	Piglet	350.00
INSERT	Piglet	NULL	NULL

Self Test Quick Answer Key

1. **B**

2. **A**

3. **B**

4. **B**

5. **D**

6. **D**

7. **B**

8. **B**

9. **C**

10. **D**

11. **C**

12. **A**

13. **B**

14. **C**

15. **D**

16. **A**

17. **B**

18. **B**

19. **B**

20. **C**

Chapter 9

MCTS SQL Server 2008 Exam 433

Working with Multiple-Source Queries

Exam objectives in this chapter:

- Using Linked Servers
- Using Four-Part Database Names
- The DTC Explained
- OpenQuery, OpenRowSet, and OpenDataSource Explained
- Multiple Sources with SQL Server Integration Services

Exam objectives review:

- ☑ Summary of Exam Objectives
- ☑ Exam Objectives Fast Track
- ☑ Exam Objectives Frequently Asked Questions
- ☑ Self Test
- ☑ Self Test Quick Answer Key

Introduction

In your working environment, it is highly unlikely that you will work with just a single SQL Server database. If your working environment has only SQL Server, you might still have to link between multiple databases. For example, in a human resources system, you need to link the payroll and attendance databases to get important information. Most users will not find it difficult to join to SQL Server databases, and in most cases, you need to work with heterogeneous database systems like Oracle or DB2, apart from SQL Server. This chapter discusses methods you can use when working with multiple-source queries effectively and efficiently.

Using Linked Servers

Linked Servers enable your SQL Server instance to execute commands against OLE DB or ODBC compatible data sources. Linked Servers can be used in the following scenarios.

- Accessing data from heterogeneous data sources like MS Access, Oracle, Sybase, and MySQL

- From Linked Servers, having the ability to issue distributed queries, updates, commands, and transactions on heterogeneous data sources

Head of the Class...

What Is the Use of Linked Servers in SQL Server Integration Services (SSIS)?

Users will often raise questions about user privileges you need to manage in order to add or drop Linked Servers. As Linked Servers are added to the SQL Server, you need to have server roles. As is obvious, the **sysadmin** server role can add or drop Linked Servers because **sysadmin** can do everything in the server, whereas the **setupadmin** server role is tailored to adding and dropping Linked Servers.

Continued

Users also often face the dilemma of when to use Linked Servers in SSIS as both options are supporting heterogeneous databases. As this is not a place to discuss features and facilities of SSIS, we will simply discuss where Linked Servers can be used.

Linked Servers can be used to update the remote server within your application. For example, if you need to update a remote server table from a trigger where the trigger is fired after an insert to the SQL Server table, **Linked Server** is the option.

You can use Linked Servers in your Web application when you need to access a remote server other than SSIS.

Also, if you want to analyze data in a remote server, most professionals prefer to use the **Linked Server** option because it will give you the luxury of tweaking data, group, Union, and so on, the way you want.

How a Linked Server Works

When a client application executes a distributed query via a Linked Server, SQL Server sends requests to OLE DB. The *rowset* request may be in the form of executing a query against the provider or opening a base table from the provider.

For a data source to return data through a Linked Server, the OLE DB provider (DLL) for that data source must be present on the same server as the instance of SQL Server.

When a third-party OLE DB provider is used, the account under which the SQL Server service runs must have read and execute permissions for the directory and for all subdirectories in which the provider is installed.

Configuring a Linked Server

You can configure Linked Servers in two different ways. The easiest way is to use SQL Server Management Studio because it provides you with the relevant screen to enter Linked Server parameters.

Here is a list of the parameters you need to configure Linked Servers in Figure 9.1.

Figure 9.1 General Page of New Linked Server

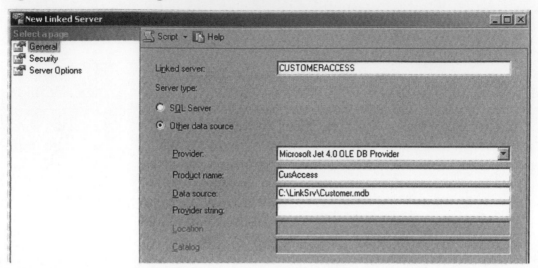

- **Provider** Select an OLE DB data source from the available list box. The OLE DB provider is registered with the given PROGID in the registry. OLE DB providers will be discussed later in the chapter.

- **Product name** The product name of the OLE DB data source to add as a Linked Server. This should be a nonempty value.

- **Data source** Name of the data source as interpreted by the OLE DB provider. In case of MS Access, Data Source is the *.mdb* file, and in Excel it is the Excel file.

- **Provider string** Unique programmatic identifier (PROGID) of the OLE DB provider that corresponds to the data source. Table 9.1 lists the parameters needed for different databases.

Table 9.1 Parameters Needed for Databases

Remote OLE DB Data Source	OLE DB Provider	Provider_Name	Data_Source	Provider String
SQL Server	Microsoft SQL Native Client OLE DB Provider	SQLNCI	SQL Server Instance Name	Database Name
Oracle	Microsoft OLE DB Provider for Oracle	MSDAORA	SQL*Net alias for Oracle	
Oracle, version 8 and later for the Oracle database	Oracle Provider for OLE DB	OraOLEDB.Oracle	Oracle database Alias	
MS Access	Microsoft OLE DB Provider for Jet	Microsoft.Jet.OLEDB.4.0	Full path of MS Access file	
ODBC data source	Microsoft OLE DB Provider for ODBC	MSDASQL	System DSN of ODBC data source	ODBC connection string (If no DSN available)
File system	Microsoft OLE DB Provider for Indexing Service	MSIDXS	Indexing Service catalog name	
Excel	Microsoft OLE DB Provider for Jet	Microsoft.Jet.OLEDB.4.0	Full path of Excel file	Excel 5
IBM DB2 Database	Microsoft OLE DB Provider for DB2	DB2OLEDB		DB2 database Catalog name

Security is a very important configuration in Link Servers. As the remote server is a different server, there is a probability that users in the SQL Server server do not exist in the remote server. Therefore, you need to map users between SQL Server and the remote server. Figure 9.2 shows the Security tab of the Linked Server.

Figure 9.2 Security Tab of Configuring Link Server

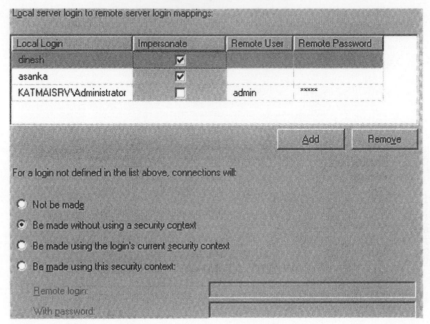

The login map will either pass the user along without transiting the login name if the **impersonate** option is checked or translate any user's login to a remote login and password if the **impersonate** option is not checked. On the external server, the login must be a valid login and must have been granted security rights in order for the link to be effective.

The default connection options for a user not mapped are as follows:

- **Not be made** This option restricts the ability to run distributed queries to those users in the user mapping list. If a user not on the user mapping list attempts to run a distributed query, he will receive an error.

- **Be made without using a security context** This option is for non–SQL Server external data sources and is not useful for SQL Server. SQL Server will attempt to connect as the user SQL without the password. If a user not on the server mapping list attempts to run the distributed query, he will return an error.

- **Be made using the logins current security context** When the local SQL server connects to the external server, it can delegate security, meaning that the local SQL server will connect to the local users' login of the SQL server. Using this method is similar to listing the user and selecting the **impersonate** option except that this uses security delegation, and to pass the security context, the login must be the exact same account and not just the same login and password.

- **Be made using the security context** This option simply assigns every nonmapped local user to a hardcoded external SQL Server login. Although this may be the simplest method, it allows every local user the same access to external SQL Server. Using this option should not violate any responsible security regulations.

Server options can be set, but most of the time you can get away with default settings. Here is a list of these default settings:

- **Collation Compatibility** Set this option to true if the two servers are using the same collation.

- **Data Access** If this option is set to false, it disables distributed queries to the external server.

- **RPC** If this option is set to true, remote procedure calls may be made to the external server.

- **RPC Out** If this option is set to true, remote procedure calls may be made from the external server.

- **Use Remote Collation** If this option is set to true, distributed queries will use the collation of the external SQL server rather than that of the local server.

- **Collation Name** This option specifies a collation for distributed queries. It cannot be chosen if collation compatibility is set.

- **Connection Time-out** The connection timeout is in milliseconds.

- **Query Time-out** The distributed query timeout is in milliseconds.

Exercise 9.1 will take you through the steps to create Linked Servers using SQL Server Management Studio. In this exercise, we will discuss how to create a Linked Server for Microsoft Access *mdb*.

EXERCISE 9.1

CREATING LINKED SERVERS USING SQL SERVER MANAGEMENT STUDIO

1. Start SQL Server Management Studio from **Program Files| SQL Server 2008**.

2. Select **Database Engine as Database Type** and the **SQL Server Database instance name** and provide the necessary user credentials to log in to SQL Server. If you supply the correct information, you will be taken to the SQL Server Management Studio.

3. If the **Object Explorer** is not visible, select the **Object Explorer** menu option from the **View** menu or press **F8**.

4. Expand **Server Object** in the **Object Explorer** and select **Linked Servers**. Right-click **Linked Servers** and select **New Linked Server** as shown in Figure 9.3.

Figure 9.3 New Linked Server Option in Object Explorer

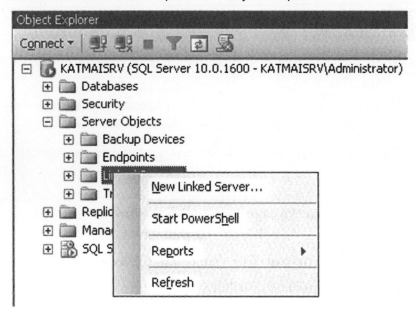

5. After selecting the name of the option, you will be taken to Figure 9.1, which is the general page of the Linked Server configuration.

6. Specify a Linked Server Name, which is the name of the Linked Server used when accessing the server.

7. Select the **Other data source** option.

8. Select **Microsoft Jet OLEDB 4.0 Provider** from the provider drop-down list.

9. Enter any text for the product name. Data Source should be the file path to the Microsoft Access *.mdb* file.

10. Leave the other two tabs with default values.

11. Click **OK** to confirm the changes.

You can drop the Linked Servers if you follow the steps in Exercise 9.2.

EXERCISE 9.2

DROPPING A LINKED SERVER IN SQL SERVER MANAGEMENT STUDIO

1. Start SQL Server Management Studio from **Program Files | SQL Server 2008**.

2. Select **Database Engine as Database Type** and the **SQL Server Database instance name** and provide the necessary user credentials to log in to SQL Server. If you supply the correct information, you will be taken to SQL Server Management Studio.

3. If the **Object Explorer** is not visible, select the **Object Explorer** menu option from the **View** menu or press **F8**.

4. Expand **Server Object** in the **Object Explorer** and select **Linked Servers**. Right-click the Linked Server you want to delete and select **Delete**.

5. Press **OK** to confirm the deletion of the Linked Server.

Similarly, you can create or drop Linked Servers using T-SQL scripts. Exercise 9.3 explains how to get the template of the Linked Server.

EXERCISE 9.3

OPENING TEMPLATE FOR LINKED SERVER IN SQL SERVER MANAGEMENT STUDIO

1. Start SQL Server Management Studio from **Program Files | SQL Server 2008**.

2. Select **Database Engine as Database Type** and the **SQL Server Database instance name** and provide the necessary user credentials to log in to SQL Server. If you supply the correct information, you will be taken to SQL Server Management Studio.

3. If the **Template Explorer** is not visible, select the **Template Explorer** menu option from the **View** menu or press **CTRL+ALT+T.**

4. In the Template Explorer, navigate to the Linked Server as seen in Figure 9.4.

Figure 9.4 Linked Server in Template Explorer

The **Add Linked Server Access MDB** template has the template to add Linked Server of MS Access MDB file to the SQL Server. **Add Linked Server Simple** template has the template for **To add a Link Server. Drop Linked Server** template has the template to drop a Linked Server.

5. Double-click the required template from the Template Explorer to enter the relevant parameters to suit your environment.

6. Execute the script by clicking the **Execute** button.

Apart from creating Linked Servers from SQL Server Management Studio, you have the option of creating them using T-SQL in Exercise 9.4.

EXERCISE 9.4

CREATING LINKED SERVERS USING T-SQL

1. Start SQL Server Management Studio from **Program Files | SQL Server 2008**.

2. Select **Database Engine as Database Type** and the **SQL Server Database instance name** and provide the necessary user credentials to log in to SQL Server. If you supply the correct information, you will be taken to SQL Server Management Studio.

3. Select the **New Query** button, which is most probably below the main menu. You will have a fresh query screen.

4. The following query will create a Linked Server named *CUSTOMERACCESS*, which is linked to Customer.MDB MS Access.

```
-- ========================================
-- Add Linked Server Access MDB
-- ========================================

EXEC sp_addlinkedserver
    @server = N'CUSTOMERACCES',
    @provider = N'Microsoft.Jet.OLEDB.4.0',
    @srvproduct = N'OLE DB Provider for Jet',
    @datasrc = N'C:\LinkSrv\CUSTOMER.MDB'
GO
```

5. The following query will set up login mapping between SQL Server and MS Access.

```
-- Set up login mapping using current user's security context
EXEC sp_addlinkedsrvlogin
    @rmtsrvname = N'CUSTOMERACCES',
    @useself = N'TRUE',
    @locallogin = NULL,
    @rmtuser = N'dinesh', --Remote User Name
    @rmtpassword = N'pa$$w0rd' -Remote user password
GO
```

6. After creating the Linked Server, you can verify by listing the tables in the Linked Server.

```
EXEC sp_tables_ex N'CUSTOMERACCESS'
GO
```

You have the option of dropping the Linked Server using T-SQL as shown in Exercise 9.5.

EXERCISE 9.5

DROPING A LINKED SERVER USING T-SQL

1. Start SQL Server Management Studio from **Program Files| SQL Server 2008**.

2. Select **Database Engine as Database Type** and the **SQL Server Database instance name** and provide the necessary user credentials to log in to SQL Server. If you supply the correct information, you will be taken to SQL Server Management Studio.

3. Select the **New Query** button, which is most probably below the main menu. You will have a fresh query screen.

4. The following query will drop the Link Server from SQL Server.

```
-- ===============================
-- Drop Linked Server template
-- ===============================
-- Drops a linked server reference to a Database Engine instance
-- Related logins will also be dropped in this example
EXEC master.dbo.sp_dropserver @server=N'CUSTOMERACESS',
@droplogins='droplogins'
GO
```

Provider Options

In addition to configuring Linked Server, you can also configure various options for each provider. These options are applied to all Linked Servers configured from the given provider. You can configure providers through the following steps in Exercise 9.6.

EXERCISE 9.6

CONFIGURING PROVIDER OPTIONS

1. Start SQL Server Management Studio from **Program Files| SQL Server 2008**.

2. Select **Database Engine as Database Type** and the **SQL Server Database instance name** and provide the necessary user credentials

to log in to SQL Server. If you supply the correct information, you will be taken to SQL Server Management Studio.

3. If the **Object Explorer** is not visible, select the **Object Explorer** menu option from the **View** menu or press **F8**.

4. Expand **Server Object** in the **Object Explorer** and expand to **Providers** in the **Linked Servers** further as shown in Figure 9.5.

Figure 9.5 List of Providers

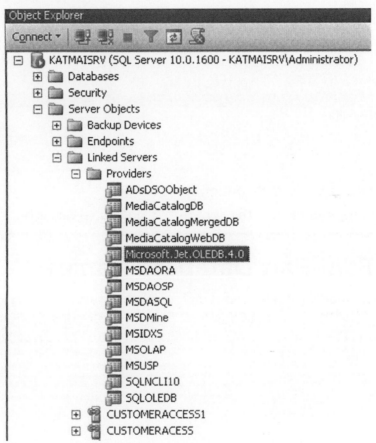

Double-click the Provider on which you want to set the configuration options and you will see Figure 9.6.

Figure 9.6 Provider Options

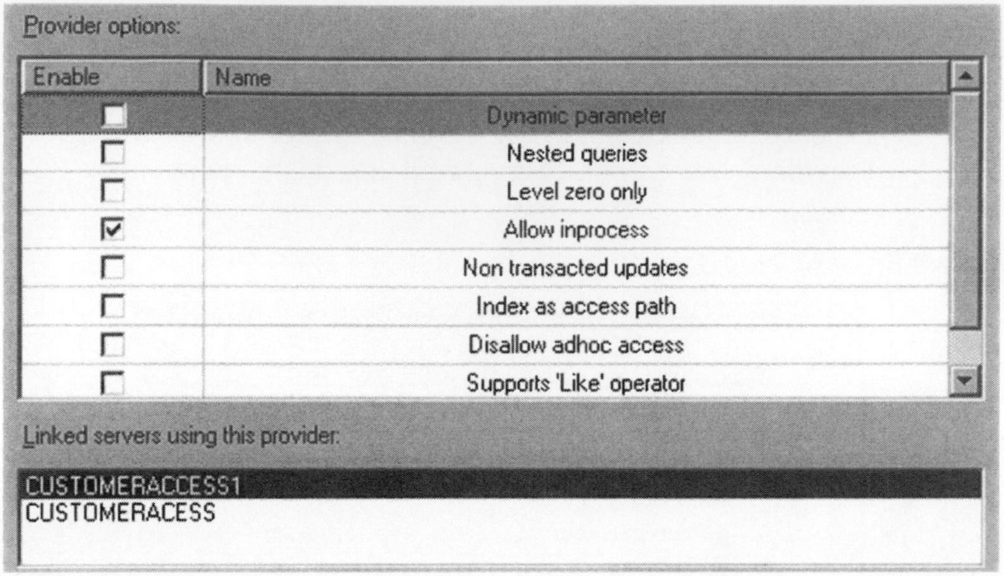

6. You can select the option from the list.
7. Also, you can see the configured Linked Server using this provider.

Using Four-Part Database Names

If the data is in another SQL server, complete the four-part name that is required to access data from the remote SQL server. *Server.Database.Schema.ObjectName* is the four-part name. The four-part name may be used in the *SELECT* or DML query. For *SELECT,* here is the query.

```
SELECT * FROM [<server_name,sysname,(local)><instance_name,sysname,\
SQLEXPRESS>].<database_name,sysname,pubs>.<schema_name,sysname,dbo>.
<table_name,sysname,authors>
GO

Example: SELECT Name, Address FROM RMTSERVER.AdventureWorks.Person.Address
```

In case of other database types, often you won't find the schema name. For example, in the MS Access example, you won't see a database and schema with a match to the SQL server. In those cases you can avoid them by notation as given in the following example.

```
SELECT * FROM CUSTOMERACCESS...Customer
```

The DTC Explained

SQL Server uses the Distributed Transaction Coordinator (DTC) to handle multiple-server transactions, commits, and rollbacks. The DTC server uses a two-phase commit schema for multiple-server transactions. Here are the steps.

1. Server is sent a **prepare to commit** message.

2. Server performs the first phase of the commit, verifying that it is capable of committing the transaction.

3. Server replies when it has finished preparing for the commit.

4. After server has responded positively to the **prepare to commit** message, the actual commit message is sent to each server.

5. DTC is required only when remote updates are occurring in the remote server.

TEST DAY TIP

There are three catalog views related to Linked Servers: *sys.linked_logins*, *sys.servers*, and *sys.remote_logins*. The most frequently used catalog view is *sys.servers*.

```
SELECT * from sys.servers
WHERE is_linked = 1
```

The preceding query will return the list of linked servers attached to a SQL server.

OpenQuery, OpenRowSet, and OpenDataSource Explained

Apart from using four dotted notations, you have three functions to access remote servers. Those functions are *OpenQuery*, *OpenRowSet*, and *OpenDataSource*. *OpenDataSource* and *OpenRowSet* commands are by default disabled, and you need to enable these options.

New & Noteworthy...

Enabling OpenDataSource and OpenRowSet Functions

As in SQL Server 2008, OpenDataSource and OpenRowSet are disabled in SQL Server 2005 by default. If you want to use these functions, you have to enable them.

In SQL Server 2005, there is a dedicated tool called SQL Server Surface Area Configuration. However, you will not find this tool with the SQL Server 2008 installation. Instead, there is a feature called Facets to enable OpenDataSource and OpenRowSet functions.

By following the steps in Exercise 9.7, you can enable these functions.

EXERCISE 9.7

ENABLING AD HOC REMOTE QUERIES

1. Start SQL Server Management Studio from **Program Files | SQL Server 2008**.

2. Select **Database Engine** as Database Type and the SQL Server Database instance name and provide the necessary user credentials to log in to SQL Server. If you supply the correct information, you will be taken to SQL Server Management Studio.

3. Right-click the server and select **Facets** from the context menu.

4. Select **Surface Area Configuration Server** from the Facet drop down. As per the RTM version of SQL Server 2008, it is the last facet in the drop down.

5. Enable **AdhocRemoteQueriesEnabled** as shown in Figure 9.7.

Figure 9.7 Enable Adhoc Remote Queries from Facets

Facet:	Surface Area Configuration	▼
Description:	Surface area configuration for features of the Database Engine. Only the features required by your application should be enabled. Disabling unused features helps protect your server by reducing the surface	

Facet properties:

AdHocRemoteQueriesEnabled	False	▼
ClrIntegrationEnabled	False	
DatabaseMailEnabled	False	
OleAutomationEnabled	False	
RemoteDacEnabled	False	
ServiceBrokerEndpointActive	False	
SoapEndpointsEnabled	False	
SqlMailEnabled	False	
WebAssistantEnabled	Property value 'WebAssistantEnabled' is not available.	
XPCmdShellEnabled	False	

OpenDataSource

Using the *OpenDataSource* function is the same as using a four-part name to access a Linked Server, except the *OpenDataSource*() function defines the link within the function instead of referencing a predefined linked server. While defining the link in code bypasses the linked server requirement, if the link location changes, then the change will affect every query that uses *OpenDataSource*(). In addition, *OpenDataSource*() will not accept variables as parameters.

```
SELECT Name FROM
OpenDataSource ('SQLOLEDB',Data Source ='Dinesh-Mob';User ID = sa;Password =sa')
.Family.dbo.Person
```

OpenQuery

For pass-through queries, the *OpenQuery*() function leverages a Linked Server. So it's the easiest to develop. It also handles changes in server configuration with changing code.

```
SELECT * FROM OPENQUERY(
LinkedServerName,'SELECT * FROM Tour WHERE Country=''Sri Lanka''')
```

You can do updates as well.

```
UPDATE OPENQUERY(LinkedServerName,
'SELECT * FROM Tour WHERE Country=''Sri Lanka''')
SET Start ='Colombo'
```

OpenRowSet

The *OpenRowSet* function is the counterpart to the OpenDataSet( ) function. Both require the remote data source to be fully specified in the distributed query.

```
SELECT Name
FROM OPENROWSET('SQLOLEDB',Data Source ='Dinesh-Mob';User ID =
sa;Password =sa',
SELECT * FROM Customers Where Cust = 1')
```

EXAM WARNING

There are several places where you can configure Link Servers. They are Facet, Provider Options, and Link Server properties. These configurations are different, and you need to make sure at which place you can do what configuration.

Multiple Sources with SQL Server Integration Services

SQL Server Integration Services (SSIS) is used mostly as an Extract-Transform-Load (ETL) tool. SSIS itself is a book title, and it will be much harder to confine SSIS to a single chapter. In this chapter, we are concerned mostly with the data source part of the SSIS.

Head of the Class...

History of SQL Server Integration Services (SSIS)

SSIS was first introduced in SQL Server 2005 as the successor to Data Transformation Services (DTS) in SQL Server 2000. In SQL Server 2005, SSIS was written from scratch, and SSIS came in the SQL Server Enterprise, Standard, Workgroup, Web, Express, and, of course, Developer editions. However, the Raw file source and XML sources are available only in Enterprise and Standard editions.

With the installation of SQL Server 2008, you will get an additional tool called SQL Server Business Intelligence Development Studio, which is used to create SSIS packages, SSAS cubes, and SSRS reports. Creating the SSIS package is described in Exercise 9.8.

EXERCISE 9.8

How to Create an SSIS Package

1. Start SQL Server Business Intelligence Development Studio from **Program Files | SQL Server 2008**.

2. Select **Projects...** from **File | New** at the main menu. You will be taken to the New Project dialog, which is shown in Figure 9.8.

Figure 9.8 New Project

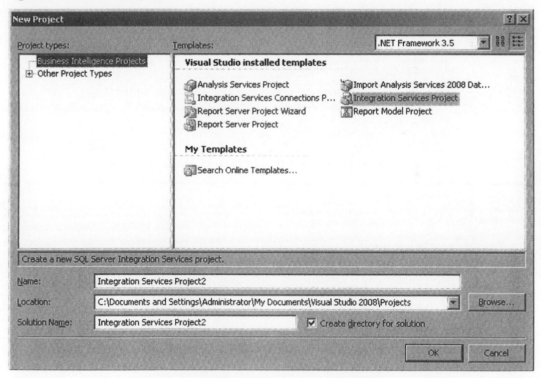

3. Select **Business Intelligence Projects** as a project type and select **Integration Services Projects** from Visual Studio installed templates.

4. Enter a name for the SSIS project and the folder location of the SSIS project and click **OK**.

5. After clicking the **OK** button, you will see the Control Flow of the package (see Figure 9.9).

Figure 9.9 Control Flow of the Package

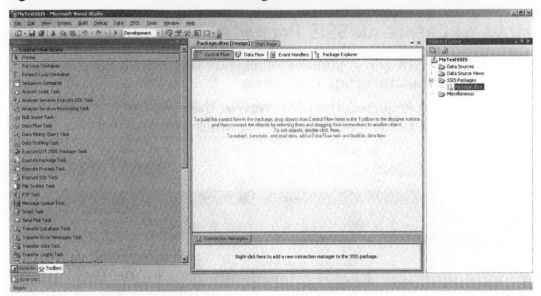

6. By default, the package name Package.dtsx is added to the project. You can rename the package and add new packages.

Here are the available sources in SSIS.

- **ADO Net source** This uses the ADO.NET connection manager to access data. In this source, you need to provide the table name or command string directly. Unlike OLE DB source, you cannot supply source in a variable in ADO net source.

- **Excel source** Excel source uses an Excel connection manager. This can be either a worksheet or a name space. Data types are assigned to each column by sampling a few rows.

- **Flat File source** Flat File source uses a Flat File manager, which can be delimited or of fixed length.

- **OLE DB source** OLE DB source uses the OLE DB connection manager.

- **Raw File source** Raw files are files written by the SSIS. Raw File Source uses these raw files.

- **XML source** Unlike other sources, XML Source does not use a connection manager; instead it uses an input file.

Exercise 9.9 will guide you in creating a connection manager.

EXERCISE 9.9

How to Create a Connection Manager

1. Create a SSIS project as mentioned in Exercise 9.8.
2. Right-click the area under the connection manager, and you will get the context menu shown in Figure 9.10.

Figure 9.10 Connection Manager Context Menu

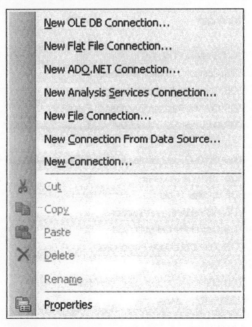

New OLE DB Connection...
New Flat File Connection...
New ADO.NET Connection...
New Analysis Services Connection...
New File Connection...
New Connection From Data Source...
New Connection...

✂ Cut
▣ Copy
▣ Paste
✕ Delete
  Rename
▣ Properties

3. Select **New OLE DB Connection** from the context menu. You will be taken to the **Configure Connection Manager** dialog box. You have the option of selecting already existing connection managers. You can create a new connection manager by clicking the **New** button.

4. Select the appropriate provider from the providers list. To create an MS Access connection manager, select **Microsoft Jet 4.0 OLE DB Provider.**

5. Browse and select the Access database.

6. In case there is a database password associated with the MS Access database, go to the **All** tab and enter the database password at the **Jet OLEDB: Database Password** as shown in Figure 9.11.

Figure 9.11 MS Access Database Password

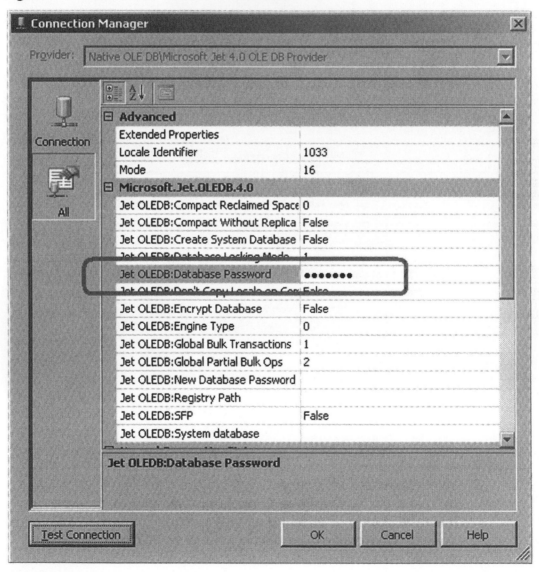

7. By clicking the **Test Connection** button, you can verify whether the connection manager is correct.

8. Clicking the **OK** button will create the connection manager.

9. You will see a connection manager at the bottom of the screen. You can rename the connection manager by right-clicking it.

New & Noteworthy...

Accessing Excel 2007 Files from SQL Server Integration Services

In SQL Server 2005, if you want to access an Excel 2007 file from SSIS, it is not straightforward.

If you want to import an Excel file, you can use Excel Source from the Data Flow Sources in SQL Server Integration Services (SSIS) and select the correct version from the available list. In SQL Server 2005, you will find only an Excel 3.0, 4.0, 5.0, and 97–2005 versions. To access an Excel 2007 file, you need to configure an OLE DB Source and select the provider **Native OLE DB\Microsoft Office 12.0 Access Database Engine OLE DB Provider** and extended properties as **Excel 12.0**.

This is much easier in SQL Server 2008 inasmuch as you have the additional version of Excel 2007 in the Excel source control and you simply have to select that version along with the filename.

SSIS provides several data flow controls that can fit your requirements (see Table 9.2).

Table 9.2 Data Flow Controls

Operation	Data Flow Controls
Union Two Data sets from SQL Server and MS Access	Union
Get Customer Name from Access database where you have the ID in the SQL Server database	Lookup
Inner Join	Merge Join
Outer Join	Merge Join
Full Outer Join	Merge Join

Exercise 9.10 will illustrate how to create an SSIS package to extract a customer name from the MS Access database where you have the Customer ID in the SQL Server table. Let us assume that the SQL Server and MS Access table names are Customer.

EXERCISE 9.10

SAMPLE SSIS PACKGE TO GET SELECTED COLUMNS FROM REMOTE DATABASE

1. Create an SSIS project and a package as mentioned in Exercise 9.8.

2. Create two connection managers, one for MS Access and one for MS SQL Server databases, as mentioned in Exercise 9.9.

3. Drag and drop a **Data Flow Control** from the data flow tasks. By default, the data flow will take Data Flow Task as its name and you can rename it any name you want.

4. Double-click the dragged control and you will be taken to the data flow control.

5. Drag and drop and an **OLE DB source** and rename it Access, as we are going to configure it to access the MS Access database.

6. Double-click the **Access OLE DB source** to configure the access OLE DB source and you will be taken to Figure 9.12.

Figure 9.12 Configuring Access OLE DB Source Editor

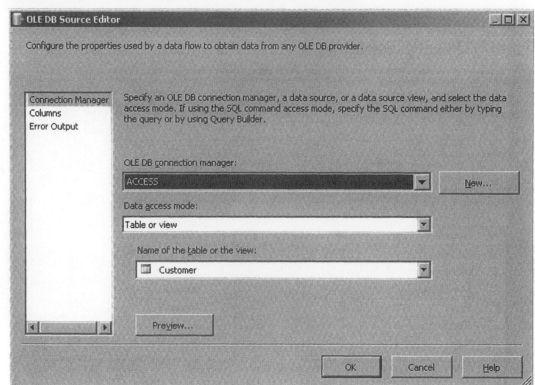

7. First select the previously created Access OLE DB connection manager. Select the data access mode as table or view. You have the option of writing a query by selecting SQL Command as the data access mode.

8. Next, select the required table from the table or view list.

9. From the column list you can select only the wanted columns so that unnecessary columns will not be used.

10. Add another OLE DB Source to configure SQL Server. The configuration will be the same as specified for MS Access.

11. For the Merge Join, you need sorted data sources; hence you need to add two Sort data flow transformation controls and connect each OLE DB source to sort and select the columns you need to order. Those columns should be the ones that are going to be joined.

12. Next, add another data flow transformation control named Merge Join and connect both data sources to it.

13. Double-click the **Merge Join control** and configure as shown in Figure 9.13.

Figure 9.13 Configuring Merge Join

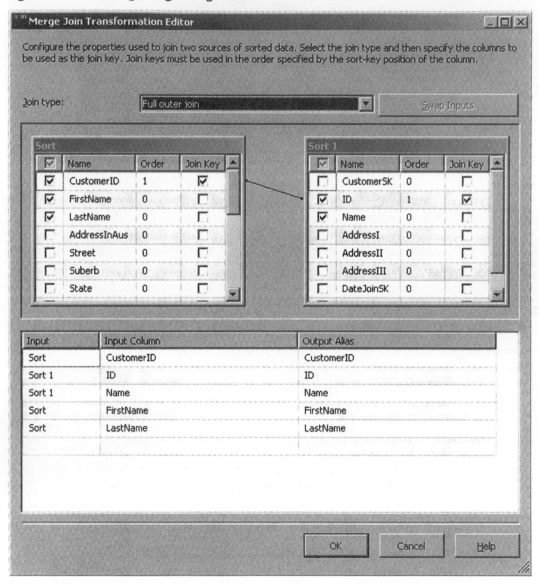

14. You have three join types, Inner Join, Left Outer Join, and Fuller Outer Join, to suit your requirements.

15. Next you have to select the columns you need to add to the data flow, and finally your data flow should look like Figure 9.14.

Figure 9.14 Data Flow

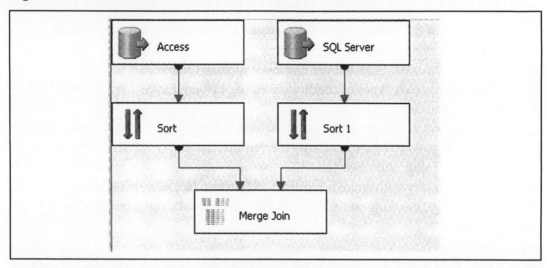

With implementation of SSIS, you will have the features of package configuration, package logging, and checkpoint configuration.

Summary of Exam Objectives

The prime aim of this chapter is to understand the methods used to connect to multiple SQL Server instances. Link Server can be used to link to SQL Server databases as well as non-SQL Server instances such as Oracle and DB2.

In this chapter, two types of methods were described: Linked Server and SQL Server Integration Services.

Linked Servers are used to create a link to the remote server, and after creating the Link Server you will have access to the remote server via the Link Server.

SQL Server Integration Services is a graphical tool through which you can access remote servers with quite a number of features. Because of the built-in controls to Merge, Lookup, and Union, working with SSIS for remote servers is easy with SSIS.

Exam Objectives Fast Track

Using Linked Servers

- ☑ Linked Servers enable your SQL Server instance to execute commands against OLE DB or ODBC compatible data sources.

- ☑ **setupadmin** or **sysadmin** server roles are required to create or drop Linked Servers.

- ☑ You can use the *OpenQuery* function to access a Linked Server, which is the recommended method.

Using Four-Part Database Names

- ☑ A four-part name is required to access data from the remote SQL Server.

- ☑ *Server.Database.Schema.ObjectName* is the four-part name.

- ☑ The four-part name may be used in the *SELECT* or DML query.

The DTC Explained

- ☑ SQL Server uses the Distributed Transaction Coordinator (DTC) to handle multiple-server transactions.

- ☑ DTC is required only when remote updates are occurring in the remote server.

OpenQuery, OpenRowSet, and OpenDataSource Explained

☑ Using the OpenDataSource function is the same as using a four-part name to access a Linked Server, except the OpenDataSource( ) function defines the link within the function instead of referencing a predefined linked sever.

☑ For pass-through queries, the OpenQuery( ) function leverages a Linked Server.

☑ The OpenRowSet function is the pass-through counterpart to the OpenDataSet( ) function.

Multiple Sources with SQL Server Integration Services

☑ SSIS can be used to access any OLE DB source, Excel, or text file with the graphic tools available with SSIS.

☑ With the installation of SQL Server 2008, you will get an additional tool called SQL Server Business Intelligence Development Studio, which is used to create SSIS packages, SSAS cubes, and SSRS reports.

☑ Lookup, Union, and Merge are data flow transformation controls used in SSIS to access remote sources mainly.

Exam Objectives
Frequently Asked Questions

Q: What service do you need to run when you need to initiate transactions in Linked Servers?

A: Distributed Transaction Coordinator (DTC).

Q: Is it possible to create Linked Servers between different versions of SQL Server?

A: Yes.

Q: Is it possible to create Linked Servers between different editions of SQL Server?

A: Yes.

Q: What is not the recommended security option to connect to Linked Servers?

A: Using hardcoded username and password for any user.

Q: What are the server roles you need to add or remove Linked Servers?

A: Sysadmin or Setupadmin.

Q: What feature can you use to enable *OpenDataSource* and *OpenRowSet* functions?

A: Facets.

Q: What data flow transformation task do you have to use when joining data flow from remote data source and SQL Server?

A: Merge Join.

Self Test

1. You have developed a payroll system using SQL Server, and you need to access attendance data that is stored in a DB2 database. It is decided to access DB2 via Linked Server. What driver should you use for better performance to access the DB2 database?

   A. Microsoft.Jet.OLEDB.4.0

   B. Microsoft OLE DB Provider for DB2

   C. MSDASQL

   D. You cannot create a Linked Server to the DB2 database.

2. You need to create a Link Server to the mySQL Database server and you find that there is no OLEDB driver for the mySQL. What driver can you use to access data from mySQL database server?

   A. Microsoft.Jet.OLEDB.4.0

   B. SQLNCLI

   C. MSDASQL

   D. You cannot create a Linked Server to mySQL database.

3. User Eric is a member of a Windows security group DBA. Both Eric and group DBA have login permission to the server. DBA group has **setupadmin** server role, user Eric doesn't have **setupadmin,** and both DBA group and Eric do not have **sysadmin** server roles. What will be the consequences if Eric tries to create a Link Server?

   A. Eric will not be able to create a Link Server.

   B. Eric will be able to create a Link Server.

   C. You cannot set up security settings as specified in the question.

4. User Eric is a member of a Windows security group DBA. Both Eric and group DBA have login permission to the server. DBA group has **setupadmin** server role, user Eric doesn't have **setupadmin,** and DBA group does not

have **sysadmin** server roles while user Eric has. What will be the consequences if Eric tries to create a Link Server?

    A. Eric will not be able to create a Link Server.

    B. Eric will be able to create a Link Server.

    C. You cannot set up security settings as specified in the question.

5. You have a SQL server, and you need to access a customer database of another SQL server that is in Chinese. You need to display it alphabetically by name. What additional configuration do you have to perform after adding a linked server?

    A. No additional configuration is required.

    B. You cannot access SQL Server data in Chinese.

    C. Set the **Collation Compatibility** option to On.

    D. Specify the Collation Name for remote servers.

6. You have a SQL server, and you need to access a production table in an Oracle database. You have decided to use the *OpenDataSource* function. After installation of SQL Server, what initial steps should you take to access data from the *OpenDataSource* function?

    A. You cannot access Oracle from the *OpenDataSource* function.

    B. By default, the *OpenDataSource* function is enabled.

    C. You need to launch SQL Server Surface Area Configuration to enable the *OpenDataSource* function.

    D. You need to enable the *OpenDataSource* function from the Facets feature.

7. You have a SQL server, and you need to get records on a product table where the category has the prefix C01. This product table is in a Sybase database, and a Linked Server is created to SQL Server on the Sybase database server with default settings. Here is the query that we try to execute.

```
Select ProductCode, ProductName, Category
From productserver…Prodcut Where Category Like 'C01%'
```

The preceding query returns an error; what might be the cause of the error?

    A. The operator is not supported by a Sybase database engine.

    B. The operator is not supported by Linked Servers.

C. The Provider option for a Sybase Provider is not set.

D. The Linked Server option for a Sybase Provider is not set.

8. You have configured several Linked Servers that are running in DB2 databases. You need to disable the access of the *OpenDataSource* function to one Linked Server and leave the other DB2 Linked Servers to have access via the *OpenDataSource* function. How can you achieve this?

A. Configure the Linked Server to enable/disable the *OpenDataSource* function.

B. Enable/disable the **Provider** option for DB2.

C. Enable/disable the Facet for *AdhocRemoteQueriesEnabled*.

D. You cannot do this.

9. You have a SQL Server database, and your production data is in a Sybase database. In SQL Server, you have the ProductCode, and you have been asked to get the product name from the Sybase database. You have decided to use SQL Server Integration Services to gather the required data from Sybase. What data flow transformation control should you use?

A. You cannot use SSIS to access data in Sybase.

B. There is no data flow transformation to gather data from Sybase.

C. The Lookup data flow transformation task.

D. The Union data flow transformation task.

10. You are a database architect of an organization where there are several branches, and they are running in different databases such as Oracle, DB2, and mySQL. You need to import all the sales data to the main database, which is in SQL Server, and you have decided to use SQL Server Integration Services. What data flow transformation control should you use?

A. You cannot use SSIS to access data in mySQL

B. There is no data flow transformation to gather data from DB2

C. The Lookup data flow transformation task

D. The Union data flow transformation task

E. The Union All data flow transformation task

11. You are developing SSIS packages to access data from multiple data sources. You are developing these packages in your development environment and need to transfer them to the production environment. What method are you going to use to store environment information such as server name and so on?

    A. SSIS Logging

    B. SSIS Package Configuration

    C. SSIS Checkpoint

    D. All of the above

12. You have an invoicing system in SQL Server 2000 where you need to update sales information in a remote SQL Server 2008 server online. You cannot afford to have a delay between data transfers. What technique should you use?

    A. Use a trigger to update a Service Broker.

    B. Use a trigger to update a Link Server.

    C. Use a scheduled SSIS package.

    D. A, B, and C

    E. B and C

13. You have an Excel file that has columns with more than 500 characters. How do you import this data to SQL Server using SQL Server Integration Services without truncating columns?

    A. You cannot import an Excel file with more than 255 characters.

    B. Change the length of the column width in the SSIS configuration.

    C. Increase the registry entry of TypeGuessRows of HKLM\SOFTWARE\Microsoft\Jet\4.0\Engine\Excel registry.

    D. Change the SSIS settings in the Settings tab.

14. You are using SSIS to access Excel files, and you have the many Excel versions from Excel 3.0 to Excel 2007. What additional steps do you need to take when accessing Excel 2007 files from SSIS?

    A. You cannot import Excel 2007 files from SSIS.

    B. You can use the Excel source and Excel 2007 as the version.

    C. You can use the Excel source and Excel 97–2005 as the version.

    D. Use the native OLE DB\Microsoft Office 12.0 Access Database Engine OLE DB provider and Excel 12.0 as the extended version.

15. You are to access an Excel file that has the following format.

RecordID	Name	Address	Postcode
1	Pablo Terry	60 West Fabeien Avenue	1237
2	Kevin Hooks	11, Second way	1987
3	Rose Mitchel	134A, Nobel Parkway	98762
.	....	....	.....
.	....	....	.....
.	....	....	.....
100	Janet Ramos		P1001

You are using *OpenRowSet* with the following query.

```
SELECT * FROM OPENROWSET('Microsoft.Jet.OLEDB.4.0',
     'Excel 8.0;DATABASE=c:\excelfiles\customer.xls', 'Select * from
[address$]')
```

However, you are getting null for postcode. What method will solve this issue?

A. You cannot access Excel files using OpenRowSet.

B. Increase the registry entry of TypeGuessRows of the HKLM\SOFTWARE\ Microsoft\Jet\4.0\Engine\Excel registry.

C. Change Excel 8.0 to Excel 9.0.

D. Add the IMEX=1 parameter to the query.

Self Test Quick Answer Key

1. **B**

2. **C**

3. **A**

4. **B**

5. **D**

6. **D**

7. **C**

8. **D**

9. **C**

10. **C**

11. **C**

12. **B**

13. **C**

14. **B**

15. **D**

Chapter 10

MCTS SQL Server 2008 Exam 433

Demystifying Data Types

Exam objectives in this chapter:

- Built-in Data Types
- Functions
- Computed Columns
- Boxing and Unboxing: The Cost

Exam objectives review:

- ☑ Summary of Exam Objectives
- ☑ Exam Objectives Fast Track
- ☑ Exam Objectives Frequently Asked Questions
- ☑ Self Test
- ☑ Self Test Quick Answer Key

Introduction

In this chapter, we'll explain the purpose of all the data types. We'll cover each of the built-in data types in depth, along with the purpose of each. We'll discuss best practices for choosing a data type, as well as how to work with and convert between data types. It's important to know how to convert data between data types both effectively and efficiently.

As database tables, SQL queries, and stored procedures are designed and implemented, a crucial task will need to be undertaken to define the appropriate data type for each column, local variable, expression, or parameter. Careful consideration must be given when choosing data types to ensure that they fit the data requirements appropriately and help provide for the most effective storage and efficient queries. A database administrator may strive to keep the use of data types consistent for each database or across multiple databases, and a developer may want to use data types that work best with the application module that he or she may be working on at that moment. It is important to define data types that work best in both situations, but consistency when assigning data types is paramount for database scalability and supportability. This chapter will start by taking a look at the available built-in data types; then describe a few string functions that are available for converting data types and working with strings; and finish up examining computed columns, filestream data, and the cost of boxing and unboxing data types.

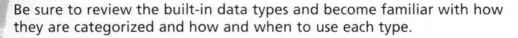

TEST DAY TIP

Be sure to review the built-in data types and become familiar with how they are categorized and how and when to use each type.

Built-in Data Types

SQL Server provides built-in data types that are organized into the following categories:

- Exact Numbers
- Approximate Numbers
- Date and Time
- Character Strings

- Unicode Character Strings
- Binary Strings
- Other Data Types
- CLR Data Types
- Spatial Data Types

See Table 10.1 for descriptions of the built-in data types for each of these categories.

EXAM WARNING

Be aware of the new data types in SQL Server 2008 and how they are used.

Table 10.1 Built-in Data Types

Data Type	Use / Description	Storage
Exact Numerics:		
Bit	Integer with either a 1 or 0 value. 9 up to 16-bit columns are stored as 2 bytes. The storage size increases as the number of bit columns used increases.	1 byte
Tinyint	Integer data from 0 to 255.	1 byte
Smallint	Integer data from $-2^{15}(-32,768)$ to $2^{15}-1(32,767)$.	2 bytes
Int	Integer data from $-2^{31}(-2,147,483,648)$ to $2^{31}-1(2,147,483,647)$.	4 bytes
Bigint	Integer data from $-2^{63}(-9,223,372,036,854,775,808)$ to $2^{63}-1(9,223,372,036,854,775,807)$.	8 bytes
Numeric	Fixed precision and scale. Valid values are from $-10^{38}+1$ through $10^{38}-1$.	Varies
Decimal	Fixed precision and scale. Valid values are from $-10^{38}+1$ through $10^{38}-1$.	Varies

Continued

Table 10.1 Continued. Built-in Data Types

Data Type	Use / Description	Storage
Smallmoney	Monetary or currency values from −214,748,3648 to 214,748.3647.	4 bytes
Money	Monetary or currency values from −922,337,203,685,477.5808 to 922,337,203,685,477.5807.	8 bytes
Approximate Numerics:		
Float	Approximate-number data type for use with floating-point numeric data. From −1.79E + 308 to −2.23E −308,0 and 2.23E −308 to 1.79E + 308.	From 4 to 8 bytes
Real	Approximate-number data type for use with floating-point numeric data. From −3.40E + 38 to −1.18E−38, 0 and 1.18E −38 to 3.40E + 38.	4 bytes
Date and Time:		
Datetime	Defines a date that is combined with a time of day with fractional seconds that is based on a 24-hour clock. Range: January 1, 1753, through December 31, 9999. Accuracy: Rounded to increments of .000, .003, or. 007 seconds.	8 bytes
Smalldatetime	Defines a date that is combined with a time of day. The time is based on a 24-hour day, with seconds always zero (:00) and without fractional seconds. Range: 1900−01−01 through 2079−06−06, January 1, 1900, through June 6, 2079. Accuracy: One minute.	4 bytes
Date*	Defines a date. Range: 0001−01−01 through 9999−12−31. January 1, 1 A.D. through December 31, 9999 A.D. Accuracy: One day.	3 bytes
Time *	Defines a time of day. The time is without time zone awareness and is based on a 24-hour clock. Range: 00:00:00.0000000 through 23:59:59.9999999. Accuracy: 100 nanoseconds.	5 bytes

Continued

Table 10.1 Continued. Built-in Data Types

Data Type	Use / Description	Storage
*Datetimeoffset**	Defines a date that is combined with a time of day that has time zone awareness and is based on a 24-hour clock. Range: 0001–01–01 through 9999–12–31, January 1, 1 A.D. through December 31, 9999 A.D. Time Range: 00:00:00 through 23:59:59:9999999. Accuracy: 100 nanoseconds.	10 bytes
*Datetime2 **	Defines a date that is combined with a time of day that is based on a 24-hour clock. Range: 0001–01–01 through 999–12–31, January 1, 1 A.D. through December 31, 9999 A.D. Time Range: 00:00:00 through 23:59:59.9999999. Accuracy: 100 nanoseconds.	Varies
Character Strings:		
Char	Character data type with fixed length.	Varies
Varchar	Character data type with variable length.	Varies
Text	This data type will be removed in a future version of SQL Server. Use varchar(max).	Varies
Unicode Character Strings:		
Nchar	Character data type with fixed length.	Varies
Nvarchar	Character data type with variable length.	Varies
Ntext	This data type will be removed in a future version of SQL Server. Use nvarchar(max).	Varies
Binary Strings:		
Binary	Binary data with fixed length.	Varies
Varbinary	Binary data with variable length.	Varies
Image	This data type will be removed in a future version of SQL Server. Use varbinary(max).	Varies
Other Data Types:		
Sql_variant	Stores values of various SQL Server-supported data types, except text, ntext, image, timestamp, and sql_variant.	Varies
Timestamp	Exposes automatically generated, unique binary numbers within a database.	8 bytes

Continued

Table 10.1 Continued. Built-in Data Types

Data Type	Use / Description	Storage
Uniqueidentifier	16-byte GUID.	16 bytes
XML	Stores XML data.	Varies
Cursor	Used for variables or stored procedure OUTPUT parameters that contain a reference to a cursor.	Varies
Table	Special data type to store a result set for processing at a later time.	Varies
CLR Data Types:		
Hierarchyid∗	Used to represent position in a hierarchy.	Varies
Spatial Data Types:		
Geometry∗	Used for storing planar (flat-earth) data.	Varies
Geography∗	Used for storing ellipsoidal (round-earth) data.	Varies

∗ **New** in SQL Server 2008.

New & Noteworthy...

New Data Types in SQL Server 2008

SQL Server 2008 has expanded the available built-in data types to include: Date, Time, DateTimeOffset, Datetime2, Hierarchyid, Geometry, and Geography.

Functions

We'll now discuss various functions that SQL Server 2008 offers.

CAST

SQL Server provides string functions that can be used to perform an operation on a string and return either a string or a numeric value. The first of these functions that we will cover will be the *CAST* function. The *CAST* function casts an expression of one data type to another data type. *CAST* is ANSI compliant, providing better compatibility when working with data across different database brands than the *CONVERT* function that we will be covering in the next section. *CAST* will also preserve decimal places better than the *CONVERT* function when converting decimal and numeric data types.

We will start with the syntax and then show an example in which a *datetime* data type is *CAST* to the *VARCHAR* data type.

The syntax for using the *CAST* function is:

```
CAST( expression AS data_type [(length)])
```

The following is an example of using the *CAST* function to cast a value from a *datetime* data type to a *VARCHAR* data type, so that the date value can be concatenated to a string. If this data type conversion is not done, you will receive a data type mismatch error message.

The SQL code is as follows:

```
SELECT 'The most recent sales promotion was: '
    + Description + ' and started on ' + CAST(StartDate AS VARCHAR(25))
FROM AdventureWorks2008.Sales.SpecialOffer
WHERE StartDate = (SELECT MAX(StartDate) FROM
AdventureWorks2008.Sales.SpecialOffer)
```

Note that our use of the *CAST* function looks like: CAST(*StartDate* AS *VARCHAR*(25)). This takes the *StartDate datetime* value and casts it to the *VARCHAR* data type.

The result we receive from this query looks like:

```
The most recent sales promotion was: Mountain-500 Silver Clearance Sale and
started on May 1 2004 12:00AM

(1 row(s) affected)
```

EXERCISE 10.1

USING THE *CAST()* FUNCTION

You have been given the task to pull a list of the sales promotions together. No special formatting is required, so you can just select the required fields from the Sales.SpecialOffer table in the AdventureWorks2008 database. You have been asked to include the Description, Type, Category, and StartDate columns. You find the StartDate column is not too attractive in the *datetime* data type with which it is stored. You also notice that you need to trim the width of each column so that there is not a lot of white space between the fields. This is not a problem because you know that you can use the *CAST()* string function to present the *StartDate* in a slightly more attractive way.

You start with the basic SQL query:

```
SELECT [Description],
       [Type],
       [Category],
       [StartDate]
FROM AdventureWorks2008.Sales.SpecialOffer
```

You find that this displays the columns spread out, and the dates look like: 2001–06–01 00:00:00.000

You need to fix the result up a little to make it more presentable, so you add the *CAST()* function to each of the columns in the *SELECT* statement.

Your revised SQL query is as follows:

```
SELECT CAST([Description] AS VARCHAR(30)) AS 'Description',
       CAST([Type] AS VARCHAR(20)) AS 'Type',
       CAST([Category] AS VARCHAR(11)) AS 'Category',
       CAST([StartDate] AS VARCHAR(11)) AS 'StartDate'
FROM AdventureWorks2008.Sales.SpecialOffer
```

You run the revised query, and the results look like the following:

```
Description                 Type                Category      StartDate
-------------------------   -----------------   -----------   -----------
No Discount                 No Discount         No Discount   Jun 1 2001
Volume Discount 11 to 14    Volume Discount     Reseller      Jul 1 2001
Volume Discount 15 to 24    Volume Discount     Reseller      Jul 1 2001
Volume Discount 25 to 40    Volume Discount     Reseller      Jul 1 2001
Volume Discount 41 to 60    Volume Discount     Reseller      Jul 1 2001
Volume Discount over 60     Volume Discount     Reseller      Jul 1 2001
Mountain-100 Clearance Sale Discontinued        Reseller      May 15 2002
                            Product
Sport Helmet Discount-2002  Seasonal Discount   Reseller      Jul 1 2002
Road-650 Overstock          Excess Inventory    Reseller      Jul 1 2002
Mountain Tire Sale          Excess Inventory    Customer      Jun 15 2003
```

This looks pretty good and satisfies the requirement. Using the *CAST()* function saved you from having to copy the data into another program for formatting.

CONVERT

The *CONVERT* function, like the *CAST* function, converts an expression of one data type to another, but *CONVERT* provides the option of applying any one of a number of styles such as displaying a date in an Italian, German, or Japanese format or *money* and *smallmoney* values with commas. *CONVERT* is not ANSI compliant.

EXAM WARNING

Remember that even though it is tempting to use the *CONVERT* function with its many available styles 100 percent of the time, if what you are doing needs to be ANSI compliant, you will need to stick to using the *CAST* function.

The syntax of the *CONVERT* function is:

```
CONVERT(data_type [ (length) ], expression [, style ] )
```

Here is an example of using the same query we used for *CAST* but this time using *CONVERT* so that we can have greater control over formatting the date that is being concatenated to the string.

```
SELECT 'The most recent sales promotion was: '
    + Description + ' and started on ' + CONVERT(VARCHAR(10), StartDate, 110)
FROM AdventureWorks2008.Sales.SpecialOffer
WHERE StartDate = (SELECT MAX(StartDate) FROM
AdventureWorks2008.Sales.SpecialOffer)
```

The result shows the concatenated string along with the promotion start date in the U.S. style of mm-dd-yyyy.

```
The most recent sales promotion was: Mountain-500 Silver Clearance Sale
and started on 05-01-2004

(1 row(s) affected)
```

When using *CONVERT* many different styles are available to help present the value in the required format. Here's an example using a style that is most often seen, the U.S.-style mm/dd/yyyy.

```
SELECT 'The most recent sales promotion was: '
        + Description + ' and started on '
            + CONVERT(VARCHAR(10), StartDate, 101)
                + '. '
```

```
FROM AdventureWorks2008.Sales.SpecialOffer
WHERE StartDate = (SELECT MAX(StartDate) FROM
AdventureWorks2008.Sales.SpecialOffer)
```

The result of using *CONVERT(VARCHAR(10)*, *StartDate*, 101) to format the date gives us a nice statement of when the most recent sales promotion started.

```
The most recent sales promotion was: Mountain-500 Silver Clearance Sale and
started on 05/01/2004.

(1 row(s) affected)
```

Head of the Class...

Always Double-Check Data Conversions

Be careful when converting data types. Always double-check the original value against the converted or transformed value to make sure that important elements are not getting inadvertently dropped. Truncated street addresses can result in very costly returned mail, and a misplaced decimal or inaccurate rounding could mean the difference between representing a $100.00 or a $1 million gain. Usually, it is best to get another opinion if the conversion is looking a little strange.

EXERCISE 10.2

USING THE *CONVERT()* FUNCTION

After supplying our result from using the *CAST()* function in the previous exercise, the requestor asked that you fix the date in the quick report that you created to have the format of: MM/DD/YYYY. Since the *CAST()* function does not give you formatting style options, you decide to use the *CONVERT()* string function. The requestor's requirements are still the same and you are required to pull a list of the sales promotions together, but the *StartDate* needs to be in the MM/DD/YYYY format.

When you select the required fields from the Sales.SpecialOffer table in the AdventureWorks2008 database this time, you include the Description, Type, Category, and StartDate columns and use the *CONVERT()* function to trim the extra white space and also apply a formatting style to the *StartDate* column.

Our revised SQL query looks like the following:

```
SELECT CONVERT(VARCHAR(30),[Description]) AS 'Description',
     CONVERT(VARCHAR(20),[Type]) AS 'Type',
     CONVERT(VARCHAR(11), [Category]) AS 'Category',
     CONVERT(VARCHAR(11), [StartDate], 101) AS 'StartDate'
FROM AdventureWorks2008.Sales.SpecialOffer
```

Since the columns other than the StartDate column are defined with the *VARCHAR* data type, a style was not necessary. The *CONVERT()* function is only being used to trim the fields to eliminate extra white space, and SQL Server help was consulted to locate the style code 101 that would give us the *StartDate* in the MM/DD/YYYY format.

Here are the query results:

Description	Type	Category	StartDate
No Discount	No Discount	No Discount	06/01/2001
Volume Discount 11 to 14	Volume Discount	Reseller	07/01/2001
Volume Discount 15 to 24	Volume Discount	Reseller	07/01/2001
Volume Discount 25 to 40	Volume Discount	Reseller	07/01/2001
Volume Discount 41 to 60	Volume Discount	Reseller	07/01/2001
Volume Discount over 60	Volume Discount	Reseller	07/01/2001
Mountain-100 Clearance Sale	Discontinued Product	Reseller	05/15/2002

The *StartDate* is now in the required format using the *CONVERT()* function.

LEN

When it is necessary to determine the length of a value to perhaps determine how many preceding or trailing zeros need to be appended, the *LEN* function is available. This function will return the number of characters in the specified string expression, excluding trailing blanks.

The syntax for the *LEN* function is:

```
LEN (string_expression)
```

This code example will simply return the character length of each last name that meets the criteria of the *WHERE* clause. This may not seem very useful, but combining the *LEN* function with an aggregate function such as *MAX()*

can be a valuable tool when analyzing data for a data conversion between legacy systems or other databases.

The *SELECT* statement looks like:

```
SELECT LEN(LastName) AS LastNameLength,
       LastName
FROM AdventureWorks2008.Person.Person
WHERE LastName LIKE '%ok'
```

This subset of the result returned by this query shows the length of data in the LastName name column along with the Last Name contained in that column.

```
LastNameLength                          LastName
--------------                          --------
7                                       Cetinok
7                                       Cetinok
4                                       Cook
4                                       Cook
```

EXERCISE 10.3

USING THE *LEN()* FUNCTION

You have been asked to double-check the data length in a few columns in a table that was imported from another database. You have run a few test queries and have found that some of the columns in question contain data that is a good bit smaller than the defined column width. You need to migrate the data into a new table and to make sure the data will fit into the destination columns. You know that you can use the *LEN()* function to return the actual data width, so you start putting your SQL query together.

```
SELECT LEN([Description]) AS 'Description_Length',
     LEN([Type]) AS 'Type_Length',
     LEN([Category]) AS 'Category_Length'
FROM AdventureWorks2008.Sales.SpecialOffer
```

Using the *LEN()* function provides exactly what you needed. The result looks like the following:

Description_Length	Type_Length	Category_Length
11	11	11
24	15	8
24	15	8
21	17	8
34	20	8

RIGHT and LEFT Functions

The *RIGHT* and *LEFT* functions can be used to return either the right part or left part of a character string with the specified number of characters.

The syntax for the *RIGHT* and *LEFT* functions is basically the same.

Here is the syntax for the *RIGHT* function:

```
RIGHT(character_expression, integer_expression)
```

In the following example, the *RIGHT* function is used to exclude the word *Lead* as well as the space that follows it by instructing the function to start at position 6 of the string.

```
SELECT RIGHT('Lead Guitar',6)
```

As shown in the following result, starting from the right side of the string and counting back six positions, the word *Guitar* has been returned.

```
------

Guitar

(1 row(s) affected)
```

The same example is used to demonstrate the *LEFT* function.

Start with the syntax that is similar to the *RIGHT* function:

```
LEFT( character_expression, integer_expression )
```

With this example, starting from the left side of the string, the function has been supplied a five-character count over.

```
SELECT LEFT('Lead Guitar',5)
```

Now the word *Lead* is returned since it is the first five characters of the supplied string.

```
-----

Lead

(1 row(s) affected)
```

Among the common uses for the *RIGHT* and *LEFT* functions is excluding suffixes or check-digits if they are similar on multiple records since that can have an undesired result when doing an *ORDER BY* or in *WHERE* clause criteria.

EXERCISE 10.4

USING THE *RIGHT()* AND *LEFT()* FUNCTIONS

You have been given a task to pull together a quick report to show the Special Offers that contain the word *Sale* at the end of the offer description. You need to include the columns Description, Type, Category, and StartDate from the SalesSpecialOffer table in the AdventureWorks2008 database. You need to limit the column widths to eliminate extra white space and to format the *StartDate* in the MM/DD/YYYY format, so you use the *CONVERT()* function to take care of those requirements. Since the text that you need to find is on the right side of the description, you know that the *RIGHT()* string function will help you find what you need.
Your SQL query looks like the following:

```
SELECT CONVERT(VARCHAR(35),[Description]) AS 'Description',
     CONVERT(VARCHAR(20),[Type]) AS 'Type',
     CONVERT(VARCHAR(11), [Category]) AS 'Category',
     CONVERT(VARCHAR(11), [StartDate], 101) AS 'StartDate'
FROM AdventureWorks2008.Sales.SpecialOffer
WHERE RIGHT([Description],4) = 'Sale'
```

The *RIGHT()* function is used in the *WHERE* clause, with the length parameter of 4 instructing the function to search four characters from the right of the string contained in the Description column.
The query result looks like the following:

```
Description                     Type                  Category    StartDate

----------------------------    --------------------  ---------   ----------

Mountain-100 Clearance Sale     Discontinued Product  Reseller    05/15/2002

Mountain Tire Sale              Excess Inventory      Customer    06/15/2003

LL Road Frame Sale              Excess Inventory      Reseller    07/01/2003

Half-Price Pedal Sale           Seasonal Discount     Customer    08/15/2003

Mountain-500 Silver Clearance   Discontinued Product  Reseller    05/01/2004
Sale

(5 row(s) affected)
```

Using the *RIGHT()* function has returned the required special offer descriptions that contain the word *Sale* in the last four characters.

You also need to provide a separate request to produce a similar result to what was returned with using the *RIGHT()* string function, but now you need to locate the records that contain the word *Mountain* in the left eight characters in the Description column of the Sales. SpecialOffer table of the AdventureWorks2008 database.

You start with the SQL query that you used with the *RIGHT()* function:

```
SELECT CONVERT(VARCHAR(35),[Description]) AS 'Description',
    CONVERT(VARCHAR(20),[Type]) AS 'Type',
    CONVERT(VARCHAR(11), [Category]) AS 'Category',
    CONVERT(VARCHAR(11), [StartDate], 101) AS 'StartDate'
FROM AdventureWorks2008.Sales.SpecialOffer
WHERE LEFT([Description],8) = 'Mountain'
```

The *WHERE* clause has been changed to use the *LEFT()* string function, and the query results look like the following:

```
Description                     Type                  Category    StartDate

--------------------------      --------------------  ---------   ----------

Mountain-100 Clearance Sale     Discontinued Product  Reseller    05/15/2002

Mountain Tire Sale              Excess Inventory      Customer     06/15/2003

Mountain-500 Silver             Discontinued Product  Reseller    05/01/2004
Clearance Sale

(3 row(s) affected)
```

Using the *LEFT()* function has provided success. The special offer records with the *Mountain* string in the first eight characters have been returned.

REPLACE

The *REPLACE* function provides an effective way to replace all occurrences of a specified string value with another string value. A great use of this function is to replace a specific value in a query result without updating the original table values. Although the *CASE* statement can also be used in many cases, *REPLACE* will be more efficient when you only need to target one specific value.

The syntax for the *REPLACE* function is:

```
REPLACE(string_expression, string_pattern, string_replacement )
```

A simple string example for using the *REPLACE* function is as follows, where the word *Lead* will be replaced with the word *Rhythm.*

```
SELECT REPLACE('Lead Guitar', 'Lead', 'Rhythm')
```

Here is the result. *Lead* has been replaced with *Rhythm*.

```
Rhythm Guitar

(1 row(s) affected)
```

Here is another example from the AdventureWorks2008 data. We've been told that the products that have "Silver/Black" as a color should not be presented that way on the product report. They should just be shown as "Silver," so we do not want to change the data in the table, but we can use the *REPLACE* function to show what is required for the report. An example of the SQL code looks like the following:

```
SELECT Name AS 'Product_Name',
       Color AS 'Original_Color',
     REPLACE(Color, 'Silver/Black', 'Silver') AS 'Replace_Color'
FROM AdventureWorks2008.Production.Product
WHERE Color = 'Silver/Black'
```

The query result shows both the original color and the replaced color.

```
Product_Name                    Original_Color          Replace_Color
-----------------               ---------------         -------------

LL Mountain Pedal               Silver/Black            Silver

ML Mountain Pedal               Silver/Black            Silver

HL Mountain Pedal               Silver/Black            Silver

LL Road Pedal                   Silver/Black            Silver

ML Road Pedal                   Silver/Black            Silver

HL Road Pedal                   Silver/Black            Silver

Touring Pedal                   Silver/Black            Silver


(7 row(s) affected)
```

EXERCISE 10.5

USING THE *REPLACE* FUNCTION

You have been tasked once again to pull together a quick report of the special offers that are stored in the Sales.SpecialOffer table in the AdventureWorks2008 database. The requirement this time is to not only supply the Description, Type, Category, and StartDate in the appropriate formats using the *CONVERT()* function, but also to replace the data value of *Excess Inventory* in the type column with the string, *Overstock*.

Because you cannot change the data in the table, you use the *REPLACE()* string function to replace the data value in the query result.

Your SQL query looks like the following:

```
SELECT CONVERT(VARCHAR(35),[Description]) AS 'Description',
       CONVERT(VARCHAR(20), REPLACE([Type], 'Excess Inventory', 'Overstock'))
AS 'Type',
       CONVERT(VARCHAR(11), [Category]) AS 'Category',
       CONVERT(VARCHAR(11), [StartDate], 101) AS 'StartDate'
FROM AdventureWorks2008.Sales.SpecialOffer
```

In order to maintain the output column width for the [Type] column, it was necessary to precede the *REPLACE()* function with the *CONVERT()* function.

The query results look like the following:

```
Description                  Type                Category     StartDate

-------------------------    ------------------  ----------   ----------

Road-650 Overstock           Overstock           Reseller     07/01/2002

Mountain Tire Sale           Overstock           Customer     06/15/2003

Sport Helmet Discount-2003   Seasonal Discount   Reseller     07/01/2003

LL Road Frame Sale           Overstock           Reseller     07/01/2003
```

The string of *Excess Inventory* has been replaced with *Overstock* as expected.

CHARINDEX

The *CHARINDEX* function can be used to search the provided *expression2* (or column) for *expression1*. If expression1 is located, the starting position within *expression2* is returned. A specific starting position can be supplied to the function if you do not want the search to start at the first position.

Here is the syntax for the *CHARINDEX* function:

```
CHARINDEX ( expression1, expression2 [, start_location ] )
```

The following code examples demonstrate use of the *CHARINDEX* function. In this first example we are searching for the string *Green* within the string contained in the *@Quote* variable.

```
DECLARE @Quote VARCHAR(25)
SELECT @Quote = 'GO Green!'
SELECT CHARINDEX('Green', @Quote)
```

The position of 4 is returned as the result due to the function finding that the string *Green* started in after *GO* (space included). A starting position was not designated, so the search began at the first position.

```
-----------
4

(1 row(s) affected)
```

In this example, because a starting position has been supplied, the search begins at position 4. The result will return a value that counts from the first position.

```
DECLARE @Quote VARCHAR(25)
SELECT @Quote = 'GO Green Now!'
SELECT CHARINDEX('Now', @Quote, 4)
```

As we see with the following result, considering that we started the search at position 4, the string *Now* begins at position 10 from position 1, including spaces.

```
-----------
10

(1 row(s) affected)
```

To demonstrate a situation in which *expression1* cannot be found in *expression2*, a resulting zero will be returned since the search criteria was not located.

```
DECLARE @Quote VARCHAR(25)
SELECT @Quote = 'GO Green Now!'
SELECT CHARINDEX('Now', @Quote, 11)
```

In the *CHARINDEX* function, 11 was provided as the starting position, but the string *Now* starts at position 10 and so the function returns a zero acknowledging that the string was not found where required.

```
-----------
0

(1 row(s) affected)
```

EXERCISE 10.6

USING THE *CHARINDEX()* FUNCTION

In order to get familiar with the *CHARINDEX()* function, execute the following SQL code in the SQL Server Management Studio in any database and experiment with the *start_location* parameter.

```
DECLARE @TestString VARCHAR(35)
SELECT @TestString = 'Testing the CHARINDEX FUNCTION!'
SELECT CHARINDEX('the', @TestString, 6)
```

Executing this SQL code will give you the result of:

```
-----------

9

(1 row(s) affected)
```

Try different string values for the *@TestString* variable and varying *start_location* values until you are comfortable with the *CHARINDEX()* function.

PATINDEX

The *PATINDEX* function returns the starting position of the first occurrence of a pattern in a specified expression, or zeros if the pattern is not found, on all valid text and character types.

The syntax is:

```
PATINDEX ( '%pattern%', expression )
```

The following code example shows the use of *PATINDEX* and indicates that we are interested in locating where the string *%ok* exists in the data value. The wildcard (%) is included since we are looking for instances of *ok* that occur after other characters. Using the *PATINDEX* function can be very helpful when looking for a location within a stored string for a specific string pattern and determining whether or not it occurs in the same location in every instance.

```
SELECT PATINDEX('%ok',LastName) AS 'PATINDEX',
     LastName,
FROM Person.Person
WHERE LastName LIKE '%ok'
```

The subset of the result of this query looks like the following:

```
PATINDEX                LastName
--------                --------
6                       Cetinok
6                       Cetinok
3                       Cook
```

As the results show, the string *ok* occurs starting at position 6 in the last name Cetinok and at position 3 in the last name Cook.

EXERCISE 10.7

USING THE *PATINDEX* FUNCTION

Execute the following SQL code in the SQL Server Management Studio in any database and experiment with the parameters of the *PATINDEX()* string function.

```
SELECT PATINDEX('%ok%', 'String functions are ok!')
```

This SQL code will produce the result

```
-----------
22

(1 row(s) affected)
```

TEST DAY TIP

Okay now, is *CONVERT* or *CAST* ANSI compliant? Be sure to know which one of these to use if you need to be concerned with being ANSI compliant.

Computed Columns

A computed column is calculated from an expression that can use other columns in the same table. The expression can be a noncomputed column name, constant, function, and any combination of these connected by one or more operators. The expression cannot be a subquery. Computed columns are virtual and are not physically stored in the table. The computed column is recalculated every time the computed column is referenced in a query. The expression used for the computed column is stored in the Computed Column Specification column properties.

An example of a computed column can be found in the Sales.SalesOrderHeader table in the AdventureWorks2008 database. See Figure 10.1 for an example of the computed column properties.

Figure 10.1 Computed Column Properties

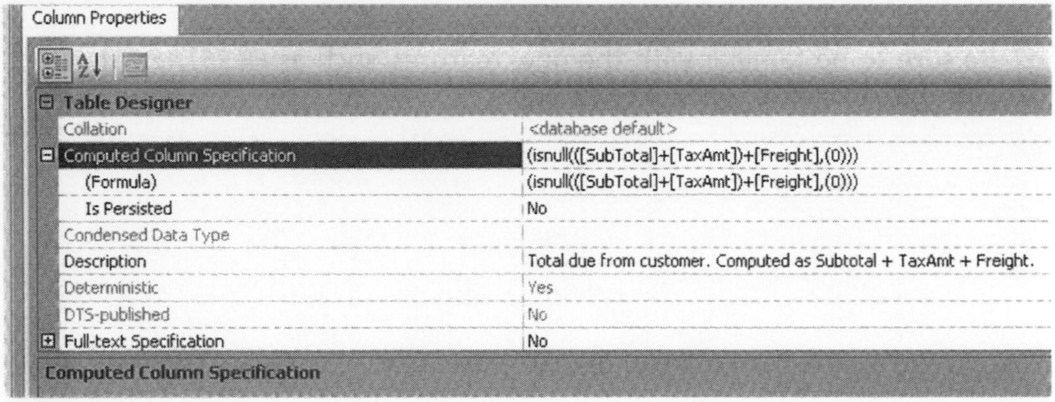

EXAM WARNING

Be able to define computed columns and explain how they are created.

Filestream Data Type

TEST DAY TIP

You have a great deal of information to keep track of. You've gotten this far ... You are doing great!

New in SQL Server 2008, the *FILESTREAM* storage attribute can be used for binary (BLOB) data to be stored in a varbinary(max) column.

Utilizing the *FILESTREAM* storage attribute has the following benefits:

- Since the data is stored on the file system, performance matches the streaming performance of the file system.
- The BLOB size is only restricted by the file system volume size.
- The *FILESTREAM* columns are fully integrated with SQL Server maintenance operations, such as backup and restore.
- SQL Server provides full transactional support between the relational data in the database and the unstructured data physically stored on the file system.
- The SQL Server security model is used to manage *FILESTREAM* data.

Exam Warning

Be sure to be familiar with the new features, such as *FILESTREAM* storage, available in SQL Server 2008.

In order for this storage attribute to be used, an attribute can be set on a varbinary column so that the data is stored on the file system. Doing this gains the benefits of the fast streaming and storage capabilities of the file system. The data is managed and accessed directly within the context of the database. The data is stored in the local NTFS file system and not in the database file.

Boxing and Unboxing: The Cost

To best explain boxing and unboxing data types, let's look at a simple example of taking a *DATETIME* value and converting it to a *VARCHAR* data type. This first conversion is considered boxing. Now you want to take the *VARCHAR* value and convert it back to the *DATETIME* value. This conversion is considered unboxing. Coding in this method can have a negative impact on query performance and should be avoided.

Exam Warning

Make sure that you understand what it means to box and unbox data type conversions and what to do to avoid the performance impact.

If the data type used on a particular column is causing you to consider doing multiple conversions, consider adding a column to the table and storing the data alongside the original column in converted format.

Configuring & Implementing...

Consistency Is Good!

Carefully planning the use of data types and maintaining a good level of consistency will reduce or eliminate unnecessary data type conversions (boxing/unboxing), which will not only optimize query performance, but also make supporting and enhancing the database and database objects much easier.

TEST DAY TIP

Review the data types presented in this chapter and make sure you are familiar with how they should be used.

Summary of Exam Objectives

The key to demystifying data types is taking the time to understand what built-in data types SQL Server 2008 has to offer and how they can be used. Designating the appropriate data type for each data requirement is vital to effectively storing data in a SQL Server database and to providing optimal query performance when retrieving data. If queries often use a date in the *WHERE* clause to retrieve data, the columns containing the dates should have one of the appropriate *Date* and *Time* data types versus having the dates stored as a *VARCHAR*. In addition, *Floats* and *Real* data types may not provide the best result for storing numbers, so a decimal data type would provide a more consistent result. Therefore, double-checking any and all data type conversions is imperative to ensuring the appropriate result. SQL Server also provides a number of string functions that enable either casting or converting the data value to a different data type, or other available functions can provide the ability to replace values or search for specific string values. Gaining a solid understanding of working with data types in SQL Server will help build effective and efficient databases and SQL code.

Exam Objectives Fast Track

Built-in Data Types

☑ The SQL Server built-in data types categories are: (1) Exact Numbers, (2) Approximate Numbers, (3) Date and Time, (4) Character Strings, (5) Unicode Character Strings, (6) Binary Strings, (7) Other Data Types, (8) CLR Data Types, and (9) Spatial Data Types.

☑ The new SQL Server 2008 data types are: (1) Date, (2) Time, (3) Datetimeoffset, (4) Datetime2, (5) Hierarchyid, (6) Geometry, and (7) Geography.

☑ The Text, NText, and Image data types will be removed in a future version of SQL Server and should not be used.

Functions

☑ The *CAST()* function casts the data type of a value to another data type.

☑ The *CAST()* function is ANSI compliant.

☑ The syntax for the *CAST()* function is: CAST(*expression AS data_type [(length)]*).

☑ The *CONVERT()* function casts the data type of a value to another data type.

☑ The *CONVERT()* function provides many options for formatting the data type.

☑ The syntax for the *CONVERT()* function is: CONVERT(*data_type* [*(length)*], *expression* [, *style*]).

☑ The *LEN()* function returns the length of a value.

☑ The syntax for the *LEN()* function is: LEN (*string_expression*).

☑ The *LEN()* function excludes trailing blanks.

☑ The *RIGHT()* function returns *n* number of characters from the right side of the string.

☑ The LEFT() function returns *n* number of characters from the left side of the string.

☑ The syntax of the *RIGHT()* function is: RIGHT(*character_expression*, *integer_expression*).

☑ The syntax of the *LEFT()* function is: LEFT(*character_expression*, *integer_expression*).

☑ The *REPLACE()* function is used to replace all occurrences of a specified string value with another string value.

☑ The syntax for the *REPLACE()* function is: REPLACE (*string_expression*, *string_pattern*, *string_replacement*).

☑ The original data value is not updated; only the value in the query results is updated.

☑ The *CHARINDEX()* function is used to search the provided *expression2* value for the supplied *expression1* value.

☑ The search starts at position 1 of the *expression2* value if a *start_location* is not provided.

☑ The syntax for the *CHARINDEX()* function is: CHARINDEX (*expression1*, *expression2* [, *start_location*]).

☑ The *PATINDEX()* function returns the starting position of the first occurrence of the supplied pattern in a specific expression.

☑ The syntax for the *PATINDEX()* function is: PATINDEX (*'%pattern%'*, *expression*).

☑ The % (wildcard) can be used with the *PATINDEX()* function.

Computed Columns

☑ A computed column is calculated from an expression that can use other columns in the same table.

☑ The *FILESTREAM* storage attribute is for binary (BLOB) data stored in a varbinary(max) column.

☑ Stored on the file system and benefits from the file system's fast streaming capabilities and storage capabilities.

☑ Stored in the local NTFS file system and not in the database file.

Boxing and Unboxing: The Cost

☑ Boxing is the conversion of the data type of a value to a different data type.

☑ Unboxing is the conversion of the data type of a value back to its original data type after being converted to a data type other than the original.

☑ Boxing and unboxing can have a negative impact on query performance.

Exam Objectives
Frequently Asked Questions

Q: To which built-in data type category does the *datetime2* data type belong?

A: The datetime2 data type belongs to the *Date* and *Time* built-in data type category.

Q: Which of the string functions, *CONVERT() OR CAST(),* is ANSI compliant?

A: The *CAST()* function is ANSI compliant.

Q: What is a computed column?

A: A computed column is calculated from an expression that can use other columns in the same table.

Q: At what position does the *CHARINDEX()* function start if a starting position is not supplied?

A: If a starting position is not supplied to the *CHARINDEX()* function, the function starts at position 1 of the string.

Q: What is boxing?

A: Boxing occurs when a value stored as a specific data type is converted or cast to a different data type.

Q: What is unboxing?

A: Unboxing occurs when a value is converted back to its original data type after it had been converted or cast to a data type other than the original data type.

Self Test

1. To which built-in data type category does the data type *Date* belong?

   A. Exact Numbers

   B. Character Strings

   C. Binary Strings

   D. Date and Time

2. To which built-in data type category does the data type *Hierarchyid* belong?

   A. Approximate Numbers

   B. Other Data Types

   C. CLR Data Types

   D. Spatial Data Types

3. Which data type is new in SQL Server 2008?

   A. Varchar

   B. Time

   C. Bit

   D. Int

4. Which data type will be removed from a future version of SQL Server?

   A. Text

   B. Bit

   C. Smallint

   D. DateTime

5. What does the *CAST()* function do?

   A. Replace a string value.

   B. Search for a specific string value.

   C. Cast a data type to a different data type.

   D. Return the length of a string.

6. What does the *CONVERT()* function do?

   A. Cast a value from one data type to another.

   B. Search for a specific string value.

    C. Return the length of a string.

    D. Convert a data type to a different data type.

7. What do the styles available for the *CONVERT()* function do?

    A. Format the converted value to any of the valid/available formats.

    B. Convert the data type back to the original data type.

    C. Return the length of the converted data type.

    D. Return the location of a specified string in the converted value.

8. What does the *LEN()* function do?

    A. Replaces a data value with a different value

    B. Returns the location of a specific string value

    C. Returns the length of *string_expression* provided

    D. Returns the starting location of a specific string value

9. What is the syntax for the *LEFT()* function?

    A. `LEFT(start_location)`

    B. `LEFT(expression1, expression2)`

    C. `LEFT(expression1, expression2, start_location)`

    D. `LEFT(character_expression, integer_expression)`

10. Which of the following is a parameter of the *REPLACE()* function?

    A. `String_replacement`

    B. `Expression1`

    C. `Expression2`

    D. `Start_location`

11. Where does the *CHARINDEX()* function start the search if a *start_location* is supplied?

    A. Character position 2

    B. Character position 1

    C. Character position 10

    D. Character position 5

12. The % (wildcard) can be used in which function?

    A. The *REPLACE()* function

    B. The *PATINDEX()* function

    C. The *LEN()* function

    D. The *CONVERT()* function

13. Where is the data stored for a computed column?

    A. In the database

    B. On the file system

    C. It is not stored.

    D. In a table

14. What is the definition of a computed column?

    A. A computed column is a virtual column that contains a value that is calculated from an expression using other columns in the table.

    B. A computed column stores XML data.

    C. A computed column stores data in the filestream.

    D. A computed column is used to stored GUIDs.

15. When is a computed column recalculated?

    A. When the table that contains the computed column is updated

    B. When a query references the computed column

    C. When the computed column data value is updated

    D. When a new data row is inserted into the table that contains the computed column

16. Where is *FILESTREAM* data stored?

    A. In the database

    B. On the file system

    C. In a database table

    D. In the database data file

17. Where is the *FILESTREAM* data managed?

    A. On the file system

    B. Windows Explorer

C. The SQL Server database

D. At the command prompt

18. Which is a benefit of using the *FILESTREAM* storage attribute?

A. Makes programming SQL code easier

B. Makes designing databases easier

C. Automatically updates the storage attributes when the file system is backed up

D. Benefits from the file system's fast streaming and storage capabilities

19. What is boxing of a data type?

A. Defining a data type for a column in a table

B. Defining a user data type

C. Converting or casting a value from its stored data type to a different data type

D. Inserting data into a table column

20. What is unboxing of a data type?

A. Changing a data type on a column in a database table

B. Converting or casting a value back to its original data type after it has been converted or cast to a different data type

C. Deleting a column from a table

D. Updating data in a table

Self Test Quick Answer Key

1. **D**
2. **C**
3. **B**
4. **A**
5. **C**
6. **D**
7. **A**
8. **C**
9. **D**
10. **A**

11. **B**
12. **B**
13. **C**
14. **A**
15. **B**
16. **B**
17. **C**
18. **D**
19. **C**
20. **B**

Chapter 11

MCTS SQL Server 2008 Exam 433

Explaining Advanced Query Techniques

Exam objectives in this chapter:

- Implementing CTE (Common Table Expression) Queries
- Applying Ranking Functions
- Controlling Execution Plans
- Managing Internationalization Considerations
- Creating and Altering Tables

Exam objectives review:

- ☑ Summary of Exam Objectives
- ☑ Exam Objectives Fast Track
- ☑ Exam Objectives Frequently Asked Questions
- ☑ Self Test
- ☑ Self Test Quick Answer Key

Introduction

In this chapter, we'll explain Common Table Expressions, ranking and partitioning, and managing performance with the Query Governor and application pools. We'll cover sparse columns and compression, and identify the advantages and disadvantages of using compression. Compression can not only save you disk space, but can also result in an enhanced performance if properly used. We'll also cover internationalization issues involving the handling of character data (collations) and the delivery of locale-specific error messages.

Implementing CTE (Common Table Expression) Queries

At first glance, Common Table Expressions (CTEs) may not seem to be much different from subqueries or views. CTEs, like subqueries, can be used as a derived table in *SELECT, INSERT, UPDATE,* and *DELETE* statements. And like subqueries, they are valid for only the life of the statement with which they are associated, and they are not stored in the database. CTEs could also be considered to be temporary views. As is true of views, CTEs have a name that can be referenced in the query. Also like views, they have an optional list of column names that can be used as aliases for the columns returned from their query definition.

So if CTEs are so similar to subqueries or views, why should we use them? Well, when compared with a complex set of nested subqueries, the CTE syntax seems much cleaner. This is because each CTE is stated before the query that uses it rather than nested inside it. This makes the "outer" or referencing query much cleaner and easier to read. CTEs can also provide a benefit over views because they don't require us to actually create a view if we only need it for a single ad-hoc query. CTEs also have one ability that neither subqueries nor views possess—the ability to be self-referencing. This ability makes it possible for us to create recursive queries! More will be said on that later; for now let's look at the basics of using CTEs.

Creating CTEs

The syntax for using CTEs is broken down into two parts: the declaration of the CTE itself and the statement that references the CTE that was just declared:

```
-- CTE DECLARATION
WITH CTE_name [ ( column_name [,…n] ) ]
```

```
AS
( CTE_query_definition )
-- CTE USE
SELECT <column_list>
FROM CTE_NAME
```

The entire block of syntax in this example represents a *single* statement, and some syntax rules particular to CTEs should be pointed out:

- When the CTE is not the first statement in a batch, the statement preceding the CTE must have been terminated with a semicolon (";"). See the sidebar titled "The Transact-SQL Statement Terminator" for more information.

- The list of "column_name" values in the CTE declaration is optional unless there are expressions in the CTE_*query_definition* that do not have explicit column names provided.

- The CTE definition is valid only for a single statement. If we want to use the same CTE for multiple statements, we must restate the CTE declaration for each of the multiple queries.

New & Noteworthy...

The Transact-SQL Statement Terminator

The semicolon (";") *Transact-SQL* statement terminator has historically been an optional syntax element in SQL Server. However as the language becomes more involved, the parser needs some help in properly interpreting our code. SQL Server 2008 Documentation states that the semicolon will be required in a future version. It would be in our best interest then to begin the habit of terminating all SQL statements with a semicolon now.

CTEs are an example of where the semicolon is required on the statement that precedes the CTE. A CTE's definition begins with a *WITH* clause. As you will see later in this chapter, the *SELECT* statement can also have a *WITH* clause for a completely different purpose when using table locking

Continued

and index hints. To help the SQL parser understand your intended use of *WITH* when creating CTEs, you must make sure that any previous statements in the same batch were properly terminated with a semicolon. It is for this reason that you may see some developers precede the CTE's *WITH* clause using a semicolon like this, ";WITH". It's important to understand that the semicolon is not a part of the CTE's declaration but rather the explicit termination of the statement that precedes the CTE's declaration in the batch.

If you fail to properly terminate the previous statement before declaring a CTE, SQL Server will let you know with the following error message:

```
Msg 319, Level 15, State 1, Line 4
Incorrect syntax near the keyword 'with'. If this statement is a
common table expression, an xmlnamespaces clause or a change tracking
context clause, the previous statement must be terminated with a
semicolon.
```

Let's look at a sample CTE. The following CTE and its referencing query answer the question, "How many products have sold a total quantity of greater than 5000 items across all orders?"

```
USE AdventureWorks2008;
GO
--CTE DECLARATION
WITH ProductsOver5000 AS
(
  SELECT ProductID, SUM(OrderQty) AS TotalQty
  FROM Sales.SalesOrderDetail
  GROUP BY ProductID
  HAVING SUM(OrderQty) > 5000
)
--CTE USE
SELECT COUNT(*) AS NumProductsOver5000
FROM ProductsOver5000;
```

The query that references the CTE is clean and easy to read. It simply references the ProductsOver5000 CTE declared above as its source. It is this clarity in the final query that often makes CTEs much easier to understand than a functionally equivalent statement written using subqueries. Let's try the same query using a subquery rather than a CTE:

```
USE AdventureWorks2008;
GO
SELECT COUNT(*) AS NumProductsOver5000
FROM
(
  SELECT ProductID, SUM(OrderQty) AS TotalQty
  FROM Sales.SalesOrderDetail
  GROUP BY ProductID
  HAVING SUM(OrderQty) > 5000
) AS ProductsOver5000;
```

Many people find the subquery version to be more difficult to understand because the "inner" query is stated in the middle of the "outer" query. It can make it difficult to figure out where one query starts and the other stops.

A single statement can have multiple CTEs declared. If that is the case, all CTE declarations must occur before the statement that references them. When defining multiple CTEs in a single statement, the *WITH* keyword only appears once, and each CTE declaration is separated by a comma (","). A benefit of multiple CTEs is that one CTE can build on the results of a previous CTE, much in the same way that nested subqueries are used. Here is an example of a query that uses multiple CTEs to answer the question, "What products were sold on the last day of business, and what was the total quantity sold for each product?":

```
USE AdventureWorks2008;
GO
WITH
-- First CTE: LastDayOrderIDs
-- Get the SalesOrderID values for all orders placed on the last day of
-- business (MAX(OrderDate))
LastDayOrderIDs AS
(
    SELECT SalesOrderID FROM Sales.SalesOrderHeader
    WHERE OrderDate = (SELECT MAX(OrderDate) FROM Sales.SalesOrderHeader)
),
-- Second CTE: LastDayProductQuantities
-- Now find the distinct ProductIDs and their total quantities for all
-- of the SalesOrderID values retrieve in the previous CTE
```

```
LastDayProductQuantities AS
(
    SELECT ProductID, SUM(OrderQty) AS LastDayQuantity
    FROM Sales.SalesOrderDetail
    JOIN LastDayOrderIDs
    ON Sales.SalesOrderDetail.SalesOrderID = LastDayOrderIDs.SalesOrderID
    GROUP BY ProductID
),
-- Third CTE: LastDayProductDetails
-- Take the ProductIDs and last day quantities from the previous
-- CTE and join it to the Product table to retrieve the product names
LastDayProductDetails AS
(
    SELECT
        Product.ProductID,
        Product.Name,
        LastDayQuantity
    FROM Production.Product
    JOIN LastDayProductQuantities
    ON Product.ProductID = LastDayProductQuantities.ProductID
)
-- Finally return the results of the last CTE
SELECT * FROM LastDayProductDetails
ORDER BY LastDayQuantity DESC;
```

The preceding query may not be the most efficient syntax for retrieving the desired result, but it does give us a way to break what may seem like a complex query down into smaller bite-size pieces (CTEs). It also allows us to do it in a top-down style notation rather than the sometimes more confusing inside-out subquery syntax. It is just another way to approach solving a problem and may allow you think around obstacles you encounter in other methods.

Test Day Tip

When taking a test you are provided with a note sheet and a pen. A helpful tip might be to write down key things you want to remember onto the note sheet before you start the test. This can help you focus your thoughts before the test as well as provide you with reminders once the test starts.

Whether we choose to write our statements using CTEs or subqueries is often just a matter of personal preference. If it is possible for us to write a statement using either a CTE or a subquery, we will probably find little difference between the CTE version of the statement when compared to the subquery version of the statement as far as SQL Server's optimizer is concerned. Assuming they both imply the same intentional result, we will likely get the same execution plan returned for both styles of syntax. Of course, that is a generalization, and when we do have a choice we should always test to see if one version of the statement has a better execution plan than the other. The CTE becomes a requirement and not an option when we want to reference the CTE multiple times in the same query (as in a self-join situation), when we want the multiple CTEs to build on the single "base" CTE, and when we want the CTE's query to be recursive.

Creating Recursive CTEs

Recursive queries are a powerful feature of CTEs. With recursive CTEs we have the ability to perform in a single set-based statement what in previous versions has typically required the implementation of procedures or functions. The recursive nature of CTEs comes from their ability to be self-referencing; something neither subqueries nor views can do. Recursive queries, though powerful, can sometimes be difficult to visualize, and if we aren't careful can generate "runaway" code. SQL Server prevents this from happening by default, but we need to be aware of what recursion means and learn how to control it. We will cover controlling recursion when we discuss the *MAXRECURSION* option at the end of this section. If you are new to the concept of recursion, read the sidebar titled "Recursion" for more information.

Head of the Class...

Recursion
Recursion is a useful programming practice for writing code that calls itself. Recursion provides a powerful mechanism for processing trees and hierarchies, building running totals, calculating factorials, and so on.

Continued

Recursion is a common tool used in many languages. SQL Server has supported recursion in stored procedures and triggers in previous versions, but CTEs now give us the ability to create recursive queries. As explained in this chapter, CTEs are named queries that can be referenced from a SQL statement. The name of a CTE can in fact be referenced from within its own query definition. By following some specific syntax rules, SQL Server can process the self-referencing CTE query definitions and traverse the parent/child relationships that are so common in relational databases.

A common example of a recursive CTE in the SQL world is one that uses the relationship between an employee and a manager. In this scenario a manager has employees, but those employees may also be managers of other employees, and so on and so forth. With a recursive query, we can retrieve the top-level (Level 0) manager in the "Anchor query" and then in the recursive operation find all the employees that report to that manager (Level 1), iterate the recursive query again to find all the employees for that report to the Level 1 employees (Level 2), and again, and again.

The structure of a recursive CTE is similar to that of a regular CTE with the exception of the CTE's query definition. Here is the basic layout of a recursive CTE query:

```
-- CTE DECLARATION
WITH CTE_name [ ( column_name [,…n] ) ]
AS
(
CTE_Anchor_member_query_definition
UNION ALL
CTE_Recursive_member_query_definition
)
-- CTE USE
SELECT <column_list>
FROM CTE_NAME
```

The preceding syntax shows that a recursive CTE's query definition has two primary components: the "anchor member" and the "recursive member." The anchor member is the query that returns rows that represent the top-level items in a hierarchy. For example, when using CTEs to recursively iterate through the manager/employee relationships in an organization, the anchor member query will return only the top-level employee (or employees if there are multiple people at the very top of the organizational chart). Anchor member queries specifically may *not* reference the CTE. Referencing the CTE is what the recursive member does.

The "recursive member" is the query that returns the details for the lower level items and maps to the "parents" of those records by joining back to the CTE itself. The recursive member is the query that references the CTE by its name and causes SQL server to perform the recursion.

The anchor member and the recursive member are separated by a *UNION ALL* operator. This continuously attaches the rows from each recursion to the final result set.

If you have read up on recursive CTE queries before, you have likely run across the standard manager / employee recursive query using the *AdventureWorks. HumanResources.Employee* table from SQL Server 2005. SQL Server 2008 has significantly changed the structure of the *HumanResources.Employee* table and how the hierarchy itself is represented. The most notable differences are the new *BusinessEntityID* and *OrganizationNode* columns. The *OrganizationNode* column uses the new *HierarchyID* data type. A discussion of it is beyond the scope of this chapter, but you can refer to the SQL Server 2008 documentation for details on it. Without further ado, here is a sample recursive query:

```
USE AdventureWorks2008;
GO
WITH OrgChart --Notice the name of the CTE is "OrgChart"
(OrganizationNode,LoginID, ManagerLoginID, Level)
AS
(
    --Anchor Member query:
    SELECT OrganizationNode, LoginID, CAST(NULL AS nvarchar(256)),
       OrganizationNode.GetLevel()
    FROM HumanResources.Employee
    WHERE OrganizationNode = HierarchyID::GetRoot()

    UNION ALL
--Recursive Member Query:
SELECT E.OrganizationNode, E.LoginID, M.LoginID,
E.OrganizationNode.GetLevel()
FROM HumanResources.Employee AS E
JOIN OrgChart AS M
```

```
ON E.OrganizationNode.GetAncestor(1) = M.OrganizationNode
)
SELECT * FROM OrgChart;
```

Let's dissect this query a little bit. First, we see that the name of the CTE is *OrgChart*. Next is the explicit list of column names that the query will return. In this example it is useful to state the column aliases here rather than in the query definitions inside the CTE's declaration. It just helps clean things up a little. Also in this query, only the *LoginIDs* of the employees and managers are being retrieved. This keeps the query simple and clean, yet still gives us a sense of "who" the managers and employees are. Remember, this is just an example.

The anchor member query returns details for employees who are at the top level of the organization. In this case we are determining that an employee is at the top of the organization by testing to see if the employee's *OrganizationNode* column value is the same as the root value of the *HierarchyID* data type (HierarchyID::GetRoot()). The last column returns the "Level" of the employee by calling the GetLevel() method of the *OrganizationNode HierarchyID* value (OrganizationNode.GetLevel()), When SQL Server processes the anchor member query, a single row is returned:

OrganizationNode	LoginID	ManagerLoginID	Level
0x	adventure-works\ken0	NULL	0

Note that in the row returned from the anchor member query definition, the *ManagerLoginID* value is *NULL*. This is because members at the top level of the hierarchy by definition do not have managers. Therefore, any manager data for those employees is empty, or *NULL*.

SQL server then moves to process the recursive member. The recursive member query joins back to the CTE by its name. In our example, the CTE now represents the row that was returned from the anchor member. SQL Server finds all employees that have an *OrganizationNode* value with the ancestor 1 level up (OrganizationNode.GetAncestor(1)) having the same value as the manager's *OrganziationNode* value. The first pass through the recursive query then returns all employees who report to "adventure-works\ken0":

OrganizationNode	LoginID	ManagerLoginID	Level
0x58	adventure-works\terri0	adventure-works\ken0	1
0x68	adventure-works\david0	adventure-works\ken0	1
0x78	adventure-works\james1	adventure-works\ken0	1

0x84	adventure-works\laura1	adventure-works\ken0	1
0x8C	adventure-works\jean0	adventure-works\ken0	1
0x94	adventure-works\brian3	adventure-works\ken0	1

SQL Server then continues to iterate the recursive member query for each row returned by its previous iteration. For example, the next iteration would join any employees that report to "adventure-works\brian3" to Brian's record and show his direct reports, giving us the following additional rows:

OrganizationNode	LoginID	ManagerLoginID	Level
----------------	----------------------	--------------------	-----
...	...	...	...
0x9560	adventure-works\stephen0	adventure-works\brian3	2
0x95A0	adventure-works\syed0	adventure-works\brian3	2
0x95E0	adventure-works\amy0	adventure-works\brian3	2
...	...	...	...

SQL Server then continues recursing into the CTE for each row returned to find that row's employees until all rows have been exhausted or the maximum depth of recursion has been reached. By default, SQL Server supports 100 levels of recursion along a single "branch" in a hierarchy. If we have hierarchies with branches that are deeper than 100 levels, we will need to override the default using the *MAXRECURSION* query option. Query options will be explained in more detail later in this chapter. We can tell if we have exceeded the *MAXRECURSION* by the system returning the following error message:

```
Msg 530, Level 16, State 1, Line 1
The statement terminated. The maximum recursion 3 has been exhausted
before statement completion.
```

Exam Warning

Don't forget about *MAXRECURSION*. Make sure to pay attention to queries that could repeat indefinitely during the exam. Recursive queries that go deeper than 100 levels along any branch will cause errors unless the *MAXRECURSION* option is used.

In Exercise 11.1 you will create a recursive CTE and test the effect of the *MAXRECURSION* option.

EXERCISE 11.1

CREATING A RECURSIVE CTE

1. Open a new query in SQL Server Management Studio
2. Enter the following code into the window:

   USE AdventureWorks2008;

   GO

   WIH OrgChart (OrganizationNode,LoginID,MLoginID) AS

   (SELECT OrganizationNode, LoginID, CAST(NULL AS nvarchar(256))

   FROM HumanResources.Employee

   WHERE OrganizationNode = HierarchyID::GetRoot ()

   UNION ALL

   SELECT E.OrganizationNode, E.LoginID, M.LoginID

   FROM HumanResources.Employee AS E

   JOIN OrgChart AS M

   ON E.OrganizationNode.GetAncestor(1) = M.OrganizationNode)

   SELECT * FROM OrgChart

   OPTION(MAXRECURSION 4);

3. Run the query and view the results.
4. Try the same query that is shown in step 2, but change the *MAXRECURSION* value from 4 to 3.

Applying Ranking Functions

Ranking functions are built-in system functions that allow us to include numeric columns in our result sets where the value in the column reflects the "rank" of the row. We determine how to rank the rows by choosing first which of the four possible ranking functions (*ROW_NUMBER, RANK, DENSE_RANK,* or *NTILE*) we wish to use, what value the rank will be based on, and optionally over what ranges or "partitions" we want the ranking to be performed. All of the functions follow the same basic format:

```
<ranking_function > OVER ( [ <partition_by_clause> ] <order_by_clause> )
```

We'll look at the general use of the functions by starting with the first one, *ROW_NUMBER.*

Using ROW_NUMBER

We will start with the *ROW_NUMBER* function because it is the most basic of the four ranking functions. It simply generates a numeric value based on the number of rows in the result.

The following examples of the ranking functions will build on a query that returns products from three specific subcategories using the *Product and ProductSubcategory* tables in the *AdventureWorks.Production* schema. The subcategories we see in the query are Bib-shorts, Bottom Brackets, and Gloves. These subcategories were chosen to help keep the result set small for demo purposes but still provide a set of data that can be used to show all the ranking functions. Here is the initial query we will use without any ranking function yet used:

```
USE AdventureWorks2008;
GO
SELECT
    S.Name AS SubName, P.Name ProdName, ListPrice AS Price
FROM Production.Product AS P
JOIN Production.ProductSubcategory AS S
ON P.ProductSubcategoryID = S.ProductSubcategoryID
WHERE S.ProductSubCategoryID IN (5,18,20)
ORDER BY S.Name, ListPrice;
```

The *ROW_NUMBER* function allows us to return a sequential row number value in our result sets. We have to indicate to the *ROW_NUMBER* function the order in which we want the rows to be numbered. For example, should they be numbered in order of list price, or should they be listed by some other sort order? We state our sorting desires using required `<order_by_clause>`. Because the ranking function gets its own `<order_by_clause>`, the ordering of the row number sequence can be different than the ordering of result set. In all of the examples, we will order the ranking functions by the ListPrice of the products where lower list prices have a lower rank value and higher list prices will have a higher rank value. Here is the same query with the *ROW_NUMBER* function added and its results:

```
USE AdventureWorks2008
GO
SELECT
    S.Name AS SubName, P.Name ProdName, ListPrice AS Price,
    ROW_NUMBER() OVER (ORDER BY ListPrice) AS ROW
FROM Production.Product AS P
JOIN Production.ProductSubcategory AS S
```

```
ON P.ProductSubcategoryID = S.ProductSubcategoryID
WHERE S.ProductSubCategoryID IN (5,18,20)
ORDER BY S.Name, ListPrice;
```

SubName	ProdName	Price	ROW
Bib-Shorts	Men's Bib-Shorts, S	89.99	8
Bib-Shorts	Men's Bib-Shorts, M	89.99	9
Bib-Shorts	Men's Bib-Shorts, L	89.99	10
Bottom Brackets	LL Bottom Bracket	53.99	7
Bottom Brackets	ML Bottom Bracket	101.24	11
Bottom Brackets	HL Bottom Bracket	121.49	12
Gloves	Half-Finger Gloves, S	24.49	1
Gloves	Half-Finger Gloves, M	24.49	2
Gloves	Half-Finger Gloves, L	24.49	3
Gloves	Full-Finger Gloves, S	37.99	4
Gloves	Full-Finger Gloves, M	37.99	5
Gloves	Full-Finger Gloves, L	37.99	6

Notice that the values in the **ROW** column are not ordered by the position of the rows, but rather by the magnitude of the ListPrice value. This is because the call to the *ROW_NUMBER* function indicated that the ranking should be ordered by the ListPrice, whereas the rows themselves are being sorted first by the subcategory name, then by list price. The *ROW_NUMBER* function call has been italicized in the preceding query to help you find it easily.

If we want the row number to number the rows in the same order as they are returned, we need to ask the *ROW_NUMBER* function to order its values using the same ordering as the *ORDER BY* clause on the query itself (S.Name, P.ListPrice), as follows:

```
USE AdventureWorks2008
GO
SELECT
    S.Name AS SubName, P.Name ProdName, ListPrice AS Price,
    ROW_NUMBER() OVER
    (ORDER BY S.Name, ListPrice) AS ROW
    FROM Production.Product AS P
JOIN Production.ProductSubcategory AS S
ON P.ProductSubcategoryID = S.ProductSubcategoryID
WHERE S.ProductSubCategoryID IN (5,18,20)
```

```
ORDER BY S.Name, ListPrice;
```

SubName	ProdName	Price	ROW
Bib-Shorts	Men's Bib-Shorts, S	89.99	1
Bib-Shorts	Men's Bib-Shorts, M	89.99	2
Bib-Shorts	Men's Bib-Shorts, L	89.99	3
Bottom Brackets	LL Bottom Bracket	53.99	4
Bottom Brackets	ML Bottom Bracket	101.24	5
Bottom Brackets	HL Bottom Bracket	121.49	6
...	...	...	...

So far, the row numbers generated are based on the entire result set (all 12 rows). We can break the ranking functions down into different subsets or "partitions" of the total number of rows much in the same way that we can group rows with the group by clause when using aggregate functions. We indicate what rows are in the same partition by stating the columns whose values the partitions will be based on in the <partition_by_clause>. For example, if we wanted to have the row number start over with each subcategory, we would use the following query:

```
USE AdventureWorks2008
GO
SELECT
    S.Name AS SubName, P.Name ProdName, ListPrice AS Price,
    ROW_NUMBER() OVER
    (PARTITION BY S.ProductSubcategoryID ORDER BY ListPrice) AS ROW
    FROM Production.Product AS P
JOIN Production.ProductSubcategory AS S
ON P.ProductSubcategoryID = S.ProductSubcategoryID
WHERE S.ProductSubCategoryID IN (5,18,20)
ORDER BY S.Name, ListPrice;
```

SubName	ProdName	Price	ROW
Bib-Shorts	Men's Bib-Shorts, S	89.99	1
Bib-Shorts	Men's Bib-Shorts, M	89.99	2
Bib-Shorts	Men's Bib-Shorts, L	89.99	3
Bottom Brackets	LL Bottom Bracket	53.99	1
Bottom Brackets	ML Bottom Bracket	101.24	2
Bottom Brackets	HL Bottom Bracket	121.49	3
Gloves	Half-Finger Gloves, S	24.49	1

Gloves	Half-Finger Gloves, M	24.49	2
Gloves	Half-Finger Gloves, L	24.49	3
Gloves	Full-Finger Gloves, S	37.99	4
Gloves	Full-Finger Gloves, M	37.99	5
Gloves	Full-Finger Gloves, L	37.99	6

Notice that the values in the **ROW** column now start back at one with each new subcategory. This is because of the `<partition_by_clause>` of *PARTITION BY S.* `ProductSubcategoryID`.

New & Noteworthy...

ROW_NUMBER() vs. IDENTITY()

The new *ROW_NUMBER()* function provides a much more flexible way to number rows in our result sets that does the *IDENTITY()* function.

The *IDENTITY()* function (similar to the *IDENTITY* property in a table column) provides a way to automatically number rows in a result set. However, the *IDENTITY()* function can only be used in *SELECT ... INTO* queries. The *ROW_NUMBER()* function, on the other hand, can be used in any *SELECT* statement and is quite configurable via the partition and order by clauses.

That is the basics of using *ROW_NUMBER* and how to use the `<order_by_clause>` and `<partition_by_clause>` for all ranking functions. Let's now take a look at those other functions.

Using RANK, DENSE_RANK and NTILE

The *ROW_NUMBER* function returned a sequential number based on the number of rows in the given "partition" and ordered by the some value. The *RANK AND DENSE_RANK* functions provide more complex numbering based on the values themselves, not just the number of rows, whereas the *NTILE* function generates numbers by dividing the rows into a given number of groups based on the total number of rows (or the number of rows in the partition if the `<partition_by_clause>`

is used) and then numbering each row with its group number. We will explain each of the functions in more detail and then present a single sample query that shows their values.

The *RANK* function generates numbers based on the values in the columns specified by the `<order_by_clause>`. The *RANK* value for a given row will be one greater than the number of rows that precede it in the current partition, except when it has the same value in the order by columns as the previous row, in which case it will have the same rank value as the previous row. This means that "gaps" can occur in the *RANK* values if one or more rows have duplicate values as other rows in columns being ranked. The following set of rows is an excerpt of a result set that shows the gaps that can occur in the rank value with the *RANK* function call of `RANK() OVER (PARTITION BY S.ProductSubcategoryID ORDER BY ListPrice)`:

SubName	ProdName	Price	ROW	RANK
Gloves	Half-Finger Gloves, S	24.49	1	1
Gloves	Half-Finger Gloves, M	24.49	2	1
Gloves	Half-Finger Gloves, L	24.49	3	1
Gloves	Full-Finger Gloves, S	37.99	4	4
Gloves	Full-Finger Gloves, M	37.99	5	4
Gloves	Full-Finger Gloves, L	37.99	6	4

Notice how the *RANK* value for the first three rows is the same (1). The column being ranked is the ListPrice column (as specified in the *ORDER BY* `ListPrice` syntax). The first three rows all have the same value for the ListPrice (24.49), so they all get the same rank value. The fourth row, however, gets a rank value that is one greater than the number of rows that preceded it in the current partition. In this case, three rows preceded it, so it gets a value of 3 + 1 or 4. The rows that follow it, however, again have the same ListPrice value (37.99), so they get the same rank value as the first row with that value (4). The end result is that gaps can show up in the ranking value. If you don't want the gaps, use *DENSE_RANK*.

DENSE RANK is similar to *RANK* in that it generates its ranking based on the column values specified by the `<order_by_clause>`, but it does not introduce gaps. *DENSE RANK* will generate rank values that are one greater than the previous rank value except where two rows have the same values in the columns being ranked. In that case, rows with the same values in the ranked columns will have the same rank values. Because subsequent *DENSE RANK* values are either the same or one greater than previous *DENSE RANK* values in the partition, no "gaps" appear. Here is the same result set excerpt as was shown for the *RANK* function above, but this time we have added a column with the *DENSE_RANK* function call of *DENSE_RANK() OVER (PARTITION BY S.* `ProductSubcategoryID` *ORDER BY* `ListPrice`):

SubName	ProdName	Price	ROW	RANK	DENSE
Gloves	Half-Finger Gloves, S	24.49	1	1	1
Gloves	Half-Finger Gloves, M	24.49	2	1	1
Gloves	Half-Finger Gloves, L	24.49	3	1	1
Gloves	Full-Finger Gloves, S	37.99	4	4	2
Gloves	Full-Finger Gloves, M	37.99	5	4	2
Gloves	Full-Finger Gloves, L	37.99	6	4	2

You can see the difference between *RANK* and *DENSE_RANK* values. When rows have distinct values in the columns being ranked, *RANK* generates a value that is one greater than the *number of rows* that precede it in the current partition, whereas *DENSE_RANK* generates a value that is one greater than *the DENSE_RANK value* that precedes it in the current partition. Both behave the same way when a row has the same value as the previous row for the column being ranked in that they receive the same rank value as the previous row. Also, if a given partition had no rows with duplicate values in the columns being ranked *RANK and DENSE_RANK* would return the same values for the partition.

The *NTILE* is based more on the number of rows in the current partition than on the actual values in the columns being ranked. In this way, it is more akin to *ROW_NUMBER* than to *RANK. DENSE_RANK NTILE*'s ranking isn't based on the magnitude of the actual value in the column being ranked, but rather the value's sort order position in the current partition. *NTILE* is different from the other ranking functions in that it does expect an argument to be passed in. The argument is an integer value that specifies how many "groups" or "tiles" each partition should be broken into. Following is again the same result set excerpt we looked at for the *RANK and DENSE_RANK* functions above, but this time with a call to the *NTILE* function of *NTILE*(3) *OVER (PARTITION BY S.* Name ORDER BY ListPrice):

SubName	ProdName	Price	ROW	RANK	DENSE	NTILE
Gloves	Half-Finger Gloves, S	24.49	1	1	1	1
Gloves	Half-Finger Gloves, M	24.49	2	1	1	1
Gloves	Half-Finger Gloves, L	24.49	3	1	1	2
Gloves	Full-Finger Gloves, S	37.99	4	4	2	2

Gloves	Full-Finger Gloves, M	37.99	5	4	2	3
Gloves	Full-Finger Gloves, L	37.99	6	4	2	3

There are a total of six rows in the Gloves subcategory. We called the *NTILE* function with an argument of "3." This means it has to break the six rows into three groups. Six divided by three is two, meaning we will have three groups with two rows each. The groups are then numbered based on the values in the columns specified in the `<order_by_clause>`. The first two rows are in group 1, the second two rows are in group 2, and so on.

If the number of rows is not evenly divisible by the number of groups requested, the additional rows are distributed among the lower order groups. This means that lower groups will have one row greater in each row than the higher groups depending on how many "remainder" rows there were. For example, if we called the above *NTILE* function with an argument of 4 rather than 3, we would get the following result:

SubName	ProdName	Price	ROW	RANK	DENSE	NTILE
Gloves	Half-Finger Gloves, S	24.49	1	1	1	1
Gloves	Half-Finger Gloves, M	24.49	2	1	1	1
Gloves	Half-Finger Gloves, L	24.49	3	1	1	2
Gloves	Full-Finger Gloves, S	37.99	4	4	2	2
Gloves	Full-Finger Gloves, M	37.99	5	4	2	3
Gloves	Full-Finger Gloves, L	37.99	6	4	2	4

Pay close attention to the *NTILE* value of the last row; it is a "4" rather than a "3" as before. With six rows being divided into four groups, we end up with four groups of one row each and two rows remaining. The two additional rows are distributed to the lower groups (group one and two) giving them each two rows, and the higher two groups (groups three and four) remain at one row only.

Exam Warning

The *NTILE()* function is the only one of the four ranking functions that requires or even accepts a parameter value. Don't be fooled by versions of the other ranking functions that have parameter values being passed in on the test.

That about covers ranking functions now that we have talked about all four of the ranking functions, *ROW_NUMBER, RANK, DENSE_RANK, and NTILE*. To wrap it up, let's look at a final query that shows all of them together so that we can easily compare their results:

```
USE AdventureWorks2008;
GO
SELECT
    S.Name AS SubName, P.Name ProdName, ListPrice AS Price,
    ROW_NUMBER() OVER
    (PARTITION BY S.ProductSubcategoryID ORDER BY ListPrice) AS ROW,
    RANK() OVER
    (PARTITION BY S.ProductSubcategoryID ORDER BY ListPrice) AS RANK,
    DENSE_RANK() OVER
    (PARTITION BY S.ProductSubcategoryID ORDER BY ListPrice) AS DENSE,
    NTILE(3) OVER
    (PARTITION BY S.ProductSubcategoryID ORDER BY ListPrice) AS NTILE
    FROM Production.Product AS P
JOIN Production.ProductSubcategory AS S
ON P.ProductSubcategoryID = S.ProductSubcategoryID
WHERE S.ProductSubCategoryID IN (5,18,20)
ORDER BY S.Name, ListPrice;
```

SubName	ProdName	Price	ROW	RANK	DENSE	NTILE
Bib-Shorts	Men's Bib-Shorts, S	89.99	1	1	1	1
Bib-Shorts	Men's Bib-Shorts, M	89.99	2	1	1	2
Bib-Shorts	Men's Bib-Shorts, L	89.99	3	1	1	3
Bottom Brackets	LL Bottom Bracket	53.99	1	1	1	1
Bottom Brackets	ML Bottom Bracket	101.24	2	2	2	2
Bottom Brackets	HL Bottom Bracket	121.49	3	3	3	3
Gloves	Half-Finger Gloves, S	24.49	1	1	1	1
Gloves	Half-Finger Gloves, M	24.49	2	1	1	1
Gloves	Half-Finger Gloves, L	24.49	3	1	1	2
Gloves	Full-Finger Gloves, S	37.99	4	4	2	2
Gloves	Full-Finger Gloves, M	37.99	5	4	2	3
Gloves	Full-Finger Gloves, L	37.99	6	4	2	3

EXERCISE 11.2

USING RANKING FUNCTIONS

1. Open a new query in SQL Server Management Studio.
2. Enter the query from the sample code above.
3. Try different configurations for the *PARTITION BY and ORDER BY* clauses.

In the last two sections, we have talked about some newer syntax we can use when submitting statements to the server. In the next section, we will look at ways that we can manage the behavior and performance of the statements we submit.

Controlling Execution Plans

One of the most powerful and beneficial features of SQL Server is its query optimizer. Part of what we are paying for when we purchase SQL Server is the expertise of the SQL Server product engineers in the form of the query optimizer. The optimizer uses a number of internal mechanisms to determine what statistically appears to be the most efficient way to execute each statement. It generates a plan for the statement's execution based on its determinations and then hands the plan off to be executed. The majority of the time we are better off letting the optimizer do its job and to just stay out of its way. There are times, however, when for one or more reasons we may need to either offer guidance to the optimizer or completely override it. This section discusses Hints, the Query Governor, and the new Resource Governor. These are tools that we can use to either guide or control the query optimizer, to limit which statements it is allowed to execute based on their cost, or to limit what resources are available to those statements as they execute.

Understanding Hints

Hints are syntax elements we can use to override the optimizer's behavior and force certain behaviors that the optimizer may not otherwise choose automatically. It is the query optimizer's job to determine the most efficient way of executing your statements. It has a number of factors to consider as it goes through the optimization process. Before the optimizer can optimize our statements, it first needs to understand the intent of the query. It does this by normalizing the syntax you submit into a more concise internal representation. It is this normalization of our syntax that makes it possible for us to write statements in ways that make sense to us rather than requiring us to adhere to specific syntax coding rules in order to optimize performance. Once the optimizer has standardized the syntax into a more normal form, it can then create an optimal execution plan for it.

As the optimizer works for the most efficient query plan, it deals with the estimated cost of the query. The cost is a number made up of both I/O and CPU costs. The optimizer uses statistics about the data in our tables and indexes. The statistics are calculated periodically by the data engine and stored as metadata in the database. Because the statistics are an approximate model of the data, they can sometimes be misleading. That leaves a small chance that the optimizer can be misguided by those statistics and actually come up with a plan that is not optimal. It is in those rare cases that we may consider overriding the optimizer with hints mixed into our syntax to guide or override its behavior. There are three different types of hints: Query Hints, Join Hints, and Table Hints. We will discuss them here.

TEST DAY TIP

Hints are to be used only in exceptional circumstances when creating production code. For that reason, unless a question is asking you specifically about how to do a hint, the answer with a hint in it is likely the wrong answer.

Using Query Hints

Query hints are included in your statements as part of the *OPTION* clause. The *OPTION* clause can be used in all of the DML statements—*SELECT, INSERT, UPDATE, DELETE,* and *MERGE.* The *OPTION* clause is always the last clause in the statement, with the exception of the *INSERT* statement where it is very near the end. The *OPTION* clause takes the format :

```
OPTION (<query_hint>[,…n])
```

We talked about a specific query hint in the Common Table Expression section when we talked about the *MAXRECURSION* option. You may recall from that discussion that the default *MAXRECURSION* value is 100, but we can override it with the *MAXRECURSION* query option. Typically, we would use that to allow hierarchies that are deeper than 100 levels to be processed. We could of course also use it to ensure that a query did *not* go deeper than a certain level by setting it to the desired depth. Here is an example of a recursive query with the *MAXRECURSION* option included:

```
USE AdventureWorks2008;
GO
WITH OrgChart (OrganizationNode,LoginID,MLoginID) AS
(SELECT OrganizationNode, LoginID, CAST(NULL AS nvarchar(256))
    FROM HumanResources.Employee
    WHERE OrganizationNode = HierarchyID::GetRoot()
    UNION ALL
    SELECT E.OrganizationNode, E.LoginID, M.LoginID
    FROM HumanResources.Employee AS E
    JOIN OrgChart AS M
    ON E.OrganizationNode.GetAncestor(1) = M.OrganizationNode)
SELECT * FROM OrgChart
OPTION(MAXRECURSION 4);
```

You may be tempted to try this query out yourself. Go ahead and give it a try! If you do, try it a second time with a *MAXRECURSION* value of 3 rather than 4 and see what happens. The important thing to take from the example is the position and syntax of the *OPTION* clause. A number of query hints can be specified in the *OPTION* clause, far too many for us to discuss in detail. You should review the SQL Server 2008 documentation regarding query hints. We will cover them at a high level, however.

One more comment about the *OPTION* clause should be discussed before we list some of the hints. That is that the *OPTION* clause affects the *entire* statement. There can also only be one *OPTION* clause per statement. If the statement is a *UNION,* the *OPTION* clause needs to be stated at the end of the last *SELECT* statement. Now let's take a quick look at some of the options.

The *GROUP, UNION,* and *JOIN* hints allow us to specify the mechanism by the optimizer to affect *GROUP BY, UNION,* and *JOIN* operations. The *FAST* hint allows us to request that the query be optimized for a certain number of rows to be returned first. The *FORCE ORDER* hint allows us to require that the optimizer use tables of multiple joins in the same order we specify them. The *KEEP PLAN, KEEPFIXED PLAN*, and *RECOMPILE* hints allow us to reduce the frequency of, disable, or require the recompilation of the plan for a given statement. There is even a *USE PLAN* hint that allows us to specify the precise plan we would like the optimizer to use. Of course, if we state a hint that makes the query unexecutable, SQL Server will raise an error (Error 8622). Again, you should review the SQL Server 2008 documentation regarding the use of query hints, which presents more complete explanations of the hints and examples of their use.

Remember that we only get one *OPTION* clause per statement, and the *OPTION* clause affects the entire statement. If we need a way to more explicitly override the behavior of different tables or views referenced in a statement, then we can use table hints.

Using Table Hints

Table hints can be used in our syntax to indicate specific behaviors on a table-by-table basis. They are much more specific than query hints in that they target a single table in a statement rather than the entire statement. As with query hints, table hints can be used in *SELECT, INSERT, UPDATE, DELETE*, and *MERGE* statements. Table hints are specified in a *WITH* clause that is stated immediately after each table reference in a statement. Note that SQL Server will permit you to state table hints without using the keyword *WITH*, but only in some cases. This style of syntax, however, has been deprecated, meaning that it will no longer be supported in future versions. For that reason we should always include the *WITH* keyword in our table hints. The *WITH* clause has the following format:

```
WITH ( <table_hint> [ [,]...n ])
```

The available table hints fall into different categories; see Table 11.1 for a list of categories and their associated table hints.

Table 11.1 Table Hint Categories

Hint Category	Table Hints
Index Usage	INDEX, FORCESEEK
Lock Contention	NOWAIT, READPAST
Lock Grain	NOLOCK, ROWLOCK, PAGLOCK, TABLOCK
Lock Mode	TABLOCKX, UPDLOCK, XLOCK
Transaction Isolation Levels	READUNCOMMITTED, READCOMMITTED, READCOMMITTEDLOCK, REPEATABLEREAD, SERIALIZABLE, HOLDLOCK

As you can see, there are a number of table hints. As with the section on query hints, you should refer to the SQL Server 2008 documentation for a complete explanation of each of them with examples for their usage. However, we can look at a couple of them here.

One hint that can be a useful tool when we are testing indexes and their benefits is the *INDEX* hint. This hint allows us to specify a specific index or set of indexes we want the optimizer to use as it accesses data in the given table. This tool should generally be used during index implementation and development. Rarely is it a wise choice to implement query hints in production code. There are exceptions to that rule, but they require significant testing and frequent review. Rather than overriding the optimizer, we should make sure it has the tools it needs (see the sidebar "Indexes and Statistics") to help it make better decisions. With that disclaimer out of the way, let's look at an example. Figure 11.1 shows two queries and their execution plans. The two queries are identical except for the table hint in the second query.

Figure 11.1 INDEX Table Hint Example

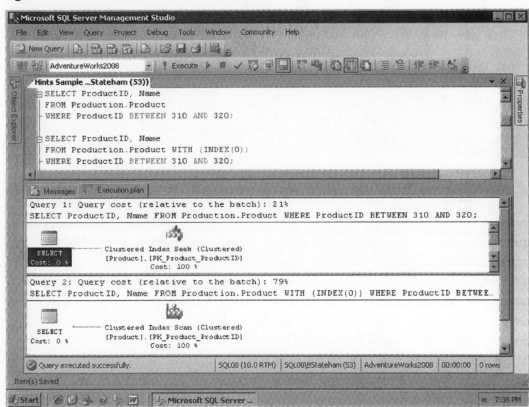

Configuring & Implementing...

Indexes and Statistics

SQL Server uses indexes in much the same way that we as humans use indexes in a book. Indexes can help SQL Server to find just the data it needs to service our queries. Books, however, usually only have a single index, where tables can have numerous indexes. The optimizer will evaluate the indexes that exist in a table as part of its optimization process to determine if any of them would be helpful in processing the statement.

The optimizer evaluates the indexes based on their statistics. The statistics are a measure of the distribution of data in the index. It tells SQL Server if there are a lot of unique values in the index or if there are a lot of duplicate values. The more unique values there are in the index, the more likely it can be used to find a few unique values out of the many. As the data in our tables change, we need to make sure the statistics of the data are being updated as well. We can use the Auto Create Statistics and Auto Update Statistics database options as well as the *CREATE STATISTICS* and *UPDATE STATISTICS* statements to ensure the optimizer has current statistics about our data.

If you read the execution plan information of the screenshot shown in Figure 11.2, you will see some interesting things. First of all, remember that the first query is the one where we did *not* include a hint. Its plan then represents the plan that the optimizer chose on its own. The second query is the one where we forced the optimizer to use *index(0)*. *Index 0* is the table itself. In other words, we requested that the optimizer scan the entire table (or clustered index in this case) rather than navigating the index to find just the rows it needed. The execution plan shows that the optimizer's plan was 21% the total cost of the batch, whereas our query with the forced table scan was 79% of the total batch cost. That means that the optimizer's plan was cheaper and therefore the better choice.

What is important to take away from the example shown in Figure 11.2 is how the table hint was stated and how it did in fact have an effect on how the query was optimized. You should refer to the SQL Server 2008 documentation to review the other table hints and their purposes and to see examples of their use.

Using Join Hints

The last kind of hint we will discuss is join hints. The optimizer has a number of different ways that it can perform join operations. This is separate from the join types of *INNER, OUTER, FULL,* and so on. Join hints instead allow us to specify what mechanism SQL Server uses internally as it performs the requested join type. The join mechanisms can be *LOOP, MERGE, HASH,* or *REMOTE.*

It is beyond the scope of this book to explain *why* you might want to use one mechanism rather than another; our purpose rather is to show *how* you can specify a join hint. The screenshot shown in Figure 11.2 shows two queries and their execution plans. The first query contains no join hints, whereas the second query specifies that a *MERGE* join operation should be performed. The execution plans have been cropped to allow you to see the important parts. You should see that the execution plan for the first query (where the optimizer chose the join mechanism) uses a "Hash Match" join, whereas the second execution plan shows a "Merge Join" operation. The most important part is the query cost of each plan; the first query was 45 percent of the batch cost, whereas the one where we forced the merge join was 55 percent of the batch cost. Again, the optimizer won.

Figure 11.2 MERGE Join Hint Example

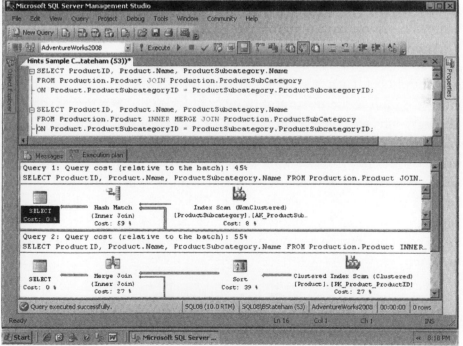

We see from these examples that while we *can* override the optimizer using hints, the optimizer more often than not will come up with a better plan. Hints are a great tool to use during development and testing, and as a learning tool to help better understand the optimizer. Before we implement hints in our production code, however, we should thoroughly test them, document them, and periodically review them to ensure they are still the best choice.

This section on hints showed us how we can change the optimizer's behavior in hopes of generating execution plans with lower total costs. In the next section we will look at the Query Governor. The Query Governor allows us to make sure that "expensive" queries do *not* run. This can save you from the accidental runaway query that gets executed in the middle of the day, and can keep it from killing your system's performance.

Using the Query Governor

The Query Governor allows administrators to specify the maximum allowable cost of the statements that can be executed on an instance of SQL Server. This server level setting helps ensure that statements with unacceptable costs do not run unless we specifically allow it.

The cost limit for the Query Governor is set at the instance level using either the **Connections** page of the **Server Properties** window in SQL Server Management Studio, or the *sp_configure* system stored procedure. It can be overridden on a session-by-session basis using the *SET QUERY_GOVERNOR_COST_LIMIT* session-level setting.

The SQL Server documentation is a little confusing as to what the value for the cost limit should be. It states in some places that the value we enter for the Query Governor cost limit is the maximum number of seconds that a query should be allowed to execute, and then in other places it states that the value is the maximum allowable query cost. Testing shows that it is in fact the maximum query cost, not a time estimate. This is a good thing because the query costs are easy to retrieve by looking at execution plans. Guessing how long a query will take is much less specific.

First, let's see how we can set the Query Governor cost limit at the instance level using *sp_configure*. The following example sets the Query Governor cost limit to 20, thus preventing any queries that have an estimated cost of 20 or higher from running:

```
EXEC sp_configure 'Show Advanced Options', 1;
RECONFIGURE;
EXEC sp_configure 'query governor cost limit', 20;
RECONFIGURE;
```

This script must first turn on the **Show Advanced Options** setting. This is because the **Query Governor Cost Limit** setting is an advanced option and can only be set when the Show Advanced **Options** setting is turned on. The *RECONFIGURE* statement after each call to `sp_configure` causes SQL Server to reload its configuration based on the new settings. This makes the new values available immediately and means we *don't* have to shut down our SQL Server instance and restart it to get the new settings.

In the preceding example, we set the cost limit to 20. Where did that number come from? What should our cost limit be? To determine the cost limit, we first need to know the "cost" of our queries. SQL Server provides a number of ways for us to view the execution plans it uses to run our statements. It is in those execution plans that we can see the estimated costs of the statements. The following script returns the execution plan for the query below it as a set of rows:

```
USE AdventureWorks2008;
GO
SET SHOWPLAN_ALL ON;
GO
SELECT TOP 1000000 *
FROM Sales.SalesOrderDetail AS OD1
CROSS JOIN Sales.SalesOrderDetail AS OD2;
```

If we run this query and look at the **TotalSubtreeCos**t column value for the first row that is returned, we will see a cost of about 4.47. That means that the *SELECT* statement has a total estimated cost of approximately 4.47 cost "units." The cost is made up of the IO and CPU costs of all steps required by the optimizer to complete the statement. We can now use that number to set the Query Governor cost limit. The following example sets the Query Governor cost limit below the estimated cost of the *SELECT* statement, thus preventing it from running. We see the error message returned below the statement:

```
USE AdventureWorks2008;
GO
SET QUERY_GOVERNOR_COST_LIMIT 4
GO
SELECT TOP 1000000 *
FROM Sales.SalesOrderDetail AS OD1
CROSS JOIN Sales.SalesOrderDetail AS OD2;
```

```
Msg 8649, Level 17, State 1, Line 1
The query has been canceled because the estimated cost of this query
(5) exceeds the configured threshold of 4. Contact the system
administrator.
```

The error message shows that the estimated cost of 4.47 we saw before was rounded up to five. The estimated statement cost of five is greater than the specified cost limit of four, and the statement is not allowed to execute. If we were to rerun the above script with the Query Governor cost limit value set to five, the query would then be allowed to execute.

The Query Governor gives us a way to prevent "expensive" queries from executing. The Resource Governor, a new feature introduced with SQL Server 2008, gives us a way to limit the resources available to clients based on certain criteria such as who they are, or what program they are using, rather than just blindly denying the execution as with the Query Governor.

Using the Resource Governor

The Resource Governor is a new feature that was introduced with SQL Server 2008. It is available only in the Enterprise, Developer, and Evaluation editions of SQL Server. Although the Resource Governor does have a name similar to the Query Governor and can limit execution of expensive queries like the Query Governor, it is a more robust resource management mechanism than the Query Governor. The goal of the Resource Governor is to be more specific in what code it limits on the server and what code is allowed to run unrestricted. We can identify the code to the server through criteria such as which user is running the query, what program the user is using, and what server or database roles the user is a member of. Based on the criteria, we can limit the code as it executes on the server by controlling things such as how many current requests there can be and how much of the available CPU and memory resources they can consume. To accomplish this goal, we will create Resource Pools, Workload Groups, and a Classifier Function.

The terms *Classifier Function, Workload Group,* and *Resource Pool,* may sound a little daunting at first, but they are easy to understand once you have gone through the process. We'll talk first about what each of these terms means and then walk through an example configuration. We'll start with Resource Pool, but first, here is a quick generalization of each term to help get you thinking:

- **Classifier Function** A user-defined function written by us. It is run every time a session starts as part of the login process, and it uses logic based on who the user is, what program the user is running, and so on, to assign the session to a Workload Group, or any other logic we feel is necessary to classify the session's workload requirements.

■ **Workload Group** Defines a "policy" for the session and its code. The policy first assigns the "Resource Pool" (see the next bullet item) from which the session will be allocated CPU and memory resources. It then defines a suballocation of the memory from the associated Resource Pool for the particular Workload Group, and sets maximum CPU time thresholds, memory resource time-outs, and maximum degree of parallelism policies.

■ **Resource Pool** Controls the availability of CPU and Memory resources to the Workload Groups assigned to use that particular Resource Group.

Resource Pools allow us to allocate a portion of the server's total CPU "bandwidth" and Memory to the statements submitted through a client connection. SQL server has two primary resources that are directly consumable by client code: CPU and Memory. Some applications, and therefore the statements submitted by those applications to the server, are "mission critical." Other applications may be important, but not critical, while still more applications may be unimportant or trivial. The problem is that sometimes it's the programs we care less about that can consume an unacceptable level of resources on the server. If that happens, they can prevent the more critical applications from having the resources they need.

Resource Pools allow us to define the minimum and maximum percentages of both CPU and memory utilization. To reflect the resources required by these three different kinds of workloads suggested above (mission critical, important, and trivial), we could create three Resource Pools. The first or, Mission Critical Resource Pool, would have a large percentage of CPU and Memory resources available. We could then create the Important Resource Pool and assign moderate percentages of CPU and Memory resources to it. Third, we could create a Trivial Resource Pool that would have a very limited percentage of CPU and Memory resources. It is important to note that the Resource Pool is a way to configure the available resources, not what code uses those resources. Client connections first get assigned to a Workload Group by the Classifier Function. The Workload Group the client session gets assigned to determines which Resource Pool the client's session will consume resources from. When multiple Resource Pools are defined, their Minimum CPU and Memory resource allocations cannot total more than 100%. The Maximum percentages are the lesser of the requested maximum and the requested maximum minus the minimum resources of the other pools.

Workload Groups allow us to enforce a policy of execution on the sessions that are assigned to it. That policy includes which Resource Pool the session will allocate resources from. Multiple Workload Groups can be assigned to the same Resource Pools and therefore "compete" for resources in that pool. For that reason, a Workload Group can be assigned an "importance" to help the Resource Governor to resolve arguments concerning which Workload Group should get a resource first. Workload Group policies determine how much of its associated Resource Pool's memory its sessions can use, how long a session can wait for memory if it is not currently available, how many concurrent requests can be open for all sessions in the Workload Group, and some others. The Workload Group can set a maximum amount of CPU time (in seconds) that a session can use, but SQL Server does not terminate code if it exceeds that time; it only generates an event that we can capture using SQL Trace and report on.

To continue our example, we could create three Workload Groups, and we could call them Mission Critical Group, Important Group, and Trivial Group. In the configuration of those Workload Groups, we could assign them to allocate resources from the Mission Critical Resource Pool, Important Resource Pool, and Trivial Resource Pool, respectively. We determine what Workload Group a client session gets assigned to by creating a *CLASSIFIER* function.

The *CLASSIFIER* function is a user-defined function that can use whatever logic we need to determine the name of the Workload Group we would like to assign the session to. As a client logs into his or her workstation and starts an application that connects to SQL Server, a session is started on the server on behalf of the user. As that session starts, during the login process, SQL Server will call the *CLASSIFIER* function we create. The *CLASSIFIER* function will use our logic to determine and then return the name of the Workload Group the server should assign the session to. The logic can be based on system functions such as *SUSER_SNAME(), APP_NAME(), HOST_NAME(), IS_SRVROLEMEMBER, IS_MEMBER(), CONNECTIONPROPERTY, GETDATE()*, as well as any other code we need to determine what kind of workload the session requires, and then direct it to the appropriate Workload Group. (If you don't know what some or all of the functions just named are, look them up in the SQL Server documentation. While you are at it, look for other useful system functions you could use to help classify your client's sessions.)

Hopefully, it is starting to make sense. Before we get started, there are a couple more things to mention:

- Resource Governor is built into SQL Server but is not enabled by default. We use the *ALTER RESOURCE GOVERNOR RECONFIGURE* statement to enable it.

- Resource Governor has two Resource Pools and Workload Groups in its initial configuration named "internal" and default." The default Workload Group is assigned to the default Resource Pool, and the "internal" Workload Group is assigned to the internal Resource Pool.

- The internal Resource Pool and Workload Group are reserved for internal SQL server processes and cannot be managed by us.

- The default Workload Group is the group to which sessions are assigned whenever there is no other Workload Group appropriate for the session, or the Workload Group name the *CLASSIFIER* function returns cannot be found.

- SQL Server provides a number of views that we can use to investigate and monitor the Resource Governor configuration. They include but are not limited to: *sys.resource_governor_configuration, sys.resource_governor_resource_pools, sys.resource_governor_workload_groups, sys.dm_resource_governor_workload_groups, sys.dm_resource_governor_resource_pools, sys.dm_resource_governor_configuration*

- Connections made via the Dedicated Administrator Connection (DAC) are not subject to the Classifier and do not run with limited resources. This can be used when the Resource Governor has been configured incorrectly or needs to be diagnosed.

To wrap it up, let's look at an example. In this example we will:

1. Create a Resource Pool that guarantees a minimum amount of CPU and Memory resources for people using the Accounting App.

2. Create a Workload Group that sets a policy for the Accounting application and assigns it to the Accounting Resource Pool made in step 1.

3. Create a *CLASSIFIER* function that uses the *APP_NAME()* function to determine if the session being created is for our accounting application, Great Plains.

4. Assign our *CLASSIFIER* function to be used by the Resource Governor.

5. Enable the Resource Governor (so it will begin to use the new configuration).

6. After connecting with Great Plains, query the server to find out what group it was assigned to.

```
USE master;
GO
-- Step 1: Create the "Accounting" Resource Pool with:
```

```
-- 25% CPU Guaranteed (Minimum)
-- 50% Memory Guaranteed
CREATE RESOURCE POOL [Accounting] WITH
    (min_cpu_percent=25,
    max_cpu_percent=100,
    min_memory_percent=50,
    max_memory_percent=100);
GO
-- Step 2: Create the "Accounting" Workload Group with:
-- High Importance
-- 30 Seconds of CPU Time threshold
-- 100 Percent of the Memory in the Accounting Resource Pool
-- 30 Seconds timeout if waiting for memory
-- Using the Accounting Resource Pool
CREATE WORKLOAD GROUP [Accounting] WITH(group_max_requests=0,
        importance=High,
        request_max_cpu_time_sec=30,
        request_max_memory_grant_percent=100,
        request_memory_grant_timeout_sec=30)
        USING [Accounting];
GO
-- Step 3: Create the Classifier Function return the Workload Group name:
-- Make sure to make the Classifier Function in the Master database
-- "Accounting" - If the APP_NAME() is like "Great Plains"
-- "default" - for everything else
CREATE FUNCTION dbo.ufnClassifier()
RETURNS sysname
WITH SCHEMABINDING
AS
BEGIN
    DECLARE @Group sysname
    IF APP_NAME() LIKE '%Great Plains%'
        SET @Group = 'Accounting'
    ELSE
        SET @Group = 'default'
        RETURN @Group
END;
GO
```

```
-- Step 4: Assign our Classifier Function to be used by the Resource Governor
ALTER RESOURCE GOVERNOR WITH (CLASSIFIER_FUNCTION = [dbo].[ufnClassifier]);
GO

-- Step 5: Enable the Resource Governor
ALTER RESOURCE GOVERNOR RECONFIGURE;
GO

-- Step 6: Query the system dynamic management views to see
-- which Workload Group and thus resource Pool
-- a live session from Great Plains was assigned to…
SELECT s.session_id, s.program_name,
       w.name AS workload_group, p.name as pool_name
FROM sys.dm_exec_sessions AS s
JOIN sys.resource_governor_workload_groups as w
JOIN sys.resource_governor_resource_pools as p
on w.pool_id = p.pool_id
ON s.group_id = w.group_id
WHERE program_name='Great Plains';

session_id      program_name      workload_group      pool_name
----------      ------------      ---------------      ----------
61              Great Plains      Accounting          Accounting
```

EXAM WARNING

The Resource Governor is available only in the Enterprise, Evaluation, and Developer editions. Test questions often like to trick you by playing with the editions available in the criteria, so pay attention!

EXERCISE 11.3

TESTING THE QUERY GOVERNOR

1. Open a new query in SQL Server Management Studio and select *AdventureWorks2008* from the list of available databases.

2. Enter the following statement into the query window:

```
SET QUERY_GOVERNOR_COST_LIMIT 4
GO
```

```
SELECT TOP 1000000 *
FROM Sales.SalesOrderDetail AS OD1
CROSS JOIN Sales.SalesOrderDetail AS OD2;
```

3. Before running it, find the estimated cost of the query by high-lighting the entire *SELECT* statement (the bottom three lines shown above) and pressing **CTRL-L** on the keyboard (or select **Query | Display Estimated Execution Plan** from the menu to see the estimated execution plan).

4. Hover over the *SELECT* icon at the left edge in the execution plan and view the **Estimated Subtree Cost** in the pop-up window that appears.

5. Based on the **Estimated Subtree Cost** found above, try different values for the SET QUERY_GOVERNOR_COST_LIMIT entry and view the results.

By using a combination of hints, the Query Governor, and the Resource Governor, we have a rich set of tools to help manage the execution of our queries. However, we don't *normally* need to use these. The SQL Server data engine does an excellent job of dynamically managing the execution of our code for normal workloads. These tools help us deal with situations that are beyond the norm. In the next section we will move on from query performance to understanding how we can deal with internationalization issues in SQL Server.

Managing Internationalization Considerations

The need to support data from sources around the world as well as to support clients from various cultures is a common need these days. SQL Server has been designed with support for these international data sets and clients out of the box. The two main features we will discuss here are the support for storing character data, or collations, and support for returning error messages to clients in an appropriate language.

Understanding Collations

Collations are the mechanism by which we tell SQL Server which characters (letters and symbols) we want to be able to work with, and how it should sort and compare values based on those characters. We have the ability to define these collation settings for each instance, database, column, and expression. To truly understand collations, we first need to understand how SQL server stores and retrieves data using data types; next we need to understand the difference between non-Unicode and Unicode data; and finally we need to understand how SQL Server sorts and compares character values.

Computers, and thus SQL Server, work with and store data as binary values. We humans don't have this capability (at least not most of us). When we ask SQL Server to store data for us in a database, SQL is responsible for properly transforming the values (words, letters, numbers, dates, etc.) that we give it into binary sequences that can be written to disk. When we later ask SQL Server to retrieve the values for us, it reverses the process and transforms the stored binary values back into the words, letters, numbers, or dates we originally gave it. SQL Server uses data types (*int, datetime, char, nchar,* etc.) to perform and manage that transformation in a consistent and formal manner. There is a set of data types specifically for storing character data; they include *char, varchar, nchar,* and *nvarchar.*

The difference between *char* and *nchar* as well as *varchar* and *nvarchar* is how many bytes each stored character takes, and from that, the range of possible character symbols that can be stored. The *char* and *varchar* types normally store characters from a limited set of 256 possible characters (determined by the selected "character set" or "code page"), with each character taking a single byte of storage. The *nchar* and *nvarchar* data types store characters from the Unicode character set that contains more than 65,000 possible characters, which each character stores using two bytes.

SQL Server makes numerous character sets from the ANSI and ISO standards bodies available for the non-Unicode *char* and *varchar* data types. Most of those character sets define a single byte per character. Some Asian character sets require two bytes per character because they have so many characters in their language. We call a non-Unicode character set that requires two bytes a Double Byte Character Set (or DBCS). With a single byte we can represent a total of 256 possible distinct values. A character maps each of the possible values to a given character. The most common ANSI code page used on North American systems is code page 1252, also referred to as Latin1. Table 11.2 shows a sample of binary values, their decimal equivalents, and the character that is mapped to it. Because different cultures and languages have different symbols, there is a problem fitting all symbols into a single set of 256. It is for that reason that we require multiple character sets. We need to then instruct SQL Server which specific character set we wish to use for each *char* and *varchar* value. Each *char* or *varchar* value can be a maximum of 8000 bytes. With each character taking one byte, that means they can store 8000 characters.

The *varchar(max)* large object data type (the successor to the old text data type) can store up to 2GB (2^{31}-1 bytes) of data, or 2^{31}-1 (more than two billion) characters.

Table 11.2 Sample Code Page 1252 Character Set Values

Binary Value	Decimal Value	ASCII Character
01000001	65	A
01000010	66	B
01000011	67	C
01100001	97	a
01100010	98	b
01100011	99	c

SQL Server also makes available the set of characters from the Unicode Consortium's Unicode character set for the *nchar* and *nvarchar* data types. Unicode stores each character as two bytes. With two bytes available, the Unicode Character set can represent 65,536 possible distinct values. With all those characters, we can represent all the symbols from the world's languages in a single character set—hence the name Unicode. This makes it an obvious choice when supporting international data sources and clients. Of course, the convenience comes with a cost. Like the *char* and *varchar* data types, the *nchar* and *nvarchar* data types can store values up to 8000 bytes. Each character, however, takes two bytes of storage, meaning they can store a total of 4000 characters each (or 2^{30}-1 characters, just over one billion) for *nvarchar(max)*. It should be mentioned that the "*n*" in-front of the *nchar* and *nvarchar* data types comes from the SQL standard's name for Unicode, which is "National Character."

So to recap, we can represent both non-Unicode and Unicode character data. The good news is that we don't have to decide to make exclusive use of non-Unicode or Unicode data. Both are supported at all times. The *char* and *varchar* data types store non-Unicode data using a code page we specify. The *nchar* and *nvarchar* data types store Unicode data.

The next step is to understand how SQL Server sorts and compares data. Specifically, how does SQL Server sort or compare two "similar" values like an uppercase letter "A" and a lowercase letter "a"? The answer is that it depends.

It depends on our preferences for case sensitivity (A vs. a), accent sensitivity (à vs. å), Japanese character kana sensitivity (Hiragana vs. Katakana), and width sensitivity (single-byte A vs. double-byte A). We could also choose to have SQL Server just sort and compare based on the binary values themselves rather than their character representations.

The case sensitivity we choose determines whether SQL Server treats uppercase "A" and lowercase "a" as equal or as distinct. The "case-insensitive" option implies that they should be treated as equals, whereas "case sensitive" implies that they should be treated as distinct. The case-insensitive option actually costs a little more in terms of procession because SQL server has to treat two things that are not the same as though they are. That takes processing to make it happen. We can cut costs somewhat by choosing a case-sensitive sort order. We can cut costs even more by choosing to sort simply by the binary values rather than by the characters they represent. Each cost-cutting step, while improving performance, adds difficulty for us as to how we specify character literals. For example if we had a case-sensitive or binary collation selected, "This" does not equal "this" because they ar not the exact same characters. The accent, kana, and width sensitivity choices follow the same pattern.

The sorting of character values is also determined by the selected collation. Different languages or cultures may sort certain values differently. For example, some Spanish-speaking cultures may choose to sort the "ch" digraph *after* cz rather than between ce and ci, as would be done in English. For example, *churro* would come after *Czech* rather than before it as would be expected in U.S. English.

We choose which non-Unicode code page we wish to use, as well as how all character data should be sorted and compared by selecting a collation. A collation combines the code page selection and sorting preferences into a single setting. SQL Server supports collations that are compatible with previous versions of SQL Server as well as collations that are compatible with your Windows operating system. Choosing between Windows and SQL Collations is based on whether you are trying to maintain compatibility with a previous version of SQL Server (SQL Collation) or with your Windows server and client operating systems (Windows Collations).

Windows Collation names take the following form:

```
<Windows_collation_name> :: =
    CollationDesignator_<ComparisonStyle>
<ComparisonStyle> :: =
    { CaseSensitivity_AccentSensitivity
      [ _KanatypeSensitive ] [ _WidthSensitive ] }
  | { _BIN | _BIN2 }
```

SQL collation names take the form:

```
<SQL_collation_name> :: =
    SQL_SortRules[_Pref]_CPCodepage_<ComparisonStyle>
<ComparisonStyle> ::=
    _CaseSensitivity_AccentSensitivity | _BIN
```

For a list of all collations, both Windows and SQL, we can run the following query (the SQL Collation names start with SQL; the rest are Windows Collation names):

```
SELECT * FROM fn_helpcollations()
```

We can specify a different collation with every character value we store, but this action is not recommended. Ideally, we would use the same collation for every character value. For that reason, we should consider what our collation should be before we install the instance of SQL Server. During the installation process, we will select a default collation that all databases, columns, and expressions will use. We can then explicitly override the default when we have a specific reason to do so. We use the *COLLATE* clause to specify which collation we wish to use. The *COLLATE* clause can be used when creating a database, defining a column, or at the end of a character expression. The following example creates a table with two character columns, each based on a different collation. The first column (col1) is based on a case-insensitive (CI) character set, whereas the second column (col2) is based on a case-sensitive (CS) collation:

```
USE AdventureWorks2008;
GO
CREATE TABLE CollateTest
(col1 nvarchar(10) COLLATE Latin1_General_100_CI_AI_KS_WS NOT NULL,
col2 nvarchar(10) COLLATE Latin1_General_100_CS_AI_KS_WS NOT NULL);

INSERT INTO CollateTest(col1,col2) VALUES ('Hello','World');

--The following query will return a single row ('Hello' and 'hello'
match when case insensitive):
SELECT * FROM CollateTest WHERE col1 = 'hello';

--This query won't return any rows ('World' and 'world' do not match
when case sensitive):
SELECT * FROM CollateTest WHERE col2 = 'world';
```

This example highlights how confusing it would be if every character value used a different collation. Not only would there be issues in sorting and matching values, but when trying to assign values from character-based column to another, corruption could occur if the target *char* or *varchar* column did not use the same code page as the source and therefore could not map some of the characters.

TEST DAY TIP

Don't let all this discussion of collations confuse you. We *want* to use the same collation in all places. They help us manage what kinds of character data we can store, and how we can find and sort that data. You are on the right track if you can pick an appropriate collation and then stick to it.

EXERCISE 11.4

TESTING DATABASE COLLATIONS

1. Open a new query in SQL Server Management Studio and select a master from the list of available databases.

2. Enter and run the following code to create a new database with a case- and accent-sensitive collation:

```
CREATE DATABASE CollationTest
    COLLATE SQL_Latin1_General_Cp1_CS_AS;
    GO
    USE CollationTest;
    GO
    CREATE TABLE TestTable
    (Col1 nvarchar(20))
    INSERT INTO TestTable (Col1) VALUES ('Some Data');
    SELECT * FROM testtable;
    GO
    SELECT * FROM TestTable WHERE Col1 = 'some data';
    GO
SELECT * FROM TestTable WHERE Col1 = 'Some Data';
```

3. Now try each of the three following queries separately. Try to understand the result you get.

```
SELECT * FROM testtable;
SELECT * FROM TestTable WHERE Col1 = 'some data';
SELECT * FROM TestTable WHERE Col1 = 'Some Data';
```

The preceding section covered the basics of working with collations. Now that we understand how we can accept and store values from international data sources, we will discuss returning error messages to clients based on their connections in culture settings.

Defining Language-Specific Custom Errors

When clients from multiple cultures connect to the same SQL Server instance, it would be beneficial to return error information to those clients in a language they can understand. When we create user-defined error messages in SQL Server, we can provide multiple versions of the error text, with each version targeting a different language.

SQL Server gives developers the ability to create error messages specific to their applications. We create the error message definitions using the sp_addmessage system stored procedure, and we then raise them using the *RAISERROR* statement. When we raise the errors in a client's connection, SQL Server can select an error message that matches the client session's culture if one is available. You can use the `sp_helplanguage` system stored procedure for details on all possible languages. To create localized versions of error messages, the following conditions must also be met:

- The U.S. English version of custom error message must be defined before any localized versions.

- The localized version must have the same defined severity as the U.S. English version.

- If the U.S. English version of the language defines parameters, the localized versions then reference the parameters by their position in the original error message. If the original message had two parameters, the localized versions refer to the first as "%1!" (without the quotes), and the second as "%2!", and so on. Notice the exclamation mark at the end of each parameter number.

The following example creates a parameterized custom error message in U.S. English, as well as in French. It then tests the error in both languages:

```
-- Create the original error message with the number
-- 50001 in US English
DECLARE @msg nvarchar(255);
SET @msg = 'This is a sample message with two parameters. ' +
          'The parameters values are %s, and %s.';
```

```
EXEC sp_addmessage
    @msgnum = 50001,
    @severity = 16,
    @lang='us_english',
    @msgtext = @msg;
-- Next create a French language version of the same error.
-- Notice the %1! and %2! parameter place holder tokens.
-- Also notice that they have been used in a different order
-- than they were defined in the original error message. That
-- is perfectly valid.
SET @msg = 'C''est un message témoin avec deux paramètres. ' +
            'Les valeurs de paramètres sont %2!, et %1!.';
EXEC sp_addmessage
    @msgnum = 50001,
    @severity = 16,
    @lang='french',
    @msgtext = @msg,
    @replace='replace';
-- Test the US English Vesrion by ensurin the session is
-- set to use US_English as the language, and then raising
-- the error with the RAISERROR statement.
SET LANGUAGE us_english;
RAISERROR(50001,16,1,'Hello','World');
-- Now try the exact same RAISERROR statement, but with the
-- session set to use the French language.
SET LANGUAGE French;
RAISERROR(50001,16,1,'Hello','World');
```

By combining the use of collations with localized versions of error messages, we have a toolset for supporting a variety of data sources and clients from around the world.

Creating and Altering Tables

In this section we look at new features in SQL Server 2008 for more efficiently storing columns with a large number of *NULL* values as well as for compressing the data in a table.

Sparse Columns

Sparse columns make it possible to store columns more efficiently where a large percentage of the rows will be *NULL*. Often, we need to include columns in our tables that only occasionally have values actually supplied for them. A column that stores an optional middle initial is an example. Most people don't bother to include their middle initial when entering their names, but occasionally somebody will. The large percentage of rows that don't have a value for the middle initial may then be *NULL*. By declaring the middle initial column with the *SPARSE* keyword, SQL Server does not consume any physical storage for the column in all rows where the column value is *NULL*.

There is a trade-off, of course. The columns that do contain values actually take more storage than nonsparse columns of the same data type. This means that there is a break-even point we must cross in terms of the percentage of rows that must contain *NULL* in that column for any actual space savings to occur. For example, the SQL Server documentation states that a nonsparse integer column that contains a value takes four bytes of storage, whereas an integer column marked as sparse requires eight bytes to store the same value. That is double the cost for each non-null integer value stored. If you do that math, then more than 50% of the rows must be *NULL* for there to be any space savings. The SQL Server documentation actually states that 64% of the rows have to be *NULL* to realize a savings. If that is the case, however, the savings could be worth it. All data types can be sparse with the exception of geography, geometry, image, ntext, text, timestamp, and user-defined data types.

If a table has more than one sparse column, we can work with all of the sparse columns using a Column Set. A Column Set is an XML column that allows us to work with all the sparse columns in the same table as a single entity. If there are a large number of sparse columns, it may be more convenient or efficient to treat them as a single set of data rather than as individual columns. For a large number of rows, working with the values as a Column Set could provide a performance increase as well. We include a Column Set by adding an XML column to the table's definition and then marking that column with *COLUMN_SET FOR ALL_ SPARSE_COLUMNS*. We can still address the sparse columns directly by name, but SQL Server defaults to showing only the Column Set column, for example, when we do a *SELECT**.

Sparse columns are good candidates for inclusion in filtered indexes. A filtered index is a special index that includes only rows that match the criteria specified in a *WHERE* clause that is part of the *CREATE INDEX* statement. Since sparse columns by definition should contain mostly *NULL* values, filtered indexes on the non-null values in sparse columns would only have to index a small percentage of the rows.

The following sample code creates a table to store demographic details we hope to collect from a customer survey. It is likely that the individuals completing the survey will leave a large number of fields empty. We want to optimize the storage of those empty (*NULL*) values by using sparse columns. Notice that the *MaritalStatus* column has not been marked sparse. The documentation states that 98 percent of the rows would have to be *NULL* for us to realize a space savings on the bit data type by marking it *SPARSE*. More than 2 percent of the surveys will likely be received with the *MaritalStatus* column completed, so we won't mark it as *SPARSE*. We will include a Column Set definition to allow us to work with all the demographic values as a single set of XML data, and finally we will create a filtered index on the income field to help us quickly find customers based on their income:

```
USE AdventureWorks2008;
GO
CREATE TABLE Person.Demographics
(
    BusinessEntityID int NOT NULL PRIMARY KEY,
    Age int SPARSE,
    BirthDate date SPARSE,
    Income int SPARSE,
    Cars int SPARSE,
    Children int SPARSE,
    MaritalStatus bit NULL,
    AllFields xml COLUMN_SET FOR ALL_SPARSE_COLUMNS
);
CREATE NONCLUSTERED INDEX FIDemographicsIncomes
ON Person.Demographics(Income)
WHERE Income IS NOT NULL;
```

The main advantage of using sparse columns is space savings. Smaller rows means fewer rows per page, fewer pages per table, less IO per query, less buffer cache per query, and so on. SQL Server 2008 now also includes the ability for us to compress the rows and pages of our tables explicitly. The next session talks about just that.

Compression

SQL Server 2008 is the first version of SQL Server that supports internal data compression. We have been able to use NTFS compression in previous versions to compress *read-only* filegroups and partitions. With SQL Server 2008, we can have the data engine itself perform compression at either the row or page level, and we can define those compression settings on a partition-by-partition basis. It should be noted that SQL Server 2008 also supports backup compression, but that is beyond the scope of this book. In this section we will talk specifically about Row and Page compression in our tables and indexes.

As with sparse columns, the big benefit of compression is a savings in storage costs. If we can compress our rows and pages, we can fit more rows per page and reduce the amount of space it takes to store the same amount of data. That storage cost savings can then translate into reduced performance costs because it requires less IO to read those pages. Of course, we don't get it for free. Compression will increase CPU costs as we compress and decompress the data. So as it is with many other things in SQL Server, there are times to compress and times not to compress.

A number of compression algorithms are available today, but two common practices to avoid taking space for empty values are to store patterns of data that repeat and to store them a single time. SQL Server can use both of these methods through its Row and Page compression options.

Row compression takes the approach of not storing "empty" bytes. It effectively treats all column values as if they were variable width. This can save a lot of space if you have columns that aren't completely full. It doesn't take an excessive amount of CPU usage to effect Row compression, so if it gives you enough of a storage savings, you won't need Page compression.

Page compression implies Row compression, but it also looks for and reduces the occurrence of redundant data. A lot more work is involved in Page compression, and so the CPU utilization will be significantly higher than that of just Row compression, but with enough redundant bytes of data, it could yield much higher space savings.

Deciding whether to use Row or Page compression comes down to a question of the amount of space saved and the amount of CPU cost to get that savings. If Row compression provides acceptable savings in space, then stay with that because it will be cheaper than Page compression. If Row compression does not offer enough space savings, however, we can then step up to Page compression.

Exam Warning

The Row and Page compression features are available only in the Enterprise, Evaluation, and Developer editions. Watch out for questions that try to trick you into the wrong answer based on the edition.

Row Compression

Row compression effectively asks that SQL Server store all fields as if they were variable length. By effectively treating every data type as if it were variable length, it is possible that we can realize an overall reduction in storage. SQL Server 2005 SP2 introduced a table option called *vardecimal*. By setting this option on a table, you could effectively store all fields with the decimal and numeric data types as if they were variable length. The new Row compression option supersedes the *vardecimal* behavior and extends the variable-width storage to all data types.

For example, imagine a table with a `char(10)` field for storing postal codes. We need all ten characters for rows where the postal code uses the "zip + 4" format (00000–0000). For the rows that have only five characters in their postal code, however, the extra five characters are wasted space. By storing the characters as a variable-width field, SQL Server could save five bytes of storage for the shorter postal codes. The variable-width data, however, has some overhead associated with it because we need a map, stored as a series of offsets, of where the data for each field is. That means that if the fields don't really vary in length (they all use "zip + 4"), it is less efficient to store them as variable-width data than as fixed width.

We indicate that a table or an index should be compressed via the respective *CREATE* and *ALTER* statements. The following example creates a table using Row compression:

```
CREATE TABLE Student
(
    SomeID int IDENTITY(1,1) PRIMARY KEY,
    FirstName nvarchar(50) NOT NULL,
    LastName nvarchar(50) NOT NULL,
    Age int NOT NULL,
    ModifiedDate datetime NOT NULL,
) WITH (DATA_COMPRESSION=ROW);
```

In this example, the storage of the FirstName and LastName fields does not change much because they are based on *nvarchar*, but other int and datetime fields can now also be stored as variable width because the Row compression option was enabled.

Page Compression

Row compression does not store empty bytes on the page. Page compression, however, actually identifies and reduces the occurrences of repeating patterns in the columns row on the page. Page compression implies Row compression, and then adds column Prefix and Page Dictionary compression methods.

In column Prefix compression, SQL Server identifies the single most common set of bytes at the beginning (from left to write) of the column values for all rows of a given column. It then stores that common set of bytes for each column in a "Compression Information" record in the page. The column values in the rows can then reference the single occurrence of the common byte sequence rather than storing it repeatedly for each row where it occurred. Rows that began with all or even some of the common bytes can be compressed based on the number of bytes they shared with the common prefix. Rows that did not begin with any or all of the common set of bytes are not compressed at all.

Since Row compression is done on a single column at a time, it can only compress data when multiple values in a column start with the same bytes. For example, if a table had a single column of first name values and only ten rows, and if each first name started with a different character, Row compression would have no benefit because there would be no common byte patterns at the beginning of the column values. With a larger number of rows, and an initial sequence of characters shared across a large number of rows, then Row compression could have a significant impact on the total storage. To find repeating patterns of data across all rows and columns, SQL Server performs Page Dictionary compression.

In Page Dictionary compression, SQL Server creates a dictionary (or list) of all common byte patterns across rows *and* columns on the page. It is no longer looking for only common prefixes on a column-by-column basis. Instead it is looking for all byte patterns that are repeated in any column of any row. It stores this list of common patterns in the same "Compression Information" structure in which it keeps the column prefix values. It then replaces any occurrences of those common byte patterns in the columns of the rows on the page, with a reference to the patterns position in the dictionary.

The following example alters the table we made in the Row compression example and changes it to Page compression:

```
ALTER TABLE Student
REBUILD WITH (DATA_COMPRESSION=PAGE);
```

Individual index and table partitions can have different compression settings. We can opt on a partition-by-partition basis to have either no compression, Row compression, or Page compression. If we have a table partitioned by time, for example, we could leave the partition with the current month's data uncompressed, use Row compression on the partitions with the month's data, and finally use Page compression on the partition with all previous data in it. The following example shows the syntax for compressing a table with multiple partitions.

```
CREATE TABLE TimePartitioned
(SomeKey int, SomeValue nvarchar(50), TheDate date)
ON TimeScheme(TheDate)
WITH
(
    DATA_COMPRESSION = NONE ON PARTITIONS (1),
    DATA_COMPRESSION = ROW ON PARTITIONS (2),
    DATA_COMPRESSION = PAGE ON PARTITIONS (3),
);
```

Turning compression on will have some implied costs in terms of both the ongoing costs to maintain compression and the initial costs to compress data already in the table or index. We should therefore first verify that we will get a benefit from compression before we enable compression.

Estimating Compression Savings

We can estimate how much space compression should save us before we actually enable it. SQL Server provides a system stored procedure named *sp_estimate_data_compression_savings*. The procedure takes a sampling of the actual pages in the target table, or index(es), performs compression on those pages, and measures the space saved. It then estimates what the compression would be for all pages based on that measurement. The following example uses the procedure to estimate how much space savings we should expect if we were to enable Page compression on all partitions (*@partition_number=NULL*) of the clustered index (*@index_id=1*) on the *AdventureWorks2008.Production.Product* table:

```
EXEC sp_estimate_data_compression_savings
    @schema_name=Production,
    @object_name=Product,
    @index_id=1,
    @partition_number=NULL,
    @data_compression=PAGE;
```

This statement returns a result similar the following (edited) result:

object_name	current_size(KB)	compressed_size(KB)
Product	120	72

EXERCISE 11.5

ESTIMATING THE EFFECT OF COMPRESSION

1. Open a new query in SQL Server Management Studio and select *AdventureWorks2008* from the list of available databases.

2. Run the sample EXEC `sp_estimate_data_compression_savings` statement shown above.

3. Try it on different tables.

4. Try changing the `@data_compression` from *PAGE* to *ROW*.

The output shows that we would go from 120KB to 72KB (60 percent of the original size) of storage for the Product table. That sounds pretty good and gives us the confidence to enable compression. If, however, the compression estimates were bleaker, we would probably opt to leave compression off.

Summary of Exam Objectives

The topics covered in this chapter include the use of Common Table Expressions, using SQL Server's new ranking functions, controlling execution plans and query performance, dealing with international data and clients, and efficiently storing null values and compressing data.

Common Table Expressions (CTEs) allow us to simplify the syntax of complex queries based on multiple sources and to create recursive queries. CTEs provide an alternative to statements based on joins or subqueries that may be hard to visualize or write. In addition, the ability of CTEs to be self-referencing now makes recursive queries possible. Recursive queries can be a powerful tool in processing hierarchical data in our databases.

SQL Server's new ranking functions give us a set of tools to include in numerical columns in our result sets that indicate the "rank" of the row. The rank can simply be based on the number of rows in the result set (using *ROW_NUMBER()* or *NTILE()*), or it can be based on the values in a given column (as with *RANK()* and *DENSE_RANK()*). The *ORDER BY* and *PARTITION* clauses allow us to specify the order in which ranks increase and to break those ranks down on subsets of rows with common values.

Through the use of Query Hints, the Query Governor, and the new Resource Governor, we have a rich set of tools to control the performance of our statements. Query Hints allow us to specify within each statement hints that control the statements' overall behavior and which join mechanisms are used, as well as to control the locking and index utilization of individual tables. The Query Governor gives us a simple cost-based threshold to prevent statements that have costs higher than that threshold from running. The Resource Governor (in the Enterprise and Developer editions only) provides us with a complete administration model for allocating CPU and Memory resources to client sessions based on what program the session is using, who the user is, and so on.

With collations we can specify which code page (or character set) we intend to work with for the non-Unicode data types (*char* and *varchar*), as well as how to sort and compare all character data including the Unicode data types (*nchar* and *nvarchar*). The instances default collation is set during installation but can be overridden with each database, column, and expression. Ideally, however, all objects and applications in a solution should use the same collation to prevent the variety of problems that can arise when characters don't match or when comparisons don't make sense. In addition to storing international data, we can create localized versions of our custom error messages and have SQL Server automatically return the appropriate error message based on the language of the client's session.

SQL Server 2008 introduced a number of new features for reducing storage costs. All editions can use the new *SPARSE* keyword when defining columns in tables. Sparse columns take no storage for *NULL* values, but have increased storage for non-null values. They are useful for columns that have a high percentage of *NULL* values. In addition, we can use Column Sets to easily work with all sparse columns as a single set.

Enterprise and Developer editions also make Row and Page compression options available. Row compression effectively treats all data types as if they were variable length. In contrast, Page compression identifies and reduces redundant byte patterns in the column values for the rows stored on the page. The storage savings provided by compression can be estimated using the sp_estimate_data_compression_savings stored procedure, and compression settings can be configured on a partition-by-partition basis for tables and indexes.

Exam Objectives Fast Track

Implementing CTE (Common Table Expression) Queries

- ☑ CTEs are an alternative to subqueries and joins.

- ☑ Follow the *WITH* clause and precede the *SELECT, INSERT, UPDATE,* or *DELETE* statement that references them.

- ☑ CTEs allow us to create recursive queries.

- ☑ Recursive queries are made up of an anchor member query to return the row(s) at the top of a hierarchy, a *UNION ALL* operator, and the recursive member query to get the child records.

Applying Ranking Functions

- ☑ There are four ranking functions: *ROW_NUMBER(), NTILE(), RANK(),* and *DENSE_RANK ()*. They all take the following basic form:

    ```
    <ranking_function > OVER ( [ <partition_by_clause> ] <order_by_clause> )
    ```

- ☑ The `<order_by_clause>` is required and identifies the column values the ranks are based on, and the order by which the rank values increase.

- ☑ The optional `<partition_by_clause>` generates ranks across subsets of rows based on the criteria specified.

Controlling Execution Plans

☑ There are three types of query hints, the *OPTION* clause controls the entire statement, merge hints control specific join operations, and table hints control locking and index behaviors on specific tables in a statement.

☑ The Query Governor sets a cost threshold below which a statement's estimated cost must be in order to execute.

☑ The Query Governor can be set at an instance level using `sp_configure 'query governor cost limit', <maxcost>`. It can be overridden in each session with *SET_QUERY_GOVERNOR_COST_LIMIT* `<maxcost>`.

☑ The Resource Governor is only available in the Enterprise, Evaluation, and Developer editions.

☑ Resource Governor Resource Pools limit the percentage of CPU and Memory resources available.

☑ Resource Governor Workload Groups suballocation resources from a resource pool and set other policies.

☑ The *CLASSIFIER* function identifies sessions based on the properties of the connection, using system functions such as *APP_NAME()* and *SUSER_SNAME()*. It then returns the name of the Workload Group that should be used by the session.

Managing Internationalization Considerations

☑ Collations specify which non-Unicode code page is used and how character values are compared and sorted.

☑ Non-Unicode and Unicode data is always available via the *char, varchar, nchar,* and *nvarchar* data types.

☑ Non-Unicode values are limited to storing characters from their assigned code page or character set, whereas Unicode values have access to characters from all the major languages in the world.

☑ We can create localized versions of our custom error messages using `sp_addmessage`.

☑ Before we can create a localized error message, the U.S. English version must first exist, and they have to use the same severity.

Creating and Altering Tables

☑ Sparse columns (columns marked with the *SPARSE* keyword) don't require any storage for *NULL* values, but they have increased storage for non-null values.

☑ All sparse columns in a table can be accessed via a single column set by adding a column of type XML with *COLUMN_SET FOR ALL_SPARSE_COLUMNS* to the table.

☑ Row and Page compression are only available in the Enterprise, Evaluation, and Developer editions.

☑ Row compression treats all data types as if they were variable length.

☑ Page compression identifies and reduces the occurrence of redundant data within the rows on the page.

☑ Each partition in a table or index can have a different compression setting (none, Row, or Page).

☑ Storage savings from compression can be estimated using the `sp_estimate_ data_compression_savings` stored procedure.

Exam Objectives
Frequently Asked Questions

Q: Can a single Common Table Expression (CTE) be used by more than one statement?

A: No, a CTE is only valid for the single *SELECT, INSERT, UPDATE,* or *DELETE* statement that references it. If multiple queries want to use the same CTE, the CTE must be restated for each subsequent query.

Q: Is there a performance benefit or cost when using CTEs?

A: Not necessarily. SQL Server normalizes, or standardizes, your statement before it optimizes it. This process generally means that whether your query uses CTEs, subqueries, or joins, the intention is likely the same, and often exactly the same plan will be used. However, at certain times one style of syntax may yield a more efficient plan. You should compare the plans of alternate syntaxes when they are available and choose the one with the lowest cost.

Q: Can views be recursive like CTEs are?

A: No, views cannot be recursive to themselves, but they can contain a CTE that is recursive.

Q: Do any of the ranking functions require an argument to be passed in?

A: Yes, the *NTILE* function requires that you supply the number of "tiles" you would like to classify the rows by. None of the other ranking functions take an argument, however.

Q: When using a ranking function, is it required to use the *OVER* clause?

A: Yes, the *OVER* clause is required, and you must specify the *ORDER BY* clause as well when using any of the ranking functions.

Q: Is *ROW_NUMBER()* the same as *IDENTITY()*?

A: No, SQL Server does have a system function named *IDENTITY()* (which is different from the *IDENTITY* property on column in a table), but it can only be used as a column expression in a *SELECT… INTO* query. The *ROW_NUMBER()* function can be used in any query and can generate partitioned row numbers.

Q: Why shouldn't we use query hints in production code?

A: The optimizer usually does a better job of figuring out what to do than we can. Occasionally, we can beat the optimizer and make it perform things more efficiently than it might otherwise choose, but those cases are the exception, not the rule. In addition, we often base our tests on unrealistic sample data. When real, more naturally distributed data becomes available, or the nature of the data distribution changes over time, the optimizer will in the long run likely make a better choice. In fact, when the data changes, the hints we hard coded can then be causing a less efficient plan to be used.

Q: If I want to control the transaction isolation level, do I have to use table hints?

A: No, generally the "Read Committed" default transaction isolation is the optimal choice. If you need to change the isolation for your entire session, you should use the *SET TRANSACTION ISOLATION LEVEL* setting. That will affect all statements submitted by your session. The table level hints should only be used when a specific table needs special locking behaviors in a statement.

Q: If I want to prevent a statement from running by setting the Query Governor cost limit, how do I determine what cost value to set it to?

A: Enter the statement you wish to prevent from running into a query window in SQL Server Management Studio. Display its estimated execution plan and read the total sub-tree cost from the last step in the plan. Round down to the nearest integer and use that as your cost.

Q: Using the Resource Governor, is it possible to limit the resources for a particular application?

A: Yes, you would need to create a *CLASSIFIER* function that tests each new session to see if the *APP_NAME()* is the name of the application you wish to limit. For sessions with your applications name, the function should return the name of the Workload Group to you along with the application to be associated with.

Q: Where does the *APP_NAME()* function get its value from?

A: When an application opens a connection, it can provide various properties values for the connection. One of those values is the "Application Name." If the client application provides it, *APP_NAME()* can show it. If, however, the client application does not supply it, *APP_NAME()* will be empty.

Q: If I never specify a collation, what collation is being used?

A: When your instance of SQL Server was installed, a default collation was selected. That collation was used for all the system databases and is the default collation for all subsequent databases, columns, and expressions. You can override the collation using the *COLLATE* clause when creating databases, columns, and expressions.

Q: I made my database using a case-sensitive collation. Now I can't query from my tables. Any ideas what is wrong?

A: When a database uses a case-sensitive collation, not only is your literal character data case sensitive, but the object identifiers (table names, view names, proc names, etc.) are also case sensitive. This is because their names are stored as data in the system tables. Those system tables use the same collation as the database and are therefore case sensitive as well.

Q: When I am creating and testing localized error messages, how can I verify the language of my session?

A: You can query the @@*LANGUAGE* function to determine your session's language.

Q: I created a table using sparse columns and a column set; now when I query from the table, the sparse columns are missing!

A: When a table has a column set defined, individual sparse columns are not returned if a *SELECT** is done on the table. However, you can reference the sparse columns by name, and they will be returned.

Q: I used sparse columns on the columns in my table, and my performance got worse! What happened?

A: Sparse columns provide optimal storage only for columns with a large percentage of the rows being *NULL*. Oddly, sparse columns actually take more space to store non-null values than they would if they were not sparse. This means that columns where most rows have values will actually increase their total storage rather than decrease. If there are multiple columns like this, and a lot of rows, you can negatively impact the storage of the table and thus performance.

Q: Is there a way to calculate the CPU processing impact of compression?

A: No, we can estimate the storage but not the CPU costs. You will have to create compressed and noncompressed versions of a table and measure the performance costs of working with both of them.

Q: If I compress a table, do all of its indexes get compressed as well?

A: No, each index would need to be created or altered to enable compression.

Self Test

1. The Recursive CTE query in the following screenshot is supposed to return the character symbols for all 256 characters in the current character set. The query is failing, however. Review the query and error message shown in Figure 11.3:

Figure 11.3 A Query and an Error Message

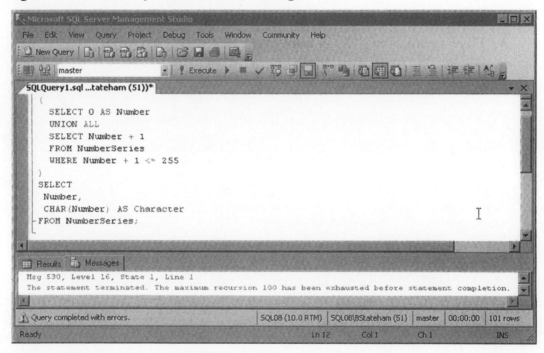

To correct the problem you should (select a single option):

A. Include an OPTION (MAXRECURSION 255) query hint in the anchor member query.

B. Include an OPTION (MAXRECURSION 255) option in the recursive member query.

C. Include an OPTION (MAXRECURSION 255) option in the referencing query.

D. Change the WHERE Clause in the recursive member to Number + 1 <= 100.

2. You receive an error when you attempt to run the following statement with two CTEs:

```
WITH LastDay AS
(SELECT MAX(OrderDate) AS LastOrderDate
FROM Sales.SalesOrderHeader),

WITH LastDayOrderIDs AS
(SELECT SalesOrderID FROM Sales.SalesOrderHeader
JOIN LastDay ON OrderDate = LastDay.LastOrderDate)

SELECT * FROM LastDayOrderIDs;
```

To correct the problem you should (select a single option):

A. Place a semicolon (";") in front of the first *WITH* keyword.

B. Remove the second *WITH* keyword.

C. Place a semicolon (";") in front of the second *WITH* keyword.

D. Remove the semicolon (";") at the end of the final query.

3. When you run the following statements as a single batch you receive an error:

```
WITH BikeIDs AS
(SELECT ProductID FROM Production.Product
WHERE ProductSubcategoryID BETWEEN 1 and 3)
SELECT * FROM BikeIDs

WITH ComponentIDs AS
(SELECT ProductID FROM Production.Product
WHERE ProductSubcategoryID BETWEEN 4 and 17)
SELECT * FROM ComponentIDs
```

To correct the problem you should (select two options):

A. Place a semicolon (";") before the first CTE.

B. Place a semicolon (";") after the first query and before the second CTE.

C. Place a semicolon (";") after the second query.

D. Place a GO between the two statements.

4. You receive an error when you run the following statements in a single batch:

```
WITH Bikes AS
(SELECT * FROM Production.Product
WHERE ProductSubcategoryID = 1)

SELECT * FROM Bikes
```

```
ORDER BY ListPrice
SELECT * FROM Bikes
ORDER BY StandardCost
```

To correct the problem you should (select a single option):

A. Separate the queries with a semicolon.

B. Place a *GO* between the two *SELECT* statements.

C. Restate the "Bikes" CTE definition for the second query.

D. Place a semicolon before the *WITH*.

5. Which of the following ranking functions should you use to generate a contiguous sequence of row numbers in a *SELECT* statement (select the best option):

A. ROW_NUMBER()

B. IDENTITY()

C. RANK()

D. NTILE()

6. Review the query and results shown in Figure 11.4.:

Figure 11.4 A Query and the Results

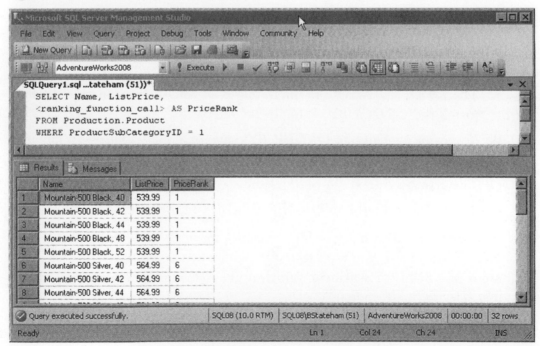

Which of the following choices should be used in place of the `<ranking_function_call>` placeholder shown in the query (select a single option):

A. *DENSE-RANK() OVER (PARTITION BY* `ListPrice)`

B. *RANK() OVER (PARTITION BY* `ListPrice)`

C. *DENSE_RANK() OVER (ORDER BY* `ListPrice)`

D. *RANK() OVER (ORDER BY* `ListPrice)`

7. The goal of the following query is to generate a row number for all the rows based on the list price of each product :

```
SELECT
  ROW_NUMBER() OVER (ORDER BY P.ListPrice) AS RowNumber,
P.Name,
P.ListPrice
FROM Production.Product AS P ORDER BY P.Name
```

Returns results similar to the following:

```
RowNumber    Name                      ListPrice
---------    ---------------------     ---------
1            Adjustable Race                0.00
310          All-Purpose Bike Stand       159.00
210          AWC Logo Cap                   8.99
3            BB Ball Bearing                0.00
...          ...                            ...
```

In the results shown, why are the row numbers out of order (select a single option)?

A. The *ORDER BY* clause in the in the *ROW_NUMBER* function doesn't match the *ORDER BY* clause for the query.

B. You cannot include an *ORDER BY* clause in a query that uses a ranking function.

C. There isn't a *PARTITION BY* clause

D. There should not be an *ORDER BY* clause in the ranking function.

8. You have created an index on the *Production.Product.Name* column called *NC_Product_Name.* You want to test the index by forcing the optimizer to use it in a *SELECT* statement. Which of the following statements should you use (select a single option)?

A. `SELECT Name FROM Production.Product.NC_Product_Name`

B. `SELECT Name FROM Production.Product USING (NC_Product_Name)`

    C. `SELECT Name FROM Production.Product WITH (INDEX(NC_Product_Name))`

    D. `SELECT NC_Product_Name(Name) FROM Production.Product`

9. You want to enforce a Query Governor cost limit for all sessions on an instance of SQL Server. You want to prevent statements that cost over 40 cost units from running. Which of the following statements should you use (select a single option)?

    A. `EXEC sp_query_governor_cost_limit 40`

    B. `SET QUERY_GOVERNOR_COST_LIMIT 40`

    C. `SET MAX_QUERY_COST 40`

    D. `EXEC sp_configure 'query governor cost limit', 40`

10. You want to use the Resource Governor to guarantee resources to your mission critical production application. The production application is a Windows program that was developed in house. It is used on various workstations and by numerous users throughout the day. Those same users run other database client applications from the same workstations. When creating a *CLASSIFIER* function, which of the following system functions would be most helpful in identifying connections from your production application?

    To correct the problem you should (select a single option):

    A. *APP_NAME()*

    B. *SUSER_NAME()*

    C. *USER_NAME()*

    D. *GETDATE()*

11. You have inadvertently set extremely restrictive Resource Pool and Workload Group policies for your application, and it is significantly affecting performance. You need to connect to SQL Server in an unrestricted session to resolve the issue. What should you do (select the best option)?

    A. Connect using sqlcmd from the SQL Server console and use the −A switch to enable a dedicated administrator connection.

    B. Shut down SQL Server and bring it up in single user mode using the −m startup option.

C. Issue an *ALTER DATABASE ... SET RESTRICTED_USER WITH ROLLBACK IMMDIATE* to force all other client connections out of the database.

D. Issue an *ALTER RESOURCE GOVERNOR DISABLe;* command to disable the Resource Governor.

12. You create a *CLASSIFIER* function to return the name of the Workload Group a session should be assigned to. Later, the Workload Group is deleted by another administrator. What will happen when a client session connects and the *CLASSIFIER* function returns the name of the now missing Workload Group (select a single option)?

A. The session will be denied, and the client application will receive an error.

B. The session will be assigned to the default Workload Group.

C. The session will be assigned to the internal Workload Group.

D. The Workload Group could not have been deleted in the first place because the *CLASSIFIER* functions are created using *WITH SCHEMABINDING*.

13. Assume you have run the following script that creates a database and a table and inserts a record into the table:

```
CREATE DATABASE TestDB
COLLATE SQL_Latin1_General_Cp1_CS_AS;
GO
USE TestDB;

CREATE TABLE TestTable
(Col1 varchar(50));
INSERT INTO TestTable (Col1) VALUES ('Sample');
```

Which of the following queries returns the row that contains the text "Sample" (select a single option)?

A. `SELECT * FROM testtable WHERE Col1 = 'Sample';`

B. `SELECT * FROM TestTable WHERE col1 = 'Sample';`

C. `SELECT * FROM TestTable WHERE Col1 = 'sample';`

D. `SELECT * FROM TestTable WHERE Col1 = 'Sample';`

14. You find that when you are copying data between two servers in different countries, the data in the destination server often has certain characters that are not the same as they were on the original server. What is most likely the problem (select one)?

   A. The databases both use Unicode data types, and that is causing certain characters to get mismapped in the copy.

   B. The databases use separate non-Unicode data types, and that is causing certain characters to get mismapped in the copy.

   C. The hard drive on one of the servers is going bad.

   D. There are problems on the network that are causing the data to become corrupted.

15. When you are creating a localized version of a user-defined error message, which of the following requirements must be met (choose three)?

   A. The localized version must use the same message number as the *us_english* version.

   B. The localized version must use the same number of parameters as the *us_english* version.

   C. The localized version must use the same severity as the *us_english* version.

   D. The *us_english* version must first exist.

16. Which of the following data types can be sparse (select two options)?

   A. int

   B. text

   C. char

   D. timestamp

17. If marking columns as sparse allows SQL Server to store the values more efficiently when they are *NULL*, why not mark all possible columns as sparse (select a single option)?

   A. Sparse columns actually have an increased cost for non-null values.

   B. Sparse columns only allow the storage of *NULL* values.

   C. Sparse columns are only available in the Enterprise edition.

   D. Sparse columns can only be referenced through the column set.

18. You are considering enabling compression on a table. What should you do to determine how much space you can expect to save by compressing the table (select a single option)?

    A. Run the `sp_estimate_data_compression_savings` stored procedure.

    B. Query the data_compression column in the sys.partitions system catalog view.

    C. Compress a copy of the data files on disk with NTFS compression to determine the new size.

    D. Export the table data to a csv file and compress the file to determine the new size.

19. Which of the following statements best describes the mechanism that Row compression uses to save space (select a single option)?

    A. It compresses the prefix bytes in a particular column across all rows in a page.

    B. It uses Dictionary compression to find common byte patterns across all columns and rows on the page.

    C. It stores all columns as though they were variable-length columns.

    D. It does not take space to store *NULL* values.

20. After reviewing the benefits of compression, you decide that you would like both Row and Page compression to be applied to your table. What should you do (select a single option)?

    A. Use WITH (DATA_COMPRESSION = ROWPAGE) when creating or altering the table.

    B. Use WITH (DATA_COMPRESSION = PAGE) when creating or altering the table.

    C. Use WITH (DATA_COMPRESSION = ROW) when creating or altering the table.

    D. None of the above; you can't compress a table with both Row and Page behaviors.

Self Test Quick Answer Key

1. **C**

2. **B**

3. **B, D**

4. **C**

5. **A**

6. **D**

7. **A**

8. **C**

9. **D**

10. **A**

11. **A**

12. **B**

13. **D**

14. **B**

15. **A, C, D**

16. **A, C**

17. **A**

18. **A**

19. **C**

20. **B**

MCTS SQL Server 2008 Exam 433

Explaining XML

Exam objectives in this chapter:

- Retrieving and Transforming XML Data
- OPENXML, sp_xml_preparedocument, and sp_xml_removedocument
- XQuery and XPath
- XML Indexes
- XML Schema and Well-Formed XML

Exam objectives review:

- ☑ Summary of Exam Objectives
- ☑ Exam Objectives Fast Track
- ☑ Exam Objectives Frequently Asked Questions
- ☑ Self Test
- ☑ Self Test Quick Answer Key

Introduction

In this chapter, we present an overall explanation of XML and how it is used in SQL Server. Keep in mind that there are whole books dedicated to XML, so if you need more in-depth information, other resources can be helpful.

We'll cover the way XML is stored and indexed in SQL server, as well as working with XML from a SQL Server standpoint.

We will also discuss XPath and XQuery. Even though these are available outside of SQL Server, they are an important concept and should be understood.

Retrieving and Transforming XML Data

You can return results as XML documents rather than a standard rowset. You can retrieve results using the *FORXML* clause in a *SELECT* statement. In your *FORXML* clause you specify an XML mode, RAW, AUTO, or EXPLICIT. Table 12.1 describes each XML mode.

Table 12.1 XML Modes Used with the *FORXML* Clause

XML Mode	Description
AUTO	Produces output with both element and attribute features in conjunction with a subquery.
EXPLICIT	Transforms the rowset that results from the query execution into an XML document. Must be written in a specific way so that the additional information about the required XML, such as expected nesting in the XML, is explicitly specified as part of the query.
RAW	Transforms each row in the query result set into an XML element that has the generic identifier <row>, or the optionally provided element name. By default, each column value in the rowset that is not NULL is mapped to an attribute of the <row> element.

In Figure 12.1, we use the *FORXML* clause with AUTO mode to produce an XML document.

Figure 12.1 Creating a Sample XML Document with FORXML

```
--Create a Temp Table
DECLARE @XML_Table TABLE (customerID INT,customerName
VARCHAR(255),customerPhone VARCHAR(255))

--Insert some values to the table
INSERT INTO @XML_Table(
      customerID,customerName,customerPhone)

VALUES

      (1,'Tommy Liddle','555-7896')

INSERT INTO @XML_Table(
      customerID,customerName,customerPhone)

VALUES

      (2,'Steve Long','555-2436')

INSERT INTO @XML_Table(
      customerID,customerName,customerPhone)

VALUES

      (3,'Monica Banning','555-4287')

--Create our XML document
SELECT customerID,customerName,customerPhone
FROM @XML_Table
FOR XML AUTO
```

When you execute the code, it returns the data in a data grid, which when you click on the hyperlink, SQL Server Management Studio brings up the XML document in another tab as a well-formed XML document.

Transforming XML Data

The introduction of the XML data type in SQL Server 2005 and the enhanced features that SQL Server 2008 has to offer make transforming XML data easier than ever. For example, if you want to find the price and quantity for all inventory items, you can use the example in Figure 12.2.

Figure 12.2 Using the *OPENXML* Clause

```
DECLARE @XMLData XML
DECLARE @Pointer INT
SET @XMLData =
            '<INVENTORY>
                    <ITEM>
                                <Description>Baseball Bats</Description>
                                <Price>55.00</Price>
                                <Quantity>3</Quantity>
                    </ITEM>
                    <ITEM>
                                <Description>Baseball Gloves</Description>
                                <Price>25.00</Price>
                                <Quantity>10</Quantity>
                    </ITEM>
                    <ITEM>
                                <Description>Baseball Hats</Description>
                                <Price>15.00</Price>
                                <Quantity>7</Quantity>
                    </ITEM>
            </INVENTORY>'
EXECUTE sp_xml_preparedocument @Pointer OUTPUT,@XMLData
SELECT Description,Price,Quantity
FROM OPENXML(@Pointer,'/INVENTORY/ITEM',2)
WITH (Description VARCHAR(255), Price money, Quantity INTEGER)
EXEC sp_xml_removedocument @Pointer
```

New & Noteworthy...

XML Tags

XML must have a starting and ending tag. For example, <ITEM> is the start-tag and </ITEM> is the ending tag. Also, XML must be HTML encoded. That means XML tags must have < and >.

In the first part of our query, Figure 12.3, we create two variables, @XMLData and @Pointer. The first variable is used to store our XML data in an XML data type, and our second variable is used as a pointer to our XML data. Then we populate our XML variable, @XMLData, with XML data using the *SET* command.

Figure 12.3 Sample XML

```
DECLARE @XMLData XML
DECLARE @Pointer INT
SET @XMLData =
            '<INVENTORY>
                 <ITEM>
                         <Description>Baseball Bats</Description>
                         <Price>55.00</Price>
                         <Quantity>3</Quantity>
                 </ITEM>
                 <ITEM>
                         <Description>Baseball Gloves</Description>
                         <Price>25.00</Price>
                         <Quantity>10</Quantity>
                 </ITEM>
                 <ITEM>
                         <Description>Baseball Hats</Description>
                         <Price>15.00</Price>
                         <Quantity>7</Quantity>
                 </ITEM>
            </INVENTORY>'
```

In Figure 12.4, we use a system stored procedure to prepare our XML document by parsing the text using the XML parser.

Figure 12.4 Using sp_xml_preparedocument

```
EXECUTE sp_xml_preparedocument @Pointer OUTPUT,@XMLData
```

Next, we construct our *SELECT* statement to provide a tabular view of the XML data in Figure 12.3. Here, in Figure 12.5, we use OPENXML, which provides an easy way to use an XML document as a data source. OPENXML allows data in an XML document to be treated just like the columns and rows of your data set.

Notice, in Figure 12.5, we use the *WITH* clause in our *SELECT* statement. The *WITH* clause provides a table format using either SchemaDeclaration or specifying and existing tablename.

Figure 12.5 *SELECT* with OPENXML

```
SELECT Description,Price,Quantity
FROM OPENXML(@Pointer,'/INVENTORY/ITEM',2)
WITH (Description VARCHAR(255), Price money, Quantity INTEGER)
```

Lastly, in Figure 12.6, we will remove the XML document we prepared. When you execute the entire script, it will produce the results shown in Figure 12.7.

Figure 12.6 sp_xml_removedocument

```
EXEC sp_xml_removedocument @Pointer
```

Figure 12.7 Results

```
Description       Price                  Quantity
--------------    --------------------   -----------
Baseball Bats     55.00                  3
Baseball Gloves   25.00                  4
Baseball Hats     15.00                  7
```

Keep in mind that XML documents are not all the same. An XML document can also contain attributes that will also need to be queried. For example, in Figure 12.8, you see that we have the same data as in the previous example but in attributes like Description, Price, and Quantity. They are not separate tags.

Figure 12.8 Sample XML

```
DECLARE @XMLData XML
DECLARE @Pointer INT
SET @XMLData =
        '<INVENTORY>
                <ITEM Description="Baseball Bats" Price="55.00" Quantity="3" />
                <ITEM Description="Baseball Gloves" Price="25.00" Quantity="4" />
                <ITEM Description="Baseball Hats" Price="15.00" Quantity="7" />
        </INVENTORY>'
EXECUTE sp_xml_preparedocument @Pointer OUTPUT,@XMLData
```

```
SELECT Description,Price,Quantity
FROM OPENXML(@Pointer,'/INVENTORY/ITEM',2)
WITH (Description VARCHAR(255) '@Description', Price MONEY '@Price', Quantity
INTEGER '@Quantity')
EXEC sp_xml_removedocument @Pointer
```

To make our query work, you will see that we made a minor change in our *WITH* clause in our *SELECT* statement. You have to specify the attribute for that column in the *WITH* clause (see Figure 12.9).

Figure 12.9 Change the Structure Inside the *WITH* clause

```
WITH (Description VARCHAR(255) '@Description', Price MONEY '@Price',
Quantity INTEGER '@Quantity')
```

OPENXML, sp_xml_preparedocument, and sp_xml_removedocument

Microsoft started supporting OPENXML in SQL Server 2000. OPENXML is a SQL Server function, which accepts a stream of XML data and provides an in-memory relational rowset view of the XML data. You specify the rowset using the *WITH* clause. OPENXML is an extension of the *SELECT* statement. OPENXML is a memory-intensive process.

The basic syntax for OPENXML is shown in Figure 12.10. Table 12.2 lists the argument available to the OPENXML function.

Figure 12.10 OPENXML Syntax

```
OPENXML (idoc int [in], rowpatten nvarchar[in],flags byte[in]) WITH
SchemaDeclaration|TableName]
```

Table 12.2 OPENXML Arguments

OPENXML Arguments	Description
Idoc	Document handle of the internal representation of an XML document
Rowpattern	XPath query used to identify the nodes to be processed as rows

Continued

Table 12.2 Continued. OPENXML Arguments

OPENXML Arguments	Description
Flags	Mapping between the XML data and the relational rowset (Optional Parameter)
	■ 0 – Defaults to attribute centric mapping
	■ 1 – Attribute-centric mapping. (Combined with XML_ELEMENTS)
	■ 2 – Element-centric mapping. (Combined with XML_ATTRIBUTES)
	■ 8 – Combined with XML_ATTRIBUTES or XML_ELEMENTS
SchemaDeclaration	The schema definition of the form
TableName	The table name that can be given, instead of Schema Declaration, if a table exists

The *WITH* clause provides a table format using SchemaDeclaration or specifying an existing TableName. The *WITH* clause is optional, and if not specified the results are returned in an edge table format. Edge tables represent the fine-grained XML document structure in a single table.

The system stored procedure, sp_xml_preparedocument, reads an XML text, parses it, and provides a document ready to be used. This document is a tree representation of elements, attributes, text, comments, and so on, in an XML document. This procedure needs to be run before your OPENXML query. The syntax for sp_xml_preparedocument is shown in Figure 12.11. Arguments for sp_xml_preparedocument are listed in Table 12.3.

Figure 12.11 sp_xml_preparedocument Syntax

```
sp_xml_preparedocument hdoc OUTPUT
[, xml]
[, xpath_namespaces]
```

Table 12.3 sp_xml_preparedocument Arguments

Argument	Description
hdoc	Is the handle to the newly created document; hdoc is an integer.
xml	Is the original XML document. The MSXML parser parses this XML document.xmltext in a text (char, nchar, varchar, nvarchar, text, or ntext) parameter. The default value is NULL, in which case an internal representation of an empty XML document is created.
xpath_namespaces	Specifies the namespace declarations that are used in row and column XPath expressions in OPENXML. The default value is <root xmlns:mp="urn:schemas-microsoft-com:xml-metaprop">.
	xpath_namespaces provides the namespace URIs for the prefixes used in the XPath expressions in OPENXML by means of a well-formed XML document. xpath_namespaces declares the prefix that must be used to refer to the namespace urn:schemas-microsoft-com:xml-metaprop, which provides meta data about the parsed XML elements. Although you can redefine the namespace prefix for the metaproperty namespace using this technique, this namespace is not lost. The prefix mp is still valid for urn:schemas-microsoft-com:xml-metaprop even if xpath_namespaces contains no such declaration. xpath_namespaces is a text (char, nchar, varchar, nvarchar, text, or ntext) parameter.

The sp_xml_removedocument removes the XML document that is specified by the stored procedure sp_xml_preparedocument. The syntax for sp_xml_removedocument is shown in Figure 12.12. Arguments for sp_xml_removedocument are listed in Table 12.4.

Figure 12.12 sp_xml_removedocument Syntax

```
sp_xml_removedocument hdoc
```

Table 12.4 sp_xml_removedocument Arguments

Argument	Description
Hdoc	Is the handle to the newly created document. An invalid handle returns an error. *hdoc* is an integer.

XQuery and XPath

XQuery is a language used to query XML data. You can query and manipulate data from XML documents or data sources that can be viewed by XML. There are four simple methods for querying XML data with XQuery:

- Query()
- Value()
- Exist()
- Nodes()

The query() method is used to return XML data that matches a query. In Figure 12.13, we will perform a query that returns everyone that has a favorite color.

Figure 12.13 Sample query() Method

```
DECLARE @xmlData XML
SET @xmlData = '<=xml version="1.0" encoding="UTF-8" standalone="yes"=>
                            <employee>
                            <person>
                                    <name>
                                    <FirstName>Addie</FirstName>
                                    <LastName>Banning</LastName>
                                    </name>
                                    <Age>21</Age>
        <FavoriteColor>Blue</FavoriteColor>
                                    </person>
                            <person>
                                    <name>
                                    <FirstName>Bill</FirstName>
```

```
                                          <LastName>Bergen</LastName>
                                          </name>
                                          <Age>99</Age>
      <FavoriteColor>Green</FavoriteColor>
                                    </person>
                                    <person>
                                          <name>
                                          <FirstName>Jennifer</FirstName>
                                          <LastName>Liddle</LastName>
                                          </name>
                                          <Age>9</Age>
      <FavoriteColor>Pink</FavoriteColor>
                                          </person>
                                          </employee>'
-- Here we create the table to hold the XML data
CREATE TABLE #tbl_xml (id INT IDENTITY PRIMARY KEY, employee XML)
-- Here, we insert the XML data into the xml column of the table
INSERT INTO #tbl_xml(employee)
VALUES (@xmlData)
-- Here, we perform our query
SELECT employee.query(
'for $p in //employee
where $p//FavoriteColor
return
<employee>
<name>{$p//FirstName}</name>
</employee>
'
)
FROM #tbl_xml
DROP TABLE #tbl_xml
```

In Figure 12.13 we created a temporary table called #tbl_xml and inserted the XML data into that temporary table. The query shown in Figure 12.14 uses XQuery to *SELECT* the information in the XML data type to list everyone that has a favorite color. Let's take a look at this query in more detail.

Figure 12.14 Query() Method In-depth

```
SELECT employee.query(
'for $p in //employee
where $p//FavoriteColor
return
<employee>
<name>{$p//FirstName}</name>
</employee>
'
)
FROM #tbl_xml
```

The first part of our query, SELECT people.query, uses a standard SQL command, SELECT, followed by the column name in our #tbl_xml document, people. We then use the method, query(), to tell our *SELECT* statement that we will be querying against this XML data column. After that, we simple write out an XPath statement and close it with the *FROM* clause. XPath will be discussed in our next section. Table 12.5 includes a description of the XQuery argument.

EXAM WARNING

You need to observe some basic syntax rules when you are writing your code. First, XQuery is case-sensitive. Pay close attention to this. Second, XQuery elements and attributes MUST BE valid XML names. Lastly, XQuery variables are always defined with a $ followed by the variable name (example: $name).

Table 12.5 Query() Method Argument

Query() Argument	Description
XQuery	Is a string, an XQuery expression that queries for XML nodes such as elements and attributes, in an XML instance.

The value() method allows you to extract a value from the XML document. This will enable you to compare XML data with data from non–XML columns. For example, in Figure 12.15, you can use the following query to return the age of 'Bill Bergen' to an integer.

Figure 12.15 Sample Value() Method

```
SELECT employee.value('/employee[1]/person[2]/Age[1][text()]', 'int')
AS Age FROM #tbl_xml
```

As you can see, the value() method requires arguments. The first argument is the XQuery expression, and the second argument is the SQL data type. Use Table 12.6 as a guide for the value() parameter.

Table 12.6 Value() Method Argument

Value() Argument	Description
XQUERY	Is the XQuery expression, a string literal that retrieves data inside the XML instance. The XQuery must return at most one value. Otherwise, an error is returned.
SQLType	Is the preferred SQL type, a string literal, to be returned. The return type of this method matches the SQLType parameter. SQLType cannot be an XML data type, a common language runtime (CLR) user-defined type, image, text, ntext, or sql_variant data type. SQLType can be an SQL, user-defined data type.

The exist() method is used to check the existence of a value in a XML document. This method will return an integer value of 1 if the value returned is a non–null value and a 0 integer for a NULL value. In Figure 12.16 we will query the sample XML document, shown in Figure 12.13, to see if the name 'Jennifer' exists. Table 12.7 includes a description of the Exist() argument.

Figure 12.16 Sample Exist() Method

```
SELECT pk, employee FROM #tbl_xml
WHERE employee.exist('/employee/person/name/FirstName[.="Jennifer"]') = 1
```

Table 12.7 Exist() Method Argument

Exist() Arguments	Description
XQuery	Is an XQuery expression, a string literal.

The last method for querying XML documents in an XML data type is the nodes() method. The nodes() method will return a rowset for each row in the query. This is helpful when you want to make your XML data type into a relational format. Every XML document has a node, and in the XML data type this is the document node. The document node is the node at the top of every XML data type. In Figure 12.17, we query the sample XML document, shown in Figure 12.13, to return rows for each person in our employee node. Table 12.8 includes a description of the Nodes() argument.

Figure 12.17 Sample Node() Method

```
SELECT T2.employee.query('.')
FROM #tbl_xml
CROSS APPLY employee.nodes('/employee/person') as T2(employee)
```

Table 12.8 Nodes() Method Argument

Nodes() Argument	Description
XQuery	Is a string literal, an XQuery expression. If the query expression constructs nodes, these constructed nodes are exposed in the resulting rowset. If the query expression results in an empty sequence, the rowset will be empty. If the query expression statically results in a sequence that contains atomic values instead of nodes, a static error is raised.
Table(Column)	Is the table name and the column name for the resulting rowset.

SQL Server 2008 provides extensions that allow XQuery to modify data using the modify() method. The modify() method includes three DML statements: insert, delete, and replace value of (see Table 12.9).

Table 12.9 Modify() Method Argument

DML	Description
insert	Inserts one or more nodes as a child. Insert allows you to insert XML before or after and existing XML node. You can also insert attributes.
delete	Delete XML elements or attributes from your XML document
replace value of	Replace a node with a new value that you specify. The node you select must be a single node, not multiple nodes.

In Figure 12.18 we use our XML document, shown in Figure 12.13, to perform and insert, delete, and replace value of. Figure 12.18 will insert the tag <HireDate></HireDate> for employee number 3, Jennifer. Notice that we use the *UPDATE* statement to perform this function and not the *INSERT* statement. The insert is performed in the XQuery command.

Figure 12.18 Insert DML for Modify() Method

```
UPDATE #tbl_xml SET employee.modify(
'insert <HireDate>5/5/1999</HireDate>
as last into (/employee/person[3])[1]')
where pk=1
```

In Figure 12.19 we will update employee number three's age from 9 to 10 using the replace value of DML.

Figure 12.19 Replace Value of DML for Modify() Method

```
UPDATE #tbl_xml
     SET employee.modify(
                         'replace value of
(/employee/person[3]/Age[1]/text())[1]
                         with "10"'
                         )
where pk=1
go
```

In Figure 12.20 we will use the delete DML. Here we will delete employee number three's HireDate.

Figure 12.20 Using the Delete DML

```
UPDATE #tbl_xml
    SET employee.modify(
    'delete /employee/person[3]/HireDate')
where pk=1
go
```

New & Noteworthy...

XML Modifications

XQuery, natively, does not support modifying XML data. Microsoft added this feature with SQL Server 2005 and modified it with SQL Server 2008.

XPath

XPath (XML Path Language) is a query language used to identify a set of nodes within an XML document. XPath can be used to compute values such as strings, numbers, or Boolean values from an XML document. It supports many different expression types. Table 12.10 describes each expression type.

Table 12.10 Expression Types for XPath

Category	Function	Description
Numeric	Ceiling	Returns the smallest integer of the values passed
	Floor	Returns the largest integer of the values passed
	Round	Rounds to the nearest integer

Continued

Table 12.10 Continued. Expression Types for XPath

Category	Function	Description
Boolean	Not	True or False value
String	Concat	Concatenates the strings passed
	Contains	Returns a true value if the first argument contains the second argument
	Substring	Returns a portion of the first argument starting at the location of the second argument
	String-length	Returns the length of a string passed
Node	Number	Returns a number for the value of the node passed
Context	Position	Returns an integer that is the current position in the sequence.
	Last	Returns an integer that is the count of the last item in the sequence
Sequences	Empty	Returns true if the argument passed, which is a sequence, is empty.
	Distinctvalues	Removes duplicates from your sequence
Aggregate	Avg	Returns the average of a set of numbers
	Count	Counts the number of items in the set and returns an integer
	Min	Returns the minimum value from a set of numbers
	Max	Returns the maximum value from a set of numbers
	Sum	Returns the sum of a set of numbers.
Constructor	Various	Allows you to create an XSD type from another type or literal
DataAccess	Data	Returns the typed value of the node
	String	Returns the value of the argument as a string

Now, let's explore some examples of how SQL Server 2008 uses XPath to calculate numbers, strings, and Boolean values. In Figure 12.21, we have created an XML document and stored it in our XML data type in the declared table @XMLTable.

Figure 12.21 Sample XML Document

```
DECLARE @xmlData XML
SET @xmlData = '<?=xml version="1.0" encoding="UTF-8" standalone="yes"=?>
                        <product>
                        <item>
                                <name>BaseBall Gloves</name>
                                <tagid>52487-1</tagid>
                                <quantity>10</quantity>
                        </item>
                        <item>
                                <name>BaseBall Bats</name>
                                <tagid>52487-1</tagid>
                                <quantity>15</quantity>
                        </item>
                        <item>
                                <name>BaseBall Balls</name>
                                <tagid>94235-1</tagid>
                                <quantity>4</quantity>
                        </item>
                        </product>'
-- Create a new table
declare @XMLTable table (pk INT IDENTITY PRIMARY KEY, colxml XML)
--Insert data into the new table
INSERT INTO @XMLTable(colxml)
VALUES (@xmlData)
```

In Figure 12.22 we will use the XPath function, *count*, in order to count the number of item nodes in our XML document.

Figure 12.22 XPath Expression count

```
-- Count the number of people
SELECT colxml.query(
'count(//item)
')
FROM @XMLTable
```

In Figure 12.23 we will use the XPath function, *contains*, to return the string that contains the word "BaseBall Bats."

Figure 12.23 XPath Expression *Contains*

```
SELECT *
FROM @XMLTable
WHERE
        colxml.exist('/product/item/name[contains(.,"BaseBall Bats")]') = 1
```

These are just two examples of all the XPath expressions you can use. To find more, refer to the Table 12.10 Expression Types for XPath.

XML Indexes

SQL Server 2008 allows for the creation of indexes only on the XML data type. It's used to optimize XQuery queries, which index all tags, values, and paths over the XML instances in the XML data type column. SQL Server provides two key types of indexing on the XML data type CREATE PRIMARY XML INDEX and CREATE XML INDEX.

EXAM WARNING

The first index on the XML type column must be the Primary XML index.

The CREATE PRIMARY XML INDEX removes the need for SQL Server to shred your XML data during every query. It should be used when you store large XML documents in each row of a table. You cannot create a primary XML index on a non–XML column, and you can only create one primary XML index on a given XML column. Figure 12.24 is the syntax for creating a CREATE PRIMARY XML INDEX.

Figure 12.24 CREATE PRIMARY XML INDEX Syntax

```
CREATE PRIMARY XML INDEX [index_name]
       ON table_name (xml_column_name)
```

New & Noteworthy...

XML Data Type

XML instances are stored in XML-type columns as large binary objects (BLOBS). These XML instances can be large, and the stored binary representation of XML data type instances can be up to 2GB.

In Figure 12.25, we have created a table and inserted some values into the table.

Figure 12.25 Sample XML Data

```
CREATE TABLE [dbo].[XML_Table](
       [pk] [int] IDENTITY(1,1) NOT NULL,
       [customerName] [varchar](255) NULL,
       [customerPhone] [varchar](255) NULL,
       [customerAddress] [xml] NULL,
CONSTRAINT [PK_XML_Table] PRIMARY KEY CLUSTERED
(
       [pk] ASC
))
INSERT INTO XML_Table (
       [customerName],
       [customerPhone],
       [customerAddress]
```

```
) VALUES (

      /* customerName - VARCHAR(255) */ 'Monica Banning',

      /* customerPhone - VARCHAR(255) */ '555-8746',

      '<customer><address1>123 Main Street</address1><city>Newark</city>
<state>DE</state><zip>14785</zip>

</customer>' )

INSERT INTO XML_Table (

      [customerName],

      [customerPhone],

      [customerAddress]

) VALUES (

      /* customerName - VARCHAR(255) */ 'Jennifer Liddle',

      /* customerPhone - VARCHAR(255) */ '555-2497',

      '<customer><address1>45 Andrew Street</address1><city>Clifton
</city><state>AH</state><zip>18783</zip>

</customer>')
```

To create the primary key for this table, we will use the code shown in
Figure 12.26.

Figure 12.26 Create Primary XML Index

```
CREATE PRIMARY XML INDEX [PK_XML_Data_customerAddress]
ON XML_Table (customerAddress)
```

Secondary XML indexes are also created on an XML data type column. There
are three types of secondary XML indexes. See Table 12.11 for more details.

Table 12.11 Secondary XML Index Types

Secondary Index	Description
PATH	XML index helps with queries that use XML path expressions.
VALUE	XML index helps with queries that search for values anywhere in the XML document.
PROPERY	XML index helps with queries that retrieve particular object properties from within an XML document.

To create a secondary XML index, you must use the *CREATE XML INDEX* statement. Figure 12.27 shows the syntax for the CREATE XML INDEX.

Figure 12.27 CREATE XML INDEX Syntax

```
CREATE XML INDEX index_name
ON table_name (xml_column_name)
[USING XML INDEX xml_index_name
[FOR {VALUE|PATH|PROPERTY}]
```

Using the table we created in Figure 12.25, we will create a secondary XML index on the customerAddress column (see Figure 12.28).

Figure 12.28 CREATE XML INDEX Usage

```
CREATE XML INDEX [SD_XML_Data_customerAddress]
     ON XML_Table (customerAddress)
USING XML INDEX [PK_XML_Data_customerAddress]
FOR VALUE
```

Along with creating primary and secondary indexes on XML data type columns, you can also modify these indexes. The *ALTER INDEX Transact-SQL DDL* statement can be used to modify existing XML indexes. In Figure 12.29, we will modify our secondary index, DB_XML_Data_customerAddress, to turn ALLOW_ROW_LOCKS OFF.

Figure 12.29 ALTER INDEX Usage

```
ALTER INDEX [SD_XML_Data_customerAddress] ON XML_Table
     SET(ALLOW_ROW_LOCKS = OFF)
```

By default, XML indexes are *ENABLED* by default, but you can *DISABLE* an XML index. To do that, you set the XML index to *DISABLE*. You *DISABLE* an index when you want to preserve the index definition but you do not want to have the index available for use within the database engine. If you want to remove the index definition from the database engine, you need to drop the index instead of disabling it. We will *DISABLE* the secondary instance we created (see Figure 12.30).

Figure 12.30 Using ALTER INDEX to DISABLE an INDEX

```
ALTER INDEX [SD_XML_Data_customerAddress] on XML_Table DISABLE
```

Of course, you can drop XML indexes. You use the *DROP INDEX Transact-SQL DDL* statement. If you drop the primary XML index, any secondary indexes that are present are also dropped. In Figure 12.31, we will drop the secondary index.

Figure 12.31 Using DROP INDEX to DROP an XML Index

```
DROP INDEX [SD_XML_Data_customerAddress] ON XML_Table
```

XML Schema

XML schemas provide a means to define the structure and content of an XML document. SQL Server supports a subset of the XML Schema and uses three DDL statements to manage XML schema collections: *CREATE XML SCHEMA COLLECTION, ALTER XML SCHEMA COLLECTION*, and *DROP XML SCHEMA COLLECTION*. XML schema collections are XML schemas that are imported into a SQL Server database and are defined using the XSD (XML Schema Definition) language.

We will first explore the *CREATE XML SCHEMA COLLECTION DDL* statement. The CREATE XML SCHEMA COLLECTION DDL uses the syntax shown in Figure 12.32. Refer to Table 12.12 for arguments and descriptions.

Figure 12.32 CREATE XML SCHEMA COLLECTION Syntax

```
CREATE XML SCHEMA COLLECTION [ <relational_schema>. ]sql_identifier AS
Expression
```

Table 12.12 *CREATE XML SCHEMA COLLECTION* Arguments

Arguments	Description
Relational_schema	Identifies the relational schema name. If not specified, default relational schema is assumed.
sql_identifier	Is the SQL identifier for the XML schema collection.
Expression	Is a string constant or scalar variable. Is varchar, varbinary, nvarchar, or XML type.

Let's examine the CREATE XML SCHEMA COLLECTION. In Figure 12.33, we created a sample XML schema collection using the *CREATE XML SCHEMA COLLECTION DDL* statement.

Figure 12.33 Sample CREATE XML SCHEMA COLLECTION

```
CREATE XML SCHEMA COLLECTION customerSchema AS
    '<schema xmlns="http://www.w3.org/2001/XMLSchema">
          <element name="root" type="string"/>
    </schema>'
```

After the schema collection is created, you can then assign it to an XML variable or a column with the schema declarations it contains. You do this by referencing the schema collection in the *CREATE TABLE* statement shown in Figure 12.34.

Figure 12.34 *CREATE TABLE* statement defining
the XML SCHEMA COLLECTION

```
CREATE TABLE [dbo].[XML_Table](
    [pk] [int] IDENTITY(1,1) NOT NULL,
    [customerName] [varchar](255) NULL,
    [customerPhone] [varchar](255) NULL,
    [customerAddress] [xml](customerSchema) NULL,
CONSTRAINT [PK_XML_Table] PRIMARY KEY CLUSTERED
(
    [pk] ASC
))
```

The ALTER XML SCHEMA COLLECTION allows you to add new schema components to an existing XML schema collection. The ALTER XML SCHEMA COLLECTION DDL uses the following syntax as shown in Figure 12.35. Table 12.13 lists all the arguments and descriptions for the ALTER XML SCHEMA COLLECTION.

Figure 12.35 ALTER XML SCHEMA COLLECTION Syntax

```
ALTER XML SCHEMA COLLECTION [ relational_schema. ]sql_identifier ADD
'Schema Component'
```

Table 12.13 ALTER XML SCHEMA COLLECTION Arguments

Argument	Description
relational_schema	Identifies the relational schema name. If not specified, the default relational schema is assumed.
sql_identifier	Is the SQL identifier for the XML schema collection.
' Schema Component '	Is the schema component to insert.

In Figure 12.36, we will add a new schema component to the customerSchema.

Figure 12.36 Sample Usage of ALTER XML SCHEMA COLLECTION

```
ALTER XML SCHEMA COLLECTION customerSchema ADD
'<schema xmlns="http://www.w3.org/2001/XMLSchema">
  <element name="customer" type="string"/>
</schema>'
```

The DROP XML SCHEMA COLLECTION removes an XML Schema from the database. You cannot drop an XML schema while it is in use. So if the XML Schema is associated with an XML-type parameter or column, the table column has to be altered without specifying the schema. If you try to drop the schema, while in use, you will receive an error. In the following example, Figure 12.37, we receive an error when we try to drop the XML Schema, customerSchema, on table XML_Table.

Figure 12.37 Sample Usage of DROP XML SCHEMA

```
DROP XML SCHEMA COLLECTION customerSchema
GO
Msg 6328, Level 16, State 1, Line 1
Specified collection 'customerSchema' cannot be dropped because it is used by
object 'dbo.XML_Table'.
```

To drop an XML schema collection, we will alter the table and remove the schema on the XML column and then drop the schema, as shown in Figure 12.38. Refer to Table 12.14 for a list of arguments and descriptions for the DROP XML SCHEMA COLLECTION.

Table 12.14 DROP XML SCHEMA COLLECTION Arguments

Argument	Description
relational_schema	Identifies the relational schema name. If not specified, the default relational schema is assumed.
sql_identifier	Is the name of the XML schema collection to drop.

To properly drop the XML Schema, customerSchema, we need to use the *ALTER TABLE* statement and then execute a DROP XML SCHEMA COLLECTION. We will use syntax shown in Figure 12.38 to accomplish this task.

Figure 12.38 The ALTER TABLE Statement

```
ALTER TABLE XML_Table ALTER COLUMN customerAddress XML
GO
DROP XML SCHEMA COLLECTION customerSchema
```

Well-Formed XML

XML is a framework for storing information in a tree. The XML document must exactly have one root tag and must have a *start-tag* (< >) and *end-tag* (</>). An XML document must adhere to the XML syntax rules, or it is not a valid document. Figure 12.39 is a well-formed XML document.

Figure 12.39 A Well-Formed XML Document

```
<person>
     <name>Steve Long</name>
</person>
```

In addition, text can be contained in the root tag. These are called attributes. For example, Figure 12.40 shows a sample XML document in which attributes are contained in the root tag.

Figure 12.40 Using Attributes in an XML Document

```
<car make="chevrolet">
     <model>cavalier</model>
     <year>2005</year>
</car>
```

XML requires that you properly nest elements in your XML document. Overlapping cannot occur, and as mentioned earlier, you need to end your XML with the *end-tag* (</>). Figure 12.41 is not a well-formed XML document. You will see that the *<year>* element overlaps the *<car>* element.

Figure 12.41 Not a Well-Formed XML Document

```
<car>hyundai<year>1997</year></car>
```

XML also has the flexibility to contain empty data. For example, in Figure 12.42, you will see that there is no price available for the car. An *empty-element tag* resembles a *start-tag* but contains a slash just before the closing angle bracket.

Figure 12.42 Empty Data Usage

```
<car make="chevrolet">
     <model>cavalier</model>
     <year>2005</year>
     <price />
</car>
```

Notice that the price does not have an *end-tag* (</>). That's because in XML there are different ways to specify the ending of a tag.

```
<price></price>
<price />
<price/>
```

XML documents must conform to syntax rules. Here are some of the rules to follow when you are creating a well-formed XML document.

- All attribute values are quoted with either single (') or double (") quotes. Single quotes close a single quote, and double quotes close a double quote.

- Tags may be nested but must not overlap. Each nonroot element must be completely contained in another element.

- Empty elements may be marked with an empty-element (self-closing) tag, such as <NoData/>. This is equal to <NoData></NoData>.

- Element names are case-sensitive.

XML Examples

```
<person>
        <name>Steve Long</name>
</person>

<car make="chevorlet">
        <model>cavalier</model>
        <year>2005</year>
        <price/>
</car>

<root>
<customer id="17" firstname="Bob" lastname="Smith">
        <address type="home" address1="763 Main Street" city="Anytown"
state="CA" zipcode="93762"/>
        <order id="17">
                <line_item part_no="12" qty="1" price="12.99"/>
                <line_item part_no="73" qty="2" price="6.95"/>
                <line_item part_no="17" qty="1" price="2.95"/>
        </order>
</customer>
</root>
```

Summary of Exam Objectives

This chapter covers a large amount of information that developers can reference when using XML in their applications. Use of XML data is growing because of its flexibility and portability. SQL Server 2008 takes advantage of these qualities by enhancing its functionality.

We looked at how to retrieve and transform XML using FORXML and OPENXML. FORXML will return results as XML documents using four different methods: RAW, PATH, AUTO, and EXPLICIT. OPENXML will return XML documents into rowsets to be compared with values. This brings together relational data with XML data.

We reviewed XQuery and XPath and discussed how they work together to query and manipulate data. XQuery uses five different methods to query and modify data: query(), value(), nodes(), exist(), and modify(). XPath helps compare string, numbers, and Boolean values.

We close the chapter with a discussion of XML indexes, XML schemas, and well-formed XML. XML documents need to be constructed using the rules of XML. Understanding the XML structure and rules around it is a critical task in preparing for this exam.

Exam Objectives Fast Track

Retrieving and Transforming XML Data

☑ FORXML is used to construct XML from relational data.

☑ FORXML uses four modes: RAW, PATH, AUTO, and EXPLICIT.

☑ FORXML is used as part of the *SELECT* statement.

☑ OPENXML exposes XML documents as a rowset.

☑ An XML document must be prepared using sp_xml_preparedocument.

☑ An XML document must be removed once completed using sp_xml_removedocument.

OPENXML, sp_xml_preparedocument, and sp_xml_removedocument

- ☑ OPENXML primarily gives the ability to insert XML data into the relational database; however, we can query the data too using OPENXML.

- ☑ sp_xml_preparedocument reads XML text, then parses the text, and provides the parsed document in a state ready.

- ☑ sp_xml_removedocument removes the internal representation of the XML document specified by the document handle.

XQuery and XPath

- ☑ XQuery uses four methods for querying XML data: query(),value(),nodes(),and exist().

- ☑ XQuery is case-sensitive.

- ☑ XQuery can be used to modify XML data using modify(), delete(), and replace value of().

- ☑ XPath is used to compute values such as strings, values, and Boolean values.

- ☑ XPath has a number of expression types.

- ☑ SQL Server 2008 does not support all expressions in XPath.

XML Indexes

- ☑ XML indexes are used to optimize XQuery queries.

- ☑ XML indexes tags, values, and paths.

- ☑ You can use two key indexing types: CREATE PRIMARY XML INDEX and CREATE XML INDEX.

XML Schema

- ☑ XML Schema provides a means to define the structure and content of XML documents.

- ☑ XML Schema collections are imported directly into a database.

- ☑ There are three DDLs to create and manage XML Schema Collections: CREATE XML SCHEMA COLLECTION, ALTER XML SCHEMA COLLECTION, and DROP XML SCHEMA COLLECTION

Well-Formed XML

☑ Well-formed XML must have one root tag.

☑ Well-formed XML must have a *start-tag* (< >) and an *end-tag* (</>).

☑ All elements in a well-formed XML document must be nested.

☑ XML documents can be any size, from a single-line blank document such as <root/> to a multi-thousand line XML document with dozens of child nodes.

☑ XML documents can contain both elements and attributes.

☑ All XML nodes are case-sensitive and must be closed with a closing tag to be valid.

Exam Objectives
Frequently Asked Questions

Q: Can I specify the format of an XML document using FORXML?

A: Yes. You need to use the EXPLICIT mode in the FORXML DDL.

Q: How many elements can be opened with sp_xml_preparedocument?

A: The number of elements that can be open at one time with sp_xml_prepare-document is 256.

Q: Can I use XPath queries in my XQuery statements?

A: Yes. The query in an XQuery statement is an XPath query.

Q: What version of SQLXML is used in SQL Server 2008?

A: The version that is used is SQLXML 4.0.

Q: Are there some features of XPath language that are not supported?

A: Yes, in Microsoft SQLXML 4.0, some features are not supported. For example, the arithmetic operator, mod, is not supported. You can see a list of Unsupported XPath features in Books Online under Using XPath Queries in SQLXML4.0.

Q: If I don't have a root tag in my XML document, is it still "well-formed"?

A: No. You must always have a root tag in your XML document.

Self Test

1. The database administrator for ABC Company is asked to create a query that will extract an XML document from the products table. The customer would like to see the following fields in the XML document, ProductID and ProductDescription. TheXML document does not have to be written in a specific way. Which query should the database administrator use?

   A. SELECT ProductID, ProductDescription FROM Products
      FORXML RAW

   B. SELECT ProductID, ProductDescription FROM Products
      FORXML AUTO

   C. SELECT ProductID, ProductDescription OPENXML RAW

   D. SELECT ProductID, ProductDescription FROM Products
      FORXML EXCEPIT

2. The database administrator for ABC Company is asked to create a relational table out of an XML column in the Products table. The customer would like to see ProductDescription and Price. The database administrator will insert the query between the sp_xml_preparedocument and sp_xml_removedocument. Which query will he need?

   A. SELECT ProductDescription,Quantity FROM OPENXML
      (@Pointer,'INVENTORY/ITEM',2) WITH (ProductDescription
      varchar(255),Quantity INTEGER)

   B. SELECT ProductDescription,Price FROM OPENXML
      (@Pointer,'INVENTORY/ITEM',2) WITH (ProductDescription
      varchar(255),PRICE)

   C. SELECT ProductDescription,Price FROM FORXML
      (@Pointer,'INVENTORY/ITEM',2) WITH (ProductDescription
      varchar(255),Quantity INTEGER)

   D. SELECT ProductDescription,Price FROM OPENXML
      (@Pointer,'INVENTORY/ITEM',2) WITH (ProductDescription
      varchar(255),Price money)

3. The main developer for ABC Company needs to confirm whether a product exists in the Products table. The product information is in an XML column named ProductsXML. Which method should the developer use in this XQuery?

    A. Query()

    B. Value()

    C. Exist()

    D. Modify()

4. The main developer for ABC Company needs to count the number of product descriptions in the Products table. The product description is in the XML column named PD_XML. Which query should the main developer use?

    A. SELECT PD_XML.query('count(//Product/ProductDescription)') FROM Products

    B. SELECT PD_XML.value('count(//Product/ProductDescription)') FROM Products

    C. SELECT PD_XML.nodes('count(//Product/ProductDescription)') FROM Products

    D. SELECT PD_XML.query('count(//Product/Products)') FROM Products

5. The main developer for ABC Company needs to replace the product description for an existing product to include some new features. Which DML should the main developer use with the modify() method?

    A. insert

    B. delete

    C. replace value of

    D. replace node of

6. The database administrator for ABC Company is creating a secondary XML index on a newly created table. He continues to receive an error when creating the index. What must the database administrator do first before he can create a secondary XML index?

    A. The database administrator must export the data, create the index, and then import that data.

    B. The database administrator must drop the table and create the table, then apply the index.

    C. The database administrator must apply a Primary XML index first.

    D. The database administrator must create a Primary Key constraint on the XML column first.

7. The database administrator for ABC Company is creating a Primary XML Index on the PD_XML column in the Products table. Which query does he need to successfully create the index=

   A. ACREATE PRIMARY XML INDEX [PK_PRODUCTS_PD_XML] ON PD_XML (PRODUCTS)

   B. CREATE PRIMARY XML INDEX [PRODUCTS] ON PD_XML ON XML

   C. CREATE PRIMARY XML INDEX [PK_PRODUCTS_PD_XML] ON PRODUCTS (PRODUCTS)

   D. CREATE PRIMARY XML INDEX [PK_PRODUCTS_PD_XML] ON PRODUCTS (PD_XML)

8. The database administrator for ABC Company needs to drop an XML index on the Products table. What DDL command should the database administrator use to drop the XML index?

   A. DROP INDEX

   B. DROP XML INDEX

   C. ALTER INDEX

   D. DROP TABLE

9. The main developer for ABC Company needs to create a schema on an XML column, PD_XML. What DDL statement must the main developer use to create the schema?

   A. CREATE SCHEMA COLLECTION

   B. CREATE XML SCHEMA COLLECTION

   C. CREATE XML COLLECTION

   D. CREATE SCHEMA

10. The database administrator for ABC Company needs to drop an XML schema collection from the Products table called [SCH_XML_PRODUCT _DESC]. Which command should be used to drop the XML schema collection?

    A. DROP XML SCHEMA COLLECTION Products

    B. DROP SCHEMA COLLECTION [SCH_XML_PRODUCT _DESC]

    C. DROP XML SCHEMA COLLECTION [SCH_XML_PRODUCT _ DESC]

    D. DROP XML SCHEMA COLLECTION ON [SCH_XML_PRODUCT _DESC]

11. The database administrator for ABC Company needs to drop an XML schema collection from the Products table called [SCH_XML_PRODUCT _DESC]. When he executes the correct command, he receives an error that the XML schema collection cannot be dropped because it is in use by the Products table. What can the database administrator do to drop the XML schema collection?

    A. The table needs to be dropped before the DROP XML SCHEMA COLLECTION DLL can be executed.

    B. The XML column needs to be dropped before the DROP XML SCHEMA COLLECTION DLL can be executed.

    C. Alter the table to remove the XML Schema.

    D. Alter the XML column to a different data type, then execute DROP XML SCHEMA COLLECTION DDL.

12. Which one of the values can XPath compute?

    A. XML

    B. Boolean

    C. money

    D. variables

13. The FORXML clause is used to do what?

    A. Return results as XML documents rather than a standard rowset.

    B. Return results as a standard rowset rather than an XML document.

    C. Insert data into an XML data type column.

    D. Delete data in an XML data type column.

14. Which DDL state do you use to delete an element from an XML document?

    A. DELETE

    B. UPDATE

    C. SELECT

    D. ALTER

15. Which is a well-formed XML document?

    A. <people>Mike</firstname></people>

    B. <people></firstname>Mike</people>

    C. <people><firstname>Mike</firstname></people>

    D. <people><firstname>Mike<lastname>Smith</lastname></firstname>
       </people>

16. What is OPENXML used for in SQL Server 2008?

    A. Used to modify data in an XML document

    B. Used to form an XML document from a relational table

    C. Used to represent a relational view of an XML document

    D. Used to remove an XML document from internal memory

17. Which stored procedure is used to prepare a document to be queried?

    A. Sp_xml_preparedocument

    B. Sp_xml_preparexmldocument

    C. Sp_xml_removedocument

    D. Sp_xml_preparedocumentquery

18. What is the ROOT directive used for within the FORXML clause?

    A. The ROOT directive tells the XPath query which column to use as the
       parent node of the document.

    B. The ROOT directive tells the SQL Server to wrap the created XML
       document within a <root> node.

    C. The ROOT directive tells the SQL Server to wrap the created XML
       document within the specified node.

    D. The ROOT directive tells the XPath query which node to use as the
       parent node or the document.

19. Which stored procedure is used to remove a document from memory?

    A. Sp_xml_preparedocument

    B. Sp_xml_preparexmldocument

    C. Sp_xml_removedocument

    D. Sp_xml_preparedocumentquery

20. Using the following XML document, which query would be used to retrieve the CustomerId and the ItemId from the query.

```
<root>
        <customer id="17" firstname="Bob" lastname="Smith">
            <address type="home" address1="763 Main Street" city="Anytown"
state="CA" zipcode="93762" />
            <order id="17">
                    <line_item part_no="12" qty="1" price="12.99"/>
                    <line_item part_no="73" qty="2" price="6.95"/>
                    <line_item part_no="17" qty="1" price="2.95"/>
            </order>
        </customer>
</root>
```

A.

```
SELECT *
FROM OPENXML (@hDoc, '/root/customer/order/line_item')
WITH (CustomerId INT '../../@id',
                     ItemId INT '@part_no')
```

B.

```
SELECT *
FROM OPENXML (@hDoc, '/root/customer')
WITH (CustomerId INT '@id',
ItemId INT './order/line_item/@part_no')
```

C.

```
SELECT *
FROM OPENXML (@hDoc, '/root/customer/order')
WITH (CustomerId INT '../@id',
        ItemId INT './line_item/@part_no')
```

D.

```
SELECT *
FROM OPENXML (@hDoc, '/root/customers/orders/line_items')
WITH (CustomerId INT '@id',
        ItemId INT '@id')
```

Self Test Quick Answer Key

1. **B**

2. **D**

3. **C**

4. **A**

5. **C**

6. **C**

7. **D**

8. **A**

9. **B**

10. **C**

11. **C**

12. **B**

13. **A**

14. **B**

15. **C**

16. **C**

17. **A**

18. **C**

19. **C**

20. **A**

MCTS SQL Server 2008 Exam 433

Performance Tuning

Exam objectives in this chapter:

- Working with Query Execution Plans
- Tracing with SQL Profiler
- Working with Database Tuning Advisor
- Using Dynamic Management Views

Exam objectives review:

- ☑ Summary of Exam Objectives
- ☑ Exam Objectives Fast Track
- ☑ Exam Objectives Frequently Asked Questions
- ☑ Self Test
- ☑ Self Test Quick Answer Key

Introduction

SQL Server 2008 is a very powerful product, and hardware vendors have released faster, more powerful servers almost every quarter for the past 10 years or more! Despite the advances in the capability of both hardware and software, building a solution that meets business performance needs is more important than ever. Performance has never been so important in these times when applications are built to service disconnected or occasionally connected mobile users and platforms need to scale better and faster than ever.

Performance tuning should be an integral part of the IT lifecycle, and even the smallest applications should go through some form of performance testing prior to release. Getting database logic and configuration right often means that users don't notice the database layer. Get the database implementation wrong, and users might be significantly affected by problems that periodically render the system useless.

Performance tuning should be included in every iteration of testing and project delivery. Attempting to retro-fit performance to an already-built solution is impractical and often expensive in terms of cost and user confidence. Goals and targets for system performance help determine acceptable thresholds for testing. Building a test environment that is representative of the production environment is critical to ensure results are trustworthy and to provide a sound basis for configuration choices and implementation. Selecting and using appropriate tools to simulate workload are very useful when validating changes or choices for system configuration.

This chapter looks at the way SQL Server evaluates options for returning query results and how it makes its selection on the best execution plan. We'll look at ways to capture and view the execution plan and how to use Database Tuning Advisor to provide suggestions for missing indexes and statistics that could improve query performance. Finally, we'll review some Dynamic Management Views (DMVs) to see what's new in SQL Server 2008 to assist with the performance tuning process.

Working with Query Execution Plans

An execution plan is a plan containing the steps SQL Server works through in order to satisfy a query. Most stored procedures or ad hoc Transact-SQL queries access more than one table, and most tables have a clustered index and usually multiple non-clustered indexes. The SQL Server Operating System has a component called the Query Optimizer, which is responsible for selecting the optimal execution plan to satisfy a query.

Getting visibility of execution plans is important since it can help developers understand several key aspects of designing a well-performing database including the following:

- Index selection

- Join type and direction

- Statistics creation/ maintenance

- Application of predicates (WHERE clauses)

Knowledge of the steps SQL Server uses to deliver query results provides insight into how the Query Optimizer functions and ideas about how you can influence the choices made to help ensure data is returned in the most efficient method possible.

When troubleshooting a poorly performing query, an execution plan provides a very helpful view of the cost of each step involved. In many situations, a query plan consists of multiple steps each with different associated costs. Performance tuning is often an iterative process of identifying the most expense step then reducing this cost, either through altering the query/ stored procedure or by making changes to indexes, statistics, an underlying table, or several of these possibilities.

Compilation and Recompilation

Compilation is the process by which the Query Optimizer determines a good plan to execute a query. Recompilation is the process by which the Query Optimizer recalculates a query plan because a condition affecting query execution has changed.

The first time a query is executed, SQL Server checks the procedure cache, an area of memory reserved for compiled query plans. If a plan is found, it will be used. Otherwise the optimizer compiles an execution plan based on statistics to determine the best method to satisfy a query. Once the query plan has been compiled, it is stored in the procedure cache for re-use in the future.

Recompilation occurs when plans stored in the procedure cache can't be used because of a change since the plan was compiled. Below is a summary of common conditions that could influence recompilation:

- Changes to statistics used to generate the cached plan

- Using sp_recompile or calling a stored procedure using WITH RECOMPILE

- ALTER TABLE or ALTER VIEW commands affecting the query

- Changes to indexes referenced by the query plan (including dropping indexes)

- Large number of inserts or deletes (exceeding a threshold value)

Cost-Based Optimization

Understanding query execution plans requires an introduction to query execution within SQL Server. SQL Server uses a cost-based optimizer where alternative relational database management systems use rule-based optimization or a hybrid of rule- and cost-based optimization.

Cost-based optimization means that a query plan is chosen based on a cost value that is placed on each of the different query plans or access methods that could be used to satisfy a query. Once the options have been evaluated (index seeks or scan, table scans, hashes and sorts, etc.), the optimizer selects and executes the execution plan with the lowest cost.

The Query Optimizer doesn't actually execute the query with many different plans; its decision is based on statistics. Statistics within SQL Server are a histogram of the data whereby values for each column are sampled at preset intervals throughout the table. Using this method, SQL Server has a view on data distribution without having to examine every row for each query.

Statistics are essentially summary data the optimizer uses to make decisions about query execution. If statistics are missing or inaccurate, the optimizer is likely to make a poor choice when executing queries. This can affect query response times and overall server performance.

When troubleshooting SQL Server performance problems, it is important to examine statistics and query plans with a view to including or eliminating statistics problems to reach a resolution. Using the Database Console Commands (DBCC) family of commands, you can determine when statistics were last updated and how many rows were sampled, as well as resample statistics to rule out statistics from the possible causes of poorly performing queries.

Capturing Query Execution Plans

Execution plans can be obtained using either SQL Server Management Studio or SQL Profiler. Depending on the nature of the problem, you'll need to determine the most appropriate tool. Queries with large execution plans are often best captured with SQL Profiler, whereas validating ad hoc changes and the impact of changes is often better suited to SQL Server Management Studio. There are two ways to display an execution plan: either in a graphical plan or in text format. The following sections describe each method, as well as how to capture and interpret the plans.

Graphical Execution Plans

Graphical execution plans provide a visual representation of the steps required to satisfy a query. More information can be drawn from the execution plan by moving the pointer over each step. To view a graphical execution plan, choose one of the following from the **Query** menu:

- **Display Estimated Execution Plan** (does not run query)
- **Include Actual Execution Plan** (does run query)

Both plans look the same or at least similar (more details are provided later in the chapter on the difference between estimated and actual execution plans). Figure 13.1 shows an actual execution plan for a query that joins three tables. Here, you can see that 61 percent of the total query execution time is spent executing a table scan on a table named "_Individual". Creating a clustered index on this table would remove the table scan and improve query completion time.

Graphical execution plans can be cumbersome to view and navigate especially for large queries or queries executed in multiple batches. It is often easier to navigate a query plan in full-screen mode: just right-click on the plan, choose **Save Execution Plan As,** and then give the file name the default extension .sqlplan. When you double-click the execution plan, it opens in full-screen view making it much easier to explore.

Figure 13.1 Graphical Actual Execution Plan

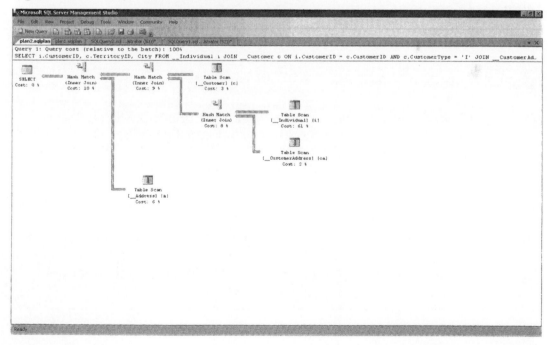

Text–Based Execution Plans

This actual query execution plan can also be captured using the SHOWPLAN_ TEXT SET option.

```
|--Hash Match(Inner Join, HASH:([ca].[AddressID])=([a].[AddressID]))
|--Hash Match(Inner Join,HASH:([c].[CustomerID])=([ca].[CustomerID]))
|  |--Table Scan(OBJECT:([AdventureWorks].[dbo].[__Customer] AS [c]),
WHERE:([AdventureWorks].[dbo].[__Customer].[CustomerType] as
[c].[CustomerType]=N'I'))
|  |--Hash Match(Inner Join, HASH:([i].[CustomerID])=([ca].[CustomerID]))
|  |--Table Scan(OBJECT:([AdventureWorks].[dbo].[__Individual] AS [i]))
|  |--Table Scan(OBJECT:([AdventureWorks].[dbo].[__CustomerAddress] AS [ca]))
|--Table Scan(OBJECT:([AdventureWorks].[dbo].[__Address] AS [a]))
```

Interpreting Graphic Execution Plans

Reading query execution plans requires an investigative approach and an understanding of how they represent decisions and steps within queries. Graphic execution plans contain icons representing operations that occur during query execution. SQL Server Books Online contains a complete list of operators; Table 13.1 lists a sample of common operators with corresponding icons and descriptions:

Table 13.1 Common Operators and Corresponding Icons

Icon	Operator	Description
	Clustered index scan	Scans a clustered index
	Clustered index seek	Seeks through a clustered index to find specific row(s)
	Non-clustered index scan	Scans a non-clustered index
	Non-clustered index seek	Seeks through a non-clustered index
	Nested loop join	Shown when a nested loop is used
	Merge join	Used to perform some inner and outer joins

Continued

Table 13.1 Continued. Common Operators and Corresponding Icons

Icon	Operator	Description
	Hash match	Represents a hash join where a computed hash table is used to match rows based on hash values
	RID lookup	Retrieves a row based on a row identifier (RID) (replaces bookmark lookup in SQL Server 2005)

Reading Execution Plans

The ability to read an execution plan takes time and practice. Use the following guidelines to extract the most interesting elements from execution plans:

- Read plans right to left and top to bottom.
- Use the + symbol in the bottom-right corner to navigate large plans.
- Mouse-over each step to get more information.
- Mouse-over connecting lines to see details such as number of rows transferred.
- Note that heavier weight connecting lines indicate more rows moved.
- Where a query consists of multiple batches, investigate the most expensive batch first.

It is essential to keep in mind the actual query. As you browse the execution plan, try to visualize how SQL Server is collecting, joining, and reducing the data from a very wide dataset (entire tables) to return just the results required to satisfy the query.

Once you're familiar with the look and feel of execution plans, try to use the plans to draw conclusions. A common approach to tuning poorly performing queries is to identify the highest cost batch and then determine alternatives—such as new indexes, statistics, or altering the query—to remove the step.

Estimated and Actual Execution Plans

Execution plans are useful in understanding how SQL Server delivers query results. There are two types of plans you can capture: *estimated plans* and *actual plans*. Estimated plans are captured by selecting **Display Estimated Execution Plan** from the Query menu. The estimated plan displays the plan the optimizer should follow if the query were executed (without actually executing the query). Actual execution plans are captured by selecting **Include Actual Execution Plan** from the Query menu.

Selecting actual execution plan executes a query and captures the actual execution plan used to deliver the query results. The output is visible in a new tab within the query results pane: select this tab to reveal the graphic actual execution plan. If the query uses any temporary tables, you'll need to use the actual execution plan because the temporary table won't be constructed if the code isn't executed. If you are using table variables instead of temporary tables, an estimated execution plan can be used.

In most cases, an estimated query plan is the same as an actual execution plan. However, there are differences in some instances usually related to statistics. Use DBCC commands to verify statistics on the objects accessed by the query and recalculate these statistics if necessary.

Tracing with SQL Profiler

Half of performance tuning is finding the problem. System Monitor (also known as Performance Monitor or PerfMon) is a performance monitoring tool provided by Windows that can be useful when measuring hardware performance or bottlenecks and when identifying a process on a server causing a slowdown. If SQL Server is running on a shared server (perhaps with a third-party application or Web server such as Internet Information Services), System Monitor can help you find the process consuming resources. If a server is dedicated to SQL Server or System Monitor identifies SQL Server as the cause of the problem, there is a more limited set of counters available for troubleshooting. System Monitor provides a server-wide overview, and it isn't possible to see exactly what SQL Server is doing at any point in time, which becomes useful when tracing.

As the performance tuning process becomes more focused, it is necessary to get visibility of activity within SQL Server, and this is when you need tracing. Tracing provides the ability to collect data about Transact-SQL (T-SQL) commands and Multi-Dimensional Expressions (MDX) executed on a database server. Additionally, it is possible to trace for information about events affecting system performance such as deadlocks, warnings, data and log file shrinks/ grows, and blocked processes. Tracing can also gather information about the way SQL Server processes requests internally such as locks, lock escalation, and query execution plans.

SQL Server Profiler (known as SQL Profiler or, simply, Profiler) is the graphic tool installed alongside SQL Server used to define, configure, and start/ stop traces.

SQL Server Profiler can be found by selecting **Start** > **All Programs** > **Microsoft SQL Server 2008** > **Performance Tools** > **SQL Server Profiler.**

Once Profiler is launched, you need to create a new trace. To create a trace, either select **File** > **New Trace** or click the left-most icon from the toolbar. The Server Connection Dialog window appears: specify the name of the server and SQL Server instance to be traced and connection credentials. After successfully connecting to an instance of SQL Server, the Trace Properties window appears (see Figure 13.2). You can provide a name that describes the trace and select options that give you control over how trace data is stored and what data is captured.

Figure 13.2 Creating a New Trace with SQL Server Profiler

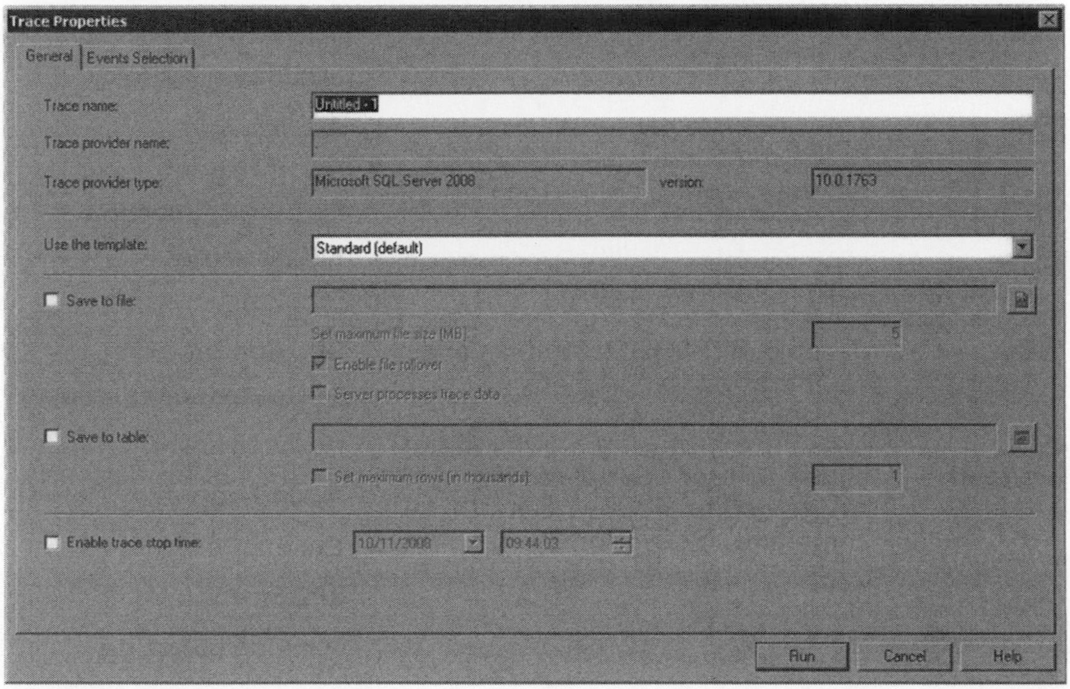

Trace Templates

The next configuration option is trace template (the Standard template is select by default). Trace templates provide a preconfigured trace definition for common trace scenarios. It is possible to create new trace templates or modify those provided with SQL Server. It is usually possible to start with a template and adjust the events and filters based on your needs. Table 13.2 contains a summary of trace templates, when you might use them, and the events captured.

Table 13.2 Trace Templates Summary

Name	Description	Events
SP_Counts	Used to trace calls to start Stored Procedures.	SP:Starting
Standard	Captures data to provide instance overview including T-SQL Statement and Stored Procedure Start and Completion.	Audit Login Audit Logout ExistingConnection RPC:Completed SQL:BatchCompleted SQL:BatchStarting
TSQL	This template captures T-SQL batch start times; useful for troubleshooting client application performance and correlating data captured from applications with SQL Server events.	Audit Login Audit Logout ExistingConnection RPC:Starting SQL:BatchStarting
TSQL_Duration	Records all T-SQL Statements and the duration to complete.	RPC:Completed SQL:BatchCompleted
TSQL_Grouped	Useful for capturing activity about a specific user or application; this template groups T-SQL commands by User or Client.	Audit Login Audit Logout ExistingConnection RPC:Starting SQL:BatchStarting
TSQL_Locks	Captures all Transact-SQL statements submitted to SQL Server by clients along with exceptional lock events. Use to troubleshoot deadlocks, lock time-out, and lock escalation events.	Blocked Process Report SP:StmtCompleted SP:StmtStarting SQL:StmtCompleted SQL:StmtStarting

Continued

Table 13.2 Continued. Trace Templates Summary

Name	Description	Events
		Deadlock Graph (Use against SQL Server 2005 or SQL Server 2008 instance)
		Lock:Cancel
		Lock:Deadlock
		Lock:Deadlock Chain
		Lock:Escalation
		Lock:Timeout (Use against SQL Server 2000 instance)
		Lock:Timeout (timeout>0) (Use against SQL Server 2005 or SQL Server 2008 instances)
TSQL_Replay	Use this template if the trace is to be replayed. Captures all events necessary to recreate statements/ workload on a different server.	CursorClose
		CursorExecute
		CursorOpen
		CursorPrepare
		CursorUnprepare
		Audit Login
		Audit Logout
		Existing Connection
		RPC Output Parameter
		RPC:Completed
		RPC:Starting
		Exec Prepared SQL
		Prepare SQL
		SQL:BatchCompleted
		SQL:BatchStarting

Continued

Table 13.2 Continued. Trace Templates Summary

Name	Description	Events
TSQL_SPs	Useful for troubleshooting poorly performing Stored Procedures; this template captures each step within the stored procedure to display execution duration.	Audit Login Audit Logout ExistingConnection RPC:Starting SP:Completed SP:Starting SP:StmtStarting SQL:BatchStarting
Tuning	This template captures T-SQL completion times; used to pass to SQL Server Database Tuning Advisor for analysis.	RPC:Completed SP:StmtCompleted SQL:BatchCompleted

EXAM WARNING

Be sure you have a good idea of what's included in the trace templates. You should especially take note of the Replay template, which is used to make a trace capture for replaying on a test server.

After choosing a trace template, you can click **Run** and server activity will begin to fill the screen. This can be useful to verify that the required events are being captured or to monitor SQL instances where activity is low (perhaps on a development workstation or test server where workload is restricted). However, reading and analyzing results captured through Profiler directly to the screen can become unwieldy on a server with even a moderate load. In this situation, consider tracing to a flat file or database table, which will speed up the trace and allow for post-capture analysis.

Trace Events

Select the **Events Selection** tab at the top of the Trace Properties window to view and control the event classes captured when a trace is running. The events already selected are those specified in the trace template. Click the **Show All Events** and

Show All Columns check boxes at the bottom right to display all events and options available for capture. You can choose any event necessary to include in the trace definition. Figure 13.3 shows some useful events to include in each trace such as Errors and Warnings, which alerts you to a number of conditions you should be aware of when troubleshooting any SQL Server problem.

Figure 13.3 Showing All Events and Columns

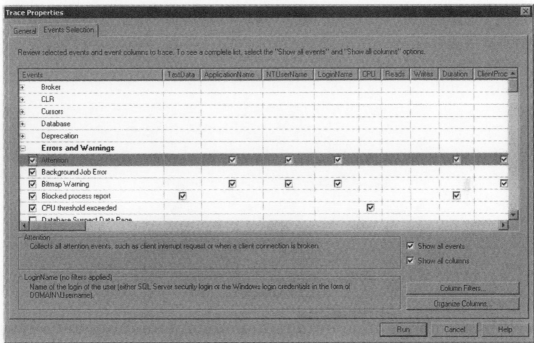

Configuring & Implementing...

Exercise Caution with LOCK Trace Events

SQL traces affect server performance. Trace as few events as necessary; you'll save overhead and capture less data to analyze! Exercise particular caution when capturing events in the LOCK event class since a busy SQL Server may acquire and release many thousands of locks per minute.

Trace Filters

Trace filters allow restrictions to be applied on the data captured by a trace. This can be useful with particularly busy or shared servers to capture activity for a single user, database, or application. Filters can be applied to include (Like) or exclude (Not Like) trace data.

To apply a filter, click the **Column Filters** button at the bottom right of the Trace Properties window and select the column you wish to filter. In the example shown in Figure 13.4, all requests from server LONDBS1 are excluded from the SQL trace.

Figure 13.4 Using Trace Filters to Include or Exclude Specific Trace Data

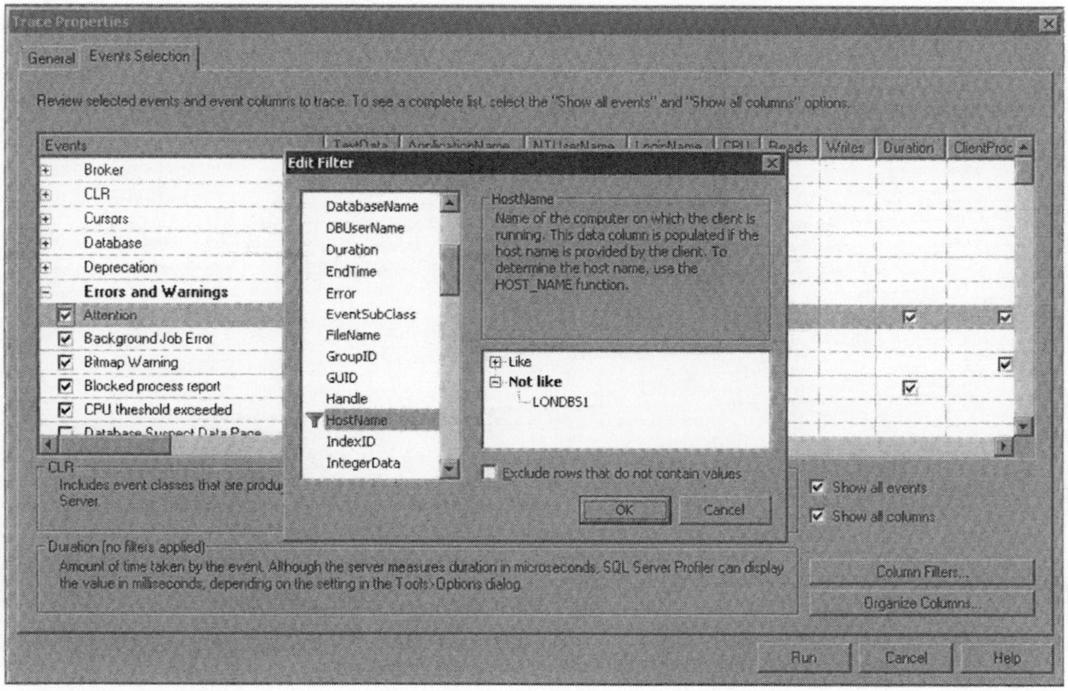

Server-Side Tracing

Server–side tracing reduces the impact of tracing and is recommended when tracing busy production servers or machines where system resources (memory or CPU) are low. Additionally, when traces are run from the server itself there is no network time involved in reporting start times for query execution. Since network time can vary (e.g., latency due to traffic of other network users), tracing across a network can produce inconsistent results.

There are two methods to create a server-side trace: as always a family of stored procedures is provided, but these can be cumbersome and difficult to translate to actual events and columns. It is possible to create a trace within Profiler and then script the trace definition. To script the trace definition, select **File** > **Export** > **Script Trace Definition** > **For SQL Server 2005 – 2008.**

After you open the trace definition in SQL Server Management Studio, you'll see the sp_trace_create statement, which is used to define the trace. Here you'll need to replace InsertFileNameHere with the path to the folder where trace files should be saved (see Figure 13.5). Try to avoid tracing to system drives or those where data or log files are stored because this type of tracing will affect performance of the database server.

Figure 13.5 Trace Definition

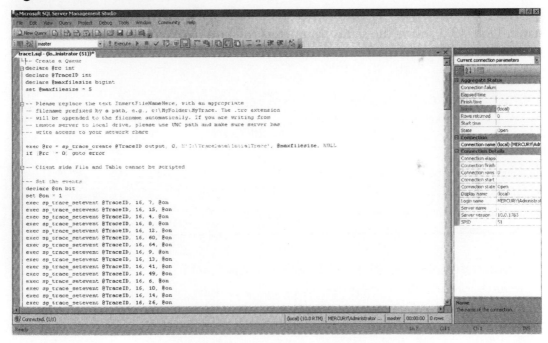

Configuring & Implementing...

Avoid Tracing to System Drives

Try to place trace files on dedicated disks that will have enough capacity for the duration of a trace. Avoid storing trace files on system drives; if the drive does fill, recovering a server from a full system partition is more difficult and time consuming that if a non-system partition fills.

Once the destination is configured, run the script and make a note of the TraceID returned by the query. The trace is now defined on the server; however there's an additional step required to start the trace. The system stored procedure sp_trace_setstatus is used to control the trace and requires parameters TraceID and status. Table 13.3 shows the status parameters to control server-side traces. In order to start TraceID 2, you must run sp_trace_setstatus(2,1).

Table 13.3 Status Parameters to Control Server-Side Traces

STATUS	DESCRIPTION
0	Stop trace
1	Start trace
2	Close trace and remove trace definition

Finally, if you lose track of which traces are running on a server, run select * from fn_trace_getinto(null) to return details of all traces. Remember that unless you've disabled it, there's a default trace (TraceID 1) running at all times to populate the Dynamic Management Views (DMVs).

Combining System Monitor and Profiler Traces

First introduced with SQL Server 2005, this excellent feature of Profiler allows administrators to combine a System Monitor trace with a SQL trace. This presents a single view of system resources (disk, memory, and CPU) with the statements executing at the time enabling administrators to, for example, correlate high-CPU conditions with a specific stored procedure or T-SQL statement.

Figure 13.6 shows the timeline from System Monitor that allows a view of hardware utilization: the red vertical bar allows administrators to jump to a particular point (e.g., a CPU spike) and the trace can identify the T-SQL command running at the moment of the spike.

Figure 13.6 Combining System Monitor and Profiler Traces in a Single View

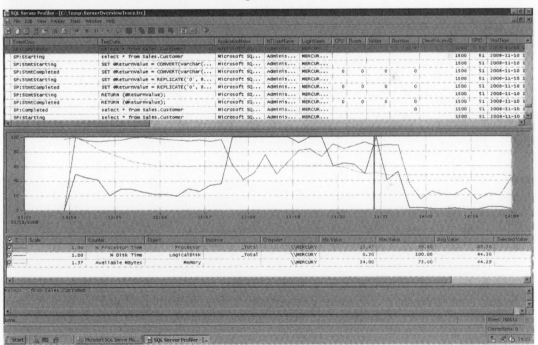

Replaying Traces

SQL Server provides the ability to replay traces. Typical scenarios involve capturing a trace from a production server and replaying the trace against a test or pre-production server. This can help when evaluating changes and also with some troubleshooting scenarios. Each statement captured in the trace is replayed against the target server, which can be helpful in verifying that a fix implemented on a test server actually resolves the problem.

A minimum set of events are required for trace playback; alternately, use the Replay trace template. Not all servers can be traced and replayed; for example, if a server is participating in transactional replication, trace replay isn't possible because of the way transactional replication marks transactions in the log.

Head of the Class...

Working with SQL Trace Data

Capturing trace data on a busy server many generate many gigabytes of data. Using a server-side trace writing to a file on a local disk minimizes tracing overhead. However, unless you're looking for a specific event in the trace, often the best way to manage the data is to load the trace data from a flat file into a table. The following function loads trace data from a file into a table:

```
SELECT * INTO srv1_trace FROM ::fn_trace_gettable
('c:\temp\trace1.trc', default)
```

Once the data is in a database, analysis with TSQL queries is much easier!

Using SQLDiag to Collect Performance Data

SQLDiag is a command line data collection utility first supplied with SQL Server 2005 that can useful for collecting performance data. SQLDiag collects the following:

- Windows event logs
- SQL Server configuration details
- System Monitor performance logs
- SQL Server Profiler trace data
- SQL Server blocking information

Essentially, SQLDiag doesn't do anything that couldn't be achieved separately: - each of these tools could be run independently, however, SQLDiag makes it easier to start and stop data collection and ensures all relevant information is collected each time data capture is run.

EXERCISE 13.1

RUNNING A TRACE WITH SQL PROFILER

This exercise will demonstrate running a trace with SQL Profiler. Initially, you'll get started with a basic trace using SQL Profiler:

1. Select **Start** > **Programs** > **Microsoft SQL Server 2008** > **Performance Tools** to launch SQL Profiler.
2. Connect to a valid SQL Server instance.
3. Name the trace.
4. Select **Standard** template.
5. Click the **Event Selection** tab.
6. Check both **Show All Events** and **Show All Columns** check boxes.
7. Enable all events in the Errors and warnings Event Class.
8. Click **Run** to start the trace.

Next, fire an error message from a query window and then correlate this in the SQL Profiler trace:

1. Start SQL Server Management Studio.
2. Connect to the same instance SQL Profiler is monitoring.
3. In a query window, run the following command:

```
raiserror('trace error text', 16,1)
```

Finally, validate the SQL trace has seen the error message:

1. Return to SQL Profiler.
2. Pause the trace to prevent any new events being added.
3. Locate the error (usually highlighted in red) with the text 'trace error text'.

Working with Database Tuning Advisor

The Database Tuning Advisor (DTA) is a tool provided with SQL Server to help Developers and System Administrators improve query performance by optimizing physical design structures such as indexes, indexed views, and table partitioning. DTA can be launched from the same folder location as SQL Server Profiler. Alternately, DTA can be started from within Management Studio, where it is located on the Tools menu.

In most cases, DTA speeds up the query it's tuning but adding indexes can have an adverse effect on inserts and deletes. Be sure to review and test the suggestions it offers.

Head of the Class...

Implementing DTA Recommendations

DTA is a useful tool in reviewing workload and making recommendations that can improve performance. However, DTA is no silver bullet. Always review recommendation and consider the impact of maintaining indexes once they've been created. For example, with one test workload, DTA could make a 90% performance improvement with 10 new indexes; however an 85% improvement could be gained with a single index—in this case we might elect to ignore the nine additional indexes.

There are two ways to use DTA: either as a workload file or as a tool to tune a specific query. Workload files can either be a SQL Profiler trace or a .sql file containing a workload (queries). To tune a specific query, load the query in SQL Server Management Studio, right-click the query, then select **Analyze Query in Database Tuning Advisor** from the menu (see Figure 13.7).

Figure 13.7 Provide a Specific Query to DTA for Analysis

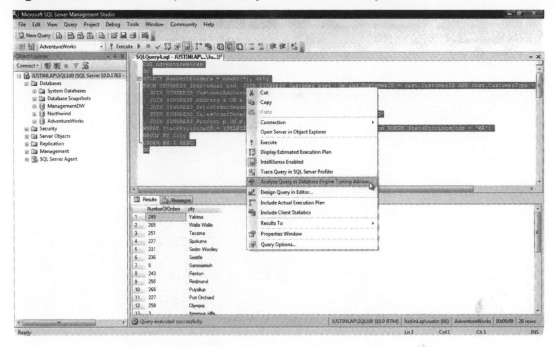

Capturing a Workload

One of the most useful features of DTA is workload analysis. This gives developers and administrators the ability to capture a trace from a production system and analyze it to identify changes that could improve the performance of the workload. The effort required to capture and use DTA to analyze the workload trace is relatively little compared with the potential performance gain. Additionally, the right-click analyze query – DTA function provides developers with opportunity to evaluate a query prior to changing the query in production – actively looking for missing statistics or indexes.

To achieve the best results, a workload trace should contain activity from the live application where optimization is to be performed. Using the Tuning trace template within SQL Profiler provides sufficient detail to enable analysis with DTA as shown in Figure 13.8.

Figure 13.8 SQL Profiler Trace Using Tuning Template

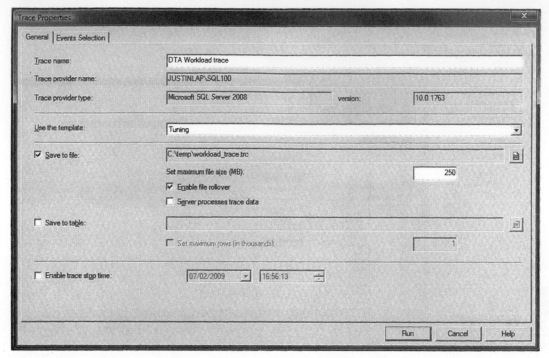

If you prefer to define a trace manually, include the following events:

- RPC:Completed
- SP:StmtCompleted
- SQL:BatchCompleted

Trace files can be provided to DTA as .trc files (the native trace output files from SQL Profiler) or from a table within a database (if you've traced from SQL Profiler directly to a table). The performance burden on the live system is minimized by tracing to a flat file.

Performing Analysis with DTA

Once the workload has been captured to a trace file or a specific query has been identified for review, launch DTA and connect to the SQL Server instance where the database to be analyzed resides.

Configuring & Implementing…

Use a Test Server for Tuning

During the tuning process, DTA can make multiple calls to the Query Optimizer within the database engine to determine benefits and impacts of physical design structure changes to query plans. If you run DTA against a production server, performance could be affected during analysis. It's recommended that you run DTA on a test server from a restored database backup to avoid any performance degradation.

Use the **General** tab within DTA to locate the workload file (i.e., the file containing tsql workload or the trc file created using SQL Profiler). If there are multiple trace files (created using the file rollover option within SQL Profiler), select the first file, and then subsequent files will be read in sequence automatically. Next, select the checkbox alongside the target database for tuning. If you're tuning a specific query or .tsql workload file, you can save time during analysis by narrowing the selection of tuning tables within the database. If the workload file is a SQL trace, this may not be possible since there's no easy way to determine the tables involved in the contents of the trace workload. In this case, run DTA against the entire database (see Figure 13.9).

Figure 13.9 Select the Workload File
and Target Database for Tuning within DTA

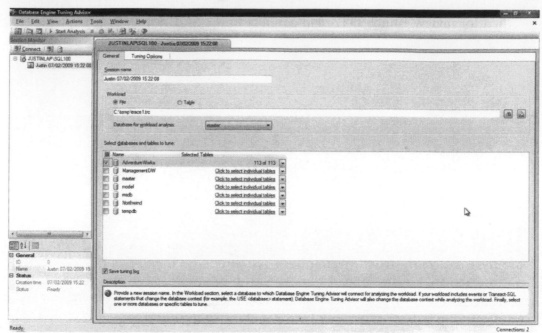

Select the **Tuning Options** tab to review a number of alternatives. Click the **Limit tuning time** check box and indicate a stop time of one hour in the future to be certain you receive results within a reasonable period of time (see Figure 13.10). Additionally, review the three categories that follow in the window to indicate your objectives and ensure any restrictions within your operating environment can be satisfied by the recommendations generated from DTA. To continue, click **Start Analysis** on the menu bar.

Figure 13.10 Review Tuning Options within DTA

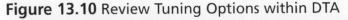

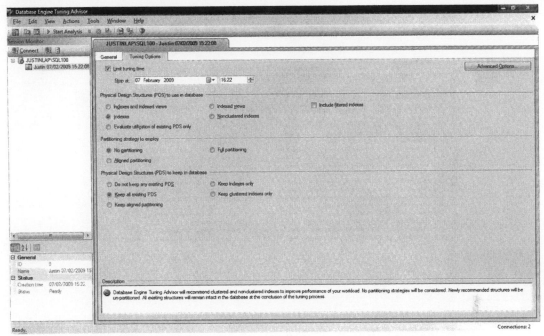

During analysis, the Progress tab displays each step undertaken by DTA. If there are any errors reading the workload files or missing events in the case of SQL traces, these are displayed with hyperlinks for further information on remediating the problem.

Following completion of your analysis, the Recommendations tab is displayed. Note at the top of the recommendations screen, DTA makes an estimation of the improvements that could be achieved by implementing the recommendations. In Figure 13.11, there is a combination of indexes and statistics recommended by DTA: the default DTA object naming convention shows new indexes with prefix _dta_index_<objectidentifier> and statistics within prefix _dta_stat_<objectidentifier>.

Figure 13.11 DTA Displays
Recommendations Following Successful Analysis

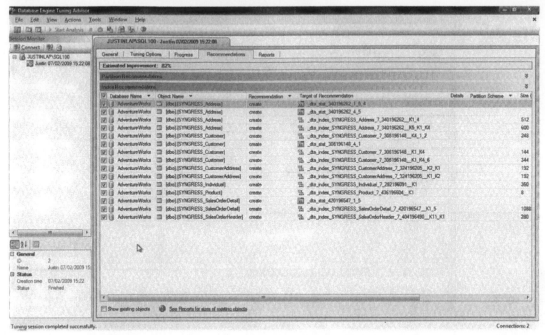

Finally, select the **Reports** tab for a summary of the analysis including details of the recommendations (such as information about proposed indexes including sizes, definition, and number of rows). Additionally, there are reports available to summarize events within the workload file such as tables and column access reports.

Implementing DTA Recommendations

Once DTA has run the analysis, its recommendations can either be applied immediately or scripted to be tested and applied at a later date. Script recommendations by selecting **Save recommendations** from the Actions menu.

Using Dynamic Management Views

Dynamic Management Views (DMVs) are almost certainly the single most useful tool for troubleshooting and performance tuning SQL Server databases. DMVs and Dynamic Management Functions (DMFs) provide administrators with simple, yet powerful insight into the workings of SQL Server and hardware resources (disk, memory, and CPU). There were 89 DMVs introduced to SQL Server 2005 and 47 new DMVs with SQL Server 2008, which can be grouped into two broad types: server scoped (requires VIEW SERVER STATE permission on the server) and database scoped (requires VIEW DATABASE STATE permission on the database).

Most DMVs can be categorized as follows:

- Common Language Runtime
- Cryptographic
- Database Mirroring
- Execution
- Extended Events
- Filestream
- Full-Text Search
- Index
- I/O
- Query Notifications
- Replication
- Service Broker
- SQL Server Operating System
- Transaction

As mentioned previously in this chapter, there's a SQL trace running continuously and cycling itself in the background while SQL Server is running. This trace also gathers the data used by the DMVs. Some DMVs provide snapshot information, whereas others provide cumulative data since the last service restart. Trace data is not persisted anywhere within SQL Server, although this is possible.

DMVs often provide information that could only be accessed otherwise by querying metadata or system tables. SQL Server administrators often like a real-time view of current server activity. They might use the Activity Monitor within Management Studio, or it they have a background with SQL Server 2000 or earlier—they'll probably use SP_WHO or SP_WHO2—both provide session level activity view. There are, however, a couple of DMVs in Table 13.4 that provide this information plus much more.

Table 13.4 Using DMVs to View Current Activity within SQL Server

Dynamic Management View	Purpose
sys.dm_exec_requests	Provides information about a request currently executed by SQL Server.
sys.dm_exec_sessions	Provides an overview of all current sessions (SPIDs) within SQL Server.

It's easy to select all data within a DMV; however, there are great opportunities to write useful queries to interrogate DMVs. One such example is sys.dm_db_index_physical_stats. This DMV shows the level of index fragmentation. In previous versions, this was available through the DBCC SHOWCONTIG command; however, it was very intensive for Disk IO, and the results were cumbersome and difficult to manipulate without significant effort. The following example shows a query that categorizes index fragmentation as High (more than 30 percent), Medium (less than 30 percent), or Low (less than 5 percent) placing the results with greatest fragmentation first since this is where we should pay most attention:

```
SELECT

    OBJECT_NAME(indstat.object_id, indstat.database_id) AS obj_name,
    QUOTENAME(sysind.name) [index_name],
    CASE

      WHEN avg_fragmentation_in_percent < 5 THEN 'LOW'
      WHEN avg_fragmentation_in_percent < 30 THEN 'MEDIUM'
      ELSE 'HIGH'

END as frag_level,
indstat.*

FROM sys.dm_db_index_physical_stats (DB_ID(), NULL, NULL, NULL, 'LIMITED')
AS indstat
INNER JOIN sys.indexes sysind ON indstat.object_id = sysind.object_id AND
indstat.index_id = sysind.index_id
ORDER BY avg_fragmentation_in_percent DESC
```

The output of the sys.dm_db_index_physical_stats can be used as the input to an index maintenance job. In this scenario, it is possible to build a SQL Server Agent job that takes action based on the output of sys.dm_db_index_physical_stats such as an index reorganize (for indexes with low or medium fragmentation) or rebuilding indexes (for those indexes with heavy fragmentation).

Providing additional indexing maintenance, SQL Server can also suggest indexes that would help improve query performance. This information is provided by a group of DMVs, the most useful of which is sys.dm_db_missing_index_details. Using the output from this DMV, we can generate a CREATE INDEX statement to add the new index and improve performance. However, there are numerous limitations to the missing indexes feature, for example, -it doesn't consider the cost of maintaining an index nor does it specify an order for columns to be used in the index.

There are DMVs such as sys.dm_os_* that reflect aspects of the SQL Server Operating System and can be a useful barometer for understanding more about SQL Server internals, system memory consumption, and other requirements. The following query uses the sys.dm_exec_query_stats DVM to display the top 10 queries consuming the most CPU power:

```
SELECT TOP 10
    SUM(qrystat.total_worker_time) AS Total_CPU_Time,
    SUM(qrystat.execution_count) AS Number_of_Executions,
    COUNT(*) as Number_of_Statements,
    qrystat.plan_handle
FROM
    sys.dm_exec_query_stats qrystat
GROUP BY qrystat.plan_handle
ORDER BY sum(qrystat.total_worker_time) DESC
```

Configuring & Implementing...

Review of Useful DMVs

These DMVs are each important in troubleshooting server performance and can be useful in initially identifying poorly performing queries and then to review bottlenecks for problem queries. Look at the following DMVs to become familiar with the contents:

```
sys.dm_exec_requests
```

Continued

`sys.dm_exec_sessions`   Both sys.dm_exec_requests and sys_dm_exec_sessions can be used to view active sessions and requests running on a server. Use these DMVs to identify long running, or currently poorly performing sessions.

`sys.dm_exec_query_stats` This DMV can be useful because it returns details of query execution statistics from the plan cache plan, rather than just considering current queries and sessions.

`sys.dm_exec_sql_text`   Once you've identified the worst performing query, use this next DMV to return the query text. It's an alternative to DBCC INPUTBUFFER and accepts a query handle as input (can be retrieved from any of six DMVs including sys.dm_exec_requests and sys.dm_exec_query_stats).

`sys.dm_os_wait_stats`   This DMV is useful for reviewing serverwide wait statistics, a useful tool in identifying resource bottlenecks across the server. Identifying sources of contention is really helpful in indentifying where improvements can be make to assist overall server performance.

`sys.dm_db_index_usage_stats`   This DMV shows usage statistics (scans and seeks) for each index, and it can be useful in identifying never-used or rarely used indexes. These indexes can often be candidates for disabling or dropping because they can be more expensive to maintain than beneficial. However, remember DMVs are cumulative since the instance last restarted; don't drop lots of indexes if SQL Server hasn't bee running more than a few weeks!

`sys.dm_db_missing_index_details`   This DMV is great for suggesting new indexes, based on past workload. The DMV will actively suggest new indexes and can be used to generate CREATE statements that can be executed to add the new indexes.

Summary of Exam Objectives

This chapter looks at SQL Server performance tuning in detail. The chapter considers some of the internals of the SQL Server operating system, including the Query Optimizer, statistics, indexes, and plan caching. Capturing and examining execution plans are valuable steps in performance analysis and improvement. Incremental and iterative performance improvement is often the best approach—you review and improve the worst performing query with each iteration.

Using SQL Profiler, Database Tuning Advisor, and Dynamic Management Views, you'll have a good insight into SQL Server performance problems such as missing indexes, resource contention, missing statistics, and the options for resolution.

Confident control and appropriate use of these tools will enable you to tackle the most complex and demanding performance problems with SQL Server. In each case, select the most appropriate tool and adopt an iterative approach, making a plan and implementing change with each iteration.

Exam Objectives Fast Track

Working with Query Execution Plans

- ☑ Capture estimated or actual query plans using SQL Server Management Studio.
- ☑ Capture text-based plans using SHOWPLAN or SQL Profiler.
- ☑ Look for the most expensive batch and try to find major bottlenecks.

Tracing with SQL Profiler

- ☑ Use SQL Profiler to capture the statements being executed on a server for performance review/analysis.
- ☑ There can be an overhead with running traces; consider how many events you capture, any filters you apply, and where the trace is run.
- ☑ Trace data is saved directly to a database or to a file and then imported into a database for easier analysis.

Working with Database Tuning Advisor

☑ Database Tuning Advisor (DTA) can be used to analyze database performance and recommend indexes and statistics to improve performance.

☑ Server workload captured with SQL Profiler or specific queries can be analyzed with DTA.

☑ Remember to apply common sense with the DTA recommendations and consider the maintenance overhead required to maintain indexes.

Using Dynamic Management Views

☑ DMVs and Dynamic Management Functions (DMFs) provide a view on SQL Server internals and can be used for troubleshooting and fault diagnosis.

☑ DMVs can be server-scoped or database-scoped reflecting the data tracked within the DMV.

☑ DMVs run continually in the background with a very low overhead; data provided is either cumulative (since last service restart) or a snapshot view.

Exam Objectives
Frequently Asked Questions

Q: What's happening when SQL Profiler reports missing events?

A: This happens occasionally with very busy servers when tracing to a table or to SQL Profiler. In this situation the SQL Profiler tool is unable to keep up with the volume of events that are generated. Consider using a server side trace and saving the trace to a flat file, local to the database server.

Q: How big will the trace file grow?

A: The size of trace files is determined by the workload, events, and columns included in the trace definition. A very busy server with only a few events defined can produce a file as large as a quiet server with many events included. Be sure to monitor the growth of trace files to ensure they don't fill any drives, and if you're leaving a trace unattended (e.g., overnight) ensure that there is plenty of disk space to include activities such as nightly maintenance or data loads.

Q: Is it safe to run Database Tuning Advisor on my production server?

A: No. It's a good idea to run DTA on a test server because it can make heavy use of the Query Optimizer to calculate alternative execution plans. Production performance could suffer during this time.

Self Test

1. You're the DBA for a sales and marketing organization that has a high rate of data change (lots of INSERTS and DELETES). Over the past few weeks the SQL Server has gradually become slower. Which DMV could help identify the cause?

    A. sys.dm_os_schedulers

    B. sys.dm_os_slow_tasks

    C. sys.dm_db_index_physical_stats

    D. sys.dm_exec_requests

2. You're troubleshooting a slow running problem, and you'd like to see which indexes, if any, are being used by the slow query. You're configuring a SQL Profiler trace. Which events should you include to see the actual execution plan in XML?

    A. Showplan XML Statistics Profile

    B. SQL:BatchCompleted

    C. Showplan XML

    D. RPC:Completed

3. Users complain that the database server is slow to respond or causes timeouts, so you've been running a server-side trace to capture details of query performance. The server is busy and you've generated 10 × 1 GB trace files. What's the best way to find queries with the longest duration?

    A. Open each trace file in Profiler and find the one with the longest duration.

    B. Open the trace in Excel and sort by duration.

    C. Use `fn_trace_gettable` to load the data into a table, then analyze with TSQL queries.

    D. Run the trace again with a filter.

4. You're working with an external vendor on a patch to their application. They've applied the patch to the test environment and would like to simulate some production-like workload to assess the success of the patch. You've decided to capture a SQL trace. Which trace template will you use?

    A. TSQL_Replay

    B. Tuning

    C. Standard (default)

    D. Capture_test_server

5. You're responsible for SQL Server performance and one of the developers reports INSERTS are particularly slow. You suspect that a previous developer has created some redundant non-clustered indexes that are hindering INSERT performance. How can you tell if an index is used?

    A. Sys.dm_db_index_usage_stats

    B. Sys.dm_db_index_request_count

    C. Sys.dm_redundant_indexes

    D. Sys.dm_db_missing_index_details

6. There is blocking occurring on your production SQL Server. You've found the session at the head of the blocking chain and retrieved the SQL_HANDLE. Now you need to find the query executed by the user. Which DMV can help?

    A. Sys.dm_exec_requests

    B. sys.dm_exec_sql_text

    C. sys.dm_db_query_plans

    D. sys.dm_stored_proc_text

7. What's the best method to run a SQL Trace with minimum overhead on the server being traced?

    A. Run SQL Profiler from your desktop.

    B. Run SQL Profiler from the server.

    C. Run a server-side trace to a database on the server.

    D. Run a server-side trace to a file on a fast local disk.

8. What command would you use to generate a text showplan from SQL Server Management Studio?

    A. SET SHOWPLAN_ALL ON

    B. SET SHOWPLAN_ALL TRUE

C. ENABLE SHOWPLAN TEXT

D. SET SHOWPLAN=ON

The correct answer is **A.** None of the other options are correct.

9. What does SQL Server use when preparing an estimated execution plan?

A. Actual data

B. Statistics

C. Approximations

D. Rules

10. Which of the following tools could be used to capture an actual execution plan?

A. SQL Server Management Studio

B. SQL Profiler

C. SHOWPLAN_TEXT

The correct answers are **A, B,** and **C.** All answers are tools that could be used to capture an actual execution plan.

11. What types of workload can be analyzed by DTA?

A. T-SQL files

B. SQL Error logs

C. SQL Profiler traces

D. Estimated Execution Plans

12. How can recommendations be applied from within DTA?

A. Apply all recommendations immediately.

B. Schedule a time in the future to apply the recommendations.

C. Save the recommendations.

13. What tools are provided with SQL Server to assist performance tuning?

A. SQL Profiler

B. Database Tuning Advisor

C. SQL Optimizer

D. Execution Plan Analyzer

14. What type of query optimization is used by SQL Server?

    A. Rules-based optimization

    B. Cost-based optimization

    C. Hybrid of rule- and cost-based optimization

15. How could you determine whether out-of-date statistics are affecting query plan selection?

    A. Use DTA

    B. Compare estimated and actual execution plans

    C. Examine statistics using DBCC commands

    D. View statistics using sp_showstats

16. What conditions could cause a recompile?

    A. More than 10 executions of the same query

    B. Changes to statistics

    C. Schema changes

    D. Large number of inserts/ deletes

17. What is a recompile?

    A. When SQL Server drops statistics

    B. When SQL Server creates a new query plan

    C. When SQL Server adds a new index dynamically

    D. When SQL Server reuses an existing query plan

18. DTA is particularly useful for

    A. Creating missing indexes

    B. Creating filegroups

    C. Creating missing multi-column statistics

    D. Suggesting partitioning schemes

19. When reading an actual execution plan from a poorly performing query, what should you look for first?

    A. Nested loops, they are expensive

    B. High row counts, they consume IO

    C. Tables scans, they are slow

    D. High costs, they are bottlenecks

20. SQL Server uses the procedure cache to store what type of information?

    A. Data pages

    B. Hashed security credentials

    C. Execution plans

    D. Statistics

Self Test Quick Answer Key

1. C

2. A

3. C

4. A

5. A

6. B

7. D

8. A

9. B

10. A, B, and C

11. A and C

12. A and C

13. A and B

14. B

15. B and C

16. B, C, and D

17. B

18. A, C, and D

19. D

20. C

Index